MINERAL WEALTH

Brown & Dey, *India's Mineral Wealth, frontispiece*

BAWDWIN, THE MINING CAMP OF THE BURMA CORPORATION LTD.

MINERAL WEALTH
India, Pakistan,
Bangladesh and Burma
A Guide to the Occurrence and Economics
of the Useful Minerals
(In Two Volumes)
(Volume-1)

J. COGGIN BROWN
Superintendent, Geological Survey of India

A.K. DEY
Superintendent, Geological Survey of India

ISHA

ISHA BOOKS
Delhi-110009

Mineral Wealth : India, Pakistan, Bangladesh and Burma

Rs. 1800 (Set)

© J. Coggin Brown and A.K. Dey

ISBN: 978-81-8205-483-7 (Set)
ISBN : 978-81-8205-484- 4 (Vol. 1)

First Published 1923 Title: India's Mineral Wealth

Reprint in 2008 in India by
ISHA Books
B-63, 1st Floor, New Gupta Colony,
Near DDA Market,
Delhi-110009
Phone: 9212142040
ishabooks@hotmail.com

Lasser Type Setting by: Rudra Computer Graphics, Delhi
Printed at : Vishal Kaushik Printers, Delhi-93

CONTENTS

v

Part V
WATER AND SOILS

MAPS

PLATES

GRAPHS

TABLES

GRADES AND ANALYSES

IMPORTS AND EXPORTS

PRODUCTION

RESERVES

MISCELLANEOUS

INTRODUCTION

ALTHOUGH there is abundant evidence of the skill and industry of the ancient miners of India in winning gold, extracting and smelting the ores of the commoner metals and in recovering diamonds from deposits of various kinds, but little systematic mining, as the term is understood today, had been attempted in India, Pakistan or Burma before the last decades of the nineteenth century. The author of the pioneer work on Indian economic geology, published in 1881, states that mining for metallic ores by public companies had not been successful up to that time, though coal and salt mining and the quarrying of building materials had been carried on both by the Government and by private concerns, with in many cases very great profit. ' It would seem, however,' he added, ' that as regards the metals there is a new era about to commence, and that the capabilities of India, not only as a gold-producing country, but also in reference to other metals, will in the course of the next few years be for the first time fairly tested.'

Valentine Ball read the signs of his time correctly, for later developments in the course of the next few years fully justified the truth of his prediction. Mineral deposits of many kinds were discovered and explored; the platitude that they were as a whole too lean to support large-scale treatment died a natural death, and although exploitation for a time resulted mainly in the export of raw products to foreign countries, the advantages to be gained by dealing with them on the spot came to be realized, and India began to advance to her proper position amongst the mineral-producing and metallurgical nations of the world.

By 1899 the growth of prospecting necessitated the issue by the Government in that year of rules to govern the grant of prospecting licences and mining leases, and the number of concessions taken up by private individuals and companies, over lands in which the mineral rights had been retained by the State, rapidly increased from an average of 370 per annum for the first decade of the present century to 706, the corresponding figure for the ten years ending 1930. Over the eight years ending 1938 the average had fallen to 555, of which nearly half had been granted in Burma. The separation of Burma from India took place on 1 April 1937, and it became an independent Union of States in 1948, but the Japanese invasion in 1942 completely shattered its prosperous mining and metallurgical industries, and internal unrest has hitherto prevented their restoration to any semblance of their former importance.

To register the progress of the mineral industry over the whole vast region now occupied by India, Pakistan and Burma, a *Review of the Mineral Production of India* was issued annually by the Reporter on Economic Products to the Government of India for the four years 1894-7, but in 1898 it was decided to publish reviews of progress at wider intervals, covering periods long enough to permit of the determination of any secular variations. The first of these reviews, dealing with the six years 1898-1903, appeared in the *Records of the Geological Survey of India* in 1905, and since then quinquennial reviews of the same character have been forthcoming. In addition to these, a brief annual statement of the quantity and value of all the minerals raised, for which returns are available, has appeared in each annual volume of the *Records* since 1906, accompanied of later years by trade statistics which enable the consumption of any particular product within the country to be gauged. By the end of 1946 no less than 2,090 mineral concessions had been granted in the area which now constitutes the Indian Union, of which 213 were prospecting licences, 1,165 mining leases and 712 quarry leases ; moreover, these figures refer only to Government-owned lands and do not include any concessions granted over *zamindari* lands or in the Indian States. This great increase was partly due to the stimulus of war and partly to the urge to render the country free of imported supplies, but it has its dangers when concessionaires are speculators more anxious to sell out at a profit than fulfil their obligations to prospect and develop the properties granted to them.

A great and growing literature exists on both the scientific and economic aspects of the mineral deposits of India, Pakistan and Burma. Apart from the papers scattered through the eighty-three annual volumes of the *Records of the Geological Survey of India* available to date, or the monographs devoted to such separate subjects as coal, oil, manganese, mica, etc., or again, those dealing with the mineral resources of separate States, such as Madras, Orissa, Madhya Pradesh, etc., to be found amongst the eighty volumes of the *Memoirs* of the same Department, a mass of information regarding them is to be found in the forty-six volumes of the *Transactions of the Mining, Geological and Metallurgical Institute of India,* in those of the *Geological, Mining and Metallurgical Society of India* and in many other publications too numerous to be detailed here. A synopsis of the literature available up to 1916 is to be found in Part II of the *Bibliography of Indian Geology and Physical Geography,* by T. H. D. La Touche, and this has been kept up to date by the publication of lists of later papers as appendices to the *Annual Reports of the Geological Survey of India.*

But few readers, apart from professional specialists, have either the time or the opportunity to search for information in a multitude of official reports or the transactions of learned societies, which in any case are only obtainable in the larger libraries. For this and

other reasons, summaries of all the salient facts are needed from
time to time in which the growth of the mineral industry itself can
be recorded; the progress of those others dependent on it for their
basic materials reviewed; its impact on the economic life of the
country generally examined, and any likely means of increasing
its extent for the benefit of the community at large indicated.

In 1908 Sir Thomas Holland published a *Sketch of the Mineral
Resources of India,* and in 1923 one of the present authors (Coggin
Brown) was instructed by the Director of the Geological Survey
of India at that time, the late Sir Edwin Pascoe, to prepare an
account on the same lines in as condensed and popular a form as
possible. This was published by the Oxford University Press, in
its *India of To-Day* series, under the title *India's Mineral Wealth,* but
whereas Sir Thomas Holland dealt with 54 distinct mineral products, it was then found necessary to consider 77. In a greatly
enlarged second edition of this work written with the approval of
the Government of India and again published by the Oxford
University Press in 1936, the total had increased to 110.

About 1908 the total annual value of minerals raised in India
as it then was amounted to an annual average of about Rs 10½
crores (£7 million); about 1928, the corresponding figure was
almost Rs 32 crores (£24 million) and by 1938, the last complete
year before the outbreak of the second world war, it had risen again
to some Rs 44 crores (about £33 million), to which Burma contributed approximately Rs 10 crores. Over the three decades thus
covered remarkable progress had been achieved; several new
coalfields had been developed; fresh oilfields drilled and the
unknown depths of existing ones explored; the enormous iron ore
fields of Bihar and Orissa had been proved and a great iron and
steel industry with its attendant satellites had been established.
Metallurgical centres had arisen at Maubhandar in Bihar, where
the copper ores of Singhbhum were smelted and refined copper and
yellow metal products manufactured, and at Nam Tu, in the Shan
States, where the ores from Bawdwin were made to yield their
contents of lead, silver, copper, antimony and nickel, and zinc
concentrates were also prepared. The wolfram deposits of Lower
Burma had proved to be of wide extent and richness, while the
associated tin ore was being recovered both by mining and dredging methods. The beach sands of Travancore, the largest and
richest in monazite in the world, were also being treated for their
content of ilmenite and zircon. The gold mines at Kolar were
becoming the deepest in the world, and India continued to head
the list of the world's mica producers, while her manganese ore
deposits gave her the same position from time to time. With the
growth of the iron and steel industry the demand for refractory
materials had resulted in the creation of works specializing in the
production of such goods, while Indian cement works satisfied
most of the country's needs. In other directions, however,

progress had been disappointingly slow, and vast quantities of materials, made in other lands from mineral products obtainable in India, continued to be imported.

Such were the general outlines of the position when the world was convulsed by the outbreak of war in 1939. The momentous changes which followed it, the freedom of India from British control, the division of the subcontinent between India and Pakistan in 1947, the foundation of an independent Burma in 1948 and the birth of the Republic of India on 26 January 1950—great dynastic events of such magnitude could not fail to have profound effects on the mineral industries of the countries concerned. Yet the total value of the minerals and ores produced in the Republic alone continued to increase and had reached a total of over Rs 83½ crores in 1950 and Rs 105 crores in 1951. In the case of Pakistan, incomplete figures register an increase from over Rs 1½ crores in 1948 to more than Rs 2⅖ crores in 1950.

Most of the successful mineral industries in India, Pakistan and Burma today owe their origin to the pioneering explorations of the Geological Survey of India which celebrated its centenary in 1951; yet, before the war in 1939, its scientific staff numbered but 27 officers, called upon to work anywhere from the confines of China to those of Iran (and occasionally to cross them), or from Travancore to the frontiers of Tibet and Afghanistan. The attitude of the New India towards the development of its mineral heritage is revealed in the increase in the cadre of the Survey to 150 officers and a total staff of 550, by 1948, as part of a reorganization not yet completed. The whole territory of the Republic is now covered by five independent circles each with its own Survey Party. In addition to these, two separate bodies of specialists deal with the problems of Mineral Development and of Engineering Geology and Ground Water, the former including geophysicists, etc. The headquarters of the whole Department, now under the control of Dr M. S. Krishnan, are in Calcutta and here also are the usual laboratories and workshops, drawing office, library and museum, as well as the Mineral Information Bureau which provides free advice on the uses and processing of raw materials and on their availability for any particular purpose. The publication of its Journal, *Indian Minerals,* now in its sixth volume, commenced in 1947, its main object being the dissemination in non-technical language of facts and correct information relating to its title.

In the Five-Year Plan of the Government of India the bearing of the mineral industry on the future industrial progress of the country is stressed; furthermore, a definite mineral policy has been adopted in which both the further investigation of resources and the proper appraisal of the known reserves have priority. The Mines and Minerals Regulation and Development Act became law in 1948, and the obsolete Rules regarding the grant of Mineral Concessions were replaced by new ones more in keeping with the times in 1949. A Bureau of Mines was created in order to secure co-ordinated working of leased and prospecting areas under efficient technical control, and to ensure that due regard is paid to the prevention of waste and to proper principles of conservation. The importance attached to research is sufficiently indicated by the formation of the Fuel Research Institute at Digwadih, near Dhanbad, the National Metallurgical Laboratory at Jamshedpur, the Central Glass and Ceramics Research Institute at Calcutta, the Central Electro-Chemical Research Institute at Karaikudi, in addition to the National Chemical and Physical Laboratories, at Poona and Delhi respectively.

In its Statement of Industrial Policy of 2 April 1948, the Government of Pakistan indicated that the mineral industry would be subjected to central planning, a decision which was implemented by the Regulation of Mines and Oilfields and Provincial Development (Federal Control) Act, 1948. A Department of Mineral Concessions was instituted in June 1949 to administer the Act, and appropriate Rules governing the grant of prospecting licenses and mining leases have been promulgated. The nucleus of the Geological Survey of Pakistan was formed in Quetta, in 1947, by a super-intending geologist, six assistant geologists and a few clerks and technicians from the Geological Survey of India; today it contains 25 gazetted officers in a department subordinate to the Ministry of Industries. Several valuable reports of its operations have already been published as *Records* of the Geological Survey of Pakistan.

In the Two-Year Plan of Economic Development of Burma issued in April 1948, great emphasis was laid on the development of mineral resources. It was considered that ' a scientific and accurate assessment of the mineral resources of Burma is essential to the evolution of a comprehensive, fully co-ordinated policy of economic development. The means for such an assessment were sadly lacking in the past and this deficiency must be remedied as early as possible '. The Government has planned to expand both the Geological and Mining Departments. In the Geological Department there are at present one Senior Geologist and two Junior Geologists. The recruitment of a Deputy Director who will later fill the post of the Director and of two Field Geologists has already been sanctioned. In the Mining Department there is now one Mining Adviser and a Junior Mining Adviser. In the meantime the Government engaged, on 27 August 1951, an American consulting firm for two years to make a thorough survey of the mineral resources of the country. According to its policy of ' joint ventures ' with foreign interests, stated early in 1951, the Burma Corporation has become a joint enterprise with govern-mental participation. Later, in 1952, a Mineral Development Corporation of Burma was founded to plan the development of all the mineral resources of the country.

Indian mineral statistics were for long grouped into two classes, those for which approximately trustworthy returns were available, and those for which regular and complete returns were not forthcoming. This system, which commenced in 1894, continued until 1938, but with the efflux of time and the growth of more effective measures for collecting production figures, the number of minerals included in the first class gradually increased at the expense of those in the second one. In 1938, therefore, the dual system was abandoned, though it must be admitted that for minerals still won by primitive methods, though they may form the bases of extensive industries, carried on by a large number of persons working on a small scale independently, in a large number of places, the accuracy of the returns still leaves much to be desired. Accurate statistics and their timely publication are essential for the information of industrialists and others concerned with the mineral trade, as well as for Government itself in framing administrative policy and planning further development. With the consolidation of the pre-Independence Provinces and the Princely States into the Indian Union, and the extension of the Indian Mines Act to all its territories except Jammu and Kashmir, it has become possible to adopt a uniform system of collection and collation of information, and in the near future it will be possible to obtain a much clearer picture of the economics of Indian mining and the mineral industries than at any time during the past fifty or sixty years.

Another innovation also appeared in 1938, when a system previously adopted only in the case of the Shan States was adopted for the whole of India. Under this system the values of the raw ores and minerals are inflated by the addition of the values of the metallic products made from some of the ores; for example, the total value of the mineral production in 1937 using the older method of computation was Rs 21,20,31,432 (£15,942,213), but under the newer one it becomes Rs 30,49,43,161 (£22,928,058), a rise of no less than 43.8 per cent. Such a system is of very doubtful validity and if adopted should logically be extended to every ore and mineral in the list, but as this is manifestly impossible, in order to avoid misinterpretation and confusion, it is advisable to maintain two lists, one for ores and raw minerals and the other for metals smelted or products made from them, in cases where accurate figures of their production are obtainable. This is the method which happily has been followed in more recent annual reports of Indian mineral production. Another cogent reason for the collection of accurate mineral statistics lies in the fact that without them the correct assessment of royalty is not possible. The rate of royalty generally assessable on the various minerals produced in India today is five per cent of their sale value at the pit's mouth, though in the case of the ores of iron, lead, zinc and copper, the rate is somewhat higher. Taking the minimum rate of 5 per cent, the total revenue from this source payable to the various State

Governments and Zamindaris increased from approximately Rs 3¾ crores in 1949 to Rs 4 crores in 1950 and Rs 5¼ crores in 1951, the royalty on petroleum being omitted in the two latter years.

In the table on pp. xx-xxi, the average annual values of a series of minerals and their products belonging to the first class are tabulated over a series of eleven periods, ranging from 1898 to 1951 and thus representing roughly half a century of progress. The only ones which, appearing early in the list, have disappeared entirely from it, are the antimonial lead, nickel speiss, tin ore, amber, jadeite and rubies from Burma, though the marked reduction of values for silver, lead, wolfram, zinc concentrates and petroleum, after the period 1934 to 1938, is due to the same cause, for at the time of the separation of the two countries Burma was responsible for about 23 per cent of the total value. The separation of Pakistan did not have the same effect, for in 1946, the last complete year before that change took place, the Indian Union alone produced approximately 97 per cent of the combined total value of the mineral production of both countries, the chief items on the debit side as far as India was concerned, after separation, being petroleum, salt and other natural compounds of sodium, chromite and gypsum. Such mineral statistics as are available for Burma and Pakistan since they became independent lands, are not included in the table but are to be found in later pages under the titles of the particular minerals concerned.

Collections of statistics of this kind are of internal, comparative value only, as indications of general trade trends. When compared with the absolute values of the mineral products of other countries, they are liable to be misleading without further explanation. As examples: the value of the coal raised over by far the greater part of the whole period, represents an approximate pit's mouth figure, which bore little resemblance to its selling price in the Indian market. The value of the petroleum too was for many years greatly underestimated. The figures given for salt are exclusive of its duty, the principal value of the commodity to the Government of the day, and over a long period equal to seven times the 'production' value. The export values attributed to mica were not connected in any apparent way with the declared production values at the mines. The figures for jadeite are not complete, and those for rubies and associated gems represent the output of a single European company, as no attempt was ever made to tabulate the results of a flourishing indigenous industry. Further instances might be added, but these will suffice to demonstrate the necessity of a separate analysis in each case before any attempt is made to visualize future tendencies.

Developments of major importance in the last few years include the connexion of unworked coalfields with the railway system, the introduction of measures for the conservation of coking coals, the discovery of an extensive lignite field in Madras, of

AVERAGE ANNUAL VALUES OF CERTAIN INDIAN MINERALS AND THEIR PRODUCTS (*In thousands of Rupees*).

METALS AND ORES

	1898-1903	1904-8	1909-13	1914-18	1919-23	1924-8	1929-33	1934-8	1939-43	1944-8	1949-51
Antimonial Lead & Antimony Ore	..	..	..	..	..	2,77	2,44	3,31	2,07†	1,24§§§	..
Chromite	..	1,36	64	3,02	6,72	6,36	5,05	5,83	7,73	7,56†	6,87
Copper Ore & Matte	..	..	..	1,86	3,62	39,56	59,18	59,84	59,91	70,16	1,41,60
Gold	2,85,71	3,39,94	3,36,28	3,38,80	2,71,92	2,25,01	2,26,29	3,02,67	3,73,11	4,15,26	5,88,80
Ilmenite	..	..	..	..	..	3,27	5,99	9,61	8,83	20,22	40,18
Iron Ore	2,04	2,06	4,43	5,22	15,54	47,38	43,89	39,71	55,19	72,88	1,63,26
Lead & Lead Ore	..	..	19,32	53,85	1,18,35	2,22,16	1,55,46	1,62,40	1,64,82†‡	2,29	10,96
Manganese Ore*	11,92	94,76	1,23,43	1,57,86	2,57,33	2,72,58	97,20	1,29,17	1,95,18	1,41,85	10,21,68
Nickel Speiss	..	..	..	..	..	1,42	8,19	13,05	12,61†‡	..	..
Silver	..	..	1,40	20,40	84,97	1,01,99	73,16	77,86	44§	50	64
Tin & Tin Ore	1,03	1,65	4,52	11,01	27,48***	47,44	47,71	99,11	..	..	..
Wolfram	..	..	11,47	69,25	15,81	4,87	13,58	56,05	1,24	47''	52
Zinc Concentrates*	..	..	..	..	3,67	50,55†	28,74	38,06	21,51	..	2,25

FUELS

	1898-1903	1904-8	1909-13	1914-18	1919-23	1924-8	1929-33	1934-8	1939-43	1944-8	1949-51
Coal	1,83,85	3,20,89	4,45,40	6,62,88	12,33,32	11,21,84	7,87,90	7,50,61	12,23,96	36,81,21'''	48,24,11
Petroleum	27,87	88,93	1,39,21	1,61,04	9,24,11	8,45,95	5,78,73	6,48,92	1,85,43§§	1,30,71¶	..

GEMS AND SEMI-PRECIOUS STONES

	1898-1903	1904-8	1909-13	1914-18	1919-23	1924-8	1929-33	1934-8	1939-43	1944-8	1949-51
Amber	5	11	3	4	11	17	2	3	1	..	..
Diamond	..	42	13	18	92	36	74	73	1,88	2,33	4,09
Jadeite*	6,72	9,21	8,31	11,17	14,76	4,45	3,43	1,54	..	..	..
Ruby & Sapphire	13,40	12,66	9,49	6,27	7,82	3,55	1,01	1,64	..	..	..

OTHER MINERALS

Graphite	1,80	1,93	2,45	9	3	94	1	12	41	1,68¶	1,62
Gypsum	..	..	..	..	..	11	96	1,14	2,25	4,93¶	12,53
Kyanite	..	10	36	1,14	2,16	2,90	73	4,30	2,22	4,84	35,56
Magnesite	8	25,52	34,61	56,01	79,09	99,40	83	1,26	3,27	5,85	14,73
Mica	12,02	..	5,37	6,80	3,48	42	59,37	97,25	2,33,60	3,81,43	9,51,29
Monazite	..	..	76,09	1,35,39	1,20,36	99,94	28	1,40	..	84¶¶	..
Salt**	52,18	67,70	36,04	71,13	44,26	17,22	1,19,25	1,12,16	1,15,26	2,92,37	4,85,11
Saltpetre*	39,39	40,20	..	..	..	61	10,92	12,21	17,44	6,94¶¶¶	31,91
Zircon	..	..	..	..	..	..	83	54	53	32¶¶	..
TOTAL	6,38,06	10,07,44	12,58,98	17,73,41	32,35,83	32,22,22	23,30,17	26,30,52	26,88,90	52,45,88	83,38,71

* Export values.
** Prices without duty.
*** Production of metallic tin ceased in 1922.
† Production figures.
‡ Estimated value of antimony ore from Chitral and stated value of antimonial lead from Burma for 1939 and 1940 only.
‡‡ Average values of metallic lead and nickel speiss from Burma for 1939 and 1940 only.
§ Average value of Indian production only, excluding Burma.
§§ Assam and West Punjab fields only.
§§§ Antimony ore from Pakistan (Chitral). Average for 1944, 1945 and 1946 only.
″ Chromite figures for 1946, 1947 and 1948 from the Indian Union only.
″ Production ceased in 1946. Average for three years only.
‴ Coal for 1946, 1947 and 1948 from the Indian Union only.
¶ Pakistan not included after 1946.
¶¶ Averages for two years only. Later statistics have not been published.
¶¶¶ Average of saltpetre exports for 1944 to 1947 inclusive and production figures for 1948.

Note. For more recent figures see Appendix.

new oilfields in the West Punjab and of a great gasfield in Baluchistan, the revival of lead and zinc ore mining in Rajasthan, the smelting of lead ores in Bihar and of antimony ores from Chitral in Bombay, the inauguration of aluminium production, the proof of the continuation of the manganese ores of Madhya Pradesh in depth, the revival of gold mining in Hyderabad, the introduction of modern methods of mining and recovery into the diamond field of Vindhya Pradesh, the discovery of emeralds in Rajasthan, the manufacture of ammonium sulphate on a great scale in Bihar, the production of ferro-alloys in Mysore, the opening of a factory to process the uranium and thorium-bearing rare earth minerals in Travancore, and of another to make titanium white from ilmenite, the growth of the alkali industry and the marked progress of the cement, refractory, ceramic and glass industries. Attention may also be drawn to the proposals to increase the production of pig iron, steel and ferro-alloys of various kinds, to the installation of large oil refineries, to the decision to erect atomic reactors, to the many hydro-electric projects either under construction or contemplated, and to the extended utilization of the ground water supplies of both India and Pakistan. In Burma, it is proposed to explore the coalfields of the Chindwin valley, and the association of the Government of that country with the companies to whom the oilfields and the silver-lead-zinc-copper ore deposits of the Shan States are leased, augurs well for their future progress.

Much remains to be done: great tracts of territory still await detailed geological mapping and prospecting in all three countries, as, for example, in the great mineralized zone of the Himalayas, at present only vaguely outlined from various occurrences of the ores of a number of non-ferrous metals in Sikkim, Nepal, Kumaun, Garhwal, the Kulu valley, Kashmir and Chitral, or, again, in the probable continuation of the wolfram and tin ore-bearing belt of Burma, stretching from Lower Tenasserim through Karenni into the Southern Shan States, and in other areas favourable for ore deposition in the Burma-China frontier tracts. These are by no means the only regions awaiting investigation by the economic geologist. In their own interests, exploratory work of this kind demands initiation, guidance and control by the Governments concerned, if adequately equipped and financed private enterprise fails in the task, for though no single country can hope to be entirely self-sufficient in strategic minerals, there is room for considerable improvement of existing conditions.

In the pages which follow each useful mineral found hitherto in India, Burma or Pakistan is considered individually, its chief occurrences are briefly described, the history of its commercial exploitation is outlined, tables and graphs of production and values are included where necessary, and, with the exception of the commoner metals, its uses in modern industry are explained. Metallurgical processes are considered in cases where they have

been introduced, comparisons made between indigenous and imported articles where they are essential to the proper appreciation
of the economic position, and, for the benefit of those on
whom the task of searching for new deposits now lies, short notes
on the important questions of origin have been incorporated.
Both authors of this book have spent many years in the investigation and study of the mineral deposits described and connected
subjects, and they are convinced that such knowledge is the surest
foundation for successful field work. They also accept responsi-
bility for statements regarding the future development of any particular mineral industry, unless the opinions of others are quoted.

In view of the urgent necessity of increasing food supplies,
chapters dealing with the geological aspects of soil formation and
of water supplies have been added. The bearing of the former on
this problem is self-evident and needs no emphasis: regarding the
latter, A. H. Kazni, in a recent report on the Water Supply of
Baluchistan, has written: ' There can be no progress in this Province, whether social, educational, economic or otherwise, unless
suitable attention is paid to the development of her most precious
mineral, water.' The best means of directing such attention are
also matters of grave concern in the arid tracts of the Indian
Peninsula and in the Dry Zone of Burma. Geologists can render
much assistance in the study of such problems and this is the reason
for a brief consideration of the principles involved here.

In a conspectus of this kind information has to be drawn from
many sources and in case of unintentional omission of acknow-
ledgement in its proper place, our thanks are tendered here to all
past and present officers of the Geological Surveys of India, Pakistan
and Burma, and to those others whose work has been utilized.
To the Chief Geologists of the leading oil companies operating in
Burma, Assam and Pakistan, Mr P. Evans and Dr E. S. Pinfold,
and their ungrudging help, is largely due the section on petroleum,
the most authentic short account of the oilfields concerned yet
available. The publication of the book would have been impossible
without the official sanction which was kindly obtained for us by Dr
W. D. West, to whom and the authorities concerned we are indeed
grateful. To Dr West's successor, Dr M. S. Krishnan, Director
of the Geological Survey of India, we are particularly indebted
for his interest in its preparation and his unfailing assistance in
our endeavours to make it as authoritative and up-to-date as
possible. In order to supply accurate particulars of the manifold
uses of the metals and minerals concerned, including many new
applications which have become established during and since the
last war, it has been necessary to consult many specialists, manufacturers and Government Departments in India, the United Kingdom, Canada, Australia and the United States, and it is pleasing
to record that we have received the fullest co-operation in every
instance.

In appendices, besides the latest figures of mineral output, a number of references to literature are given, as they may prove useful to the reader desirous of following a subject further than our limited space permits. In some of these, and in the *Bulletins of Economic Minerals,* published as Vol. LXXVI of the *Records of the Geological Survey of India* during the last war, the Indian producer will find explanations of the manner in which manufacturers are accustomed to obtain supplies of raw ores and minerals, details of the various systems of buying and selling, the regulations of the mineral trade associations, the standard contract forms of metallurgical firms and ore dealers, the recognized market grades and the units of sale. A section of the periodical *Indian Minerals* is regularly devoted to Trade and Commercial Intelligence and to a Review of the Metal Markets. Herein will also be found accounts of new finds as they are discovered as well as digests of scientific and technical progress, both at home and abroad, as it affects the progress of the mineral industry in India and neighbouring lands.

The main object of this book is to draw attention to the commercial and industrial potentialities which the mineral deposits of the three countries possess, in the hope that under administrations aware of their importance, capital and enterprise will be forthcoming in full measure for their future development, with all that it means for the lasting advantage of the peoples of India, Pakistan and Burma.

PART I

THE MINERAL FUELS

CHAPTER I

THE MINERAL FUELS

COAL

COAL is India's most valuable mineral product and its winning one of her more important industries. Over 320,000 workers find employment in and about the mines in normal times and over 98 per cent of the output is consumed in the country. The railways are the largest users and take approximately one third of the total. They are followed by the iron and steel industry, while the remainder supplies power for a host of other undertakings, mills and factories of every description. After the United Kingdom India is the largest coal-producing unit of the Commonwealth; thus her output of approximately 29·7 million tons in 1946 compares with 22 millions from South Africa, 18·3 millions from Australia and 16·7 millions from Canada.

Coal was known to exist in the Raniganj field in 1774 and was actually worked in 1777, though little was done in the way of regular mining until 1814. In those early days the coal was transported to Calcutta by boats on the Damodar river, and the completion of the East Indian Railway to Raniganj in 1855 really created the demand for the fuel. As the railway systems extended, other fields were opened, and by 1881 production had reached about one million tons annually, though the imports of coal into India from abroad still averaged over 800,000 tons for the same period. Rapid expansion followed. Over two million tons were raised in 1890, the export trade began to develop, and by 1900 a yearly output of over six million tons was reached: imports by that time had fallen to about 200,000 tons and exports had increased to nearly half a million tons. (See tables on pp. 75ff.) Later statistics are arranged in tabular form below, and from them it is evident that uninterrupted progress was registered until 1919, with its output of 22,628,037 tons. The decline which then set in following the first world war was due to the cumulative effects of many causes, shortage of railway wagons, inadequacy of labour supplies, prolonged strikes and increasing imports. At the same time the collieries were for a period unable to meet the home demand, and the prices obtained for good coals from 1920 to 1924 were the highest received up to that time: indeed in 1921 the domestic shortage became so acute that exports were temporarily prohibited. Production began to increase again in 1924, and in

1929 and 1930 reached totals of over 23 million tons, when the effects of a world depression in trade spread over the industry. As a result of this, prices slumped to such an extent that the 20 million tons raised in 1932 were worth only half the value at the pit-head of the 19 million tons raised a decade earlier. This state of affairs continued until 1936 and by that time pit-head prices had collapsed to those of the early years of the century. A long overdue improvement was registered in 1937 and from then onwards prices have risen consistently. As the table on p. 75 demonstrates, production of coal has had its fluctuations, but in spite of the unprecedented difficulties of transport and distribution caused by the confused conditions of the second world war, the trend in general has been upwards, reaching 31,695,375 tons in 1949 and 32,307,481 tons in 1950.

Owing to the division of India on 15 August 1947, the coalfields of Baluchistan, the North-West Frontier Province and the West Punjab passed to Pakistan on that date and their production does not appear in the Indian returns from 1947 onwards. For the five years ending 1946, the coalfields of these three regions had contributed an average of less than one per cent per annum to the general total, an amount of little significance to India but of some importance to Pakistan with its coal deficiencies.

The demands on India's coal reserves are great and growing and were estimated by the Indian Coalfields Committee of 1946 as likely to increase to about 41 million tons per annum from 1956 onwards. Amongst other recommendations of this Committee designed to facilitate the required expansion and to reserve the coking coals for metallurgical purposes, the following are noteworthy: the continuation of the Colliery Control Order by which prices and distribution were fixed in 1945; the acquisition by the State of all coal below 2,500 feet, with suitable compensation for working mines; the introduction of various methods of conservation, including the reservation of the coking coals for the use of the iron and steel industry; the prohibition of the export of coking coals and of their use as bunker fuels on steamships; the compulsory introduction of underground sand stowing in mines where it is needed; the use of coals of inferior quality for thermal, electrical power production, and of better-quality non-coking coals in railway locomotives; the systematic investigation of the physical and chemical characteristics of all the known coal seams, and of the problem of the desulphurization of the Tertiary coking coals of Assam; the reorganization of the existing system of the collection of mineral statistics, together with various suggestions regarding the welfare of mining labour and the development of better transport facilities.

India's reserves of coal down to 1,000 feet below the surface, in seams not less than four feet in thickness and containing not more than 25 per cent of ash, are believed to be of the order of 20,000 million tons. Of better-quality coals with not more than 16 per cent of ash, in seams not less than four feet in thickness, there are calculated to be some 5,000 million tons. These estimates refer only to coals of Gondwana age, and, in addition to them, there are reserves of Tertiary coals of the order of 10,000 million tons. As workable coal may be found to extend to depths of 4,000 feet, the actual reserves are probably considerably greater than the figures given. The probable reserves of workable Tertiary coal in Pakistan were computed recently to be 165½ million tons.

India's reserves of good coking coals, however, give cause for anxiety for most of her Gondwana coals are of non-coking types. The Coalfields Committee estimated the reserves of good coking coals at 700 to 750 million tons, which at the present rate of extraction and wholesale use for all kinds of purposes will be exhausted in some 65 years. Some authorities would double this estimate to 1,500 or 1,600 million tons, adding that by blending weak with strongly coking coals, and careful washing of the inferior grades of coking coals, it should be possible to raise the total to 2,000 million tons. This is the final, overall, most optimistic assessment of the position. In the words of Dr M. S. Krishnan, Director of the Geological Survey of India, however: 'Unless drastic steps are taken to curtail the consumption of coking coal for non-metallurgical purposes, the Indian steel industry will be reduced to the position of having to seek for metallurgical coke from foreign lands.' To this timely warning may be added the unanimous opinion of the members of the Committee on the Conservation of Metallurgical Coke, that the reserves of 2,000 million tons may well be halved unless precautions, particularly compulsory sand stowing, are taken in the mines themselves, and unless those measures of beneficiation already mentioned are adopted with the weaker coking coals when they reach the surface.

The enormous reserves of high-grade iron ores in India, perhaps the largest of their kind in the world, contrasted with the comparatively low reserves of the only fuel by which they can be smelted profitably, have troubled geologists and exercised the minds of the metallurgists of the iron and steel industry for the past thirty years. At present the iron and steel works consume 3½ million tons of coking coal annually, but the country as a whole is burning about 10 million tons of such coal yearly and so reducing the probable life of the reserves to 200 years. Extensions of Indian steel-making capacity, however, are already being built, or contemplated in the not distant future, which will raise its requirements to 8 million tons per annum, so that if used for this purpose alone, the life of the reserves would be some 250 years. But if during the next 50 years steel production is increased tenfold, and as far as iron ore supplies are concerned there is no reason why this should not be done, the coking coal requirements will become 35 million tons per annum, and the probable life of the reserves will then be not more than

55 years. This is a summary of the considered views of the latest Committee of Enquiry into the subject, and they are again followed by a reiteration of the warning that the probable life period may be halved unless the conservation measures recommended are put into practice forthwith.

Fortunately the position is now officially appreciated. Sand stowing of worked-out areas in the mines is widely practised, both as a measure of conservation and on the grounds of safety. Already in 1939, the Coal Mines Safety (Stowing) Act created a Board to administer funds collected for this purpose by the levy of a cess on coal and coke. Wider powers still are conferred on a new Coal Board established under the Coal Mines (Conservation and Safety) Ordinance of 1951, which can now enforce any measures, including stowing, which it considers either necessary or desirable. These, combined with the more general and rational use of the non-coking coals for such purposes as they are best suited, the progress of research into the problems of Indian coal beneficiation by modern methods of washing and blending, together with the fundamentally important work of resurveying and reclassifying the known seams, in which the Geological Survey and the Fuel Research Institute must share, should reduce, if not remove, existing apprehensions. Moreover, it is still possible that scientific research may solve the problem, for it was announced at the Fourth Empire Mining and Metallurgical Congress, in July 1949, that investigations recently made on some of the South African coals, which like those of India are of Gondwana age, have shown that it is possible to produce a satisfactory coke for use in smelting operations from coals which have hitherto been regarded as quite unsuitable for coke manu-facture. The coking coals of the quality required by the iron and steel works are found in the Raniganj, Jharia, Giridih, and East and West Bokaro fields; the semi-coking coals come from all these fields, and in addition, from those of Karanpura and the Kanhan Valley. The question of the production of liquid hydrocarbons from coal has received considerable attention in India, particularly in view of her inconsiderable petroleum resources, but the proposal to utilize third-grade, high ash coal for this purpose awaits exami-nation of the high cost factor involved in the initial expenditure on the plant required.

Over 98 per cent of the coal is won from the Lower Gondwana rocks of the Peninsula and the remainder from Tertiary strata of regions outside it. The chief Gondwana exposures are distributed in linear fashion along the valleys of the Damodar and Mahanadi, the Godavari and the Wardha. The former two converge, and coalescing in southern Baghelkhand continue to the west, on the lower side of the Narmada valley, hidden at intervals under the blanket of later Deccan Trap flows, until they finally disappear about Long. 78°. The coalfields are fragments, pre-served mainly by faulting, of four great basins of freshwater deposition which existed over these and probably much more extensive tracts, in Lower Gondwana (Permian) times. One such basin enclosed the areas now drained by the Son, Damodar and their tributaries; a second covered the Chhattisgarh-Mahanadi region; a third the Godavari-Wardha valleys and a fourth the Satpura region. Coalfields of Lower Gondwana age occur thus in the States of West Bengal, Bihar, Madhya Pradesh, Hyderabad, Vindhya Pradesh, Orissa and Andhra (see Map II). As a general rule the coal seams are thick, in some cases exceeding 100 feet. Quarrying on a large scale is done by mechanical methods but mainly on the outcrops of seams of inferior quality. Underground mining has now attained maximum depths of over 2,000 feet, and in the past the bord and pillar system was usually adopted for the extraction of the coal, but the introduction of coal-cutting machines, of which there were over 300 at work in 1947, had led to the adoption of long wall methods at some collieries. Screening plants designed to give marketable products in the eight sizes recognized by the Indian Mining Association are installed at many of the larger collieries. Two large coal washing plants with a capacity of over two million tons of coal per annum were installed for the Tata Iron & Steel Co. Ltd, at West Bokaro in 1951 and Jamadoba in 1952, and another is under construction at Lodna for Messrs Turner, Morrison & Co. Ltd.

Under various enactments full provision is made for the safety and health of the mining labour force. A compulsory provident fund scheme to provide for some 250,000 miners in old age is in operation. A Coal Mines Labour Welfare Fund was instituted in 1944 and derives its income from cesses on both coal and coke dispatches. It is administered under such provisions as housing hospitals and public health of the mining community generally.

The total amount of coal and coke exported from India between 1900 and 1946, inclusive, was 28,694,000 tons, of which Ceylon took 48·3 per cent, the Straits Settlements 14·3 per cent and a number of other countries mainly in eastern Asia under 10 per cent each. The full details of the export trade are tabulated on pp. 8off. It reached its zenith in 1940 when over two million tons were shipped, mainly to Ceylon, Burma, the Straits Settlements, Hongkong and China. For the five years ending 1948 exports averaged 420,605 tons per annum, the full destinations of which are not available, though with the exception of West Pakistan, which began to import coal from India after the division of the country, they probably did not differ greatly from the earlier and normal ones. In 1949, of an exported total of 1,264,963 tons, Pakistan took 38·5 per cent and Ceylon 24·6 per cent. In 1950 no coal was exported to Pakistan and exports fell to 903,145 tons, of which Ceylon took 32·6 per cent while other destinations included Japan, Egypt, South Korea and Aden. Italy, Libya, Denmark, Argentina and the United Kingdom all received Indian coal in 1951. The export of coal from India was suspended for a time in 1949 and this gave South African coal, always a serious competitor, unhindered access to the Far Eastern markets. In September 1949 the Government of India took over the control of all export transactions. It is difficult to forecast the future trend of the export trade. India will need her own coking and high-grade gas coals for her own expanding metallurgical and chemical industries. Whether distant foreign markets will accept lower grades will depend in the long run largely on their processing to reliable, standardized grades at competitive prices; in any event geographical proximity to Pakistan and the comparatively short sea leads, as well as long established trade relations with Ceylon, Burma, Malaya and other countries bordering the Indian Ocean, indicate the natural as well as the potential markets of the future should they be required.

The total imports of foreign coal into India between the years 1900 and 1950, inclusive, amounted to 10,669,761 tons, of which 44·7 per cent came from the United Kingdom and 26·7 per cent from South Africa. The statistical data are analysed in the table on p. 79, their most striking feature being the dwindling of the import trade into insignificance at the end of the period. Imports of foreign coal into Pakistan are not included in this table.

A Coal Grading Board, constituted under an Act of the Legislature in 1925, provides for the classification, grading and certification of coal, particularly if it is intended for export. A certificate of the Grading Board is a guarantee of quality for the overseas buyer. The following grades fixed by the Board illustrate the general composition of various kinds of Indian coal.

GRADES OF INDIAN COAL

Low Volatile Coal	High Volatile Coal
Jharia (Barakar Series)	Raniganj Series
Giridih	Karanpura
Karanpura	
Bokaro	

SELECTED GRADE

Up to but not exceeding 13% ash, and over 7,000 calories.	Up to but not exceeding 11% ash, over 6,800 calories, under 6% moisture.

GRADE I

Up to but not exceeding 15% ash, and over 6,500 calories.	Up to but not exceeding 13% ash, over 6,300 calories, under 9% moisture.

GRADE II

Up to but not exceeding 18% ash, and over 6,000 calories.	Up to but not exceeding 16% ash, over 6,000 calories, under 10% moisture.

GRADE III
Any coal from these coalfields inferior to the above.

During the last war and as a guide to the fixation of prices another classification was adopted. Under its provisions coals of the Raniganj field with ash and moisture content not exceeding 17·5 per cent were classified as Selected Grade A. When the ash and moisture content exceeded 17·5 per cent but did not exceed 19 per cent they were placed in a Selected Grade B, while Grade I coals were those in which ash and moisture combined exceeded 19 per cent but did not exceed 26 per cent. With the exception of those of Tertiary age, Indian coals are usually low in sulphur and phosphorus contents. Typical analyses are given under the descriptions of the separate fields and general ones in the table on p. 75.

India has a population of over 357 millions and Pakistan of some 76 millions, yet it is doubtful if their combined consumption of domestic fuel greatly exceeds one million tons annually. Various efforts have been made to popularize the use of soft coke in place of the traditional fuel of the home, the burning of which in itself constitutes a grievous loss to the agricultural economy, and in 1929 legislation was enacted providing for the levy of a cess on all soft coke dispatched by rail from the coalfields of West Bengal and Bihar. The funds obtained from this cess are used for promoting the sale and improving the methods of manufacture of soft coke, the demand for which is growing in northern India, for while the average dispatches from the two coalfields concerned over the ten years 1940 to 1949, inclusive, were 644,430 tons, they amounted to 1,066,697 tons in 1949 and rose to 1,250,324 tons in 1950.

The production of hard coke for the metallurgical industries, principally iron and steel, exceeded over 2¼ million tons in 1941, and for the five years ending 1946 averaged 1,764,373 tons per annum, in making which 2,514,611 tons of coal were consumed. Of this tonnage no less than 93·4 per cent was drawn from the Jharia field, about 4 per cent from Raniganj, 1·4 per cent from Giridih, 1·1 per cent from Bokaro and the remainder from the Namdang Tertiary field of Assam. For the four years ending 1950, the average annual production of hard coke was 1,866,335 tons, representing 2,631,833 tons of coking coal. The production of hard coke in 1950 was 2,103,212 tons. By-product coking dates from about 1910 when the first battery of ovens was erected at the Kulti works of the Bengal Iron Co. Today there are fifteen installations in operation or under construction in India, comprising over 600 ovens, capable of carbonizing some 3½ million tons of coal annually and owned either by colliery companies or by the iron and steel concerns. The coke-oven gas of the latter is used to heat the steel furnaces; of the other by-products, which include benzole and ammonium sulphate, an average of 71,778 tons of coal tar were produced in the five years ending 1950.

The Coal Measures of the Lower Gondwanas are found in the rocks of the Damuda Series, itself the middle of the three divisions

(Talchir, Damuda and Panchet) which form the lower part of the System. The Damuda Series itself is subdivided into three Stages which are displayed in the Raniganj and Jharia coalfields as follows:

SUBDIVISIONS OF THE COAL-BEARING DAMUDA SERIES

RANIGANJ COALFIELD	JHARIA COALFIELD
Raniganj Coal Measures (up to 3,400 feet)	Raniganj Coal Measures (1,840 feet represented)
Ironstone Shales (1,200 feet)	Barren Measures (2,080 feet)
Barakar Coal Measures (up to 2,100 feet)	Barakar Coal Measures (2,000 feet)

The Barakar Coal Measures of these two fields comprise some 2,000 feet of feldspathic sandstones, conglomerates, clays, fireclays, occasional bands of ironstone and most of the country's important coal seams, and in the central and southern coalfields, not shown in the above table, they vary from a few hundred to over 1,000 feet in thickness. The Barren Measures of the Jharia field are thicker than indicated, if they are taken to include certain beds of both under- and overlying stages which are coal-bearing in Raniganj but not so in Jharia.

Over most of the vast region occupied by this section of the Gondwana rocks in Permian times, the accumulation of the vegetable debris, from which the coal seams were formed, ceased at the end of the Barakar Stage, and the succeeding strata consist of sandstones, shales and ironstones. In the eastern part of what is now the Damodar valley, however, this sequence of barren strata, considerably over 1,000 feet thick, was followed during Upper Permian times by conditions in which coal formation again became possible, represented today by the Raniganj Coal Measures, up to 3,400 feet thick in the type area from which they take their name and which are further represented by a thickness of 1,840 feet in the Jharia field.

The coals of the eastern fields of the Damodar valley have been grouped by E. R. Gee as follows:

(a) RANIGANJ COAL MEASURES (upper and middle seams together with the lower seams of the eastern end of the Raniganj field):–Non-caking to poorly caking, long flame, bituminous to sub-bituminous coals.

(b) RANIGANJ COAL MEASURES (of the Jharia field, together with the lower seams of the western and middle parts of the Raniganj field):–Caking to poorly caking, long flame, bituminous coals.

(c) BARAKAR COAL MEASURES:–Hard-caking, relatively short flame, bituminous coals.

In the fields of the more western parts of the Damodar valley, such as Hutar, Daltonganj and others, the Barakar coals alter in composition and approach those of the eastern parts of the Raniganj field; as such they become long flame, bituminous to sub-bituminous types and possess only poorly caking properties. Such qualities also characterize many of the Barakar seams of the more southern fields of the Peninsula.

Ash percentages under 10 per cent are exceptional for Indian run-of-mine coal and 11 to 13 per cent is the normal figure for best quality coal in marketable quantity. The Barakar seams of the eastern fields contain from 25 to 35 per cent of volatile matter and 65 to 75 per cent of fixed carbon. The Raniganj seams range from 40 to 46 per cent of volatile matter and 54 to 60 per cent of fixed carbon. These percentages are calculated on a moisture and ash free basis. The coking coals of the Barakar Stage are also excellent steam coals, while those of the Raniganj Stage are very suitable for gas manufacture.

The Eocene coals of India and Pakistan possess a lignitic character, except in the case of the Jammu fields of Kashmir where well matured bituminous to anthracitic types occur. Many of the Assamese coals have less than 5 per cent of ash while those of West Punjab and Kashmir usually contain over 10 per cent. Their caking properties vary from strongly caking in the case of Assam to the poorly caking or non-caking coals of West Punjab etc., but unfortunately, most of the Eocene coals possess unusually high percentages of sulphur. As free burning coals, easily pulverized and low in moisture, they have high calorific values and have proved very suitable for cement manufacture.

LOWER GONDWANA COALFIELDS

BENGAL, BIHAR, ORISSA

The coalfields of these three States accounted for 86·7 per cent of the 1,022 million tons raised in India between 1900 and 1950, both years included. The major portion of the Raniganj field lies in the western part of West Bengal and smaller parts of it encroach into Bihar. The more important coalfields of Bihar are Jharia, Bokaro, Ramgarh and North and South Karanpura, though there are others of lesser degree. They are all isolated fragments of the once continuous Gondwanaland, faulted down into the crystalline floor and arranged in a broken band stretching roughly east and west along the valley of the Damodar river. Other fragments of Gondwanaland are found in the Mahanadi and Brahmini valleys of Orissa, and although the two coalfields of the State—Talchir, which is partly in Angul, and Rampur, in

MAP IV

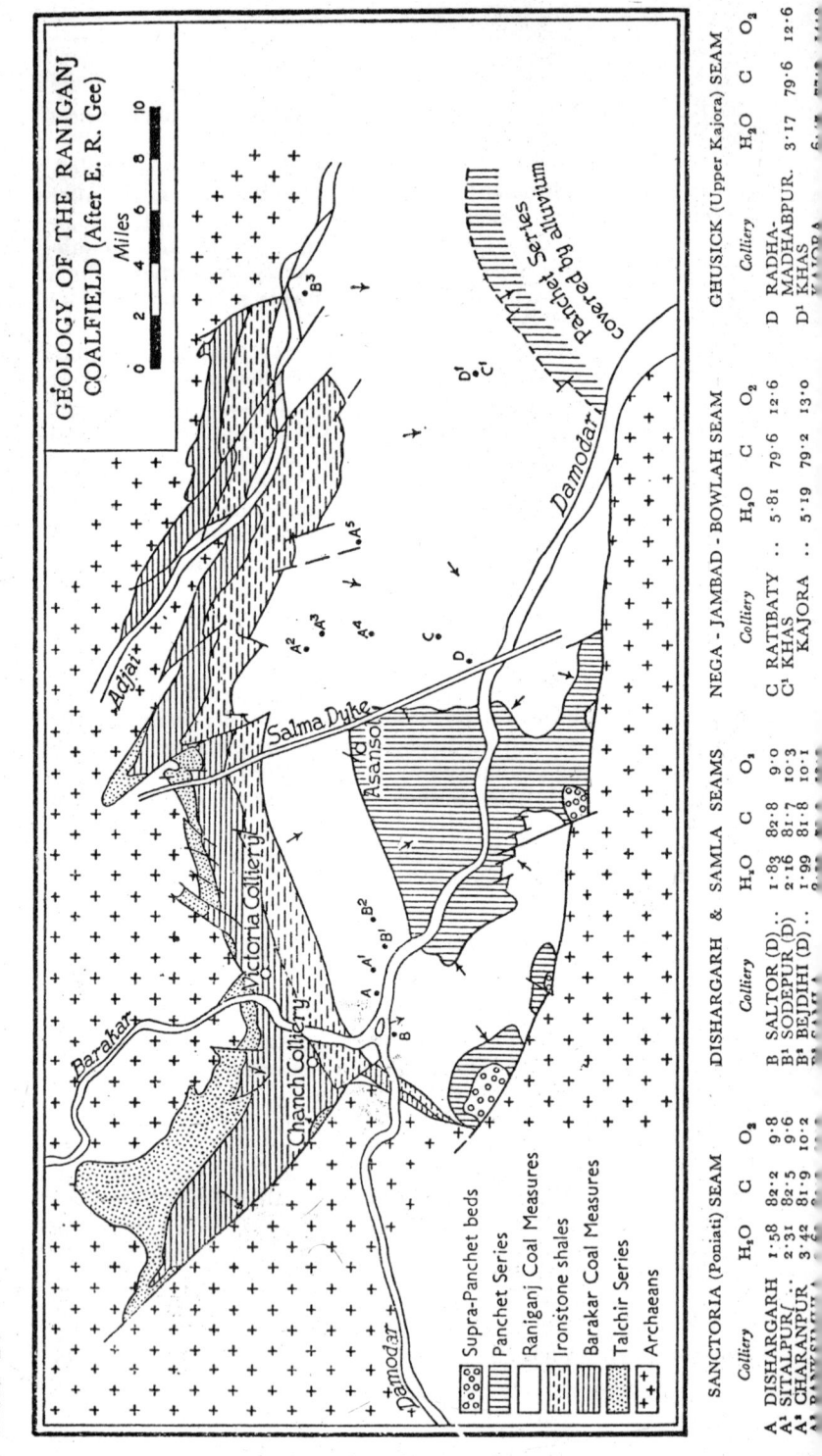

GEOLOGY OF THE RANIGANJ
COALFIELD (After E. R. Gee)

Miles
0 2 4 6 8 10

Supra-Panchet beds
Panchet Series
Raniganj Coal Measures
Ironstone shales
Barakar Coal Measures
Talchir Series
Archaeans

Panchet Series
covered by alluvium

SANCTORIA (Poniati) SEAM

Colliery	H₂O	C	O₂
A DISHARGARH	1·58	82·2	9·8
A¹ SITALPUR	2·31	82·5	9·6
A² CHARANPUR	3·42	81·9	10·2

DISHARGARH & SAMLA SEAMS

Colliery	H₂O	C	O₂
B SALTOR (D)	1·83	82·8	9·0
B¹ SODEPUR (D)	2·16	81·7	10·3
B² BEJDIHI (D)	1·99	81·8	10·1

NEGA - JAMBAD - BOWLAH SEAM

Colliery	H₂O	C	O₂
C RATIBATY	5·81	79·6	12·6
C¹ KHAS KAJORA	5·19	79·2	13·0

GHUSICK (Upper Kajora) SEAM

Colliery	H₂O	C	O₂
D RADHA- MADHABPUR	3·17	79·6	12·6
D¹ KHAS KAJORA			

Sambalpur, are now separated, it is certain that the coal-bearing rocks of both were at one time connected. The Rampur coalfield lies at the eastern extremity of a further extension of the Gondwanas, across Gangpur into Madhya Pradesh and Rewah. Brief descriptions of the coalfields now follow.

Raniganj. The easternmost of its group, this coalfield lies from 120 to 150 miles north-west of Calcutta, partly in the Birbhum and Burdwan districts of West Bengal and partly in the Manbhum district of Bihar. It has an area of 619 square miles though its eastern limits, buried as they are under younger strata, are not definitely known. It was the first coalfield to be worked in India, in 1777, and until 1905 was the leading producer. In 1906, its output, then 37 per cent of the Indian total, was surpassed by that of Jharia, with 42 per cent. In 1940 it yielded 9,344,877 tons, or 31·8 per cent of the total, and in 1950, 10,583,885 tons, or 32·76 per cent; its total production up to the end of that year being of the order of 350 million tons.

Its Lower Gondwana rocks are divided in ascending order into the Talchir, Damuda and Panchet Series, and the general classification of the middle, coal-bearing Damudas into the Barakars or Lower Coal Measures, the Ironstone Shales and the Raniganj or Upper Coal Measures has been given on page 10. In the Lower (Barakar) Measures there are seven separate coal-bearing horizons, according to Dr E. R. Gee, whose exhaustive memoir on the field was published in 1932, though they are not all found in every part of the field, while the seams themselves vary greatly in thickness and to a lesser extent in composition, as they are traced from one area to another. The productive seams include the Chanch Laikdih, Ramnagar, Damagaria and Salanpur, which average 20 feet in thickness, and like the others, are known under a variety of confusing synonyms in various parts of the field. The productive seams of the Raniganj Measures are more numerous and in them Gee has correlated nine main coal-bearing horizons. The same disorder of seam nomenclature exists, but the more important ones include the Dishargarh (18 feet thick), Sanctoria or Poniati (10 to 15 feet), Ghusick (10 to 20 feet) and Raniganj (10 to 20 feet).

Coals of Barakar age have relatively low moisture, comparatively low volatile contents ranging from 21 to 30 per cent, and a high proportion of fixed carbon, usually between 52 and 64 per cent, a figure about 55 per cent being common. All the seams of the Barakar Measures are coking coals, while parts of the Laikdih and Ramnagar seams, in particular, yield good, hard cokes: all the better quality seams give good steam coals. In some parts of the field the quality tends to deteriorate owing to a higher ash content, but it should be possible to improve this by suitable cleansing methods.

TYPICAL ANALYSES OF BARAKAR COALS (LOWER MEASURES), RANIGANJ

Seam	Moisture	Volatile Matter	Fixed Carbon	Ash	Fuel Ratio	Calorific Value	Remarks
Chanch ∴	1·63	28·96	56·02	13·39	1·93	..	Strongly caking
Ramnagar	1·61	27·99	58·15	12·25	2·08	7,022	ditto
Laikdih ..	1·58	28·74	60·27	9·41	2·10	7,408	ditto
Laikdih (†)	1·40	26·00	62·00	11·40	2·41	7,632	ditto
Damagaria	1·24	23·00	62·00	15·00	2·70	7,149	Caking

(†) bottom 17 feet of the seam.

Coals of the Raniganj or Upper Measures vary considerably in composition both vertically in the sequence and laterally in individual seams. Compared with the Barakar coals they have, as a rule, more moisture, which ranges from 3 to 10 per cent (though the Dishargarh seam often contains only 1·35 to 3 per cent), and considerably higher volatile contents, varying in the better grades from 29 to 38 per cent: their fuel ratios are in all cases lower than those of the coals from the Barakar Measures. As the seams are followed from east to west of the field there is a progressive increase in moisture content and their caking properties diminish. The Dishargarh and the Sanctoria-Poniati seams yield excellent gas coals and free-burning steam-raising fuels; mixed with a strongly caking Barakar coal they give hard, metallurgical cokes. The remaining seams of these Upper Measures are either non-coking or produce only a very soft coke.

TYPICAL ANALYSES OF UPPER MEASURES (RANIGANJ) COALS

Seam	Moisture	Volatile Matter	Fixed Carbon	Ash	Fuel Ratio	Calorific Value	Remarks
Dishargarh	1·83	35·95	50·54	14·68	1·41	7,074	Gives a hard porous coke
Sanctoria	2·31	34·78	51·07	11·84	1·47	6,983	ditto
Ghusick ..	4·10	33·80	53·50	12·70	1·58	6,791	Poor coke
Raniganj..	5·81	33·14	45·90	15·15	1·39	6,067	Very poor coke
Jambad ..	5·19	36·98	45·59	12·24	1·23	..	ditto

The Coal Measures of Raniganj, like those of the other fields of the eastern part of the Damodar valley, Jharia and Giridih, were intruded by ultrabasic dykes and sills during the later part of the Mesozoic period, which in many instances have resulted in the production of large quantities of *jhama*, the local name for partially coked coal.

Gee estimated the reserves of the Raniganj field as follows:

RESERVES OF THE RANIGANJ COALFIELD (1932)

	To a depth of 1,000 feet	To a depth of 2,000 feet
Caking coal of superior quality ..	81,791,000 tons	249,905,000 tons
Non-caking coal of superior quality	963,644,000 ,,	1,570,730,000 ,,
Coal of inferior quality	4,631,142,000 ,,	6,859,291,000 ,,

The estimates of 'coal of inferior quality' were limited to seams and portions of seams of proved economic value, and the term ' caking coal of superior quality ' includes not only coals which yield good metallurgical coke without admixture, but also those reserves of good coal which when mixed with a strongly caking, low volatile coal have proved to yield a good coke. Recent surveys by A. N. Banerjee and others place the reserves of straight coking coal in the Laikdih, Ramnagar and Begunia seams at a round figure of 103,000,000 tons, of which some 84 million tons are recoverable if underground stowing is adopted.

Jharia. The Jharia coalfield, with an area of 175 square miles, of which 105 square miles are occupied by coal-bearing rocks, lies about 30 miles west of the Raniganj field, and although coal was known to occur here before 1858, mining was not undertaken seriously until 1894, when the field became linked to the railway system. From that time production has risen from 15,000 tons to a maximum of 12,692,234 tons, or 39·3 per cent of the Indian total, in 1950, the total yield of the field to the end of that year being 453,461,681 tons, omitting the two years 1895 and 1896, for which separate data are not available.

As in the case of the Raniganj field, the coal-bearing Damuda rocks of Jharia display a threefold subdivision, though with certain important differences. Thus, the Lower or Barakar Measures, about 2,000 feet thick, contain a far greater total thickness of coal, probably exceeding 200 feet, and all of low volatile, coking quality. Secondly, the Ironstone Shales of Raniganj are here represented by a thick series of unproductive sandstones termed the Barren Measures, and thirdly, above these Barren Measures only the lower part of the Upper Measures of the Raniganj sequence occurs in the Jharia field and its coal seams are relatively unimportant by comparison. Intrusions of mica-peridotite dykes are numerous and have burnt many millions of tons of coal into natural coke or *jhama*, which, however, may not be without its economic value in the future. The two groups of Coal Measures are divided into the following Stages.

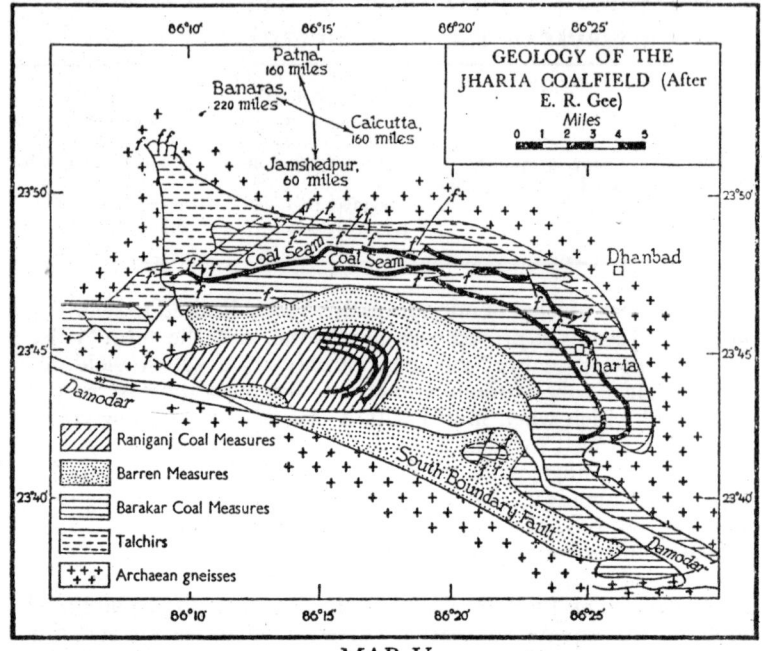

MAP V

THE BARAKAR (LOWER) COAL MEASURES OF THE JHARIA FIELD

No. 4.	Bhagaband Stage	700 to 900 feet of strata, the uppermost Barakars. Includes coal seams XVI to XVIII, mainly of superior quality.
No. 3.	Jialgara or Barari Stage ..	250 to 300 feet of strata. Includes seams XIII to XV, mainly of superior quality.
No. 2.	Gareira or Nardkarki Stage	300 to 350 feet of strata. Includes seams VIII to XII, of moderate quality, except seam XII which is of good quality.
No. 1.	Muraidih or Golakadih Stage	500 to 600 feet of strata, the basal Barakars. Includes seams I to VII, mainly of inferior quality.

These Barakar Measures contain not less than 24 separate seams, each with not less than four feet of coal, while many of them are of considerable thickness and often exceed twenty feet. In some cases two thick seams are separated by only a thin sequence of sandstones and shales. In the seams of the Jialgara and Bhagaband Stages there exist some of the best coking and steam-raising coals of the Republic, and until recently the Indian iron and steel industry depended in great measure on cokes made from seams XV, XIV A, and XIV, with XVII and XIII, as well as XVIII, in the order named. They are ' Selected Grade A ' kinds, banded, bright and dull coals of better quality than any other varieties of Gondwana age, with the exception of the coal from the Lower Karharbari seam of the Giridih field. Later it has been found that seams X and XI of the Gareira Stage, as well as XVI and XVIA of the Bhagaband Stage, also contain satisfactory coking coal in restricted areas though they generally require careful preparation by washing.

THE RANIGANJ (UPPER) COAL MEASURES OF THE JHARIA FIELD

No. 4. Lohpiti and Kangra sandstones, thickness 200 feet, uppermost.
No. 3. TELMUCHA and PATHARGARIA Coal Measures, thickness 200 feet.
No. 2. Jamdiha and Kumardih sandstones, thickness 500 feet.
No. 1. BAMANGORA and MURULIDIH Coal Measures, thickness 720 feet, basal.

At Telmucha there are three seams, the uppermost being 7 feet thick and the lower ones 3 to 4 feet thick each. In the Bamangora Stage there are seven seams of which three are potentially workable with an average total thickness of 15 to 16 feet.

In 1934, Sir Cyril Fox calculated the reserves of the field as follows:

RESERVES OF THE JHARIA COALFIELD (1934)

Series	Stages		Millions of Tons at Depths of		
			500 ft.	1,000 ft.	2,000 ft.
Upper Measures	Telmucha ..	..	17	29	29
	Murulidih ..	..	36	61	61
	Bhagaband	..	115	225	225
Lower Measures	Jialgara ..	..	293	568	731
	Gareira ..	..	580	1,100	1,550
	Muraidih ..	..	630	1,103	1,575
	Extras ..		36	36	36
	TOTAL ..		1,707	3,122	4,207

' Making allowances for loss from fires and subsidences, and including the coal left in pillars, it may be broadly stated ', wrote Fox, ' that for every ton of coal raised from the seams in question, an equal quantity has been rendered unavailable by existing methods of working.' The ' seams in question ' were those of the Bhagaband and Jialgara Stages supplying most of the coking coals, and Fox was driven to the conclusion that at the rate they were then being mined, the reserves of roughly 800 million tons, to a depth of 1,000 feet, must be exhausted within 40 to 50 years, unless mining methods were quickly improved.

Much attention has been devoted to this problem in more recent years and a Working Party of the Geological Survey of India, after making a new computation in 1951, concluded that the reserves of coking coal *in situ* still amount to some 1,200 million tons of Selected Grades A and B (including 325 million tons in unworked areas), and some 766 million tons of Grades I and II (including 85 million tons in unworked areas). It is stressed, however, that without the adoption of stowing as mining proceeds, only 508 million tons of the former and 383 million tons of the latter grades are likely to be won. Even under the best mining practice the losses are likely to amount to one-fifth of the total quantity. As regards reserves of coking coal lying at greater depths than 2,000 feet below the surface, Dr E. R. Gee has suggested that they may be of the order of 1,000 million tons, after allowing for losses caused by igneous intrusions and in mining, but until the results of deep boring tests are available, this question must remain highly speculative.

TYPICAL ANALYSES OF JHARIA, LOWER MEASURES (BARAKAR) COALS

Stage	Seam (*)	Moisture	Volatile Matter	Fixed Carbon	Ash	Fuel Ratio	Calorific Value
Bhagaband ..	XVIII	1·80	24·60	65·00	10·40	2·64	7,608
,, ..	XVII A	1·68	26·85	63·30	9·85	2·35	7,634
,, ..	XVII	1·70	26·70	62·30	11·00	2·33	7,517
,, ..	XVI	2·10	24·35	52·65	23·00	2·16	6,410
Jialgara ..	XV	1·24	22·10	64·66	13·24	2·92	7,693
,, ..	XIV	1·08	24·32	60·65	15·02	2·49	7,185
,, ..	XIII	0·80	21·20	66·40	12·40	3·13	7,403
Gareira ..	XII	0·90	19·80	62·80	17·40	3·17	7,004
,, ..	XI	1·08	20·65	64·47	14·88	3·12	7,291
,, ..	X	1·20	20·20	59·40	20·40	2·94	6,681
Muraidih ..	V to VII	1·02	15·15	63·90	20·95	4·22	6,607
,, ..	V/VI	0·65	14·20	68·00	17·80	4·79	7,141

(*) The collieries which supplied the 12 samples quoted were, in descending order :—Dharmaband, Baliari, Jamadoba, South Baliari, Lodna, Bhalgora, Banjora, Chetudih, Katras, Kujura, Behaldi East and Matiagara North. All the samples are coking coals.

TYPICAL ANALYSES OF JHARIA, UPPER MEASURES (RANIGANJ) COALS

Stage	Seam	Moisture	Volatile Matter	Fixed Carbon	Ash	Fuel Ratio	Calorific Value
Telmucha ..	D.	2·11	28·40	52·80	18·80	1·86	6,607
Murulidih ..	Hatudih	2·07	32·20	52·75	15·05	1·64	7,084
,, ..	Bamangora	1·64	28·75	55·10	16·15	1·92	6,944
,, ..	Koradih	2·20	27·68	57·20	15·12	2·07	7,403

Brown & Dey, *India's Mineral Wealth, facing p. 19*

V.P. Sondhi, G.S.I.

THE 100-FOOT KARGALI SEAM OF THE BOKARO COALFIELD

The small area of Barakar rocks at the extreme western end of the Jharia field, isolated from it by a narrow strip of Talchir strata, is sometimes referred to as the Chandrapura coalfield. It is but an outlying fragment, less than one square mile in extent, and it contains nine seams with about 10 million tons of coal, mostly of inferior quality.

Bokaro. Two or three miles west of Jharia lies the Bokaro coalfield, occupying an area of 220 square miles in the Hazaribagh district of Bihar, and including a long strip of Gondwana rocks stretching westwards for 40 miles, from Chirudih and in the catchment of the Bokaro river. Its rock sequence includes some 2,750 feet of sandstones and shales of Middle Damuda age, corresponding to the Barren Measures of the Jharia field and like them containing no coal, but they are followed downwards by the coal-bearing Barakar (Lower Damuda) Series, with a total thickness of 2,694 feet. These Barakar rocks were subdivided by Sir Lewis Fermor as follows:

(d)	Upper Sandstones and Shales.	982 feet thick with 68 feet of coal in 10 thin seams.
(c)	Middle ,, ,, ,, .	863 feet thick with 232 feet of coal in 6 thick seams.
(b)	Lower Grits, ,, ,, ,, .	396 feet thick with 25 feet of coal in 7 thin seams.
(a)	Basal Grits and Conglomerates.	128 feet thick.

Later work has proved that the seams vary considerably from place to place, the most important ones occurring in the Middle Stage (c), and in downward succession comprising the ' A ' seam, 12 feet in thickness, the Kargali seam which varies from 41 feet to the enormous total of 123 feet, the Bermo seam from 40 to 46 feet thick, and the Karo seam which is again remarkable for its great thickness of from 70 to 120 feet. In some localities the Kargali seam splits into two sections, separated by comparatively narrow bands of rock. As in the case of the other fields of the Damodar valley already described, dolerite and mica peridotite dykes are common in the Coal Measures. The eastern part of the field has been developed to a greater extent than its western section and very largely by collieries belonging to the State Railways.

By 1910 three collieries were under development in this field and its output jumped from 10,000 tons to almost 200,000 tons per annum on the approach of a railway in 1916, through communication being finally established in 1919. Over one million tons were raised in 1922, or 5·46 of the Indian total for that year. Its highest output was 2,775,286 tons (9·34 per cent of the total) in 1946. In 1950, 1,864,960 tons were won, and the total quantity of coal taken from the field up to the end of that year was 55,598,000 tons, approximately.

Upwards of 90 per cent of the output comes from the Kargali and Bokaro collieries, the property of the Indian Government Railways, and to deal with the extraordinarily thick seams, mechanized outcrop mining has been adopted. On the Kargali seam, which varies from 70 to 110 feet in thickness on this particular property, ten electrically or Diesel-driven excavators operate on a series of four benches, loading directly from the coal face into broad-gauge railway wagons. Besides the Kargali seam, the Karo and Bermo seams, with thicknesses of 120 and 45 feet respectively, occur at these mines.

It has been estimated that in 15 square miles of the Bokaro field there are at least 3,000 million tons of coal of all descriptions, but unfortunately the ash content tends to be high—about 16 per cent in the case of the Kargali and over 27 per cent in that of the Bermo seam, which nevertheless, according to A. B. Dutt, contains some 220 million tons of coal. The Kargali coal can, however, be washed to yield a coke acceptable to the iron and steel makers and its present reserves are estimated to be 583 million tons. Several seams of coking coal are known to occur in the western part of the field, ranging from 9 to 11 feet in thickness, the proven reserves totalling some 88 million tons with an ash content of about 15·6 per cent. A modern coal-washing plant, using the Chance process, is in operation in this section for the Tata Iron & Steel Company. A typical sample of coal from the Kargali seam of West Bokaro contains: moisture 1·6, volatile matter 23·57, fixed carbon 58·96 and ash 16·31 per cent.

Ramgarh. The Ramgarh coalfield, in the Hazaribagh district, lies along the valley of the Damodar river, about 5 miles south-west of Bokaro, and it has an area of some 40 square miles, including 30 square miles of Barakar Coal Measures. Its more prominent seams include the Upper and Lower Ranta, each averaging 20 feet in thickness; the Upper and Lower Sugia, 25 and 15 feet thick, respectively; the Upper and Lower Semabera, 25 and 50 feet thick, respectively; and the Upper and Lower Mael seams, 40 to 60 feet in total thickness. The coals are of medium quality and are said to be of semi-coking varieties. The reserves so far proved total 188 million tons down to relatively shallow depths. Production from Ramgarh first appeared in the annual returns in 1943, and from that time until the end of 1950, 486,397 tons had been won.

North and South Karanpura. A few miles west of the Bokaro field and in the Upper Damodar valley lie the two coalfields of North and South Karanpura, with areas of about 475 and 75 square miles respectively. Mapped by T. W. H. Hughes of the Geological Survey of India, in 1867–8, they were resurveyed by A. Jowett in 1915–18, and the Coal Measures again found to include rocks of both the Barakar (Lower) and Raniganj (Upper) Series, separated, here as elsewhere, by a thick series of barren strata.

The most important seams occur in the Barakar Series, which in the southern field, lying in the Hazaribagh district, has a thickness of 2,500 feet, of which 280 feet are of coal. Included amongst these seams are the Nakari (7 feet), the Semana (12 feet), the Argada, ranging in thickness from 50 to 120 feet, and the Sirka, which in some cases is 20 feet thick and in others ranges up to 50 feet approximately.

Production commenced in 1925 and rose rapidly with the provision of railway communication to a maximum of 978,695 tons, or 3·25 per cent of the Indian total, in 1947. The total output up to the end of 1950 was 13,494,877 tons. Hughes estimated that 8,750 million tons of coal were available, while according to Jowett, the total quantity of first and second class coal in the Karanpura fields must amount to between 5,000 and 10,000 million tons, to a depth of 2,000 feet. Several open-cast and underground workings have been developed by railway companies and others of late years in the Argada and Sirka seams of South Karanpura. The coal is high in ash—about 20 per cent—but is a useful steaming variety which yields a fairly hard coke. Recent estimates put the reserves of the Argada and Sirka seams at 450 million tons to a depth of 1,000 feet, but they are not included in the official figures of the Republic's reserves of good coking coals.

The North Karanpura field, lying partly in the Hazaribagh and partly in the Palamau district, is known to contain several thick coal seams similar to those of South Karanpura, but remains to be exploited. The economic value of the thin seams of the Upper Measures (Raniganj) of both fields is doubtful.

Chope and Itkhori. Lying to the north of the Karanpura fields and on the Hazaribagh plateau are the two, tiny, unopened coalfields of Chope and Itkhori. The coal-bearing Barakar rocks of the former cover less than one square mile and contain a seam, 4 feet thick, of impure coal. The latter, smaller still, has three seams, one of which is 8 feet and the other 4 feet thick. Hughes estimated the reserves at 1½ million tons of coal.

Sahajuri, Jainti and Kundit Karaia. Forming, as it were, outliers to the great fields of the Damodar valley proper, and actually in the valleys of the Adjai and Barakar rivers, tributaries of the Damodar, are the coalfields of Sahajuri, Jainti, Kundit Karaia and Giridih. The three first-named, in the Santal Parganas, are sometimes grouped together as the Deogarh coalfields and possess a combined area of 28½ square miles, of which 11½ square miles are occupied by Barakar rocks. The opinion of T. W. H. Hughes in the case of Jainti, that in any summary of the coal resources of India it must occupy a very subordinate position, probably applies equally well to all.

Coal was obtained from Jainti in 1886, but organized mining dates from 1914: the record output was reached with 152,941 tons, in 1919 (0·69 per cent of the Indian total): the total production to the end of 1950 was 2,011,751 tons, and that for 1950 alone, 13,710 tons. According to H. S. Dutta, the field contains 5 seams, all of which have been mined at one time or another, while their average thickness appears to be about 5 feet. P. K. Chatterjee, writing in 1934, stated that 2 million tons of good quality coal were then available, of which half is coking coal. The same geologist estimated the workable reserves of the Sahajuri field at 22 million tons, contained in two seams of 18 to 25 feet in thickness, but this coal is inferior in quality and high in ash. The Kundit Karaia field possesses two thin seams of very inferior coal.

Giridih. The Giridih coalfield, in the Hazaribagh district of Bihar, was first brought to notice by McClelland in 1848, and though its area is only about 11 square miles, of which 7 are occupied by Barakar rocks, it has been of great importance by reason of its favourable geographical position and the fact that it yields some of the best coal in India. Systematic mining was initiated in 1851, and its geological survey was undertaken by Hughes in 1868. A railway reached it in 1871 and its exploitation has continued vigorously since then.

The principal seams are the Lower Karharbari, varying between 10 and 24 feet in thickness; the Upper Karharbari, from 4 to 10 feet thick, and the Bhaddoah, averaging about 6 feet. There are other seams with an aggregate thickness of 66 feet, but much of this is of poor quality. The two Karharbari seams have between them provided India with much of its finest metallurgical coking coal in the past. In 1934, Fox estimated the total available coal at about 49 million tons, but as far as good coking coal is concerned, only 17 million tons were left in 1950. For a great many years the whole of the Giridih lump coal was used as locomotive fuel by the railways, while the slack was converted into coke, slack coal from other fields being brought to the Giridih collieries for their own power-raising purposes.

By 1880 the output from the field had reached 400,000 tons and in 1946, at 464,658 tons, it was not much greater: in 1950, 335,581 tons were raised, being 1·04 per cent of the total production. Its record output was 950,045 tons (4·2 per cent) in 1919 and from 1900 to 1950, inclusive, 35,784,440 tons of coal have been taken.

Rajmahal Hills. To the north of the Damodar valley coal measures of Barakar age are exposed over an area of about 70 square miles, in a number of small isolated patches on the western margin of the Rajmahal Hills of eastern Bihar: to the west of them the underlying ancient crystalline floor crops out, while above them to the east are basaltic lavas gently dipping in that direction. They include Hura, near the northern end of the Hills, with two seams 4 and 16 feet thick respectively; Jilbari, where two seams of poor coal, one of which is 6 feet thick, have been worked spasmodically in the past; Chuparbhita, where several seams up to 9 feet in thickness, but all of poor quality, are known; Pachwara, where coal is won on a small scale for local brick burning; the Mahuagarhi Tract, about which little is known but which presumably contains coal, and the Brahmani field, in which, according to Chakravarti, there are about $29\frac{1}{2}$ million tons of impure coal in a seam with a maximum thickness of 4 feet. V. Ball, as long ago as 1869, calculated that 210 million tons of coal could easily be won from these fields, but Fox concluded in 1934 that the material is not attractive even on a moisture-free basis. Exploitation is confined to the extraction of small quantities of outcrop coal for local uses. The production in 1950 was 1,443 tons, and from 1898 to the end of that year had attained a total of 108,523 tons, omitting the period 1915 to 1918 for which production figures are not available.

Auranga, Hutar and Daltonganj. The main belt of the coalfields of the Damodar valley continues westwards into that of the Koel river and its tributaries, affluents of the Son. These three fields are often referred to as the Palamau group, from the name of the district in which they are situated. Auranga, with an area of over 100 square miles, was surveyed by Ball in 1878 and then by Dunn in 1928, who states that it was described as a ' coalfield ' because it consists of Lower Gondwana rocks which contain a few, rare, coal bands. The seams, although up to 40 feet thick, consist largely of carbonaceous shale and the coal itself is so high in ash and moisture that its large-scale systematic exploitation is said to be doubtful. Be this as it may, a colliery, at which operations were started in 1944, supplies fuel to brick works and cement factories.

The Hutar field, 12 miles west of Auranga, covers an area of about 80 square miles, and five seams are known in its Barakar rocks; thin over much of their spread but occasionally thickening to more than 13 feet. One seam, 8 feet thick, of first-class coal is known, but most of the others are of lower grade. Dunn estimated that over an area of 4 square miles, 32 million tons of average, Indian-quality coal are available. Known since 1779, parts of the field have been explored from time to time and it will unquestionably attract more attention in future. The Sone Valley Portland Cement Co. commenced mining at Barichatan in 1946, in two seams which were originally opened up by the Bengal Coal Co. in 1925. The coal, said to contain $31\cdot4$ per cent volatile matter, $51\cdot8$ per cent fixed carbon and $16\cdot8$ per cent of ash, with a calorific value of 6,600 calories, is brought to Barwadih railway station by ropeway for use in the cement works at Japla.

In the Daltonganj field the coal-bearing Barakars crop out over an area of 32 square miles. Coal was known to occur here in 1829, was mined between 1842 and 1848, and later still by the Bengal Coal Company whose colliery at Rajhara was wrecked in 1857. In those early days the coal was transported by boat down the North Koel river, as a railway did not reach the field until 1901. A boring, 450 feet deep, near Rajhara, penetrated 14 coal seams ranging from 6 inches to 5 feet in thickness, but mining has been limited to the Rajhara seam which locally reaches a maximum of 29 feet. The coal is a non-coking kind and of second-grade quality. As in the case of other semi-explored fields, estimates of its reserves vary widely and the available amounts will not be known definitely until a large-scale geological survey and systematic boring over the whole area is undertaken. According to La Touche (1891) there are about 9 million tons of coal of fair quality in one square mile near Rajhara. For many years production was maintained between 70,000 and 80,000 tons per annum; the record year was in 1908 when 96,391 tons were raised, but output gradually fell away and ceased entirely between 1932 and 1937. Between 1938 and 1950 inclusive, 279,424 tons were won from the two fields of Daltonganj and Hutar. The total production of the Palamau fields between 1900 and 1950, inclusive, was 1,744,930 tons.

Darjeeling. Coal-bearing rocks of Damuda age are found in the Outer Himalayan ranges of the Darjeeling district and of other regions further to the east, such as Bhutan and some of the hilly frontier tracts of north Assam, where, as far as is known, they are of no particular value. Many coal seams, varying in thickness from 2 to 11 feet, were discovered by F. R. Mallet, in 1874, in the 30 miles of country between Pankabari and Daling. The coal itself is in a powdery condition, though P. N. Bose's later researches, in 1890–1, proved that some of it has coking properties. In the Lish valley, near Bagrakot, coal has been exploited since 1943, at an annual rate of 15,000 to 25,000 tons: the production for the four years ending 1950 was 79,022 tons. Thin, steeply dipping seams of powdery coal also occur in the Phagu and Lethi blocks of the Kalimpong Forest Division.

Sikkim. To the north of the Darjeeling district, in the interior ranges of the Lesser Himalaya of western Sikkim, lies the Rangit Valley field in which Coal Measures of Lower Gondwana age extend over an area of 40 or 50 square miles. First visited by T. H. D. La Touche in 1909, the significance of its age was not at that time appreciated and it was not until 1953, when A. M. N. Ghosh published a preliminary account of his investigations, that reliable data of its structure and resources became available.

The field contains several seams, usually from 8 to 12 feet thick, though one, about three-fourths of a mile north-north-east of the confluence of the Rishi *khola* and the Rangit river, attains a thickness of almost 25 feet. The coal, as might be expected from the

intensive mountain-building movements in which these Gondwana
rocks have taken part, is of a semi-anthracitic character, an average
analysis of eleven samples from various seams showing moisture
3·65, volatile matter 8·13, fixed carbon 57·36 and ash 30·86
per cent. It is non-coking, requires a good draught to commence
ignition, burns with a short, smokeless flame, provided a draught
is maintained, and has a calorific value varying between 8,730
and 12,335 British Thermal Units with the particular seam tested.
According to A. M. N. Ghosh at least 240 million tons are available, assuming a workable thickness of 6 feet.

Although the southern boundary of the Rangit Valley field
is only about 6 miles north of Darjeeling, it lies some 6,000 feet
below the level of the town and this will necessitate the construction
of an aerial ropeway, unless the use of the coal is to be restricted
to tea gardens in the neighbourhood of the field.

Talchir. This coalfield, the most easterly member in the
Mahanadi-Gondwana zone, lies in the valley of the Brahmani,
some 65 miles north-west of Cuttack. The earliest discovery of
its coal was announced in 1827, and its first survey was made by
the Blanford brothers and W. Theobald, in 1855, with disappointing
results, though they have the distinction of forming the subject of
the first memoir published by the Geological Survey of India,
dated 1856. The field covers an area of at least 200 square miles;
its coal-bearing Damuda Series is about 1,800 feet thick, is said to
belong to the Barakar Stage, and is overlain unconformably by
Upper Gondwana rocks of the Mahadeva Series.

A systematic drilling campaign conducted by Villiers Ltd of
Calcutta between 1919 and 1923 proved that the productive seams,
at least in the area examined, are confined to the lower section of
the Barakar rocks, but only 11 square miles to the west of Talchir
town have been thoroughly prospected and found to contain about
184½ million tons of recoverable coal, after allowing for a loss of
40 per cent in extraction. Production commenced in 1923, two
seams of 9 and 13 feet in thickness, separated by about 12 to 35 feet
of strata, being mined. The record output was 512,375 tons, or
1·74 per cent of the Indian total in 1941: in 1959, 232,440 tons
were won and the total amount of coal taken from the field up to
the end of that year was 7,113,212 tons. Though comparatively
low in ash, the Talchir coals are non-coking and have a high
moisture content, but they have proved of practical value for
use as locomotive fuels, indeed, the Duelbera (Talchir) colliery
has been operated by the Indian Government Railways since
1937.

Rampur-Hingir. The Rampur coalfield forms the central part
of the long belt of Lower Gondwana rocks stretching north-westwards up the Mahanadi valley into Madhya Pradesh. Lying as

it does across administrative boundaries which have themselves been changed from time to time, it suffers from a confusing multiplicity of names bestowed on all, or parts of it, both by Government Departments and geologists. Sir Cyril Fox in 1934 proposed to restrict the name Rampur (or Ib River) coalfield to its extreme eastern tip, which now lies in the Sambalpur district of Orissa; to separate a narrow strip of its Barakar rocks on the north as the Hingir field; to name a similar portion of Barakar rocks on the north-west as the South Raigarh field; while the main portion which lies in Madhya Pradesh should, he suggested, retain the name of Raigarh. For present purposes the nomenclature adopted by the Geological Survey of India in its more recent publications is followed. In any case, these separate areas of Barakar rocks are probably continuous under the younger Gondwanas which now superficially divide them.

As a whole the field covers some 200 square miles in Sambalpur and Gangpur (Orissa) and about a further 200 square miles in Raigarh (Madhya Pradesh); the greater part of it has still to be mapped on a large scale and but little is known of its real potentialities. Surveys of part of the area were done by V. Ball in 1871 and 1875, and a series of borings made under the superintendence of W. King between 1884 and 1886 were not particularly encouraging, though thick seams of inferior coal were proved. The accidental discovery of a coal seam during sinking operations for the foundations of the railway bridge over the Ib river led to another survey by G. F. Reader in 1900, when four seams, varying from 4 to 17 feet in thickness, were found by boring. The Ib Bridge seam, however, was the only one with a low enough ash percentage to be worth working. In 1936, Fox calculated that it contains at least 140 million tons of coal within a depth of 600 feet from the surface. Mining commenced in 1929 at the Rampur-Hingir colliery, while a second, the Ib River colliery, began operations in 1940. The highest production was in 1942 with 146,733 tons, while the total amount of coal taken from the field up to the end of 1950 was 2,430,245 tons. Air-dried coal from the Rampur-Hingir colliery has the following composition: Moisture 9·49 per cent, volatile matter 27·74 per cent, fixed carbon 49·19 per cent, ash 13·58 per cent.

VINDHYA PRADESH

The only coal-bearing rocks of Lower Gondwana age within the limits of Vindhya Pradesh are those of the Rewah region, embracing the coalfields of Umaria, Sohagpur, Johilla, Korar and Singrauli. Of the 1,022,364,245 tons of coal raised in India during the first fifty-one years of the present century, 13,572,735 tons, or 1·3 per cent, were derived from the producing fields of Umaria, Sohagpur and Johilla.

Umaria. Deriving its name from the Umrar river, a tributary of the Son, on which it lies 36 miles south-east of Katni, this field was surveyed by Hughes between 1881 and 1884. It has an area of 6 square miles, but its Barakar rocks, which contain six coal seams, dip under younger strata and may be continuous with those of the Korar field, three miles away. Of its six seams, four are workable and range from 3 to 4·5 feet (No. IV), to 8·5 to 13 feet in the case of No. III, but the coal is relatively high both in moisture and ash. Because of its location on the railway between Katni and Bilaspur, the field attracted early attention and mining commenced in 1884. In 1885, its reserves were believed to be 55 million tons, but in 1934 Fox calculated the future available supply at 24 million tons. The record output was 200,285 tons (1·16 per cent of the total) in 1916, but since then there has been a decline, more than compensated, as far as the region as a whole is concerned, by production from Sohagpur and developments on the Johilla field. The output from Umaria in 1950 was 105,603 tons, and the total production from 1884 to 1950 has been 7,439,192 tons, including that from Johilla between 1898 and 1902.

Korar. The small undeveloped field of Korar, surveyed by Hira Lal and Hughes in 1882, has an area of 9½ square miles and lies about 7 miles north-by-east of Umaria. Four seams, ranging from 4 to 8 feet thick, have been proved by boring to a depth of 50 feet.

Sohagpur. Sohagpur is the largest of the coalfields of Rewah and, as mapped by Hughes in 1880, covers 1,600 square miles, but parts of it which cross the borders into Madhya Pradesh have been given separate names. To avoid confusion it has to be borne in mind that the Jhagrakhand coalfield (see page 29) is but the south-eastern corner of the Sohagpur field and that the Sanhat and Jhilmili fields (see pp. 29 and 32) are its eastern extensions into Korea and Surguja respectively. As thus reduced the Sohagpur field occupies about 1,200 square miles in Rewah. Nine-tenths of this extensive area is covered by Barakar rocks, and details of many coal outcrops have been given both by Hughes and by K. P. Sinor (1923). As far as existing information goes it is safe to state that a number of seams of workable thickness exist, some of which are of promising quality, while their low dips and great areal extent lead to the belief that when detailed explorations come to be made the reserves are likely to amount to very large figures. Thus at Rajnagar near Dola in the easternmost end of the field, in an area of 5 square miles leased to Messrs Dalchand Bahadur Singh, a seam 5 to 15 feet thick, with 9 to 10 per cent ash, is estimated to contain about 50 million tons of coal. Another, about 32 feet in thickness, exposed in a small portion of the leased area, is said to contain 12 million tons but the ash content is 25 to 30 per cent.

The south-western part of the field has railway communications, and mining was commenced on a 10-foot seam of the Burhar-Amlei area in 1921. Sohagpur, with an output of 131,174 tons, passed the Umaria production in 1924 and reached its peak of 379,227 tons (1·25 per cent of the total) in 1948. In 1950, 358,988 tons were won (1·11 per cent) and from the beginning to the end of that year its total raisings amount to 5,961,845 tons.

Johilla River Fields. The Barakar Coal Measures occur again in two separate tracts in the valley of the Johilla river, near Birsingh-pur, on the Katni-Bilaspur line. The northern area covers 11½ and the southern one 3¼ square miles. A few borings in the northern area led Hughes to conclude that at least 20 feet of coal exist, from which 100 million tons might be available within a depth of 500 feet, but this estimate was reduced by Fox to 30 million tons in 1934. Later borings were encouraging; systematic production commenced in 1940 and has steadily increased, reaching 327,592 tons (1·01 per cent of the Indian total) in 1950. The whole recorded output up to the end of 1950 was 1,426,397 tons, omitting the small production over the years 1898 to 1902, included in the Umaria figures.

Singrauli. The area of the Singrauli field, originally surveyed by R. D. Oldham and P. N. Dutta about 1895, and later examined by K. P. Sinor and A. L. Coulson, covers about 900 square miles, extending from Rewah into the south-western corner of the Mirzapur district of Uttar Pradesh. Several coal seams are known to exist, especially near Parari and Naunagar, one of which, originally reported to have a thickness of 18 feet, has recently been found to be 40 feet thick: an exposure located by F. Ahmad, in the Pipraunhi *nala*, displays over 50 feet of coal and may be an extension of the same seam.

Many years ago small quantities of coal used to be extracted and carted to Mirzapur for use on the Ganga river steamers, indeed a small colliery was working near Kota in 1857, but the isolation of the field has hindered its proper exploration let alone development. The reserves of the field will certainly be very large and there is already evidence that some of the coal is of attractive quality. The completion of through railway connexion between Barwadih, to the south of Daltonganj, and Anuppur, on the Katni-Bilaspur line, would enable the Singrauli field to be reached by a short feeder line.

MADHYA PRADESH

The producing coalfields of Madhya Pradesh accounted for 6 per cent of the total Indian production of over 1,022 million tons of coal raised from 1900 to 1950, though by 1950 alone the proportion had risen to 9·41 per cent of 31,885,096 tons. The fields fall into four natural groups, which include those portions of the Rewah-Gondwana basin stretching across into Madhya Pradesh; those fields lying for the most part in the valleys of the tributaries of the Son, and which form, as it were, a zone joining the western prolongation of the Damodar valley fields to those of the Brahmani-Mahanadi line; the fields of the Satpura region; and, finally, the Wardha valley group.

GROUP I

The accident of a political frontier divides part of the coalfields of the Rewah-Gondwana basin which lie in Vindhya Pradesh from their neighbours in Madhya Pradesh, the State formerly known as the Central Provinces. Coal-bearing Barakar rocks occupy four distinct areas within the boundaries of Korea: they comprise about 416 of its area of 1,647 square miles and are termed the Sanhat, Jhagrakhand, Kurasia-Chirmiri and Koreagarh fields. The two former fields are eastern extensions of the great Sohagpur field of south Rewah.

Sanhat. The largest field of the group with its area of 330 square miles, the Sanhat field occupies the plateau across the central portion of Korea. Surveyed originally by Hughes and Hira Lal in 1885, it was re-examined by Fermor in 1914 and by Coulson in 1923, and although parts of it are leased for mining and others are being prospected, development cannot proceed until railway communication is established. According to K. K. Dutta, about 35 million tons of selected and first-grade coal, 37 millions of second-grade and at least 22 million tons of inferior coal have already been proved.

Included in these estimates are the reserves of certain seams in the Kutkona, Churcha and Sardih sections of the field, which lie on its eastern boundary and about 8 miles further to the west, respectively. The first-named has a seam of $4\frac{1}{2}$ feet separated from a lower one, 13 feet in thickness, by 154 to 164 feet of strata. This lower seam has about 9 million tons of selected grade coal. In the Churcha section, two seams of 4 and 8 feet thickness are capable of yielding 1,700,000 tons of selected coal and 1,800,000 tons of a slightly lower grade. In the Sardih section about 6 million tons are available from a seam approximately 12 to 14 feet thick, assuming a workable thickness of 6 feet. It is anticipated that further prospecting will increase these estimates greatly.

Jhagrakhand. The Jhagrakhand field includes some 30 square miles of Barakar rocks in the south-west of Korea, which are continuous north and west with strata of the same age in the main Sohagpur field. Coulson, who surveyed it in 1923, described three coal-bearing horizons, the lowest of which, extending over 4 or

5 square miles, he believed contained 30·8 million tons of good coal per square mile, in seams of 4 and 6 feet thickness. The coal of the second horizon was of lower grade, while the lateral extent of the highest one was limited and its seams thin. According to K. K. Dutta, there are only two seams, of which the lower, 5 to 7 feet thick, is of superior quality and workable below an area of almost 7 square miles. Some 36 million tons of selected and first-grade coals have already been proved in a portion of the northern section of the field. Both the Jhagrakhand and the Kurasia-Chirmiri field, described below, are now in an advanced stage of development and are served by a feeder line from Anuppur on the Bilaspur-Katni branch of the Eastern Railway.

Kurasia-Chirmiri. In 1884, Hughes gave the name Kurasia to the detached area of 50 square miles of coal-bearing Barakar rocks lying within Korea, 4 to 6 miles south of the Sanhat field; today the field is also called the Chirmiri, after the Chirmiri Colliery started in 1930. Fermor, after a detailed examination in 1915, wrote of the considerable quantities of excellent coal in the field as well worth the expenditure on boring. This has now taken place and six areas in the field are today leased for exploitation. The most important lease is the Chirmiri Colliery of the Ballarpur Collieries Co. Ltd. It comprises an area of 4·75 square miles and mining commenced in 1930 on a 20-foot seam, which now has reserves of about 85 million tons.

The Gorghela area, about 10 square miles in the south-east, leased to the Tata Iron & Steel Co. Ltd, contains according to the Company's geologists eleven coal-bearing horizons: VIII— 'Duman', VIIA, VII—'Kotmi', VIA, VI—'Gorghela', V, IVA, IV—'Loharin', III, II, I. But there are only four workable seams, the Loharin (IV) averaging 5 feet in thickness with 11 per cent ash; the Gorghela (VI) 5 to 11 feet with 13 per cent ash; the Kotmi (VII) made up of a number of bands aggregating about 11 feet in thickness and containing 17 per cent ash, and the Duman (VIII) exposed on the east at an altitude of about 2,150 feet and over with a thickness of about 5 feet and containing 18 per cent ash. Tata's Lachman-Jharia lease in the north-eastern part of the field has an area of about 2·5 square miles and contains only two important horizons: the Lachman-Jharia (VIA) of 3 feet thickness with 18·5 per cent ash and the Bijora (VIIA) containing 8 to 17 feet of coal in two bands separated by a parting of sandstone or shale, 1 to 7 feet in thickness; the ash content of the Bijora seam is about 14 per cent. The total reserves of coal available in the Gorghela and Lachman-Jharia areas are of the order of 40 million tons. North of Tata's Lachman-Jharia lease, three seams, 7½, 6½, and 4 feet thick respectively, are exposed in the Tipkapani *nala*, and according to K. K. Dutta at least 7·5 million tons of coal are available here. In the Kurasia Colliery, a sub-lease from Tata's

Gorghela and originally held by the Bombay, Baroda & Central Indian Railway Company and now by the Government of India and producing since 1932, there are three seams: Nos. 1, 2 and 3 from the top, with thicknesses up to 4, 11 and 23 feet respectively, in an area of about 1·25 square miles. The coal generally is of first-class to selected grade in quality, with 9 to 13 per cent ash, and the total reserves available at the time of writing were of the order of 40 million tons. The Chitajhor area (West Chirmiri Colliery) of 1,792 acres in the north of the field, held under lease by Indra Singh & Sons Ltd, has a seam 10½ to 20 feet in thickness with 11 per cent ash and reserves of nearly 27 million tons. The Bijaurajharia lease (North Chirmiri Colliery) of the United Collieries Ltd has a seam split into three bands with thicknesses of 3 to 4 feet, 7 feet and 4 feet respectively from below upwards, average ash content being 13 per cent and reserves of coal about 30 million tons. The New Ponri Hill Colliery of Sir M. Dadabhoy, producing since 1942, has reserves of almost 74 million tons; and the Sajapahar Colliery of the Central India Coalfields Ltd, which commenced mining in 1945, about 9·5 million tons. The total reserves of the field, as far as they are now known, are 313 million tons, a total which may be expected to rise as development proceeds. The coal is generally selected grade.

Output from the Korea fields, all the coals of which are non-coking, commenced with 3,517 tons in 1930 and increased rapidly to more than one million tons in 1938: the record output was in 1942 with 1,283,356 tons (or 4·63 per cent of the Indian total); in 1950 it was 1,023,570 tons (3·17 per cent), and the total production up to the end of that year was 16,869,412 tons.

Koreagarh. The Koreagarh field, with an area of 6 square miles, lies 3 miles south-east of Kurasia-Chirmiri. Its two, or possibly three, thin seams do not appear to be of much economic importance.

GROUP II

In the next group the coalfields concerned, commencing from the north, are Tatapani-Ramkola, Jhilmili and Bisrampur, sometimes referred to as the coalfields of north-east Surguja, and a number of others sometimes classified as the fields of south-west Surguja and north-east Bilaspur, and including Lakhanpur, Sendurga, Hasdo-Rampur, Mand River, Korba and Raigarh. They lie for the most part in tributaries of either the Son or the Mahanadi, in isolated and inaccessible regions, which caused little attention to be paid to them in the past. The construction of the railway link, however, between Barwadih and Anuppur, commenced in 1947, which will tap many of them, has altered this state of affairs and prospecting has recently become active.

Tatapani-Ramkola. These two coalfields are formed by two separate areas of Damuda rocks, in a tract of Gondwanas situated about 15 miles west of the Hutar coalfield (see page 23) between the Kanher andRehar rivers, northerly flowing tributaries of the Son, in the north-east of Surguja. As the Barakar Coal Measures of Tatapani in the north are only separated from those of Ramkola in the south by a strip of cover rocks belonging to the Panchet and Mahadeva Series, it is legitimate to regard the two as one compound field.

The Coal Measures crop out over an area of about 100 square miles and they were first examined by Griesbach in 1878–9, but although numerous seams were found, few were of workable thickness or quality. Dr A. L. Coulson traversed them again in 1922–3, as geologist accompanying the Central Coalfields Railway Survey, without finding any better material. In 1951, however, Mukti Nath described a seam, 6 feet thick, one mile west-north-west of Mitgain with the following composition: Moisture 10·98 per cent, Volatile Matter 36·46 per cent, Fixed Carbon 44·06 per cent, Ash 8·50 per cent, Calorific Value 5,911. The possibilities of the field will remain doubtful until it is mapped on a large scale and tested by borings.

Jhilmili. This coalfield, recognized by V. Ball about 1872, described from his notes by Hughes in 1885, and re-examined by Coulson in 1923, forms the eastern part of the Sohagpur field lying within the Jhilmili *tahsil* of Surguja—an area of 71 square miles with its Coal Measures continuous with those of the Sanhat field of Korea (see page 29). In the second edition of this book (1936), after referring to the four coal-bearing horizons then known, and the possible existence of others of good quality, it was stated that no estimates of quantities were possible until the field had been bored.

In the intervening years this has been done and four separate areas in it leased for mining, particulars of the proved seams being tabulated below:

COAL SEAMS OF THE JHILMILI FIELD

Lease	Horizon	Seams	Extent		Reserves	Quality	
Baskurpara .. (D. B. Singh)	I	13-14 feet	5½ sq. miles		75m.	16-18% ash	
	II	8-9 ,,	5½ ,, ,,		45m.	16-18% ,,	
	III	5-6 ,,	4½ ,, ,,		24m.	10-12% ,,	
	IV	5 ,,	6 ,, ,,		30m.	10-12% ,,	} ? caking
	V	7 ,,	6 ,, ,,		42m.	10-12% ,,	
Khadapara .. (N. S. Singhi)	—	—	5 ,, ,,		45m.		
Kundhour .. (N. S. Singhi)	—	5 ,,	3 ,, ,,		15m.	13% ash	
Goknai .. (R. S. Singhi)	—	7½ ,,	3 ,, ,,		24m.	11% ,,	
	I	11 ,,	4 ,, ,,		44m.	—	

The reserves as known at present thus amount to 344 million tons. The Goknai area in the north of the field is not yet fully proved, but there are geological grounds for suspecting the existence of Horizons III to V at depth which, if proved by boring, will add considerably to the reserves.

Bisrampur. In the Bisrampur field of central Surguja, V. Ball, in 1872, found the Barakar Coal Measures extending over 400 square miles with good coal in fair abundance, though in his time it had been known for at least 25 years. Coulson gave a summary of such seams as he saw during his traverse in 1922, but in 1936 it was only possible to state the obvious facts that a detailed geological survey and borings were necessary before any reliable estimates could be made.

During the years 1945–7, the Tata Iron & Steel Co. Ltd prospected an area of 180 square miles round Dejagir, Khargaon, Badauli, Patpahari and Pasang, and found the following sequence of coal horizons: Dejagir, Bedra, Barbaspur, Khargaon, Tulsi, Banki-Raima and Badauli. The last one is referable to the Pasang and Patpahari horizons on the west and to the Lainijoba and Barkadharia horizons on the east. Only the Badauli, Khargaon and Dejagir are workable. The Badauli contains two bands with a sandstone split. The upper band is 14 feet thick and contains 5 to 8 per cent Moisture, 34·24 per cent Volatile Matter, 56·56 per cent Fixed Carbon, 5,922 Calorific Value. The lower one is 4 feet with about 5 per cent Moisture, 37·16 per cent Volatile Matter, 54·64 per cent Fixed Carbon, 8·20 per cent Ash, 5,555 Calorific Value. The Khargaon seam, which is about 5 feet thick, contains 38·44 per cent Volatile Matter, 53·40 per cent Fixed Carbon, 8·16 per cent Ash, 6,546 Calorific Value. The Dejagir horizon contains four bands separated by fireclay. The bottom seam is 16 feet thick with an average ash content of 23 per cent, 5,555 Calorific Value. The other three seams have an aggregate thickness of about 14 feet but with higher ash content.

Bansar. A small area of 10 square miles of Barakar rocks, lying 5 miles to the east of Bisrampur, was mapped and named by Hira Lal in 1888–9. It is known to contain at least one thin coal seam and deserves thorough re-examination.

Lakhanpur. The Lakhanpur field lies to the south of Bisrampur, partly in Surguja and partly in the Bilaspur district. It has an area of 135 square miles and was reconnoitred partly by Ball in 1870-1 and partly by Hira Lal in 1887-8. Beyond the fact that several outcrops of coal seams, ranging from 3 to 9 feet thick, have been located, next to nothing is known of its possibilities. Much the same applies to most of the remaining fields of Group II, to be mentioned below.

Panchbhaini. This small area of 4½ square miles of coal-bearing rocks of Barakar age, found and named by Hira Lal in 1885-6, lies to the west of the Lakhanpur field. It contains several seams of good quality coal, up to more than 3 feet in thickness.

Damhamunda. Another small area of about the same size as Panchbhaini, lying further west still and in which Hira Lal located some thin coal seams.

Sendurgar. The Sendurgar field, lying five miles west of the Hasdo river, a tributary of the Mahanadi, in northern Bilaspur, has an area of 20 square miles in which seams of 4 feet and 10 feet thickness are known to occur. Hira Lal was of the opinion that most of the area is underlain by the former seam, but if this is halved, the reserves cannot be less than 40 million tons. The coal is of first-class quality and further exploration is desirable.

Hasdo-Rampur. This coalfield spreads from the Rampur *tappa* of Surguja, in the Arand (Rer) valley, to beyond the Hasdo river, in Bilaspur, and covering an area of nearly 400 square miles, partly in that district and partly in Surguja, it crosses the watershed of the Son and Mahanadi rivers. To avoid confusion with the Rampur-Hingir field of Orissa (see page 25), it would be preferable to refer to it as the Hasdo field, the name suggested originally by Hira Lal for its greater part. The Coal Measures of its eastern and south-central sections are separated from those of the Mand River and Korba fields by younger rocks, though they are probably continuous beneath this superficial cover. The Sendurgar field lies beyond its western end and the outliers of Damhamunda and Panchbhaini are situated to the north between it and the Lakhanpur field. E. R. Gee, writing in 1945, recalls that our knowledge of this field is very limited. Several coal seams of workable thickness and variable quality have been observed, but samples from outcrops are not reliable guides to true composition. ' Further investigations ', adds Gee, ' are obviously necessary to obtain anything like a true picture of the position '.

Mand River. The Mand River field lies to the north-west of the Rampur-Hingir field (see page 25), the Supra-Barakar rocks separating them having a minimum width of but 8 miles. It derives its name from that of the tributary of the Mahanadi which bisects it from north to south, and it has an area of roughly 200 square miles. Mentioned by Blanford in 1870, explored by Ball in 1882, and bored in preliminary fashion by W. King and Hira Lal in 1886, it is known to possess a large number of coal seams, but owing to the high ash contents of two of them, the Jubilee Seam, 19 feet thick and the Hira Lal Seam of 13 feet, investigations then ceased and attention was directed to the Korba field.

Korba. A ridge of Supra-Barakar rocks, under which the Coal Measures are doubtless continuous, divides the valley of the Mand river from that of the Hasdo, the next large tributary of the Mahanadi, 16 miles further west. This stream traverses the Korba coalfield, which also extends into the valleys of its tributaries, the Aharan and the Kurung, while a narrow strip of Barakars on the south directly unites it with the Mand River field.

It covers an area of over 200 square miles, and in 1870 Blanford had already found an outcrop exposing 50 feet of coal of good quality. Lala Hira Lal examined the field in 1886-7, when several borings were made. In more recent years it received further attention from prospectors, both Indian and European, but it remains undeveloped though barely 24 miles from the main line of the Bengal-Nagpur railway. At Korba itself a 70-foot seam crops out on the right bank of the Hasdo just below the town, but available analyses of its alternations are not encouraging. A seam, 150 feet thick, has also been recorded 8 miles to the west of Jatraj, itself on the west bank of the Hasdo, south of Korba, and at other places. A 5-foot seam of coal of good quality has been found near Ghordewa, and another, 20 feet thick, to the north-east of the same place. East of the Hasdo, a seam at least 6 feet in thickness exists near Rajgamar, the outcrop samples of which contained under 10 per cent of ash. There are known to be at least 50 million tons of good coal available within quite a small area, while the lower-grade reserves must total many hundreds of millions of tons. The field appears to be singularly free from dislocations and no igneous intrusions have been reported.

The small amounts of coal appearing under ' Bilaspur ' in the annual Mineral Returns, over the nine years 1941 to 1949, and reaching a total of only 20,383 tons, probably come from small outcrop quarries on this field.

Raigarh. As explained on page 26, Raigarh is the name given to that portion of the Rampur-Hingir field of Orissa which crosses the border into the north-eastern corner of the Raigarh district of Madhya Pradesh, in which it occupies about 200 square miles. It was examined by V. Ball in 1871, and again in 1875, but most of the seams he found were thin and associated with carbonaceous shales. It has not been bored and must await detailed examination before its resources can be properly assessed. Small amounts of coal have been taken from it since 1933, usually at the rate of 2,000 or 3,000 tons yearly, the highest amount being 3,898 tons in 1940. In 1950, this had fallen to 2,358 tons, and the total recorded production up to that time was 38,683 tons.

South Raigarh. This is a narrow strip of Barakar rocks south of the Raigarh field and contains so far as known poor-quality coal.

GROUP III

Between the isolated Mandla mass of the Deccan Trap in the east and its main great expanse on the west lie the Gondwana rocks of the Satpura basin, in which the Coal Measures appear at intervals from under the margins of the younger groups, over a distance of 170 miles; particularly on the north near Mohpani, in the Narsinghpur district, and in the south in Betul and Chhindwara. The coalfields concerned are the following: Mohpani, in the Narsinghpur district; Shahpur, in the Betul district and the fields of the Tawa, Kanhan and Pench valleys; Tawa lying partly in Betul and partly in Chhindwara district, as well as in the Narmada basin, while the others are in Chhindwara and belong to the Godavari river system. Further south there is abundant evidence of a concealed coalfield near Kamptee in the Nagpur district.

Mohpani. The exposed Barakar Coal Measures of this, the most northerly field of the group, cover rather more than one square mile. Discovered by J. R. Ouseley in 1835, mining commenced in 1862 and continued in the four seams of an area known as the Old Field until 1902, the total amount raised being 450,845 tons. In 1892, a second area, the New Field, was discovered as a result of the work of F. L. G. Simpson and T. D. La Touche, in which seams, aggregating 27 feet in thickness, spread over a considerable expanse. Up to the end of 1903, when the mines were sold by the Narbada Coal & Iron Co. Ltd to the Great Indian Peninsula Railway Co. Ltd, the output from this had been 181,080 tons, and from that date until operations ceased in 1926, a further 1,402,987 tons had been won. The highest production was reached in 1921, with 89,623 tons, or 0·47 per cent of that year's total. The coal was somewhat inferior in quality to the average Damodar valley coal, and for locomotive purposes $1\frac{1}{4}$ tons of Mohpani coal were taken as equivalent to 1 ton of Bengal coal. It was probably this economic reason which led to the closing of the collieries, for although the area of the field is not large, occurring as it does on a faulted anticline of Barakar rocks, there are still, according to Fox, some seven million tons of workable coal left in it.

Shahpur, Tawa, etc. The Shahpur fields, with an exposed area of about 26 square miles, lie in the valley of the Tawa river between Betul and Hoshangabad, and their thin coal seams were first noticed by J. Finnis in 1834. J. G. Medlicott, in 1863, and Blanford in 1868, found numerous narrow seams, and H. B. Medlicott surveyed the region in 1875, but discovered nothing likely to be profitable. Borings in 1881 led to no better results, but later work about 1920, on the Pathakhera field, an area of about 16 square miles of Barakar rocks, in the Ranipur reserved forest of Betul, proved three seams of $4\frac{1}{2}$, 6 and 13 feet thickness respectively, lying within 200 to 450 feet of the surface. According to Fox, the thickest of these is of fair quality and more or less proved over about 3 square miles, so that allowing a loss of 50 per cent for dykes, faults and waste in mining, he concluded that 15 million tons may be looked on as the available reserve in the southern and eastern portions. E. R. Gee, writing in 1925, concluded as follows: 'This area appears to represent a large tract which promises well to exploiters, certainly the most promising tract, so far as our present knowledge goes, of the Tawa valley coal-bearing strata; considering its nearness, 7 to 10 miles, from the Betul-Itarsi railway, it is surprising that its exploitation has not already been taken up more enthusiastically.'

The remaining small coalfields concerned include Sonada, Gurgunda or Suki River, Mardanpur or Machna River, Dulhara, Bamhanwara-Khapa and Tandsi. Small quantities of coal have been taken from them for local uses at intervals in the past; between 1921 and 1927, 6,001 tons were so removed; and between 1938 and 1943, 20,504 tons appeared in the official returns.

Kanhan Valley. The coalfields of the Chhindwara district lie on the southern flanks of the Satpuras in the valleys of the Tawa, Kanhan and Pench rivers, stretching from close to the Shahpur fields in the west, at intervals in an easterly direction for 50 miles, to a point 10 miles north of Chhindwara itself. They were discovered by Jerdon and R. H. Sankey in 1852, described by W. T. Blanford in 1866, A. Sopwith in 1867 and E. J. Jones in 1887, sampled by G. V. Hobson in 1924 and resurveyed by Sir Cyril Fox and W. D. West in 1923–5. Officially grouped together for statistical purposes as the Pench Valley fields, they are here separated, following the classification proposed by Fox in 1934, under which the Kanhan Valley fields proper include the Damua-Kalichhapar, Ghorawari-Nimkhera, Panara-Jinaur, Datla-Jamai and Hingladevi areas. As in the fields of Betul further west, the coal-bearing Barakars are overlain in some of them by higher stages of the Lower Gondwana succession, notably the Motur clays and sandstones and the Bijori sandstones and shales.

On the first of them, a seam of moderate quality, 10 to 15 feet thick, has been mined at the Damua colliery since 1932, while the Kalichhapar colliery has been in production since 1936, and the Rakhikol colliery since 1939. The second tract forms the eastward continuation of the Damua-Kalichhapar outcrops, and on it both Top and Ghorawari seams are mined and quarried at the Hirdagarh colliery, which has been producing since 1930, and the Ghorawari Kalan colliery where work commenced in 1943. The Ghorawari seam is about 15 feet thick, separated from it by 15 feet of sandstone is another coal seam 10 feet thick, followed in its turn by 45 feet of sandstone and then by the Bottom seam, again 10 feet thick.

Following closely on the Ghorawari-Nimkhera area is the Panara-Jinaur field where the Ghorawari seam again makes its appearance near the village of Panara. It is mined near Jinaur at the Junnordeo colliery where operations started in 1945. The Datla-Jamai area has a colliery at Dongaria and a seam of somewhat poor quality, about 5 feet thick, has been worked on the Hingladevi field near Ghogri.

Kamptee. As long ago as 1867, W. T. Blanford advised the Chief Commissioner of the Central Provinces (Madhya Pradesh) that borings to a depth of 200 or 250 feet within a few miles of Nagpur would settle the question whether the Barakar rocks, which he suspected to underlie the thick alluvial surface deposits, contained coal or not. He also indicated several suitable locations for such trials.

There the matter remained until a few years ago when a 300-foot borehole searching for water, north of Kanhan railway station, near Kamptee, in Nagpur, cut through several coal seams including one 21 feet thick, 81 feet from ground level, in Barakar rocks lying directly below the alluvium. This discovery led to further borings and in two holes just west of Kandri, a few miles to the north of Kanhan railway station, seams up to about 29 feet in thickness were intersected. In these cases lower Kamthi strata intervene between the surface and the coal-bearing Barakar rocks and the seams are at depths of from 75 to 150 feet below ground level. An analysis of the coal from a shaft sunk later in the same neighbourhood shows: Moisture 7·84, Volatile Matter 30·90, Fixed Carbon 38·53 and Ash 22·72 per cent with a calorific value of 9,140 British Thermal Units. Although a minimum of one million tons of coal is assured here, further exploration is desirable on account of the proximity of the concealed field to Nagpur.

ANALYSES OF KANHAN VALLEY COALS

COLLIERY	MOISTURE	VOLATILE MATTER	FIXED CARBON	ASH	CALORIFIC VALUE	REMARKS
Kanhan ..	2·44	30·76	49·58	17·24	6,515	gives a hard coke
Ghorawari ..	2·40	28·66	50·14	18·80	6,348	,, ,, ,, ,,
Hirdagarh ..	3·20	29·50	50·35	16·95	6,671	fairly hard coke
Rakhikol ..	1·22	25·08	54·15	19·55	6,308	soft coke
Junnordeo ..	3·76	29·80	39·96	26·48	5,226	non-caking
Dongaria ..	4·56	29·84	42·46	23·14	5,602	gives a hard coke
East Ghogri	6·10	28·22	41·84	23·84	5,372	non-caking

In the Kanhan Valley as a whole, although three or four coal seams of workable thickness occur, only one, states Fox, is both thick and of good enough quality for profitable exploitation, and most of the mining has been confined to this, the topmost of the group. Moreover, the whole tract is sliced by parallel faults, so that each property is usually faced with the problem of working a narrow strip of bearing ground between them. Much of the coal has coking properties and is of fair quality generally, though not equal to the first-grade coals of the Raniganj and Jharia fields. A. B. Dutt has recently estimated that in the Ghorawari and Damua-Rakhikol group of collieries alone there are reserves approaching 66 million tons of coal possessing moderately good caking properties. A railway extension reached the valley in 1915 and its production is included with that of the Pench Valley.

Pench Valley. The Pench Valley fields are practically continuous with those of the Kanhan Valley, indeed some of the coal exposures classed by Fox in the eastern end of the latter might equally well be included in the former. The geological sequence is identical, the Barakar Coal Measures, probably 300 to 400 feet thick, being succeeded by a much greater thickness of the Motur sandstones and clays, the equivalents of the Barren Measures of the middle division of the Damuda Series of the Damodar valley of Bihar and West Bengal. The Coal Measures extend in a continuous, easterly trending strip from Barkuhi through Chandameta and Parasia to the Pench river near Chinda, a distance of 11 miles as the crow flies. In addition to this there are disconnected areas of Barakars near Gajandoh, eastwards from Eklaira, near Setia, at Sirgora and other places.

The Barakars, as usual, consist of coarse sandstones, carbonaceous shales, grey shales, seams of shaly coal and of good coal. 'Although several seams of coal occur,' writes Fox, ' only four of these are recognized at present as possibly workable, and only one, near the top of the series, is worked. It varies from 5 to 12 feet thick and occupies a position about 120 to 150 feet below the base of the Moturs. The lower seams occur within 100 feet below the main seam.' Coal was quarried from the outcrop of one of the seams about 1862. Encouraging prospecting operations by private firms and the provision of through railway communication in 1905 were soon followed by systematic mining: the Chandameta and Barkuhi collieries have been in production from that year and today there are many others at work. The principal sub-areas concerned are Barkuhi, where the seam being mined is 6 to 7½ feet thick; Bhandaria-Bhutaria, where the seam includes 8 feet of coal of which the bottom 5½ feet are worked; Chandameta-Dongar Chikhli, where 6 feet of coal are mined, and the Eklaira-Newton Chikhli area. North of Parasia, a bore hole proved 3 seams, 6, 4 and 4½ feet thick respectively, all within 133 feet of the surface. A deeper bore to 375 feet encountered 7 seams, from 3 to 4½ feet thick, without reaching the base of the Coal Measures. In two

square miles of the Barkuhi, Chandameta and Dongar Chikhli
area, Fox calculated that 5 million tons of coal are still available;
the southern strip, from Bhutaria to Bhandaria, may perhaps include
another half million tons, but if the 3 square miles of coalfield
concealed under the Deccan Trap between Bhandaria and
Gajandoh is included, the additional amount would be of the order
of 10 million tons. In the Eklaira-Newton Chikhli area, the same
authority placed the reserves at a total of 7 million tons, allowing
for losses, adding that there is little doubt that the Coal Measures
extend further, within workable depths, ' far out under the Pench
river '.

ANALYSES OF PENCH VALLEY COALS

COLLIERY	MOISTURE	VOLATILE MATTER	FIXED CARBON	ASH	CALORIFIC VALUE	REMARKS
Barkuhi ..	7·38	29·98	44·52	18·12	5,649	non-coking
Chandameta ..	7·48	31·24	44·24	17·04	5,688	,, ,,
Dongar Chikhli	9·60	28·94	44·28	17·18	5,544	,, ,,
Eklaira.. ..	6·98	28·47	45·14	19·41	5,668	,, ,,
Newton Chikhli	7·93	31·20	42·82	18·05	5,650	,, ,,
Rawanwara ..	5·55	29·84	49·35	15·26	6,286	,, ,,
Jamui-Datla ..	3·96	29·42	50·69	15·93	6,836	,, ,,

Progress on the Pench Valley fields has been steady from its
inception, output rising without a setback to over one million tons
(1,117,942 tons, or 5 per cent of the Indian total) in 1934, and
thence to a peak of 1,524,818 tons (5·18 per cent) in 1942. After
that time somewhat lower figures were recorded until 1948 and
onwards, when they rose to the record of 1,659,999 tons, or 5·14 per
cent of the total in 1950. From the commencement in 1903 to
the end of 1950, 33,331,917 tons of coal have been mined in the
Pench and Kanhan Valley fields.

Sir Cyril Fox computed that the coal reserves of all kinds in the
Satpura region as a whole—Mohpani to the Kanhan and Pench
Valleys—amount to a round figure of 1,000 million tons, though he
reduced this academic calculation to 150 million tons of workable
coal, in the absence of deep borings along the northern edge of the
Pench Valley.

GROUP IV

The Wardha Valley coalfields are situated in the Chanda and
Yeotmal districts of Madhya Pradesh and form part of the Godavari-
Gondwana zone. R. R. Simpson, at one time Coal Mining
Specialist to the Government of India, summarized the occurrences
as follows: ' They occupy the valley of the Wardha river for a
distance of about 72 miles in a straight line, the total area being

1,600 square miles. The coal-bearing rocks (Barakars) have a thickness of only 250 feet, their distribution is very broken and their surface area small. There appears to be only one coal horizon, and it occurs near the top of the Coal Measures. The thickness of the coal varies from nothing up to 90 feet, the average being about 30 feet. Our knowledge of the fields is almost entirely due to T. W. H. Hughes, who between 1870 and 1876 mapped the area and superintended the boring operations.' In the Chanda district are situated the Bandar, Warora and Ballarpur fields, the last crossing into Hyderabad. In the Yeotmal district there are the fields of Wun and its related areas, while the Ghugus-Telwasa fields lie partly in both districts.

Bandar. The Bandar field, about 6 square miles in area, lies 30 miles north-east of Warora, and four seams of coal of workable thickness are known, as the result of boring, to occur in it. Fox estimated its available reserves to be at least 54 million tons but owing to its isolated location it remains undeveloped.

Warora. The Coal Measures of the Warora basin, which is 62 miles south of Nagpur, are largely concealed by younger rocks and alluvium. Borings between 1870 and 1873 proved two seams, averaging 15 and 12 feet in thickness, only 46 feet apart and within 232 feet of the surface. Collieries were worked between 1873 and 1906 and, after raising about three million tons of coal, had to be abandoned owing to the influx of water, underground fires and a large subsidence brought about by mining both seams at the same time. Hughes estimated the reserves in 1877 as 20 million tons, with probable extensions to the south raising the total to 60 or 100 million tons. The coal is inferior to Raniganj and Jharia coal by reason of its higher moisture and lower fixed carbon contents.

Wun and Related Areas. Across the Wardha river, in the neighbourhood of Wun and other places in the Yeotmal district of Berar, coal has been proved to occur within the Barakar rocks lying beneath the members of the Kamthi Group, mainly sandstones with no coal seams, which are the local representatives of the Panchet Series of the Damodar valley coalfields. Sometimes, however, in this region the Coal Measures lie directly underneath the alluvium. ' On the Wun side of the Wardha ', wrote Hughes, ' a much larger area has been tested than on the Chanda side and the coal has been proved to be much less irregularly distributed. An average of 20 feet may be admitted for 20 square miles and 30 feet for 60 miles, making a total of 2,100 millions of tons.' From direct evidence 105 million tons were estimated to occur between Wun and Papur (7 square miles) and 150 million tons in 5 square miles between Junara and Chicholi, all within 500 feet of the surface. Near Pisgaon, 27 to 31 feet of coal were found at a depth of 77 feet, and at Rajur, 18 to 30 feet of coal, within 160 feet of the surface. The coal is non-coking, high in moisture and contains some 15 per cent of ash. Reviewing the evidence in 1934, Fox concluded that there are 240 million tons of coal in 12 square miles from beyond Pisgaon to Warora, of which half may be considered available.

A colliery commenced working in 1927, after rail communication had been established, but separate production figures for the Yeotmal district do not appear in the returns until 1938, with the exception of the years 1925 to 1927, when an output of 2,355 tons was obtained. The production in 1950 was 23,411 tons, and the total tonnage won from 1939 to 1950, both years included, was 521,244 tons.

Ghugus-Telwasa. Of small extent as far as visible outcrops are concerned, Ghugus-Telwasa is in reality a concealed field occupying an area of about 100 square miles, in which a seam, over 50 feet thick in places, including its shale bands, has been proved at shallow depths. Estimating on what he regarded as a safe figure of 15 feet of coal, Sir Cyril Fox concluded in 1934 that there are 1,000 million tons available, adding 'surely the possibilities render this [area] one of the most attractive for testing'. The Mayo mine was opened here in 1870 but only worked until 1873, when it was abandoned in favour of Warora colliery. New borings were made after the 1914–18 war and with the construction of a railway from Tadali, on the Ballarshah-Wardha line, to Ghugus, new workings were established about a mile south of the old Mayo mine. No. 1 Pit proved 11 feet of coal at a depth of 109 feet—the top of the thick seam, and No. 3 Pit, 17½ feet at 225 feet. These Coal Measures dip to the west under the Wardha river and should be found again in the Yeotmal district. The coal is non-caking and resembles that from Ballarpur in composition; its production is not shown separately in the official returns, being included apparently with that of Ballarpur and Chanda.

Chanda. Although Chanda town itself, the headquarters of the district of the same name, is supposed to lie on Kamthi rocks, there has always been some doubt about it. In any case, borings at Mahakali on the eastern outskirts of the town found 19 feet of coal at a depth of 81 feet, and 26 feet of coal at 120 feet below the surface. A colliery commenced operations here in 1927, and a second one at Babupeth, to the south-east of the town, sometime before 1934. The extent of the Coal Measures is unknown and the production of the mines is not shown separately in the official returns.

Ballarpur. The Ballarpur field lies for the most part in Hyderabad, where it is known as the Sasti field. In 1868, Blanford found a coal seam, 6 feet thick, on that side of the Wardha river, that is to say in what were then the Nizam's dominions, but borings on the other bank in Indian territory at that time failed to reach it. In 1900, however, in anticipation of the closure of Warora colliery, systematic re-boring was undertaken in the area and two seams, 17 and 14 feet thick, with a sandstone parting of one foot between them, were proved at a depth of 62 feet, at a point opposite Sasti. Nearer Ballarpur and on the other side of some faulted ground, several seams of workable thickness were met with. The first shaft was sunk in 1903 and the second in 1906 when mining at Warora ceased; through railway communication was established in 1908 and the seams at Sasti were also developed, the coal being carried across the Wardha river from the Hyderabad side by an aerial ropeway to Ballarpur. Mining operations have been continuous, the record annual output having been attained in 1933, with 356,344 tons, or 1·29 per cent of India's total for that year. In 1950, 331,012 tons were raised, and the grand total to the end of that year was 8,088,765 tons. It is to be noted that the totals from 1941 to 1946, inclusive, appear in the official returns under ' Chanda ', though before and after that period they are classified under ' Ballarpur '

Covered as it is by younger rocks, the exact limits of the Ballarpur field are not known, but in the 2 square miles proved, there were reserves of 40 million tons in 1934. The total area involved, however, may well be of the order of 200 square miles with a corresponding multiplication of these figures.

Other large tracts of country where further concealed coal-bearing rocks are believed to occur include Wamanpalli, Lathi and Dabha, the southward continuation of the area lying to the south-east of Chanda town.

ANALYSES OF WARDHA VALLEY COALS

Field	Moisture	Volatile Matter	Fixed Carbon	Ash	Calorific Value	Remarks
Warora ..	10·40	30·40	41·12	18·06	..	No. 2 seam, 15 feet
,, ..	9·78	29·60	43·72	16·88	..	No. 3 seam, 10 feet
Wun ..	10·91	35·30	49·30	15·40	6,539	....
Ghugus ..	11·00	34·30	49·58	16·12	6,114	....
Ballarpur ..	9·64	35·35	50·50	14·15	6,371	....

Note :—Calorific values are in calories and, being determined on moisture-free samples, are appreciably higher than the true heating values of the coals.

HYDERABAD

Of the 1,022 million tons of coal produced in India between 1900 and 1950, inclusive, Hyderabad was responsible for 38,474,825 tons, or 3·7 per cent. Its Coal Measures form part of the Pranhita-Godavari Gondwana belt, a continuation towards the south-east of those of the Wardha valley region already briefly outlined. They are of Barakar age, occur at numerous localities, but in nearly every case are overlain by younger Gondwana rocks, the Kamthi sandstones and shales, so that their real extent is not known and indeed cannot be delineated until proved by deep and extensive boring. Complications are introduced by the erosion which the coal-bearing rocks suffered to a varying degree before the Kamthis were deposited upon them, and by the faulting which took place afterwards. Strata of Gondwana age—mainly Kamthi sandstones—form a continuous strip through Hyderabad, where they occupy a region covering some 3,800 square miles, into Andhra, where they have an areal extent of about 600 square miles, but in both States exposures of the Barakar Coal Measures are few and far between. The discovery of the coalfields was due to the labours of W. T. Blanford, T. W. H. Hughes and W. King between 1860 and 1880. The producing fields are those of Sasti, Tandur, Singareni and Kothagudium, but there are several other localities in the Adilabad and Warangal districts where rocks of Barakar age come to the surface but which have no coal seams actually exposed, or where fragments of coal have been found in stream beds, derived from outcrops of seams which still have to be located. Though of little economic interest at present, such occurrences are of great geological importance, especially as a guide to future exploration by boring.

Sasti. The Sasti field is a continuation, on the south side of the Wardha river, of the Ballarpur field in the Chanda district of Madhya Pradesh, the coal occurring in two basins between Sasti and Paoni. Part of the area was bored between 1871 and 1874 and coal with an average thickness of 40 feet proved over an area of 1½ square miles, but the shafts at Sasti colliery found only 27 feet of coal at a depth of 78 feet, as the top of the seam had been denuded. A 60-foot seam was also proved at Paoni. Hughes calculated in 1877 that 30 million tons of coal are available in the 1½ square miles mentioned. Systematic mining commenced in 1920, the area having been leased by the Hyderabad (Deccan) Company to the proprietors of the Ballarpur colliery on the other side of the Wardha river. The total production to the end of 1950 was 1,611,557 tons, the highest output being in 1938 when 90,782 tons were raised.

Antargaon-Aksapur. In the south of the Sasti field the Coal Measures disappear below the covering of Kamthi rocks to the north of Rajur, but they appear again some 10 miles to the south-east as a narrow strip, stretching for approximately 12 miles. To this exposure Fox gave the name of Antargaon-Aksapur coalfield,

the latter part of the compound appellation from a small outlier
10 miles further south, which may be continuous with the rest
under the Kamthis. Beyond the fact that a coal seam, 6 feet
in thickness, crops out in the Wardha river at Lathi Ghat, nothing
further is known about the potentialities of this field.

Tandur. Twelve miles south of Aksapur, and still in the
Adilabad district, the Coal Measures come to the surface again,
outcropping once more as a narrow strip which reaches from beyond
Kairgura, south-eastwards through Tandur, to east of Belampalli
railway station, with the small outlier of Waripet to the west. The
exploitation of this field dates from the completion of the Kazipet-
Ballarshah railway, which passes through Tandur, in 1927. Two
seams, averaging 6½ feet in thickness and separated by 140 feet of
strata, are mined both by inclines and shafts. Production commenced in 1931 with 46,530 tons, attained a peak of 369,421 tons,
being 1·26 per cent of the country's total, in 1942, and was 306,654
tons in 1950 (0·95 per cent of the total). From the commencement
of operations until the end of 1950, 5,347,054 tons had been raised.
   A certain amount of iron pyrites occurs as layers and lenses in
the Tandur coal but is picked out by hand on a travelling belt.
Otherwise Hyderabad coals are usually low in sulphur and in
phosphorus and as a general average contain about 6 per cent
Moisture, 24 per cent Volatile Matter, 56 per cent Fixed Carbon
and 14 per cent Ash, with a heating value of 6,500 calories.

Chinur-Sandrapali. From the overlap of the Kamthis on to the
Coal Measures at the southern end of the Tandur field, to their
next appearance at the surface along the same line of strike, to the
north-west of Chinur, is a distance of approximately 18 miles, and
yet again the Barakars are exposed as a long narrow strip between
members of the Talchir Group on the west and the Kamthi sandstones on the east. Striking to the south-east they cross the
Godavari into the Karimnagar district of Hyderabad and continue
to beyond Sandrapali, a total distance of 16 miles. Fragments
of coal are common in the river below the outcrop but the seams
whence they are derived remain undiscovered.
   From a point above the junction of the Godavari with the
Pranhita and to the south and west of the confluence, an expanse
of Kamthi rocks, 16 or 20 miles in width, continues across the valley
of the Pengadi river for over 70 miles, south-east to below Cherla.
' That coal seams exist in the Barakars below the Kamthis ', wrote
Sir Cyril Fox, ' cannot be seriously questioned.'

Kamaram. This is the name of a small outlier of Barakar rocks
which lies approximately on a line joining the Tandur and Singareni
coalfields, 45 miles from the former and 25 miles from the latter as
the crow flies. It contains two seams, 9 feet and 6 feet thick,

respectively, containing 1,132,500 tons of coal, but, in the words of W. King, 'ill-placed in every way for its development'. To the east and south-east of Kamaram, coal has been reported from the region between Bandala and Allapalli, in the Kinarsan valley.

Singareni. The Singareni field, in the Warangal district and 146 miles from Hyderabad city, was discovered and described by W. King in 1872. It occupies a narrow strip of Lower Gondwana rocks, sometimes referred to as the Yellandlapad exposures about 12 miles long and 2 miles wide, of which the Barakar Coal Measures cover 9 square miles. King persuaded the Government to prospect this area by boring, and four seams were proved within 50 to 250 feet of the surface. The top one of good coal was 6 feet thick, the second and third averaged 3 feet each, while a very thick bottom seam, the Singareni seam, was also reached. Later borings and actual workings revealed that the Singareni seam is about 70 feet thick, including some variable shale and sandstone bands. Below it follow the New Seam (5 to 8½ feet), the Stone Coal (3½ to 7½ feet), the King Seam (5 to 6 feet of high quality coal), and finally another seam, 2½ feet thick, 340 feet below the Thick Coal and 140 feet below the King Seam. Mining was commenced in the King Seam in 1886, at first by inclines and by shafts after 1894. In that year Saise estimated that it contained 36 million tons: by 1900 the annual production was over 460,000 tons, and ten years later it was more than half a million tons. The peak was passed with 768,420 tons, or 3·28 per cent of the total Indian output, in 1929, and annual tonnages were maintained between one half and three quarters of a million tons until 1941, when with a sudden fall to 154,164 tons, operations on the field ceased ' on the exhaustion of the King Seam '. History does not relate why the Thick Seam was not mined. The coal was a hard, dull, non-coking steam coal largely consumed by railways and mills in southern India, and the total amount raised from 1886 to 1941 was 26,354,733 tons. Small-scale operations started again in 1948, with an output of 14,235 tons, rising to 77,135 tons in 1950, with a total of 149,959 tons for the three years concerned and bringing the grand total for Singareni to 26,504,692 tons.

Kothagudium. In 1925, borings at Kothagudium proved the presence of the Coal Measures under about 150 feet of Kamthi strata, 24 miles east of Singareni, the King Seam lying at a depth of about 400 feet, while the Thick Seam was found to be strongly intercalated with shaly bands. Mining commenced soon after-wards, but in the meantime a railway had reached the Tandur field where preliminary work had been commenced in 1927. For these reasons the Kothagudium colliery was abandoned, only to be restarted again in 1937, when it became apparent that Singareni was approaching its end. Today the workings consist of four inclines and one shaft and they are connected to Dornakal junction by a branch line. The coal is utilized by railways and other large consumers, besides being distributed in Hyderabad, Bombay, Andhra and Madras. Production quickly increased to 844,598 tons in 1942 (2·87 per cent of the total) but had fallen to 778,717 tons (2·41 per cent) in 1950. Between 1937 and 1946 inclusive, 7,622,494 tons had been raised.

Other Exposures of Coal Measures. Twenty-five miles south-east of Singareni a small exposure of Coal Measures is known to occur on the north-eastern end of the Kannegiri Hills, near Maddukuru. To the east of the Kothagudium field and some 25 miles from it, Coal Measures appear again on the right bank of the Godavari about Damercherla and Madhavaram: these rocks cross the river into the Totapalle-Gaviridevipeta region of the East Godavari district of Andhra and are dealt with below.

ANALYSES OF HYDERABAD COALS

Field	Moisture	Volatile Matter	Fixed Carbon	Ash	Calorific Value	Remarks
Sasti ..	12·06	31·76	52·71	15·53	6,148	(*)
Tandur ..	7·25	28·50	55·40	16·10	6,463	(*)
Singareni ..	7·18	28·75	50·30	13·77	5,984	King Seam
,, ..	5·86	24·12	55·85	14·17	6,433	(†)

(*) Ash, Volatile Matter (less Moisture) and Fixed Carbon total 100. Calorific values determined on moisture-free samples.
(†)Average composition of a large number of samples as loaded for dispatch.

POSSIBLE COALFIELDS OF ANDHRA

Dr M. S. Krishnan summarized our existing knowledge of the coalfields of Andhra in 1949, and the following brief notes are derived from his writings. (See Bibliography.)

Lingala Area. A small area of Coal Measures occurs around Lingala, in the East Godavari district, immediately south of the confluence of the Talperu river with its parent stream. The discovery of pieces of coal in the river bed in 1857 led to a visit by W. T. Blanford in 1867 and the subsequent location of four seams, three of 2 feet and one of 5 feet thickness. Seventy tons of good coal were removed from a trial pit in 1891. The whole region was mapped in 1944–5 by V. Subramanyam and S. N. Sen of the Geological Survey, who also uncovered a thin coal seam in a prospecting trench. The possibilities of this small field will remain problematical until it is systematically bored. It lies 40 miles north of Bhadrachalam, itself 20 miles by road from the railhead at the Kothagudium colliery in Hyderabad.

Gaviridevipeta (Totapalle). This small field, ten square miles in extent, is a continuation, on the Andhra side of the Godavari river, of the Damercherla and Madhavaram Coal Measures of Hyderabad, where they cover a further 8 or 9 square miles. The village from which it takes its name is situated 15 miles east-south-east of Bhadrachalam on the Kunavaram road. A few shallow borings were made hereabouts in 1871 at the suggestion of W. T. Blanford, and at least one of them cut through a seam of coal, 18 feet thick. Between 1890 and 1895, the Godavari Coal Co. Ltd sank a shaft and extracted 3,576 tons of coal from a 6-foot seam. V. Subramanyam mapped the field under the supervision of Dr M. S. Krishnan in 1944-5, but until deeper boreholes are drilled through to the underlying basement, be it Talchirs or Metamorphic rocks, this too must remain a problematical field.

Bedadanuru. This area has the distinction of containing the most southerly exposures of the Barakar Coal Measures in the Indian Peninsula. Its name-village, in the Polavaram Agency of West Godavari, is 10 miles north-west of Zangareddigudem, itself some 32 miles from the railhead at Ellore. Discovered by W. T. Blanford and examined by W. King in 1871-2, it was mapped by Dr Krishnan and R. N. P. Arogyaswamy in 1941-2, when it was found to cover an elliptical area of about 6 square miles, overlapped from north-west to south by the younger Kamthi rocks, probably as a rather thin covering. Sixteen boreholes were drilled in it under official auspices in 1874-6, the deepest reaching only 356 feet, and six seams of poor-quality, shaly coal revealed. In 1900, five more holes were bored by the Ellore Syndicate, but they appear to have been badly located and added no new information. Four deeper borings, made in 1922-4 by the Hyderabad (Deccan) Co., in the Swarnavarigudam area, through the overlying Kamthi blanket, from one to two miles south of the Barakar outcrops, reached a maximum depth of about 900 feet, but only proved a 10½-foot seam of very poor quality coal, at a depth of 220 feet in one hole, and at 818 feet in another, further down the dip. Other borings have been made in the Koyyalagudam area (in 1923) and in the Yernagudam taluk, near Komatigunta and Gollagudam, in both cases without finding true coal seams. For details of these and their bearings on future exploration Dr Krishnan's work must be consulted. He has concluded that the possible occurrence of workable seams can be settled only by boring down to 2,000 feet.

JURASSIC, CRETACEOUS AND TERTIARY COALFIELDS

Although less than 1½ per cent of India's coal is derived from these younger rocks, as compared with the remainder from the Permian Gondwanas, they supply all the coal mined in West Pakistan and their fields are of great economic importance to the regions in which they occur, and in which mining is done in them, such as those of Assam, Rajasthan, the West Punjab and Baluchistan, while fields still unworked are found in Kashmir and Burma.

ASSAM

Wo: able coal occurs in Assam at three separate geological horizons, two of which are in the Lower Eocene and the other in the Upper Eocene, possibly extending into the Oligocene. The rocks concerned belong to the Jaintia Series which is about 3,000 feet thick and is well displayed in the southern and south-western portions of the Shillong Plateau region. This series is divided into three stages known, from below upwards, as the Tura Sandstones, the Sylhet Limestones (up to 1,000 feet thick) and the Kopili Beds (1,000 to 1,500 feet). The older geologists classified the Tura Sandstones with the Cretaceous beds of Upper Senonian age which underlie them, when they do not rest directly on crystalline rocks, but they are now thought to belong to the Lower Eocene. They contain important Coal Measures and the oldest of the coal seams of Assam. The Kopili Beds, which are of Khirtar age, also include some thin coal seams: thus coal is found in Assam both above and below the Sylhet Limestones.

The formation of coal during Lower Eocene times was confined mainly to the western areas of the Garo, Khasi, Jaintia and Mikir Hills, but in Upper Assam, along the southern side of the Brahmaputra valley, east of Dibrugarh, it took place in Upper Eocene times, giving rise to the thick seams of the Naga and Patkoi Hills. These Upper Eocene rocks form the Barail Series which occupies a very large area in Upper Assam, showing much lateral variation and necessitating the employment of many local subdivisions as they are followed from the Surma valley, through north Cachar, into the Naga Hills. In the north-east, the subdivisions consist of the lowest or Naogaon Stage, followed by the Bargolai and then by the Tikak Parbat Stages, which together form the Coal Measures and which in their type area are about 11,000 feet in thickness, the thick seams being confined to the lower 400 feet in the Namdang-Ledo area.

THE GARO HILLS

The Garo Hills form the western termination of the Assam Range, around which the Brahmaputra takes its great bend from the Assam valley into the plains of Bengal. Immediately north of the gneissic range, running westwards from the Khasi plateau and forming the culminating ridge of the Garo Hills, the Cretaceous and Lower Tertiary rocks with their Coal Measures occupy a series of detached basins in the gneiss. James Bedford drew attention to the coal of the Garo Hills in 1841, H. B. Medlicott examined the region in 1864, and T. D. La Touche mapped part of it in 1883. Coal seams have been found in many places, even westwards and northwards of Tura, the chief town of the. Hills, for the Tura Sandstones cover large tracts between the Ringgi and Kalu rivers, but the seams of the Karaibara area to the south-west are seldom over 3 feet thick. To the east of Tura and north of the main range, with its peak Nokrek (4,633 feet), are the fields of Rongrenggiri and Daranggiri.

Rongrenggiri. This field lies in the Simsang valley about 20 miles east of Tura, and its sandstones with a cover of Sylhet Limestone extend roughly over 25 square miles, but its seams are described as thin and of no practical value.

Daranggiri. A few miles below Rongrenggiri and on both sides of the Simsang river, above the head of the gorge where it cuts through the main range, lies the Daranggiri field, doubtless connected at one time with its northern neighbour. It is about 10 miles across from east to west, and 6 miles from north to south, with a few outliers to the south. La Touche, in 1883, gave the thickness of the single workable seam as $5\frac{1}{2}$ feet and estimated its contents at 76 million tons above main drainage level. The coal is of excellent quality and R. R. Simpson, writing in 1913, stated that the only bar to its exploitation was its distance from a railway. Its western portion was re-examined by B. Laskar and G. V. Rao in 1949–50, who reported the presence of a main seam $4\frac{1}{2}$ to 5 feet thick of hard, splintery coal, with an upper seam, $1\frac{1}{2}$ to 2 feet thick, some 200 feet higher in the sequence. The main seam dips at very low angles and its reserves, in an area of $18\frac{1}{2}$ square miles, were estimated to be 84 million tons. The eastern portion was examined at the same time by R. N. P. Arogyaswamy, S. N. Sen, A. S. Ramiengar and S. N. Puri who found it dissected into eight small areas as a result of uplift and erosion. They reported little variation in the average thickness of the main seam and estimated its reserves at 31 million tons in 8·89 square miles. The composition of the Daranggiri coal is approximately as follows:—Moisture 8·8 per cent, Volatile Matter 36·3 per cent, Fixed Carbon 49·8 per cent, Ash 5·1 per cent.

Siju. On its southern slopes the main range is flanked by the Lower Eocene strata and the Coal Measures (Tura Sandstones) are visible at many places over the 36 miles between Tura and Siju. R. N. P. Arogyaswamy and A. S. Ramiengar investigated part of this region in 1949–50, locating many exposures between Siju Songmong and Table *nala* and concluding that reserves of the order of 117 million tons may be expected in 26 square miles, though verification by drilling is recommended.

THE KHASI AND JAINTIA HILLS

Part of the Daranggiri field lies within the Khasi Hills, for the Simsang and its tributary, the Rongdi, form the administrative boundary between them and the Garo Hills to the west. There is no break in stratigraphical continuity and the Coal Measures extend up the Rengchu valley into the Nongstoin area of the Khasi Hills. The Tura Sandstones with their capping of Sylhet Lime-stone occur on Asilgaon Hill (1,739 feet), where at least two coal seams extend over 3 square miles. The lower one contains not less than 15 million tons of partly coking coal, assaying Moisture 4·65 per cent, Volatile Matter 35·2 per cent, Fixed Carbon 60·4 per cent and Ash 4·4 per cent.

Langrin (Umblay). The gently inclined coal seams of the massif of Pendengru, in the Garo Hills, extend into the extreme south-western corner of the Khasi Hills to form the Langrin coalfield. Mentioned by W. Jones in 1829, visited by Godwin-Austen in 1869 and mapped by La Touche in 1884, it builds a plateau, deeply trenched by several streams, 1,500 feet above the plains to which it descends steeply on the south. It covers about 30 square miles and has at least four seams with an aggregate thickness of 20 feet. No estimates of its reserves have been made but large quantities of coal of fair quality, some of which possesses caking properties, undoubtedly exist.

Other Small Fields. A number of small fields exist in the neigh-bourhood of Shillong, the capital of Assam, both to the north and south. They include Um Rileng, with an area of half a square mile, where the Tura Sandstones carry two seams, with a total of 8 to 10 feet of coal, and reserves of one million tons in the lower 5-foot seam; and Maobehlarkar, 20 miles south of Shillong, to which it supplied fuel for many years, of small extent and of little conse-quence. At Cherrapunji, where coal has been known since 1815, small-scale mining has been carried on since 1834. The area of the field is only 136 acres and in 1889 its reserves were estimated at 1,185,000 tons, in a seam varying from 3 to 9 feet in thickness. Other localities in the same neighbourhood include Rongsanoba, Laitrango and Mawlong. Their seams, like those of Cherrapunji itself, occur in sandstones which lie above the Sylhet Limestone and thus belong to the Kopili Stage of the Lower Eocene. As a rule they are strongly caking coals of good quality with a low ash content. Since 1935, Cherrapunji coal has been won by the Cherra-Chhatak Ropeway Co., and transported by ropeway to Bholaganj and thence by boat traffic. In 1884, the output from the field was 4,200 tons, but in the period covered by the official mineral statistics, the whole production of the Khasi and Jaintia Hills never exceeded a few hundred tons per annum, until it reached 1,005 tons in 1930, since when it has greatly increased. In 1950 it was 50,694 tons and the total tonnage raised between 1930 and 1950, inclusive, was 402,747 tons.

THE JAINTIA HILLS

Coal seams of the same age as those just described, and usually 2 or 3 feet in thickness, occur in the Jaintia Hills of central Assam, a region which also includes the north Cachar Hills and continues into the Mikir Hills of south-east Nowgong and west Sibsagar. Amongst other localities are those of Jaram, 10 miles south of Jowai; Bapung, 7 miles east of the same place; Satunga, 15 miles to the east-south-east and Lakadong, barely 10 miles east-north-east of Jaintiapur on the plains of Sylhet. Further east, in the valley of the Kopili, the stream separating the Jaintia Hills from those of north Cachar, and in that of its tributary the Diying, it is known that Eocene coal occurs, but the region has still to be mapped in detail.

THE MIKIR HILLS

Of the eight coal occurrences found in the Mikir Hills by F. H. Smith in 1897, only two are of sufficient thickness to be of economic interest. They are at Longloi, where 12 feet of rather poor coal are visible, and Nambor, where the high ash content renders profitable exploitation improbable. Longloi, in the centre of the south Mikir Hills, is close to the Jamuna river and 12 miles north-north-east of Lumding on the North Eastern Railway. Further to the east, two seams, 3 to 4 feet thick, are known in the Dissoma valley. It is also reported that coal occurs in quantity in the Jahenri and Koliani river valleys, which drain the hills west of Golaghat, in western Sibsagar district. At Koilapahar, 17 miles west-north-west of Manipur Road, in the Mikir Hills of west Sibsagar, a 5½-foot seam is mined at the Koilajan colliery. All the coals of the Mikir Hills belong to the Lower Eocene and probably to the Cherra (Tura) Sandstone Stage.

COALFIELDS OF UPPER ASSAM

Leaving the Mikir Hills and continuing north-eastwards into Upper Assam, the broad valley of the Brahmaputra, bounded on the north by the foot-hills of the eastern Himalaya and on the south by the Naga Hills and the offshoots of the Patkai Range, no further examples of the Lower Eocene Coal Measures are met with, but only those belonging to the upper part of the same system, continuing perhaps into the Oligocene. They form part of the Barail Series—a great thickness of mainly arenaceous beds in which coal first shows its presence as thin, inconstant streaks in the sandstones and as carbonaceous shales. These, however, when followed to the north-east from the Zubza valley, across the valleys of many other streams which flow from the Naga Hills to unite in the Sibsagar plains and join the Brahmaputra, become more abundant, until in the valley of the Dayang stream, thin coal seams, up to 1 foot in thickness, make their appearance. At Sanis, on the watershed between the Dayang and the Baghti, a 10-foot seam occurs, while at Chohuisan and in the near-by Disai valley, five or six seams, up to 4 feet thick, are known. The extent of the Disai field has still to be determined, but the proven length of coal outcrops is about 5 miles. The coals themselves have the following average composition: Moisture 6·8 per cent, Volatile Matter 33·8 per cent, Fixed Carbon 52·9 per cent, Ash 6·5 per cent.

Further on in the same general direction the following coalfields are known, Jhanzi, Nazira, Jaipur, Makum and Namchik.

Jhanzi. In this field two or three thin seams have been traced for rather less than 3 miles. The occurrence is about 15 miles south-east of Amguri railway station.

Nazira. About eight miles north-east of Jhanzi, lies the Nazira field in which steeply dipping coal-bearing rocks have been followed for 16 miles. This area, drained by the Dikhu, Tiru and Saffrai rivers, was known in 1848, examined by Mallet in 1876 and by Simpson in 1906. Mallet estimated the reserves of the Saffrai portion, over a length of 4½ miles, at an average thickness of 51 feet, in 5 seams, and within 350 feet of the outcrop, at 20 million tons, but these reserves refer only to a portion of the area. The coal is a high-grade, caking variety with Moisture 4·85 per cent, Volatile Matter 39·15 per cent, Fixed Carbon 53·70 per cent, Ash 2·30 per cent, and a Calorific Value of 7,448: as usual with Assamese coals, the sulphur percentage is high. The coal seams in the collieries of Borjan and Konjan are in the lower part of the Tikak Parbat Stage of the Upper Eocene. The mines actually lie in the Naga Hills, but they are connected with the North Eastern Railway at Sibsagar Road station by a branch line 15 miles in length, terminating at Naginimara, to which the coal is conveyed by an aerial ropeway, 4 miles in length, from the workings which are situated about 1,000 feet above the level of the railway. The output from 1913 to the end of 1950 was 1,110,109 tons, the highest production being in 1924 with 60,083 tons, but of late years there has been a marked decline, the annual average for the five years ending 1950 being only 20,843 tons.

Jaipur. After a gap of about 16 miles, across which the Coal Measures have not yet been traced, probably because of the maximum difficulties of prospecting in the virgin forest, dense thorny undergrowth and thick soil caps which the Naga Hills present, they are known again, stretching north-eastwards from the Tiyok stream, across the Disang valley, where they leave the

Sibsagar district and enter that of Lakhimpur, thence across the
Dihing for approximately 4 miles beyond Lakhimpur, a total
distance of some 25 miles.   This band forms the Jaipur field, in
the southern portion of which, especially near Barpeta, Disam,
Hapjan and Jaipur itself, a town on the railway, the coal seams are
of considerable thickness, though north of the Dehing, near
Dhekiajuli and Seraipung, they are very much thinner.

Known in 1838, the field for many years supplied the factories
of the local tea estates with fuel from outcrop quarries.   In 1876,
Mallet estimated that between Tipam and Boruarchali, a distance
of 15 miles, allowing an average workable thickness of 15 feet,
there was a total of 20 million tons of coal within a depth of 450 feet.
Today the Coal Measures are known to extend not for 15, but for
25 miles.   In a limited area of one square mile, known as the
Disang-Borhat area, Simpson, in 1906, allowing 25 feet of workable
coal, considered that 1¼ million tons could be profitably extracted
from a total of 2,676,830 tons, pointing out at the same time that it is
very probable the seams continue to be of economic value for many
miles beyond the limit he was able to prospect.   During 1949-50, T.
Banerjee re-examined the area between the Dihing and Dikhu rivers
and estimated the available reserves at 3,850,000 tons.   Practically
the whole of the coal, however, lies below water level.   A small
mine was opened at Hapjan in 1910, the coal being conveyed to
Namrup by a tramway 4 miles in length, but it was not a profitable
venture.   The proprietors of the Bemolapur tea garden quarried
the outcrops of two seams, measuring 6 and 4 feet in thickness,
near their property for a short time.   The Dilli colliery, which
was taken over by its present owners in 1945, contains a number of
distorted seams, aggregating a total thickness of 25 feet, near the
Disang river.   The coals from this mine contain: Moisture 5 to
10 per cent, Volatile Matter 36 to 42 per cent, Fixed Carbon
42 to 53 per cent, Ash 2 to 18 per cent.   Their sulphur content is
about 2·5 per cent.

Coal production from the Sibsagar district appears in the
official returns as a total of 4,283 tons for the years 1917 to 1919,
and then again from 1942 onwards: up to the end of 1950 a total
of 193,859 tons had been raised, the output for 1950 being 26,944
tons.

Makum.   The Namdang-Ledo, or Makum coalfield, lies to
the east of Jaipur, and the Coal Measures occupy a narrow strip
some 18 miles long and one mile broad.   Mallet, in 1876, found
the best outcrops in the 5½ miles' stretch between the Namdang and
Tirap streams.   According to Evans (1932), thick coal seams with
carbonaceous shales, shales and sandstones form the lower part
of the Tikak Parbat Stage, while the workable seams are limited
to a small part of the succession.   The lowest or 'Thick' coal is
often termed the '60-foot seam' and in many places it is divided

into three separate ones. Above this coal there are two comparatively thin seams, followed by the ' 20-foot ' coal, which, in its
turn, is also followed by several thinner seams. In some areas,
parts of the ' Thick ' coal are missing, and the 20-foot seam has
been eroded over a large area near Baragolai. The average dip
is high, but the outcrops, being often some hundreds of feet above
the plains, permit of mining by means of adit levels. In 1900,
G. E. Harris estimated that in the stretch of ground mentioned
above there is a total of 90 millions of tons of coal above natural
drainage level. According to Sir Cyril Fox, not less than a further
100 million tons exists between Ledo and Tipong, while ' taking
the whole area involved from the longitude of Makum to the
hairpin bend of the Tirap, say 50 square miles, the quantity of
coal within a depth of 2,000 feet must be of the order of 1,000
million tons '.

Mining commenced in 1881 when collieries were opened at
Ledo and Tikak and a little later at Namdang. A metre-gauge
railway, 77 miles in length, was made to the fields from the Brahmaputra valley near Dibrugarh, and more collieries followed later,
at Baragolai (in the Thick Seam of Makum), at Lakhpani (in the
Lakhpani seam) and at Tipongpani (in the Makum Thick and
20-foot Seams). The coal is of excellent quality, a valuable gas-
producing material which also furnishes a hard, porous, low ash
coke; its only defect is its large sulphur content. A recent analysis
of a dried sample showed: Volatile Matter 44·38 per cent, Fixed
Carbon 52·92 per cent, Ash 2·70 per cent. Moisture in original
sample 2·06 per cent, Sulphur 2·89 per cent. The average
theoretical calorific value of ten samples of Makum coal, quoted
by R. R. Simpson, is 7,447 calories, compared with the value of
6,526 calories calculated for thirty-one samples of Raniganj coal.
Makum coal is consumed by railways, river steamers, tea factories,
and rice and oil mills in Assam. In 1884, the output was 19,493
tons and by 1900 it had risen to 215,962 tons: for the next twenty
years it fluctuated between 250 and 305 thousand tons per annum.
The highest production was 307,414 tons in 1930, and in 1950,
303,584 tons, being 0·94 per cent of the total Indian output for
that year, were raised. The total tonnage taken from the field
between 1900 and 1950 was 13,125,970 tons.

Namchik. The discovery of coal in the Namchik valley, close
to its junction with the Dehing river, and but 18 miles in a straight
line from Ledo, by W. Griffith and H. Bigge, was announced by
the latter to the Asiatic Society of Bengal in 1837. Later, the
seams were described by Medlicott in 1865 and examined by Sir
Edwin Pascoe in 1911. He reported five groups of seams within
360 feet of strata: their total thickness is 60 feet, of which only
5 or 6 feet are of poor quality; the best seam is 21½ feet thick but it
contains 3 thin clay bands. The average analysis of the coal is:

Volatile Matter 44·4 per cent, Fixed Carbon 52·9 per cent, Ash 2·7 per cent.   The Coal Measures are an extension of those of the Makum field and they have also been traced further east still in the Namphuk valley, where 600 million tons of workable coal are said to be available, and on to the slopes of the Miao Bum range, though here they appear to be thinning out.   All these localities lie beyond the eastern border of the Lakhimpur district and in the Sadiya Frontier Tract.

ANALYSES OF ASSAMESE COALS

LOCALITY	MOISTURE	VOLATILE MATTER	FIXED CARBON	ASH	REMARKS
Garo Hills ..	5·64	40·90	50·72	2·74	average of 4 samples, 2·72% sulphur
Cherrapunji ..	4·14	50·38	42·71	2·77	....
Nazira ..	4·35	48·00	45·70	1·95	Borjan colliery
Namdang ..	2·25	42·27	54·27	1·21	Makum colliery
Ledo ..	1·80	40·15	55·59	2·46	sample of 49 feet of coal
Tikak ..	2·09	37·25	58·99	1·67	sample of 47 feet of coal

TERTIARY COALFIELDS OF KASHMIR

The next Tertiary coalfields to be described lie in the Jammu Province of Kashmir, but it is necessary to mention the recent discovery of an intermediate occurrence near the base of Maha-bharat Lekh, in the Sallyana district of west Nepal, where G. N. Dutt has found coal seams of Eocene age up to 8 feet in thickness and with about 12 per cent of moisture, 21 per cent of volatile matter, 31 per cent of fixed carbon and 36 per cent of ash.

The Coal Measures of Jammu occur on the flanks of elongated domes, strung out roughly east and west, over a distance of 40 miles across the hills some 20 miles north of Jammu city.   There are six of these structures: the large Riasi dome, bisected by the Chenab river from north to south, and its isolated representative of Dandli; the smaller domes of Mahogala, Metka and Kalakot, and finally the subsidiary northern group of Dhanswal-Sawalkot, found in 1924.   Visited by Medlicott in 1859, various reports have been written on them including those by La Touche (1888) and Simpson (1904).   Middlemiss, in 1929, investigated in fuller detail the three smaller domes and noted briefly on the Dhanswal-Sawalkot, Chakar and Chinkah fields, the two latter forming part of the Riasi dome, west of the Chenab.   The Coal Measures underlie the Nummulitic limestone and are divided into an Upper Series, probably of Lower Eocene age, about 120 feet thick, and an irregular Lower Series, 4 to 24 feet thick, also known as the Bauxitic Series as shown in the following Table.

COAL-BEARING SEQUENCE OF KASHMIR

NIMADRIC BEDS (MURREES & SIWALIKS)	Miocene and younger.

.... unconformity ....

NUMMULITIC LIMESTONES & SHALES ..	About 400 feet (Eocene).

PROBABLY LOWER EOCENE	UPPER COAL MEASURES	Carbonaceous shales with coal seams and ironstone bands. Total thickness about 120 feet.
	BAUXITIC SERIES WITH LOWER COAL MEASURES	Bauxite, bauxitic clays and kaolin with local ironstone and coal in thick seams at certain places. Thickness 4 to over 24 feet.

BRECCIA	Chert fragments in calcareous or siliceous cement; 20 to 30 feet. Age unknown.
GREAT (RIASI) LIMESTONE	Massive grey limestone. Probably Permian.

NOTE :—On the flanks of the domes the coal-bearing Eocene rocks are overlain by the sandstones of the Murree Series. In their inner parts the underlying Great (Riasi) Limestones crop out.

In the Dandli field, described by C. M. P. Wright in 1905 and by D. N. Wadia, in part, in 1928, which crosses into Poonch, there are two or three inconstant, lenticular seams, from 6 to 36 inches thick, of extremely crushed coal, which in Wright's opinion offer no inducement to exploitation. The only workable portion of the Ladda-Sanganmarg field of the Riasi dome, according to Simpson, lies between Ladda and the Anji valley, east of the Chenab, where a seam, averaging about 31 inches in thickness, probably contains about $1\frac{3}{4}$ million tons of workable coal and possibly $3\frac{3}{4}$ million tons above free drainage level. In the years 1902–4, 2,407 tons were taken from this Ladda field.

In the areas west of the Chenab, outcrops of a seam of workable thickness occur at several places between the river and Chakar, near the western end of the Riasi dome, and over a distance of some ten miles. Middlemiss thought that the region around Chinkah, near the river itself, should yield 6 million tons. The Upper Measures of the Chakar field have two seams, each about 5 feet in thickness, with a reserve of about 9 million tons.

Five miles west of the Chakar field lies that of Mahogala where the seams of the Lower Measures are sporadic and poor, but the Upper Measures, especially to the north and east, have two main seams of low volatile coal of excellent quality, though it is soft and friable. The two seams total about 12 feet in thickness and 4 million tons of coal are regarded as 'reasonably in sight' in them.

The Metka field, one mile west of Mahogala, has three separate seams in the Upper Measures with a total, average thickness of 5 feet, from which 5 million tons of mainly friable, semi-anthracitic coal may be obtainable.

Kalakot is the most westerly member of the main, southern group, situated 1½ miles west of the Metka field. Its Lower Measures contain a seam of good-quality, hard, semi-bituminous coal, varying up to 17 feet in thickness, with estimated minimum reserves of 1 million tons. An upper seam in the Upper Measures is from 4 to 7 feet thick and should yield about 6 million tons of second-class fuel, for though a low volatile, bituminous to semi-bituminous type, it is relatively high in ash. A thin, 2- to 2½-foot seam occurs, still in the Upper Measures, though 40 feet below the former one. Both it and another middle seam are said to contain a further 2 million tons of very good coal, perhaps all of which, however, will require briquetting before being marketed, if it ever comes to be mined.

The outlying Dhanswal-Sawalkot field stretches to the east-south-east from Dhanswal to Lodhra, a distance of about 12 miles, and in it the main seam, up to 7 feet in thickness, rests on the Bauxitic Series. Its coal is greatly crushed and powdery, of an anthracitic character, with only about 10 per cent of volatile matter and a high ash content. Its possible reserves have been given as 9 million tons. About 40 feet above this seam there is another thinner one. In calculating the reserves of the Kashmir fields, an arbitrary limiting depth of 1,000 feet has been taken, but there is no apparent geological reason why the seams should not extend to greater depths than this.

· About 1945, the Mining Department of Kashmir announced the discovery of a seam of good coal, 4 feet thick, at Khuiratta, some 18 miles to the west of the Kalakot field, and of another steeply dipping seam of similar quality, 10 feet thick, at Jangalgali, about 42 miles by road, north-north-east of Jammu. Departmental mining by underground methods commenced at Kalakot and Jangalgali, both of which are in the Riasi district, about 1945, and open-cast quarrying of outcrop material at Dandli, in the Nurpur district, in 1943. While the coal from Kalakot is hard and lumpy, that from Dandli is a semi-anthracitic powder which is used in brick kilns. The coal from Jangalgali too is powdery, but it can, however, be coked. The total output of coal recorded from Kashmir between 1939 and 1949 was 35,827 tons.

The Eocene coals of India and Pakistan are largely of a lignitic character, but in Kashmir as well as certain other Himalayan areas, higher rank coals occur, the change having been brought about by the pressures developed during the earth movements which accompanied the growth of the range, mainly during late Tertiary times. Thus it comes about that the Jammu coal has a semi-bituminous and anthracitic character while most of it is very friable with a marked foliated structure. It burns with little flame or smoke, and when washed and briquetted forms a fairly good steam coal. Some varieties coke strongly and most appear to contain a high percentage of sulphur.

ANALYSES OF KASHMIR COALS

Locality	Moisture	Volatile Matter	Fixed Carbon	Ash	Remarks
Ladda ..	1·03	12·42	69·74	16·81	average of 6 samples
Metka ..	1·96	12·60	71·54	13·90	average of 10 samples
Mahogala ..	3·78	14·76	71·60	9·86	average of 6 samples
Kalakot ..	0·63	12·25	78·12	9·00	Lower Measures
„ ..	4·62	14·54	69·44	11·40	Upper Measures

TERTIARY COALFIELDS OF THE WEST PUNJAB, PAKISTAN

The events which led to the formation of coal seams in southern Kashmir during early Eocene times were not confined to that region, but affected a wider part of north-western India including the West Punjab. The retreat of the sea towards the end of the Mesozoic period and the formation of a land surface, typified in Jammu by the Bauxitic Series and the coal seams which follow it, has its counterpart in the Lower Eocene (Ranikot) laterite and the associated Makerwal coal seam of the trans-Indus Salt Range beyond Kalabagh.

After its formation there were further encroachments of the sea, marked by the foraminiferal limestones, marls, shales and subordinate sandstones which follow it, but local estuarine and marshy conditions disturbed this particular marine phase during late Ranikot and succeeding Laki times. It was during a marine recession of the Upper Ranikot that the Dandot seam was formed over what is now the eastern Salt Range and parts of the Kala Chitta area, while during the ensuing Laki period several thin seams had their origin in parts of Baluchistan and Sind.

The Coal Measures of the West Punjab in Pakistan then are found at two distinct geological horizons of Lower and of Upper Ranikot age, though both are not productive in the same fields. The coals themselves are lignitic in character and either non- or poorly caking; sometimes banded and bright, liable to marked variation of composition from place to place, and often in a single seam, and relatively high both in moisture and sulphur. The seams crop out mainly in the scarps overlooking the Jhelum plain in the eastern Salt Range and that of the Indus, in the Mianwali district, in its western extension. Early accounts of the Punjab Salt Range coal were given by A. Fleming between 1848 and 1853, while a later list made by T. Oldham, the first Director of the Geological Survey of India, mentions thirteen localities, many of which, however, have no economic significance.

Eastern Salt Range. In the middle part of the Salt Range scarp, the Dandot seam is found associated with shales lying between limestones of Ranikot and Laki ages, respectively; it is thus somewhat younger than the Makerwal seam of the trans-Indus range described below. The Dandot seam is fairly constant eastwards as far as the Bhaganwala area but westwards it is shaly and is not mined. It continues northwards beneath the underlying Laki limestones and shales of the plateau, and being horizontal, or only gently inclined, lies within depths of 250 and 450 feet. As a result of the rugged topography and the intersection of the plateau by deep gorges, various separate areas have to be mentioned though only one seam is concerned and the workable area, as far as is known, is confined to a distance of 3 to 5 miles from the scarp face, though the Coal Measures come to the surface again 12 to 15 miles to the north on the slopes of the Diljabba range.

Bhaganwala Area. This includes the small plateau 8 square miles in extent, around Ara, in the eastern part of the range, and originally the outcrop of the seam could be traced for about a mile. In 1893, La Touche estimated a reserve of 88,000 tons of proved and available coal, in a seam which varied from practically nothing up to a maximum of 7 feet in thickness. Between 1877 and 1893 about 2,000 tons of outcrop coal were removed, and in the latter year the North-Western Railway Co. commenced mining, connecting its pits with the Sind-Sagar line at Haranpur, about 1896. The maximum production was 13,145 tons, in 1897, but operations ceased in 1900 owing to the poor quality of the coal.

Dandot Area. From Bhaganwala the Coal Measures continue cropping out to the west-south-westwards around the scarp, and the next area of mining activity includes the tracts around Dandot, Pidh and Manihala, where the seam varies from 2 to 4 feet in thickness. It was mined beneath the Laki limestones both at Dandot and at Pidh, 3 miles to the north-east, by the railway company between 1884 and 1911, when the collieries were sold to a private firm. Various small concerns continue to work in this area, and it has been proposed that the existing tramway system, which terminates on the Pidh platform, should be extended and linked with the upper terminus of a new overhead ropeway to convey the coal down the scarp to Dandot railway station. The total output from 1900 to 1946 was 2,283,219 tons; the record annual output during that period was 81,218 tons in 1899, and the production for 1946 was 76,852 tons.

Chittidand Area. On the Chittidand plateau, just to the west of Makrach, about 4 miles west of Dandot, as the crow flies, the Eocene limestones form another basin several square miles in extent. The coal seam below them again varies up to about 4 feet in thickness. The output from the drifts here is moved by tramway to the railway at Golpur, and it is counted as part of the Dandot production.

Dhak-Katha Area. From the Chittidand plateau the Coal Measures again continue westward, cropping out along the scarp slopes past Sardahi and Nurpur, to the Dhak-Katha area of the Sargodha district. Numerous small mines have been at work for many years north-north-west of Katha, as at Tejuwala near the crest of the scarp, and at Jhakarkot, $3\frac{1}{2}$ miles further south-west, where a variable seam averages about 3 feet in thickness. They are connected by a tramway with the railway at Dhak station to the south. From 1905, when separate statistics commenced, to 1946, a total of 268,772 tons had been won, the annual outputs steadily increasing to a maximum of 12,280 tons in 1946.

A firm of consulting mining engineers, engaged by the Government of West Pakistan in 1949, has estimated the workable reserves of coal in the Salt Range of the West Punjab as follows:

WORKABLE RESERVES OF SALT RANGE COAL

Area	Reserves (tons)	Area	Reserves (tons)
Dhak-Katha	5,250,000	Diljabba	4,000,000
Pidh-Dandot	10,500,000	Dalwal	3,450,000
Rakh Drengan & Rakh Dewan	13,800,000	Chittidand	3,000,000
Rakh Manihala	18,500,000	Nurpur	3,700,000
North & west of Ara ..	7,500,000	Total ..	69,700,000

Note.— The successful recovery of these reserves is dependent on the provision of capital, the introduction of modern mining methods and the construction of proper surface transport facilities.

Trans-Indus Ranges. The thin coal and coaly shale bands which occur in the Jurassic rocks, north of Kalabagh on the west bank of the Indus, and also above Kutch a few miles further north, in the Mianwali district, are of little economic interest and workable coal seams are confined to the Lower Eocene. The general direction of the Salt Range on this side of the Indus, where it is known under a variety of names, is at first northwards and then westwards from Kalabagh to beyond Chapri and later it turns southwards to the Kurram river, the Coal Measures cropping out in the scarps overlooking the alluvial plain of Isa Khel. The Dandot seam of the eastern Salt Range lies above the Ranikot limestones, but the Makerwal seam of the trans-Indus section lies

in the basal Eocene sandstone below them. The horizon of the
Dandot seam itself, both here and in the western half of the cis-
Indus range, is merely represented by carbonaceous shale. The
Makerwal seam is on the whole similar to the Dandot one, though
in places of somewhat superior quality. It varies greatly in thickness, being entirely absent in some parts and usually up to 3 feet
thick, but in the south of the Makerwal area it is said locally to
attain a thickness of 12 feet, including a shaly parting about its
middle. The greater part of the outcrop of the Coal Measures lies
within the Isa Khel *tahsil* of the Mianwali district of the West
Punjab, but around and south-west of Chapri, the beds dip northwards and westwards beneath the limestones of the Kohat district,
in the North-West Frontier Province. It is again necessary to
consider separate areas as follows:

Kalabagh-Chichali Area. A thin seam, 2 to 3 feet in thickness,
occurs at the base of the Eocene near the top of the scarp north of
Kutch, and it has been opened up by a few small workings. Eocene
rocks continue for about 7 miles along the strike to the south-west
to the Chichali pass, where a similar thin seam is exposed on the
eastern slopes.

Kurd-Malla Khel Area. Commencing 4 or 5 miles west of the
Chichali Pass, this area embraces the whole sweep of the Maidan-
Surghan part of the range, as it changes its direction from north-
east to south, a distance in a straight line of 13 miles. Several
small workings have proved the seam to vary rapidly up to a few
feet in thickness, though in some localities it has not been found.

Makerwal Area. This area lies 4 miles directly south of Malla
Khel, and from it both to the west and north-west of the town of
Sultan Khel, more than half of the Punjab's production of coal
has been won in recent years. The seam underlies the massive
sandstones of the Lower Ranikot Stage and locally attains a thickness of 10 feet, though it usually varies between 4 and 8 feet. R. R.
Simpson's prediction, in 1904, that successful mines might be
established here has been fulfilled. The production of 765 tons
in 1907 rose to 7,000 tons in 1912, to over 30,000 tons in 1932 and
to a record of 117,000 tons in 1939. The total output from the
commencement to the end of 1946 was 1,519,115 tons. The area
between Makerwal and Malla Khel has been developed more
recently. The mines are served by a metre-gauge track, about
30 miles long, from Mari station on the Indus. The Makerwal
collieries, covering a lease of 1,691 acres, were taken over by the
Punjab Government in 1948 and later by the Central Government
of Pakistan. The workable reserves of the trans-Indus fields are
estimated at 18,870,000 tons, of which 6,270,000 tons are in the
Makerwal area: proved and readily available reserves above water

level amount to 1,100,000 tons. Just south of Makerwal colliery the Coal Measures disappear beneath alluvium. The West Punjab and Baluchistan between them account for practically the whole of the coal production of Pakistan and statistics published by its Department of Mineral Concessions, in 1950, give the total output for the fifty years ending 1950 as 7,059,458 tons, of which 4,689,857 tons, or 66·4 per cent, came from the West Punjab.

COALFIELDS OF BALUCHISTAN

Thin coal seams of Eocene age occur in various parts of Baluchistan though easily accessible areas containing workable seams are not numerous. They include the Khost-Sharig-Harnai group, the Sor Range and Digari fields and the Mach area. The seams occur within the Ghazij Shale Stage of Laki age and are thus at a higher horizon within the Eocene sequence than those of the Punjab. They are associated with a great thickness of gypsiferous, olive-green shales and sandstones, themselves overlain and under-lain by Eocene limestones: above the latter follow the shales, sandstones and clays of the higher Tertiary, Gaj and Manchhar Stages.

Khost-Sharigh-Harnai Belt. The Coal Measures of this belt, which is situated some 30 to 40 miles east of Quetta, and about 4,000 feet above sea level, extend from beyond Khost in the north-west, through Sharigh and Nakus, to Harnai in the south-east, a distance of 25 or 30 miles along the general strike of the strata. They dip at high angles to the south-west and are approachable from the Sibi-Zardalu section of the North-Western Railway, which runs more or less parallel to them. A large number of thin coal seams and bands of coaly shale occur but many of them are only a few inches thick. In the Khost-Sharigh section thin seams of 1½ to 2, 2 to 3 and 4½ feet thick, respectively, have been worked. The Sharigh portion of the belt, according to S. T. Ali and N. M. Khan, who examined it in 1948, has a lateral extension of 6 miles. In the Nakus section, farther south-east, a seam, 1½ to 2 feet in thickness, has been proved over a distance of 1½ miles, while in the Harnai section there is a 2½ to 3-foot seam which has been followed for more than 4 miles. M. Haque, of the Geological Survey of Pakistan, mapped the Harnai and Nakus areas of the Sibi district in 1948, and discovered a new 2½ to 3-foot seam, traceable for about 6 miles. The consulting engineers to the Pakistan Government estimate the workable reserves of the Khost-Sharigh belt at 39,900,000 tons. Collieries were opened by the North-Western Railway Co. in 1877 at Khost; at Sharigh in 1894 and at Harnai in 1910, but owing to disturbed ground, variations in the seams themselves and the liability of the coal to spontaneous combustion, they were later abandoned. Owing to its friability much of the

Khost coal was briquetted before use. Today there are many small, separate, producing units, working the outcrop coal at shallow depths by primitive, hand-to-mouth methods. In 1900 the output was 17,664 tons and it rose to a maximum of 45,585 tons in 1913, gradually falling away to 17,085 tons in 1925. The collieries were closed about this time, though a few thousand tons continued to come annually from the region. A pronounced revival occurred in 1942, with an output of 26,234 tons. The production in 1946 was 23,075 tons and from 1900 to the end of that year, a total of 1,008,240 tons had been obtained.

Sor Range. Over a distance of 7 miles along the scarp of the Sor Range, 10 to 15 miles east of Quetta, there are a number of small mines exploiting two seams from their outcrops: the upper of the two is 2½ feet thick and the lower one 4½ to 5 feet thick, though it is not present everywhere. The intervening shales vary from a few feet to about 100 feet in thickness and the dip is from 40° to 50°. Here, as elsewhere, the workings follow the dip of the seams and their extent is usually limited by the underground water level. A metalled road joins Spin Karez with Quetta and a fair-weather road, maintained by the lessees themselves, connects the various workings with it. The coal is usually slack and powdery; the ash content is often low, but there is an appreciable amount of sulphur, rising in some cases to as much as 4 per cent.

Digari. The Digari field is 6 miles south of the Sor Range, in the Quetta-Pishin district and the Kalat State, about 18 miles from Spezand Junction. When R. D. Oldham visited the field in 1890, the mines had been worked fitfully for many years and the workings were at that time strewn along more than a mile of outcrop. M. Haque and M. I. Ahmed investigated the field in 1941–2 and reported the presence of three or four seams at Digari, of which only two are workable: a lower one, 5 feet thick, and an upper one, 2½ feet thick, separated by shales and sandstones up to 40 feet in thickness. Both seams are pyritic with a sulphur content ranging between 1·8 and 4·1 per cent; the ash varies from 4·8 to 7·1 per cent. About a mile north of Digari, two seams are mined at Sherin Ab; separated by 50 to 100 feet of sandstones, they are 2½ feet thick in the case of the upper one, and 5 feet thick in the lower one, although this also contains some shaley bands. The coal of the upper seam contains 14·8 per cent of ash and 1·9 per cent of sulphur, and, like most Digari coal, consists of lump and slack in roughly equal proportions. The total probable reserves of workable coal are given as 17,990,000 tons in the Sor Range and 3,990,000 tons in the Digari-Shirin Ab area.

Mach. The existence of coal at Mach, in the Bolan Pass, was noted by Hutton in 1846 and the occurrences are within a few miles of the main railway line to Quetta. There are a number of thin seams up to $3\frac{1}{2}$ feet thick, but only three or four of them are workable. As the whole of this area has been subjected to great tectonic disturbance, the Coal Measures in the soft Ghazij Shales, mostly unprotected by harder, overlying beds, have suffered severe folding and faulting, so that mining becomes unusually complicated and the small workings generally end within a few hundred feet of the outcrops. The coal is friable with sulphur contents up to 6.5 per cent. Assuming a total length of 3 miles and an aggregate thickness of 4 feet, a quarter of a million tons should be obtainable within a depth of 100 feet. The mining consultants to the Government of Pakistan, however, compute the total, workable reserves as 15,050,000 tons, though to obtain this, capital, as well as modern mining methods and machines, will be necessary. Official coal statistics as published do not separate the small production of the many individual mines, often operated by petty lessees and small sub-contractors, in the Sor Range, Mach and Kalat areas. At the commencement of the present century, the aggregate total output was about 5,600 tons per annum and with minor fluctuations it increased to over 13,000 tons in the next twenty years. The largest recorded output of those days was in 1922, with its 26,269 tons, and thereafter it varied widely between 5,000 and 17,000 tons until the forties. The second world war and subsequent events greatly stimulated the industry, production jumping from $10\frac{3}{4}$ thousand tons in 1942 to 40,000 in 1943, passing 100,000 tons in 1944, and reaching 173,563 tons in 1946, giving a grand total of 898,831 tons for the period 1900 to 1946, inclusive. Since that time output has continued to rise, particularly in the coalfields of Baluchistan as a whole.

The total output of the West Punjab and Baluchistan for the 50 years 1901 to 1950, was, as already stated, 7,059,458 tons, and to this total Baluchistan contributed 33.6 per cent and the West Punjab 66.4 per cent, but these figures give no indication of a marked change which has taken place. In the earlier years the output of the West Punjab generally greatly exceeded that of Baluchistan, but since 1945 Baluchistan production has approached, and in some years passed, that of the West Punjab. Thus, for the five years ending 1950, while the average annual production from the West Punjab was 176,890 tons, that from Baluchistan was 171,780 tons, compared with 151,604 tons and 62,201 tons, respectively, for the previous quinquennium, ending 1945. These are small figures as coal tonnages are reckoned but they are of some economic significance in a region where fuel is so scarce, the distances to the important Indian fields so great, and the local demand so much in excess of internal supplies. The Department of Mineral Concessions of the Government of Pakistan estimated in 1950 that the demand for coal of all types was about $3\frac{1}{2}$ million tons per annum at that time.

COALFIELDS OF SIND

Jhimpir. A thin, lenticular seam of lignitic coal, 9 to 30 inches in thickness, occurs amongst the sandstones and shales forming the uppermost division of the Lower Eocene, Ranikot Series, about Jhimpir, Meting and other places in the Karachi district of Sind, about 80 miles north-east of Karachi itself. It is unusually high in moisture, contains 6 to 8 per cent of ash and is liable to spontaneous combustion. The seam, with a low and uniform dip, lies 50 to 70 feet below a series of low hills and is mined from short adits over an outcrop length of 12 miles. The Jhimpir portion of the field is about 6 miles from the railway station of the same name. The consultants of the Pakistan Government have recommended the drilling of the Jhimpir field as a matter of primary importance to prove its extent and resources. Production commenced with 6,245 tons in 1944 and 73,984 tons had been won by the end of 1950.

OTHER COAL OCCURRENCES IN PAKISTAN

The Coal Measures of the Mianwali district of the West Punjab continue down dip into the Kohat district of the North-West Frontier Province and are found on the crest of the Surghan range, just under which the outcrops are worked. The seam also crops

ANALYSES OF COALS OF THE WEST PUNJAB, PAKISTAN

LOCALITY	MOISTURE	VOLATILE MATTER	FIXED CARBON	ASH	CALORIFIC VALUE	REMARKS
Dandot ..	5·87	43·65	38·04	12·44	..	....
Pidh ..	4·44	40·38	38·70	16·48	..	....
Rakh						
Drengan ..	5·3	38·8	41·6	14·3	11,100	....
Chittidand ..	5·1	40·8	38·1	16·0	11,100	....
Katha Mine..	5·2	37·7	44·8	12·3	10,900	....
Makerwal ..	2·80	42·34	36·94	17·92	..	6·35% sulphur
,, ..	3·04	43·43	44·29	9·24	..	5·90% sulphur

ANALYSES OF COALS FROM BALUCHISTAN, PAKISTAN

LOCALITY	MOISTURE	VOLATILE MATTER	FIXED CARBON	ASH	CALORIFIC VALUE	REMARKS
Khost ..	2·29	41·51	46·52	9·68	..	....
Sharigh ..	6·80	40·80	47·60	4·80	..	Picked sample
Nakus ..	2·4	44·5	43·8	9·3	12,400	5·5% sulphur
Shirin Ab ..	11·9	38·8	43·1	6·2	10,700	2·1% sulphur
Mach ..	10·9	33·1	41·0	15·0	..	....

NOTE.— Coals of the West Punjab and Baluchistan are either non-caking or poorly caking.

In the case of coals dispatched from the mines, the ash content is often appreciably higher than that shown by the above analyses, owing to lack of care in removing shale bands.

out in the Baroch gorge of Kohat where it is 2 feet and 10 inches in thickness.

The coal of the Cherat Hills, Nowshera, Peshawar district, was investigated by N. M. Khan and J. M. Master in 1948, and though originally a thin seam it is now broken up into lenses of small dimensions through the action of earth movements. Their discontinuity and thinness together with the crushed condition of the surrounding ground do not warrant mining operations.

An irregular seam of coal, greatly crushed and sheared, crops out among shales which underlie Nummulitic limestone, in the Dore valley, east of Abbottabad, in Hazara. It varies greatly in thickness, from nothing up to 17 feet; most of it is of very poor quality with a high ash content. Small quantities have been mined in the past for local brick-burning and lime kilns, but attempts to exploit it on a larger scale have not been profitable.

COALFIELDS OF BURMA

COALS OF JURASSIC AGE

Panlaung Valley and Loian. Coal seams of Jurassic age occur in the Panlaung valley, on the edge of the Southern Shan plateau, and some of the exposures were described by E. J. Jones in 1887. They were examined in 1932 by V. P. Sondhi, who found that the Coal Measures build the Legaung ridge for a distance of 8 miles, and stretch in a band, 3 to 3½ miles wide, across the Toklet valley and through the Wetpyuye forest into the Panlaung valley proper, a distance of 13 miles. The coal is scattered in pockets, streaks and lenticles and at only one locality, 1½ miles south of Legaung, is it considered worth further examination.

In the southerly extension of the same Coal Measures, between Myinka and Konhla, the best known locality is the Loian coalfield near Kalaw, but it is a very disturbed region in which the Coal Measures themselves are tucked into the axes of reversed folds in older limestones, or faulted down into them. Extensive underground exploration was carried on here about 1922 but without commercial success, the seams proving exceedingly irregular, crushed and broken. Most of the Shan Jurassic coals are more or less powdery and could not be marketed without briquetting, though some of them form a good, hard coke.

Henzada. The Jurassic coal seams of the Henzada district were described by Murray Stuart in 1910. Perhaps the best occurrence is that near Kywezin, where a seam 8 feet thick is exposed, but the strata are greatly contorted and the coal so crushed that its volatile contents have been diminished while its fixed carbon percentage is high. Attempts at mining here have not been successful and large-scale tests of the coal have been disappointing. There are other seams of minor importance at Hlemauk and Posugyi.

ANALYSES OF BURMESE JURASSIC COALS

LOCALITY	MOISTURE	VOLATILE MATTER	FIXED CARBON	ASH	REMARKS
Loian ..	0·7	26·4	60·2	12·7	mean of 7 samples
Kywezin ..	1·68	17·59	74·44	6·29	„ „ 3 „

COALS OF TERTIARY AGE

Tertiary coal seams are known in several districts of Burma. Thin, crushed and shaly seams were examined in 1896 by Sir Henry Hayden at Mithwe in Bhamo, while in the adjoining district of Katha, F. Noetling, in 1893, had already reported the presence of several seams, including one of fair quality, 4 to 5 feet thick, at Yuyinbyat, near Pinlebu. Near Kyaukset, in Minbu district, there is stated to be a seam 4 feet 7 inches thick, while from the Yaw river valley in Pakokku, G. de P. Cotter and Rao Bahadur Setu Rama Rao, in 1914, described seams varying from 5 to 6 feet in thickness but with numerous shaly partings and of low calorific value, near Letpanhla and Tazu. The irregular seam of Lime Hill, near Thayetmyo, and the thin ones of Cap Island, Cheduba, and Ramree, in Arakan, are probably worthless.

Kabwet. T. Oldham, in 1855, visited three coal outcrops a few miles west of Kabwet in the Shwebo district, and they were certainly mined by the Burmese before the British occupation of Upper Burma, i.e. before 1885. The coal-bearing area lies between the Kabwet bend of the Irrawaddy and its tributary the Man Chaung, and mining was confined to a single seam about 6 feet thick. A company carried on operations here at intervals between 1891 and 1904, when the workable coal is said to have been exhausted. The annual output varied from 10,000 to 15,000 tons, though in 1896 23,000 tons were extracted.

Upper Chindwin. The most extensive coalfields of Burma proper lie in a very isolated part of the valley of the Upper Chindwin and probably for this reason have remained undeveloped. The Coal Measures are of Eocene age and they occupy the valleys of the Nantahin, Peluswa, Maku and Telong streams, to the north of the Kale river, a tributary of the Chindwin, for a distance of 55 or 60 miles. According to Noetling (1889), seams of 2 feet and under are the general rule, but thicknesses up to 12 feet occur. In the Nantahin-Peluswa tract, with an area of 25 square miles, a total thickness of 48 feet of coal was considered to be available, and on the assumption that this could be worked to an incline depth of

1,000 feet from the outcrop, Noetling estimated that there are 210 million tons of workable coal in this limited portion of the Upper Chindwin field.

ANALYSES OF BURMESE TERTIARY COALS

LOCALITY	MOISTURE	VOLATILE MATTER	FIXED CARBON	ASH	REMARKS
Yaw River ..	18·73	34·15	35·86	11·26	mean of 22 assays
Kabwet (Shwebo).	12·27	37·45	38·97	11·31	,, ,, 2 ,,
Chindwin ..	10·14	34·59	49·95	5·32	,, ,, 13 ,,

LIGNITE

The lignites, or brown coals, represent an early stage in the transformation of plant tissues into the black coals, and as in most instances the Eocene coals of India, Pakistan and Burma have not matured beyond the lignitic stage, it would not be incorrect to classify such examples here. But in some cases their composition has been greatly changed through the influence of the intense tectonic pressures to which they have been subjected, as in the semi-anthracitic coals of southern Kashmir, and it becomes difficult to draw a strict line of division. Thus the grouping adopted here is purely an arbitrary one and under the term ' lignite ' are included the fuels of Miocene or younger age, formed under shallow-water, estuarine conditions in some parts of southern India; the resinous, woody coal of Eocene age, occurring in Bikanir, Rajasthan; and others, found mainly in Kashmir and Burma, which were laid down for the most part in areas of more or less enclosed drainage, under lacustrine or fluvio-lacustrine conditions.

As a group such lignites are characterized by high moisture contents, volatile constituents ranging from about 30 to 50 per cent and fixed carbon under 50 per cent. They are light in weight, often dark brown in colour, of tough structure and sometimes displaying a wood-like, fibrous structure. They weather rapidly on exposure, splitting easily into thin layers, and readily fall into powder-defects which can be remedied by briquetting before their use as fuel.

LIGNITE FIELDS OF SOUTHERN INDIA

Cuddalore-Pondicherry Area, Madras. The occurrence of lignite under the coastal flats between Pondicherry and Cuddalore has been known since 1884, when W. King published an account of assays and trials of local lignite made for a French firm, who proposed to compress the material into briquettes for fuel, a venture which was not carried to a successful conclusion. The lignite had been proved in three boreholes at the following localities: Bahur, 5 miles north-north-west of Cannanore; Aranganur, 2½ miles north of Bahur, and Kanniyakovil, 3 miles north of Cannanore. The depth of the seam from the surface and its thickness were, at Bahur, 257½ feet and 35 feet; at Aranganur, 203 feet and 27 feet; at Kanniyakovil, 330 feet and 50 feet. From these depths it is calculated that the seam has a dip towards the south-south-east of 50 feet per mile. A second seam, 5¼ feet thick, was encountered in the borehole at Kanniyakovil at a depth of 330 feet. One of the better of several available analyses shows: Moisture 16·28 per cent, Volatile Matter 38·55 per cent, Fixed Carbon 37·72 per cent, Ash 7·45 per cent, Calorific Value 5,318 calories. Seven samples of the lignite analysed in Paris showed an average ash content of 8·35 per cent.

South Arcot. Lignite was found again about 1934 during boring operations for artesian water in the neighbourhood of Neyveli, near Vriddhachalam, South Arcot district, some 120 miles south of Madras. Three or four boreholes made by Messrs Binny & Co. (Madras), Ltd led to the further recognition of lignite of good quality, and systematic drilling by officers of the Geological Survey of India, under the direction of Dr M. S. Krishnan, were commenced in 1943 and completed in 1947, after proving a reserve of 320–400 million tons in an area of about 16–20 square miles in the taluks of Vriddhachalam and Cuddalore. Since 1947, the Government of Madras have been continuing the investigation and H. K. Ghose, their Mining Engineer, proved the extension of the field to a further 80–86 square miles, making a total of about 100 square miles with estimated reserves of 2,000 million tons. Since October 1951, the services of Paul Eyrich of the U.S. Bureau of Mines have been made available to the lignite investigation, as a mining consultant under Truman's Point-Four Programme.

About the middle of 1954, the Government of India, under the Colombo Plan, obtained the services of Messrs Powell Duffryn Technical Services Ltd, London. Their report, submitted in November 1954, is under examination by the Central and the State Governments. The experimental excavation for lignite which started with equipment obtained on loan from the Government of India in 1952 has gone to a depth of over 145 feet below ground and the results of the excavation will soon be available.

The field as at present defined is centred around Neyveli station on the Southern Railway, 27 miles from Cuddalore and 11 miles from Vriddhachalam, and though its northern and north-western limits are known, its extension to the south and south-east beyond the Vellar river has still to be proved. The area is occupied by Cuddalore Sandstones of Miocene age, alternations of soft, often waterlogged sandstones and grits with clays of various colours.

The country is practically flat with a very gentle seaward slope displaying occasional banks of lateritized sandstone. The lignite occurs as a regular seam, varying from 0 at the field boundary to 90 feet in thickness, with a low dip towards the east-south-east, and showing a tendency to thicken in this direction; it is nowhere found at a depth of less than 140 feet from the surface. When fresh the material is black and compact but it becomes dark brown and cracks on drying. The range of assay values from the drill cores was as follows:

Moisture (dry air)	..	..	11 to 15·5 per cent
Volatile Matter	..	..	40 to 53 per cent
Fixed Carbon ..	..	..	30 to 38 per cent
Ash	..		3 to 6 per cent
Phosphorus	..	..	traces
Sulphur	..	..	0·5 to 1·4 per cent
Calorific Value ..	..	..	9,000 to 9,900 British Thermal Units.

The moisture content *in situ* is approximately 45 to 50 per cent. The presence of strong water sands under artesian conditions caused considerable technical difficulties during boring operations and later when a shaft was sunk to the lignite seam. In both cases these difficulties were surmounted successfully, and during November, 1951, 120 tons had been raised for testing purposes. The thickness of the seam at the shaft bottom is stated to be 65 feet, and the depth of the shaft, including the seam itself, is 240 feet. No water under pressure was encountered above the lignite seam, but below it, under an intervening layer of clay varying in thickness between 0 and 35 feet, a sandstone carries an artesian aquifer under pressure.

The present experimental working lies about one mile north of Neyveli railway station and adjoins the site of the completed 10-foot shaft noted above. It covers an area of 600 × 600 feet, has a more or less tank-like form and is intended to expose an area of lignite covering 100 × 100 feet. This working, commenced on 5 March 1953, will afford data of the actual slope of the seam, its water contents and at the same time provide some idea of probable working costs. Such studies are necessary as a basis for the development of more extensive operations.

The overburden in this area will be about 180 feet, exposing a seam of lignite 60 feet in thickness. This gives an overburden to coal ratio of 3 : 1, which the advisory engineers consider well within the limits of economic recovery. The overburden itself carries two layers of refractory clays which will also be exploited. Any water accumulating during the course of the mining operations will be stored in ' tanks ' which already exist in the neighbourhood, and directed from them for irrigation purposes.

The presence of lignite in the areas described in Pondicherry and South Arcot leads to the view that it may also be present in the Cuddalore Sandstones which occupy several scores of square

miles in the districts of Tiruchirapalli, Tanjore and Ramanathapuram, and that these areas should be systematically investigated for
this purpose.

Lignite Deposits of the West Coast. The Cuddalore Sandstones
of the East Coast have their counterparts on the West Coast,
where they are known as the Warkalli (Varkala) Beds which are
found not only at and around Varkala and Quilon, in Travancore,
but also extend northwards into Malabar and South Kanara.
As long ago as 1910, I. C. Chako and E. Massillamani, the State
Geologists of Travancore at that time, estimated the presence of
276 million tons of lignite beneath an area of 41 square miles,
near Varkala and other places. Moreover, lignite is known to
occur near Beypore and Cannanore in Malabar and near Kasargod
in South Kanara.

LIGNITE OF RAJASTHAN

Palana (Bikaner). A seam of dark brown, resinous, woody to
peaty lignite was discovered at Palana, 13 miles south-west of
Bikaner city, during well-sinking operations in 1896. It varies
up to a total of about 20 feet in thickness, lies beneath foraminiferal
limestones and is probably of Lower Eocene age. Mining commenced in 1898; railway connexion was established with the
Jodhpur-Bikaner line and production commenced in 1900. Since
that time it has continued without interruption, the fuel being
mainly consumed on the railway after briquetting. Up to the end
of 1950, a total of 1,509,318 tons had been won; the record output
was 72,371 tons in 1948 and the average annual production for the
five years ending 1949 was 60,187 tons. As mined, the lignite
contains from 40 to 45 per cent of moisture, but a few days' exposure
to the climate of the Rajasthan desert reduces this to 15 per cent
or less. The seam is flat, and as the area is largely covered by
desert sand, little is known about its possible extensions. Sir Cyril
Fox mentions, however, that lignite has been proved at Madh,
nearly 20 miles west of Palana, at a depth of 100 feet, while another
seam has been found near Chaneri, 32 miles away, 180 feet below
the surface. Thus it may well prove that the lignite resources of
Bikaner are of considerable magnitude.

ANALYSES OF BIKANER LIGNITE

	MOISTURE	VOLATILE MATTER	FIXED CARBON	ASH
Dry Lignite	12·55	46·67	36·38	4·40
Briquette (1)	14·84	40·64	38·78	5·74
Briquette (2)	9·32	44·36	38·80	7·52

LIGNITE OF KASHMIR

Shaliganga and Handwara. The lignite fields in the Karewa formation of the Vale of Kashmir, which are of late Tertiary age, were described by C. S. Middlemiss in 1923. In the Raithan and Lanyalab basins of the Shaliganga area, a minimum amount of 4 million tons is available, while the Handwara area contains 32 million tons, in continuous seams from $2\frac{1}{2}$ to 6 or 8 feet thick, down to easily workable levels. The areas mentioned are 40 miles apart, but if, as seems probable, lignite also occurs in the higher, south-western, disconnected, Karewa basins, over the greater part of the Valley of Kashmir, the quantities would become very large indeed. It is a low-grade, rather impure fuel, earthy in appearance, of a dark brown to black colour and of a slabby structure, averaging some 15 per cent Moisture, 28 per cent Volatile Matter, 27 per cent Fixed Carbon and 30 per cent Ash. It can be burnt under favourable conditions in stoves and furnaces and may prove useful for distillation in the future. The Mining Department of the Kashmir and Jammu Government has marketed the raw lignite for local consumption since 1944, from workings at Nichoma and Raithan, in the Handwara and Badgam *tehsils* respectively. The total production from 1944 to 1946 was 6,403 tons.

LIGNITE OF EAST PAKISTAN

Sylhet and Mymensingh. Irregular, lenticular beds of lignite have been found along the banks of certain rivers and lakes, at about water level, in deltaic deposits of the Ganga and Brahmaputra rivers, over an area of about 170 square miles, in the Sylhet district of East Pakistan, extending northwards into the Mymensingh district. The average thickness which is visible above water, within a depth of 10 feet from the surface, is $2\frac{1}{2}$ feet.

LIGNITE OF BURMA

MERGUI DISTRICT

Theindaw-Kawmapyin. The Theindaw-Kawmapyin field of Mergui, the southernmost district of Lower Burma, in which shales, sandstones and conglomerates of late Tertiary age, deposited in old river valleys, corresponding generally with the existing courses of the more important streams, and its associated seams of lignite, have been the subject of numerous reports, extending over a period of almost one hundred years. The more important of these were summarized by A. M. Heron in 1919, together with the results of his own investigations. A number of seams, from 4 to 15 feet in thickness, are known, while their enclosing rocks cover an area of about 30 square miles. Practical tests of the fuel are said to have given good results, but until the field has been bored it is impossible to assess its potentialities. Similar lignites occur in the Lenya valley of the same district.

THE SHAN STATES

The lignite-bearing rocks of the Northern Shan States occupy a number of separate basins grouped around the mountain Loi Ling. They have originated from peaty deposits more or less *in situ* in lacustrine and fluvio-lacustrine deposits, the formation of which is still proceeding in the lakes which yet remain, both in the Southern Shan States and in the adjoining Chinese territory of Yunnan. Thus they range in age from late Pliocene to Recent times.

Lashio. The Lashio field, with an area of about 50 square miles, lies in the valley of the Nam Yau river, about 5 miles to the north of Lashio, the terminus of the Northern Shan States branch of the Burma Railways. It was surveyed by La Touche and Simpson in 1904–5 and they found several outcrops of brownish-black lignite, with a distinctly woody structure, varying from 3 to 25 feet in thickness. Tests of the outcrop material in a locomotive were not successful, but this is not surprising as the fuel had not been briquetted and the fire-box of the engine was of the normal type used for burning Bengal steam-raising coal.

Namma. The Namma field, with an area of 50 square miles, lies 11 miles south of the Lashio field and was investigated by Simpson in 1905. The principal seam of lustrous black lignite has been traced for about half a mile and varies from 7 to 17 feet in thickness. A portion of this field was explored by the Burma Corporation Ltd some 35 years ago, and two seams of 12 and 21 feet in thickness proved. According to E. L. Moldenke (1922), in the small area concerned there are 50 million tons of lignite in the lower seam and 30 millions in the upper one, but it has not yet been used on a commercial scale.

Mansang and Mansele. The Mansang and Mansele fields, 16 and 27 miles south and east of the Namma field respectively, are each about 13½ square miles in extent. Surveyed by Simpson in 1905, they are known to contain numerous outcrops of lignite up to 4½ feet in thickness.

ANALYSES OF BURMESE AND SHAN LATE TERTIARY LIGNITES

LOCALITY	MOISTURE	VOLATILE MATTER	FIXED CARBON	ASH	REMARKS
Kawmapyin (Burma).	13·87	35·74	43·75	6·64	mean of 2 samples
Lashio (Shan States)	20·65	35·63	31·08	12·64	,, ,, 6 ,,
Namma ,, ,,	16·58	36·90	38·81	7·71	,, ,, 5 ,,
Mansang ,, ,,	14·23	35·13	36·32	14·32	,, ,, 6 ,,
Mansele ,, ,,	14·73	38·83	34·22	12·22	one sample

AVERAGE COMPOSITION OF INDIAN COALS

	Non-Caking Coals		Coking Coals	
	Bengal (a)	Central India	Bihar (b)	Assam
	%	%	%	%
Moisture	3 to 10	4 to 15	1 to 2	1 to 3
Ash	10 to 25	10 to 25	10 to 30	2 to 10
Sulphur	0·4 to 1·0	0·5 to 2·0	0·4 to 1·0	2 to 6
Volatiles	35 to 45	33 to 40	20 to 35	45 to 50
Fixed Carbon	55 to 65	60 to 67	65 to 80	50 to 55
Carbon	78 to 84	78 to 84	86 to 91	80
Hydrogen	5 to 6	4·5 to 5·5	4·5 to 5·5	5·0
Nitrogen	2·0	2·0	2·0	1·0
Sulphur	1·0	1·0	1·0	3·0
Oxygen	7 to 13	8 to 14	2 to 6	10
Calorific Value	14,000 to 15,000	13,500 to 14,700	15,400 to 15,800	14,500

(a) Represented mainly by coals of the Raniganj Measures.
(b) Mainly Jharia and Bokaro Coals but includes some from the Laikdih Series of the Raniganj Field.
Figures for moisture, ash and sulphur are based on samples ' as received '.
The remaining figures are based on a Unit Coal Basis, that is to say on coal free from moisture and mineral matter.
Calorific Values are expressed in British Thermal Units.
These analyses are taken from a report by Dr J. W. Whitaker, Director of the Fuel Research Institute of India.

PRODUCTION OF COAL IN INDIA, 1900–50

Year	Tons	Value at Mines		Pit's Mouth Average Value Per Ton	Proportion From	
		£	Rs.	Rs. a. p.	Gondwana Rocks %	Tertiary Rocks %
1900	6,118,692	1,343,081		3·29	94·6	5·4
1901	6,635,727	1,323,372		2·99	94·4	5·6
1902	7,424,480	1,366,909		2·76	95·4	4·6
1903	7,438,386	1,299,716		2·62	95·1	4·9
1904	8,216,706	1,398,826		2 9 0	95·02	4·98
1905	8,417,739	1,419,443		2 8 0	94·95	5·05
1906	9,783,250	1,912,042		2 15 0	95·56	4·44
1907	11,147,339	2,609,726		3 8 0	96·17	3·83

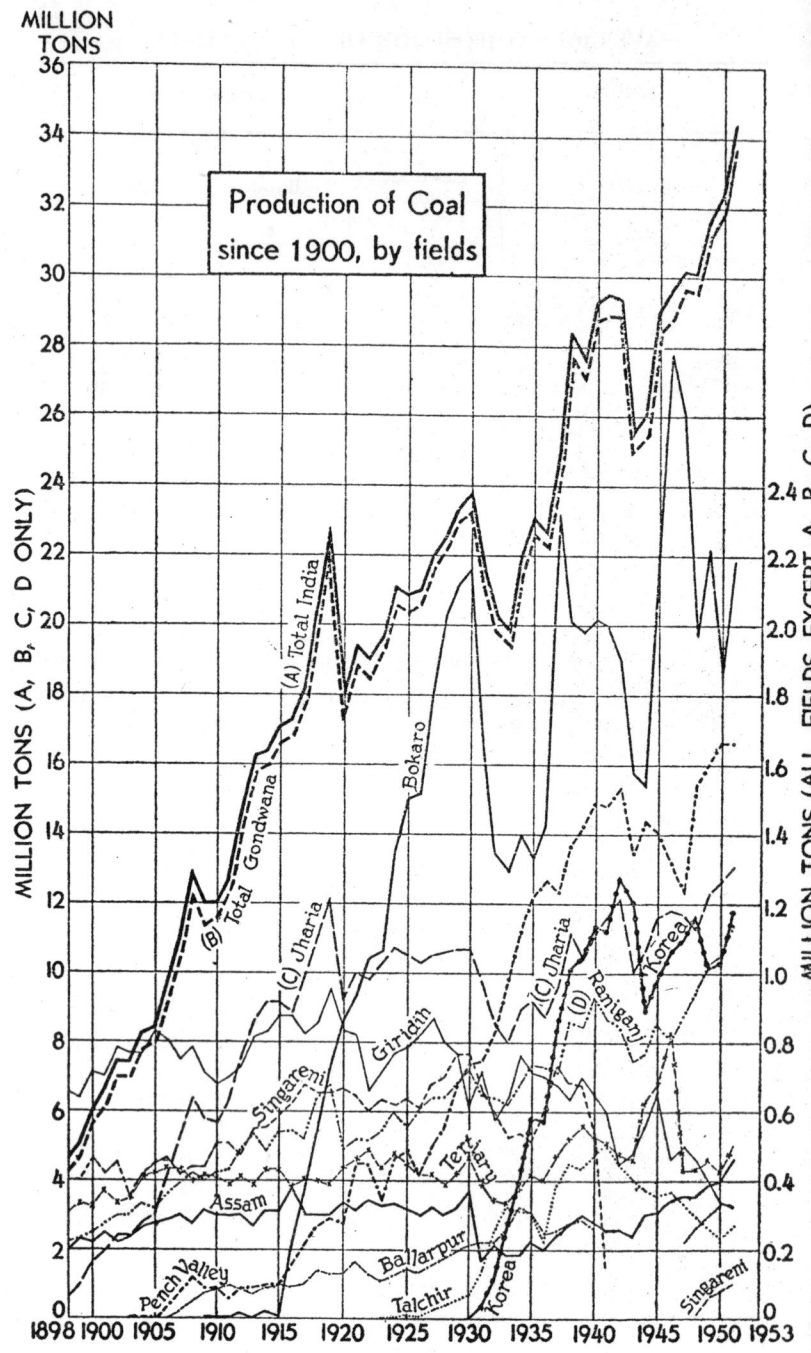

MILLION
TONS

Production of Coal
since 1900, by fields

PRODUCTION OF COAL IN INDIA, 1900–50—*Continued*

YEAR	TONS	VALUE AT MINES £	VALUE AT MINES Rs.	PIT'S MOUTH AVERAGE VALUE PER TON Rs. a. p.	PROPORTION FROM GONDWANA ROCKS %	PROPORTION FROM TERTIARY ROCKS %
1908	12,769,635	3,356,209		3 15 0	96·90	3·10
1909	11,870,064	2,779,865		3 8 0	96·57	3·43
1910	12,047,413	2,455,544		3 1 0	96·58	3·42
1911	12,715,534	2,502,616		2 15 0	96·96	3·04
1912	14,706,339	3,310,365		3 6 0	97·23	2·77
1913	16,208,009	3,798,137		3 8 0	97·57	2·43
1914	16,464,263	3,907,380		3 9 0	97·42	2·58
1915	17,103,932	3,781,064		3 5 0	97·48	2·52
1916	17,254,309	3,878,564		3 6 0	97·74	2·26
1917	18,212,918	4,511,645		3 11 0	97·81	2·19
1918	20,722,493	6,017,215		4 6 0	98·08	1·92
1919	22,628,037	8,799,353		4 8 0	98·28	1·72
1920	17,962,214	9,297,853		5 3 0	97·58	2·42
1921	19,302,947	8,673,377		6 12 0	97·62	2·38
1922	19,010,986	9,755,343		7 11 0	97·43	2·57
1923	19,656,883	9,737,316		7 7 0	97·77	2·23
1924	21,174,284	10,766,433		7 1 0	97·75	2·25
1925	20,904,377	9,503,828		6 1 0	97·82	2·18
1926	20,999,167	7,574,599		4 13 0	98·02	1·98
1927	22,082,336	7,079,852		4 5 0	98·11	1·89
1928	22,542,872	6,604,106		3 15 0	98·27	1·73
1929	23,418,734	6,668,591		3 13 6	98·22	1·78
1930	23,803,048	6,861,134		3 14 3	98·06	1·94
1931	21,716,435	6,125,804		3 12 11	98·22	1·78
1932	20,153,387	5,120,045		3 6 1	98·32	1·68
1933	19,789,163		6,11,77,739	3 2 0	98·32	1·68
1934	22,057,447		6,30,60,951	2 13 9	98·34	1·66
1935	23,016,695		6,52,20,840	2 13 4	98·22	1·78
1936	22,610,821		6,24,98,404	2 12 0	98·24	1·76
1937	25,036,386		7,81,02,439	3 2 0	98·13	1·87
1938	28,342,906		10,64,23,835	3 12 0	98·17	1·83
1939	27,769,112		9,87,23,916	3 9 0	98·01	1·99
1940	29,388,494		10,51,65,232	3 9 0	98·19	1·81
1941	29,463,742		10,76,79,014	3 10 0	98·28	1·72
1942	29,433,253		13,09,05,064	4 7 0	98·36	1·64
1943	25,511,909		16,95,07,329	6 10 0	98·22	1·78
1944	26,126,676		27,23,92,131	12 12 6	97·63	2·37
1945	29,167,152		32,80,99,008	14 3 4	97·70	2·30
1946	29,766,018		35,73,87,713	12 0 0	97·43	2·57
1947	30,144,505		43,77,20,245	14 9 0	98·61	1·39
1948	30,124,175		45,20,56,474	15 0 0	98·57	1·43
1949	31,695,375		47,56,36,921	15 0 0	98·61	1·39
1950	32,307,481				98·69	1·31
TOTAL	1,022,364,253					

NOTE :—The production of Pakistan is included up to the end of 1946.

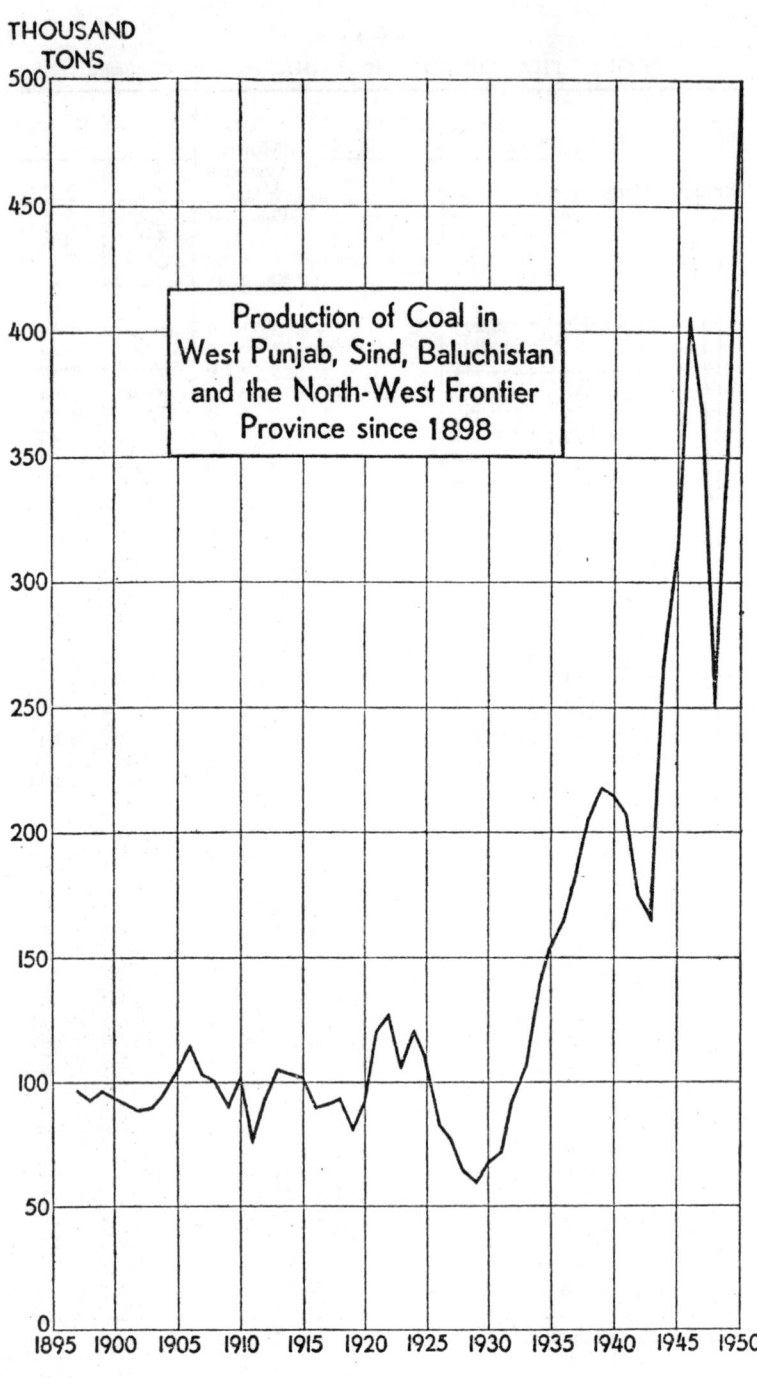

THOUSAND
TONS

Production of Coal in
West Punjab, Sind, Baluchistan
and the North-West Frontier
Province since 1898

AVERAGE ANNUAL IMPORTS OF COAL INTO INDIA, 1900-46 (Long Tons)

Arranged according to Countries

Period	United Kingdom	Australia	Union of South Africa	Portuguese East Africa	Japan	Other Countries	Total
1900–1 to 1902–3	173,515	13,520	....	....	29,460	2,442	218,937
1903–4 to 1907–8	190,158	23,643	8,030	....	21,904	4,476	248,211
1909–13	229,526	52,393	71,604	....	43,908	68,730	466,161
1914–18	47,128	20,247	29,782	29,280	10,805	11,279	148,521
1919–23	265,236	40,015	170,144	90,886	26,719	11,941	604,941
1924–8	73,061	11,792	148,560	75,787	4,666	5,048	318,914
1929–33	23,001	2,790	95,359	1,042	798	4,709	127,699
1934–8	16,657	3,472	36,265	5,591	1,070	8,296(1)	71,351
1939–43	3,126	....	8,707	....	....	2,928(2)	14,761
1944–6	193	....	2,782	....	....	337(3)	3,312
Total	4,760,589	812,320	2,850,601	1,012,930	637,730	595,372	10,669,542
Percentages	44·7%	7·6%	26·7%	9·5%	5·9%	5·6%	....

(1) includes an average of 7,308 tons from Germany.
(2) ,, ,, ,, 795 ,, of coke.
(3) ,, ,, ,, 288 ,, of coke.

Over the years 1947 to 1950 (inclusive), a total of 219 tons of coal were imported into India, all of which came from the United Kingdom.

AVERAGE ANNUAL EXPORTS OF COAL FROM INDIA, 1900-46 (Long Tons)

Arranged according to Destinations

Period	United Kingdom	Aden	Burma	Ceylon	Mauritius	Straits Settlements	Hong Kong	China
1900-3 (*)	....	40,571	....	325,897	13,064	81,624	....	....
1904-8 (*)	....	24,077	....	360,427	9,550	203,724	45,356	....
1909-13	....	8,084	....	466,965	2,423	187,525	....	....
1914-18	....	9,422	....	359,496	837	88,782	....	....
1919-23	10,272	22,954	....	282,951	....	74,284	24,308	....
1924-8	20,215	13,353	....	260,421	984	74,956	141,359	....
1929-33	....	1,496	201,799	270,352	1,575	30,879	37,662	2,294
1934-8	....	4,786	296,960	231,415	2,052	24,383	94,224	65,032
1939-43	....	2,761	....	305,648	....	87,691	....	212,457
1944-6	....	....	....	64,008	....	....	....	....
Total Exports..	152,435	556,378	2,493,795	13,858,085	126,297	4,105,992	1,714,545	1,398,915
Percentage of Total ..	....	1·9%	8·7%	48·3%	....	14·3%	5·9%	4·8%

(*) fiscal years.

PERIOD	JAVA	SUMATRA	PHILIPPINES & GUAM	EGYPT	OTHER COUNTRIES	TOTAL	VALUE Rs	VALUE £
1900-3 (a)	....	12,069	....	....	25,209*	498,434	51,39,165	342,611
1904-8 (a)	7,936	50,461	....	....	15,925**	717,456	56,78,040	378,536
1909-13	6,120	102,239	....	....	41,118	814,474	74,81,143	498,743
1914-18	8,496	52,141	....	....	20,248	539,422	49,24,260	328,284
1919-23	6,685	23,496	....	20,492	13,647	444,509	58,00,587	515,962
1924-8	....	4,045	14,416	21,142	24,631	448,528	57,64,029	428,679
1929-33	....	1,213	32,216	....	13,342	514,941	53,93,062	402,391
1934-8	....	5,295	....	....	19,850†	592,274	56,87,124	426,534
1939-43	....	....	....	20,148	206,438	1,243,647‡	1,23,96,654	929,749
1944-6	....	....	....	19,273	123,678	207,399§	37,72,274	282,920
TOTAL EXPORTS..	146,185	1,230,657	233,160	366,729	2,222,656	28,693,740	29,23,58,812	21,420,983
PERCENTAGE OF TOTAL ..	..	4·4%	....	1·2%	10·5%¶	....	....	....

GRAND TOTAL. 28,693,740 tons valued at Rs 29,23,58,812 or £21,420,983.

(a) fiscal years.

* includes 17,378 tons to British East Africa and Natal.
** „ 6,671 „ „ „ „ „ „
† „ 57 „ „ „ „ „ „
‡ includes 17,320 tons of coke.
§ „ 437 „ „ „
¶ includes the percentage of the United Kingdom, Mauritius, Java, British East Africa, Natal, the Philippine Islands and Guam, in addition to coke shipments.

ANNUAL EXPORTS OF COAL FROM INDIA, 1947-50 (Long Tons)

Year	Aden	Ceylon	Western Pakistan	Other Countries	Total	Value Rs
1947	..	137,648	..	409,983	550,526(1)	1,52,01,387
1948	1,180	249,346	372,646	311,349	948,288(2)	3,28,66,182
1949	..	312,567	487,898	464,498	1,267,267(3)	4,17,00,092
1950	6,123	295,241	..	601,781	910,844(4)	3,47,34,182
Total	7,303	994,802	860,544	1,787,611	3,676,925	12,45,01,843

(1) includes 2,895 tons coke
(2) ,, 13,767 ,, ,,
(3) ,, 2,304 ,, ,,
(4) ,, 7,699 ,, ,,

PRODUCTION OF COAL IN WEST PAKISTAN (TONS)

Year	Baluchistan	West Punjab	Total
1946	197,505	192,706	390,211
1947	182,290	175,454	357,744
1948	95,955	144,822	240,777
1949	145,350	178,722	324,072
1950	237,847	192,750	430,597

PEAT

The first stage in the development of many types of coal is represented by the peat deposits of present and comparatively recent times. They are the result of the slow accumulation of partially decayed vegetation under the waterlogged conditions prevalent in bogs, swamps and marshes in which the remains of the mosses, reeds and grasses adapted for such situations are neither removed nor thoroughly decomposed but serve as a foundation for the next crop of younger growth as season follows season. In this way a succession of layers is slowly built up—living plants at the top, their recognizable remains at lower depths, until in the bottom layers little trace of their original structures is left. When deeply buried and compressed in the course of geological time peat passes into the brown coals and lignites.

In its raw state peat contains about 80 per cent of moisture, but by suitable stacking and air-drying this can be reduced to about 20 per cent. Such air-dried peat is still used in isolated districts as a slow-burning fuel though its calorific value is stated to be only about half that of an equal weight of good coal. Even in countries possessing very extensive deposits, the problems

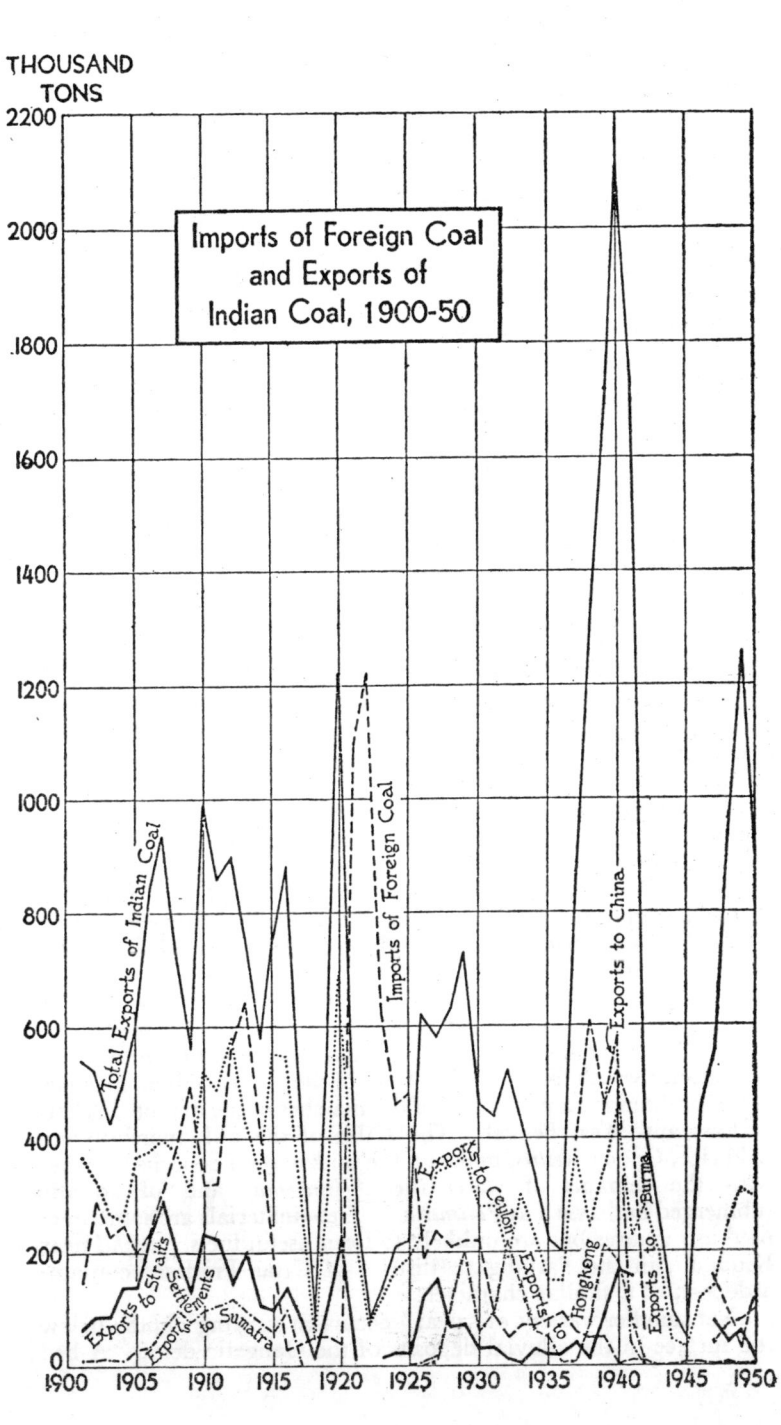

THOUSAND
TONS

Imports of Foreign Coal
and Exports of
Indian Coal, 1900-50

connected with the large-scale profitable utilization of peat for commercial purposes remain unsolved, owing to the high cost of winning, handling, drying and preparing it for the market in competition with other fuels. Owing to its absorbent properties dried peat makes a good stable litter and then forms an excellent manure. It is increasingly employed in Europe in the preparation of horticultural composts and, in the form of dust, as a packing for fruit and vegetables for transit by sea, air or railway. After the addition of chemical fertilizers it is utilized as a top dressing for grass and other farm crops.

Peat deposits are more characteristic of cold, temperate climates such as those of northern Europe and Canada than of warm tropical regions where the decay of plant life is usually rapid and complete; but even in such countries special conditions of altitude and environment are occasionally found in which peat, or deposits of an analogous character, have been laid down.

Perhaps the nearest relatives of the true peats of northern latitudes are the bog peats of the Nilgiri Hills of Madras. These lie in surface hollows at elevations of over 6,000 feet above sea level, where the local flora shows affinities with that of the Palaearctic region, where *Sphagnum* moss prevails extensively as it does in the peat bogs of northern Europe and where identical genera of associated plants are present. Dried Nilgiri peat was at one time used as fuel in Ootacamund and, about 1870, the possibility of employing it in place of coal for locomotives on the Indian railways was discussed. Beyond the fact that in places some Nilgiri peat deposits are said to be 30 feet deep, nothing is known as to their real extent or average composition.

In the Shevaroy Hills of the Salem district, Madras, peat is reported to form at elevations of over 4,000 feet. According to H. B. Medlicott, beds of serviceable peat are of frequent occurrence at various levels in the valley of Nepal, particularly about the Katwaldar gorge and to the north of Katmandu where it is used as fuel for both brick and lime kilns. Similar material has also been found in the Vale of Kashmir.

Of quite a different character are certain deposits to which the name ' peat ' has been applied, probably for want of a more suitable term. These include the masses of decayed vegetation of a peaty appearance which form at the bottom of the *jhils* of Sylhet, Cachar, of the Brahmaputra valley and of the marshes of the deltaic districts of East and West Bengal. The stalks of the tall, marsh-loving wild rice, *Oryza sylvestris*, make up the bulk of such deposits together with the remains of water-lilies (*Nymphaea*) and of aquatic submerged herbs such as *Valisneria*. These materials are sometimes used as manures but are unlikely to form useful fuels. A *jhil* near Kindauli, in the Partabgarh district of Uttar Pradesh, contains a deposit of a similar character.

Yet another variety of ' peat ' occurs at varying depths below the surface in the alluvial deposits of the Gangetic delta. A bed of this type is traceable over a wide area about 30 feet below the surface, on both sides of the Hooghly river, in the neighbourhood of Calcutta. As it contains both the stumps of coastal *sundri* trees (*Heritiera littoralis*) and of aquatic plants such as *Euryale ferox*, it appears to be of composite origin. Generally speaking it is too impure for use as a fuel, even if it were practicable or desirable to hazard mining operations in such a situation. To geologists these peat beds are marker horizons of the amount of subsidence of the land which has taken place since their formation, a matter of some importance in the vicinity of a great city.

Southern India too can furnish examples of much the same kind of buried, coastal swamp peats; thus R. B. Foote and W. King mention a peat bed exposed at low tide in the alluvium of the estuary of the Vellar river, at Tolum in the South Arcot district of Madras, in which the leaves and fruits of dicotyledonous trees are still visible. Further south still, Dr M. S. Krishnan has related how peat was discovered in the Tanjore district, in 1828, at a depth of 17 feet below the surface, at a location 'near the promontory about 20 miles from Cape Calimere'. This bed is over 5 feet in thickness, full of vegetable remains, including the bark and branches of trees, and possibly extends along the coast for upwards of 30 miles. The preservation of this particular deposit was perhaps due to the same general subsidence of the coast responsible for the submerged forest at the western end of Valimukkam Bay in Ramanathapuram district.

In West Pakistan, states W. T. Blanford, peat occurs ' about half a mile west of the station at Quetta and occupies a considerable area of marshy ground. It is not very pure as it is somewhat mixed with earth but it closely resembles that found in Europe.'

The surface peaty deposits of the Shan plateau of Burma are formed by rank growths of aquatic plants and grasses in gently undulating situations, where stagnant conditions of drainage exist, as, for example, in the vicinity of Nawnghkio, on the southern side of the Gokteik gorge. Underground peats probably exist ir the upper layers of some of the lacustrine deposits of the Shan States, as they do in the corresponding beds on the eastern side of the frontier in the Chinese province of Yunnan.

Few analyses of Indian peats are available and most of them are old, unrepresentative of the deposits as a whole and liable to be misleading. A re-examination of the whole subject would doubtless lead to results of scientific interest, but the known deposits are unlikely to prove of much practical importance.

PETROLEUM

The oil-bearing regions of Burma, India and Pakistan occur in the Tertiary rocks of the Chindwin-Irrawaddy, Assam-Arakan and Punjab-Sind-Baluchistan belts respectively, forming, as it were, a link between the oilfields of Borneo, Java and Sumatra on the one hand and those of Iran, Saudi Arabia and Iraq on the other.

OILFIELDS OF BURMA

In the extreme south, the two arms of the Tertiary belt of Burma are separated by the alluvial, deltaic deposits of the Irrawaddy, but further northwards they unite about Prome and continue northwards for over 700 miles into the Upper Chindwin valley, with a maximum width of 120 miles, bordered on the east by the outer fringes of the Shan Plateau and on the west by the foot-hills of the Arakan Yoma. The Tertiary rocks themselves are of great thickness, the Middle and Lower Eocene alone having been est-imated to possess a thickness of 25,000 feet. The Upper Eocene consists of the Pondaung Sandstones, up to 6,500 feet thick, followed by the rocks of the Yaw Stage which range between 1,000 and 2,000 feet in thickness.

Above the Eocene comes W. Theobald's ' Pegu System ', a name which he applied to all the beds between the Eocene ' Nummulitics ' and the Irrawaddy (Fossil Wood) System. The subdivisions of the Pegu System, of great consequence from the point of view of petroleum prospecting, have undergone many changes over the years, but thanks mainly to the work of the geologists of the Burmah Oil Company, they are now definitely established as shown in the Table below. Although the junction of the Yaw Stage of the Upper Eocene exhibits no apparent

THE TERTIARY SUCCESSION IN BURMA

DIVISIONS	SUBDIVISIONS	THICKNESS (feet)	EUROPEAN TIME SCALE (approx.)	
Irrawaddy System	UNCONFORMITY	More than 10,000	Pliocene and U. Miocene	
Pegu System	Obogon Alternations ..	Up to 3,000	Vindobonian	M. Miocene
	Kyaukkok Sandstones ..	Up to 5,000	Burdigalian	L. Miocene
	Pyawowe Stage ..	Up to 3,000	Aquitanian	L. Miocene
	UNCONFORMITY			
	Okhmintaung Sandstones	0–5,000	Chattian	U. Oligocene
	Padaung Clays ..	Up to 2,500	Rupelian	M. Oligocene
	Shwezetaw Stage ..	2,000–4,000	Sannoisian	L. Oligocene
Nummuli-tic System	Yaw Stage	1,000–2,000	Bartonian	U. Eocene
	Pondaung Sandstones.	Up to 6,500	Auversian	U. Eocene
	Tabyin Clays		Lutetian	M. Eocene
	Tilin Sandstones	Up to 25,000	Cuisian	L. Eocene
	Laungshe Shales with		Sparnacian	L. Eocene
	Paunggyi		Thanetian	Palaeocene
	Conglomerate		Montian	Palaeocene

This table combines the results of the Geological Survey of India and the Burmah Oil Company as given by F. E. Eames and H. R. Tainsh.

unconformity with the lowest Shwezetaw Stage of the Oligocene, the scanty fauna of the latter contrasts strongly with the richness of that of the former. The Shwezetaw Stage, from 2,000 to 4,000 feet thick, displays marked lateral variation and is followed upwards by the Padaung Clays, up to 2,500 feet of shales and mudstones, in spite of their name: of Middle Oligocene age, they are succeeded by the Okhmintaung Sandstone, attaining a maximum thickness of 5,000 feet, but varying greatly, and in some localities entirely removed by the uplift and subsequent erosion which happened towards the end of Oligocene times.

The break in the succession which divides the Pegu System into two parts at the Oligocene-Miocene boundary is no small, local event for it is even more strongly developed in Assam, where it occurs between the Barail Series and the Surma Series; it is especially pronounced in the Punjab, where the Murree Series of Lower Miocene age rests on various members of the Eocene and the Oligocene is entirely absent, and it has been recognized recently in Sind between the Upper and Lower Nari subdivisions, according to Eames (1950).

The Burmese Miocene has three subdivisions, the Pyawbwe Stage up to 3,000 feet thick, in places having a massive development of sandstones at its base, but otherwise largely of shales and sandstones, containing many characteristic Miocene lamellibranchs; the overlying Kyaukkok Sandstones, which may attain 5,000 feet, and carry a rich, molluscan fauna with a large proportion of gastropods and, lastly, the Obogon Alternations which are only present where the erosion associated with the unconformity between the Irrawaddy and Pegu Systems has been comparatively slight. The deposits of the Irrawaddy System are of continental and fluviatile types, thick conglomerates, grits and false-bedded, ferruginous sands with a few subordinate clays; silicified wood is very abundant in them and mammalian remains similar to those of the Siwaliks of north-west India are found in the lower horizons.

In studying the stratigraphy of the oilfields of Burma, it is important to remember that in late Eocene, part of Oligocene and Miocene times, the sediments deposited in the Tertiary gulf to the north of the main oilfields were generally of a non-marine character, while further to the south, the prevailing conditions were essentially marine. As Tainsh has pointed out, similar events are proceeding today in the Brahmaputra valley and the lower Irrawaddy basin, where, within much the same tectonic framework, fluviatile, deltaic and marine sediments are being contemporaneously and rapidly deposited.

The Burma Tertiary basin is divided into four structural units as follows:—(1) a Northern or Chindwin Basin, north of Latitude 22°, separated by a transverse uplift from (2), the Central Basin, lying between Latitudes 19° 30' and 22°, and separated in its turn

from (3), the Southern Basin, by an uplift about Latitude 19° 30′.
The fourth unit comprises the Pegu Yoma with its north and south
trending, packed folds, extending as far as Latitude 24°. Between
Latitudes 19° and 20° branching folds stretch north-west, across
the prevalent regional strike, and merge with the western margin
of the Central Basin. The folds on the eastern sides of the Northern
and Central Basins are usually overthrust towards the east, and on
their western sides the beds as a rule dip easterly, though there are
also strike faults and some subsidiary folding.

In the Northern Basin all the surface oil shows are in the
Upper Eocene rocks, particularly in the uppermost part of the
Pondaung Sandstones, but the oilsands of its only known field
are in Miocene or Oligo-Miocene strata. In the Central Basin,
although most of the surface oil shows are in the Eocene, there
are others at higher horizons and the production of the oilfields
comes mainly from Oligocene and Miocene rocks ranging from the
Shwezetaw to the Kyaukkok Sandstones. In the Southern Basin oil
seepages have not been found in the Eocene, but there are a few in
higher horizons, mainly of Miocene age. In the following descriptions the oilfields are traced from north to south.

Indaw. Within the main syncline of the Northern Basin and
lying across its central line is the anticline of Indaw, on which is
located its solitary oilfield, about 175 miles north of any of the
other important fields. Situated 22 miles inland from Pantha, on
the east bank of the Chindwin river in the Upper Chindwin district,
it is an asymmetrical, elongated dome with a gentle west flank
dipping about 10° to 15°, and a steeply dipping (50° to 65°) eastern
one. It is some 9 miles long and 2 miles across at its widest point,
and in its southern half possesses a subsidiary crest parallel to the
main one and about half-a-mile from it on the west. Its Pegu
rocks are predominantly sandy in character, but there are also
alternations of sands and clays, especially in the lower horizons.
The bulk of the production came from shallow sands, between
800 and 1,200 feet from the surface, and deep tests have proved
difficult owing to the presence of gas sands under high pressures
below the main oil horizon. Indeed the natural gas resources of
the field appear to be large. The oil was piped to a refinery at
Pantha and the finished products were distributed to various
markets in Upper Burma before the Japanese occupation of the
country. The Indo-Burma Petroleum Co. Ltd commenced drilling on the Indaw field in 1912, but the prevalence of malaria
and the difficulties of transport in this isolated region hampered
progress, so that it was not until 1918 that commercial production
was obtained. The output rose to a maximum of 4,040,690
gallons in 1932, after which there was a gradual decline to 2,014,072
gallons in 1938. During these 37 years of its life the Indaw field
had yielded a total of 45,638,075 gallons of oil.

Sabe-Yenangyat. These fields, together with the more southerly one of Lanywa, lie to the west of the Irrawaddy, on the long inlier of Pegu rocks which, south of the river, continues into the Singu or Chauk oilfield. They are all, together with the Yenangyaung and Miubu fields, in the Central Basin. The whole outcrop of the rocks of the Pegu System has a length of 39 miles and a maximum breadth of $3\frac{1}{2}$ miles, trending north-north-west to south-south-east with its steep eastern scarp lying for half its length close to the western bank of the Irrawaddy. The anticline is remarkably asymmetrical; its gentle, western flank rising at about $15°$ to $20°$ while its thrust-faulted eastern one is very steep, sometimes vertical and in places overturned. The pitch of the fold itself and the positions of three high portions of its crest account for the oil pools at Sabe, in the north, around Yenangyat itself, some 12 miles further south, and again in a locality about 5 miles further south still.

T. Oldham, the first Director of the Geological Survey of India, who was at Yenangyat in 1855, suggested that it might be worth while exploiting and hand-dug wells seem to have been started about 1864, though 'springs of petroleum' in this neighbourhood had been mentioned by Buckland in 1827. Machine drilling was commenced in 1893 and although the wells have often started with big initial yields, they declined rapidly and production has never been high. Most of the oilsands are shallow, from 500 to 1,500 feet below the surface, near the summit of the long, narrow, Yenangyat field proper. On the small Sabe field which was first developed in 1908, oilsands occurred down to 1,800 feet, but they proved to be thin, with poor yields, and production ceased there in 1922.

Starting with 118,400 gallons in 1893, the maximum output of the whole field was reached in 1903, with $22\frac{1}{2}$ million gallons, but the inevitable decline though slow at first became accentuated later, and in the five years ending 1928 production averaged only 1,970,434 gallons per annum. From 1928 onwards the official returns include the output for the Lanywa field, doubtless an advantage to the revenue statistician but a considerable loss to the petroleum geologist. The production of Yenangyat alone immediately before the Japanese invasion was however about 5 million gallons annually, and the field has hitherto yielded about 290 million gallons. The Yenangyat and Singu (Chauk) fields were connected by a pipeline, and the latter was joined in the same way with Yenangyaung, whence another line led to the refineries at Syriam, near Rangoon.

Lanywa. The Lanywa and Singu oilfields lie on a major dome of Pegu rocks, the axis of which is slightly *en échelon* with that of the Yenangyat field, a fact of great economic significance overlooked by the earlier investigators who considered the prospects of the Lanywa area, so far south of Yenangyat, as hopeless. The geologists of the Indo-Burma Petroleum Co., however, established the fact of this slight off-setting and decided that Lanywa belongs to the Singu rather than to the Yenangyat folding.

The anticlinal crest crosses the Irrawaddy obliquely and rich oilsands lie under its bed. In 1914 a well was started on a sand-bank in the river to the south of Lanywa but as this became submerged during the flood season, the Government of the day ordered its removal as a menace to boat traffic. In 1919 another well was drilled on a sand-bank projecting from the shore and it obtained oil from two sands. By 1929 the Company had completed an embankment for its protection, and by the end of 1930 there were 17 producing wells on the reclaimed area, with a yield for the year of $17\frac{3}{4}$ million gallons.

A total of over 100 wells has been drilled, and many of them have been inclined from the vertical to reach the oilsands beneath the river. Some of these inclined wells have deviations up to about 45° and have been completed as much as 1,700 feet away from a point vertically below the top of the well. The Indo-Burma Petroleum Company's development of the sands beneath the river represents a remarkable technical achievement. The highest production obtained was in 1935, when 23 million gallons came from Lanywa, and the total production prior to the Japanese invasion was about 250 million gallons.

Singu (Chauk). The Singu, or Chauk, oilfield is the continuation on the opposite (left) bank of the Irrawaddy of the Lanywa field just described. It comprises the southern end of the 39 miles long anticline which stretches northwards through Lanywa, Yenangyat and Sabe. This portion of the Pegu inlier, with its exposed length of about $6\frac{1}{2}$ miles and an average breadth of 2 miles, was first recognized by G. E. Grimes of the Geological Survey of India in 1897. Like its sister fields to the north, it is a pronounced, asymmetrical, elongated dome, with dips on its western flank of 10° to 15° increasing gradually to 20° to 25°, while on the eastern flank dips of 80° to vertical, or, in places, slight overturning are met with. The presence of a thrust fault in association with the steep eastern flank has been recently demonstrated. In the southern part of the field, the anticlinal crest pitches at 5° towards the saddle which lies between it and Yenangyaung.

Below the blanket of the Irrawaddian, the members of the Upper Pegu System comprising the Kyaukkok Sandstones, 500 feet in thickness, and the Pyawbwe Clays, 1,100 feet thick, are exposed, together with the upper portion of the Okhmintaung Sandstones (1,700 feet in all). The remaining stages which belong to the Lower Pegus, the Padaung Clays (3,600 feet thick) and the Shwezetaw Sandstones of unknown thickness, lie below the surface but are penetrated by the wells. The proved oilsands occur in the upper part of the Padaung Clay, which, in spite of its name, and its great thickness of marine shales, contains sandy, oil-bearing bands of varying lateral extent, 20 to 50 feet thick. Although entirely buried in the Singu-Lanywa dome, these clays are partially exposed at the surface further north in the Yenangyat field. The Shwezetaw Sandstones have only been reached by a few wells in the Singu field and have not yielded oil as yet, but they contain some producing wells in Yenangyat.

The major portion of the field was leased to the Burmah Oil Co. Ltd and the first well was drilled in 1902; since then more than 1,000 wells have been completed by this concern, the Indo-Burma Petroleum Co. Ltd, the Pyinma Development Co. Ltd and the British Burma Petroleum Co. Ltd. At the end of 1938, there were 562 wells in production. There are said to be about 35 oilsands, varying from 10 to 50 feet in thickness, the oil pools lying at depths of 1,200 to 3,800 feet on the western flank, except in an area south of a large cross fault in the south of the field where they are found at depths of from 3,500 to 5,000 feet. New wells usually flowed for short periods, but most of them were pumped or drained by gas-lift. Following the success of the training wall and reclamation on the west bank of the river at Lanywa by the Indo-Burma Petroleum Co., the Burmah Oil Co. constructed one on the east bank, no simple engineering undertaking in a river with an annual rise of 40 feet and a swift current: eighty-three acres of productive territory, since extensively drilled, were recovered by this means from the bed of the river. For the five years ending 1938, the average annual production of the Singu field alone was 101,212,170 gallons, and in that year its record of 120,769,811 gallons passed the annual production of the Yenangyaung field (113,017,514 gallons) for the first time. In 1939, Singu gave 139,792,004 gallons and during the 38 years of its existence it has yielded a total of over 2,728 million gallons of crude oil, characterized by its paraffin base and high wax content.

Yenangyaung. Thirty-five miles south of Singu lies Yenang-yaung, the richest oilfield of Burma, some 2 miles east of the Irrawaddy and near the town of the same name, in the Magwe district. It is an elongated dome of Pegu rocks on the same main line of folding as the Singu, Lanywa and Yenangyat fields. Slightly asymmetrical, with dips up to 40° on its eastern and up to 50° on its western flank, it is crossed by numerous transverse faults and is about 6 miles long and one mile wide, though its chief producing area covers only a portion of this. From beneath the overlying Irrawaddian rocks, a portion of the Lower Miocene, Kyaukkok Sandstones of the Upper Pegus, is exposed at the surface. According to Tainsh, writing in 1950 with the permission of the principal oil companies concerned, these Kyaukkok beds consist of 1,400 feet of false-bedded, coarse-grained sandstones, with alternations of sand and shale, and with gypsum-bearing shales. Under them, but not exposed at the surface, are the blue clays and shales of the Lower Miocene Pyawbwe Stage; 1,400 feet thick, they contain many thick sand beds and fossiliferous marine bands. Below the Pyawbwe Stage come the Upper Oligocene shallow water, false-bedded, marine sands of the Okhmintaung Stage, 1,000 feet thick, with subordinate shale bands and several well-known marker horizons of harder, cemented sandstones or breccias. The downward succession is completed by the rocks of the Middle Oligocene Padaung Stage, perhaps 3,900 feet thick, and by the underlying Shwezetaws about which little is known. The upper part of the Padaung Stage carries alternating bands of sand and shale, the former generally about 20 feet thick. The lower part is almost entirely shale with very few sand intercalations.

The Yenangyaung field differs from Chauk in the much smaller degree of asymmetry, the greater number of cross faults, and in the number and stratigraphical range of the oilsands. In Chauk, only the upper sands in the Padaung Clays have yet been proved to carry oil, whereas at Yenangyaung oilsands range from the lower part of the Kyaukkok Sandstones, through the Pyawbwe Stage and Okhmintaung Sandstones into the rocks of the upper part of the Padaung Stage, comprising a stratigraphical thickness of 4,500 feet of strata. No oil has yet been found in the lower part of the Padaung Stage, while the Shwezetaw Sandstones, lying at depth, have still to be thoroughly tested. Altogether there are over 50 oilsands varying in thickness from 10 to 150 feet, and found at all depths from the surface to 5,500 feet. For productive purposes they are divided into Shallow, Intermediate and Lower Sands, and the oil pools of each are developed by separate sets of wells. The shallower pools occur near the crest and are up to 2,600 feet in width. The oil pools of the Okhmintaung Stage are found at the crest in some parts of the field and on the eastern flank in others, in which case the crestal areas are gas-bearing. The pools of the Padaung Stage lie on the eastern flank with large original gas-caps.

A primitive form of oil mining has been practised for centuries by the Burmese on the Yenangyaung and certain other fields, by sinking narrow, timbered shafts to sands at depths of from 200 to 400 feet and baling the oil from them. Under the Burmese monarchs the rights to carry on oil mining were vested in 24 families and their hereditary claims over two tracts of 295 and 155 acres, known as the Twingon and Beme reserves of the Yenangyaung field, were recognized and preserved by the British Government after the annexation of Upper Burma in 1885, a specified number of well sites (circles of 60 feet diameter) being allotted to each family annually until the whole area had been distributed. The output from the hand-dug wells was about 2½ million gallons per annum in 1888. The use of modified diving dresses by the shaft sinkers enabled them to reach greater depths and to obtain more oil, so that by 1900, hand-dug production had increased to 8½ million gallons. After 1908, however, a rapid decline followed as the hereditary families sold and leased their well sites to the European companies, yet no less than 195 wells of this type were still in operation in 1938, for the oil from them has its special uses and an old-established market up and down the Irrawaddy valley.

Modern exploitation dates from 1887, when the Burmah Oil Co. Ltd commenced drilling in Khodaung, the central area which together with other parts of the field is leased to it. The first well was but 727 feet deep and others were still shallower; one of them, B.O.C. No. 8, 350 feet deep, is known to have yielded oil for over 50 years and probably could still give a small production. In 1907, the Rangoon Oil Co. Ltd began to lease well sites from the hereditary owners, and other companies soon followed suit, so that eventually the Twingon and Beme reserves became congested with wells, many of them only 60 or 80 feet apart, engaged in competitive production which gravely increased the hazards of fire and flooding. Outside the reserves, in the blocks leased to individual companies, the spacing of the wells followed more normal practice. A total of more than 4,000 wells have been drilled on the field by various concerns, including the Burmah Oil Company, the Indo-Burma Petroleum Company, the British Burmah Petroleum Company (successors to the Rangoon Oil Company) and the Nath Singh Oil Company; out of this total 2,710 wells were producing oil in 1938. In 1930, the discovery at a depth of 4,000 feet or so of an oil-bearing sand in the south of the field led to great hopes for the development of an area hitherto considered to be of little value. Although a well still further south, near the southernmost exposure of rocks of the Pegu System, found some oil at 5,000 feet, further drilling showed the southerly pitching end of the structure to be disappointing. On the eastern flank of the anticline, however, sands between 3,000 and 4,000 feet have given good yields. In the central part of the field very high pressures are met with at depth, and testing has become both difficult and expensive. Several deep wells have been drilled below the developed sands, the deepest reaching 9,705 feet; although some high-pressure water-sands were found, no deep oil had been discovered when the Japanese invasion put an end to all operations on the field.

The output of oil from Yenangyaung was 1½ million gallons in 1890 and increased gradually to 8¼ million gallons in 1897, but after 1898 there was a rapid expansion from 14½ million gallons in 1899 to 181 million gallons in 1909. The peak was reached with 203,638,000 gallons in 1916, after which there was a steady decline. By 1939 output had fallen to 106,089,250 gallons, the average for the five years ending 1938 being 126,676,207 gallons. From the commencement of drilling in 1887 to the end of 1939, over 5,675 million gallons of oil had been taken from the Yenangyaung field. The crude oil, like that from Singu (Chauk) and Lanywa, has a paraffin base, contains a high percentage of low boiling fractions and averages 7·5 per cent wax.

Minbu, Palanyon and Yethaya. A narrow, anticlinal fold in the Pegu rocks, trending approximately north and south, occurs on the right bank of the Irrawaddy and extends more or less parallel to it, 20 to 30 miles south of Yenangyaung. It is an acute fold, slightly overturned in places and overthrusted on the east, with steep dips on its western flank, except in the extreme south where they become flatter. The flexure is sharp and deeply denuded; in Sir Edwin Pascoe's words, ' not unlike that of Yenangyat but it has reached a more advanced stage '. It possesses a number of irregularities suggesting an intermittent action on the part of the forces responsible for the folding: these, and its general structure, have resulted in great compression of the beds and in the circumscribed character of the oil pools which have been found at certain favourable positions along the crest. The general direction of the anticlinal axis is 20° west of north to 20° east of south, but there are many local deviations.

In the north, near the town of Minbu, the fold is almost symmetrical with dips of 75° to 80° on the west, but a strike fault, which further south develops into a thrust, occurs a short distance beyond the crest, and to the east of it the beds are vertical or overturned. The Minbu oilfield lies on the northerly, pitching end of the fold and its shallow wells obtain production from sands between 100 and 1,000 feet below the surface. To the south of the town are the mud volcanoes and gas pools, large hollows filled with soft mud through which bubbles of gaseous hydrocarbons exude. Over much of the anticline the thrust has replaced the crest, so that the true, original crest only remains locally and for short distances. The fold also pitches in the south near Yethaya, but over a distance of some 8 miles between Minbu and this place it undulates, and small, irregular domes, often disturbed by cross faults, occur at intervals.

The small dome of Palanyon, 6 miles south of Minbu, is one of these and for several years it yielded oil from sands in the 1,000 to 2,000 foot zone. It lies near the culmination of the anticline which is here sharply asymmetrical with its steeply dipping eastern limb truncated by the thrust fault. One of its wells had an initial production of 5,000 gallons per day, in 1929, accompanied by sufficient gas to satisfy the fuel requirements of this section of the field for some time.

The Yethaya field lies some 4 miles south of the Palanyon dome, on a subsidiary structure developed in the easterly, synclinal limb of the main Minbu field. In addition to shallow wells between the depths of 300 and 600 feet which have been known for many years, several oilsands lying between 900 and 1,900 feet below the surface were exploited later. A deep test well which reached a depth of 5,000 feet, approximately, was abandoned in 1931, without obtaining oil in profitable quantities. Three miles south of Yethaya, small quantities of oil were obtained from shallow wells at Pepi (Petpe), which lies on the main Minbu structure. It remains to add that in the Minbu anticline the whole sequence of Pegu strata from the Lower Miocene, Kyaukkok Sandstones, down to the Middle Oligocene, Padaung Stage, is petroliferous, but unfortunately its structural abnormalities have either hindered the accumulation of large oil pools or have caused their dispersal after their formation. In the Minbu district as a whole there were 318 producing wells at the end of 1938. Output was first recorded in 1910 and reached a maximum of more than 6 million gallons in 1928, falling to less than half this amount, or 2,818,228 gallons, in 1938. A grand total of 107½ million gallons had been drawn from the various sections of the anticline up to the end of that year.

Padaukpin. The small oilfield of Padaukpin lies about 8 miles west-north-west of Thayetmyo, the headquarters of the district of the same name, on the west bank of the Irrawaddy, south of Minbu. It is sited on a long, steep anticline of Pegu rocks, developed in the trough of a wide, local syncline. The Upper Oligocene, Okhmintaung Sandstones of the Lower Pegus are exposed here, and small quantities of oil were obtained from hand-dug wells in them during the time of the Burmese kings. Early efforts at modern drilling yielded only negligible results, but in 1920 further tests by Indo-Burma Oilfields Ltd led to the expectation of remunerative production. Although about 36 wells were drilled, the total production averaged less than 2,000 gallons per day and within a few years sank to negligible amounts.

Yenanma. Official statistics did not separate the production of the Padaukpin field from that of Yenanma, which is located about 20 miles south-west of Minhla, a town on the west bank of the Irrawaddy, in the north of the Thayetmyo district. Three shallow wells were drilled here about 1912 though without much success, but in 1922 deeper drilling by Indo-Burma Oilfields Ltd obtained oil at depths between 300 and 1,200 feet. As there is no clearly defined anticline hereabouts, the mode of occurrence of the oil has been the subject of controversy, though the view usually accepted is that it is associated with a monoclinal structure close to strong cross faults. Four miles farther west are the mud volcanoes of Yegubwet. The total recorded production from the Thayetmyo district up to the end of 1939 was 22¼ million gallons approximately. During the better years of its earlier life, the Yenanma oilfield used to average about 1,200,000 gallons per annum, but by the period 1930-3 production was only about one tenth of this amount. About 1935, however, an extension of the then known producing area was discovered, and output quickly rose to the record of 2,712,000 gallons by 1938, dropping again to

1,990,376 gallons in 1939. The annual average for the quinquennium 1934–8 was 1,405,725 gallons.

The Arakan Islands. The islands off the Arakan Coast, long
noted for their mud volcanoes and the submarine eruptions which
occur from time to time in the neighbouring sea, contain oil
deposits of doubtful value; though within the territory of the Union
of Burma, these occurrences really form the southern land termination of the oil shows of the Assam Tertiary belt. Hand-dug
wells have been operated on some of them for an unknown length
of time. At the beginning of the present century the outputs of
the Akyab and Kyaukpyu districts were roughly 50,000 and 100,000
gallons per annum, respectively, but the output from Akyab slowly
dwindled and finally ceased in 1930, while that from Kyaukpyu
still languished at a few thousand gallons yearly. In 39 years
from 1900, the combined areas yielded a total of 1,983,582 gallons,
or less than the Yenangyaung field produced in one week in 1939.
Special rules were in existence in the days of the British administration concerning the grant of petty leases for oil in the Kyaukpyu
district, which were limited to a maximum of one acre and to a
duration of ten years.

The Akyab oil came from the Baronga Islands, and although
gas vents and oil seepages occur on all three of them, most of the
oil was obtained from hand-dug wells, about 300 feet deep, in the
southern end of the eastern island. The local rocks consist of
sandstones and shales, probably of Miocene and Oligocene age,
and the structure is of steep, narrow, overfolded anticlines.

On Ramree Island, of the Kyaukpyu district, there are two
small, oil-producing areas, near Minbyin in the northern, and at
Ledaung in the southern section, respectively, which first came to
the notice of Europeans about a century ago. Several wells were
drilled at Yenandaung, in the Minbyin area, by the Canadian
system, and although encouraging results were obtained at first,
the yields gradually diminished and the industry passed into local
hands. The productive wells, generally 250 to 300 feet deep,
though sometimes reaching 500 feet, are laid out along two parallel
bands about 300 yards apart, which appear perhaps to indicate
the presence of an oilsand in the two limbs of a sharply folded and
denuded anticline, as the whole region seems to have been crushed
into a series of steep, narrow and contiguous folds. At Ledaung,
there are two similar bands from which oil has been obtained by
means of a few, shallow, hand-dug wells. In the opinion of Sir
Edwin Pascoe, folding and denudation have been too severe in
these regions to warrant the expectation of oil in large quantities.

In addition to the main oilfields thus briefly described, petroleum
is known to occur at many other places in Burma, particulars of
which are obtainable in the memoirs by the late Sir Edwin Pascoe,

G. de P. Cotter and E. L. G. Clegg. We also wish to acknowledge our indebtedness to the publications of the geologists of the Burmah Oil Co. Ltd, including those by G. W. Lepper, H. M. Sale, P. Evans, F. E. Eames and H. R. Tainsh.

On 1 April 1937, Burma separated from the former Indian Empire, but the production figures for the oilfields already described have been given up to the end of 1939, the year which witnessed the outbreak of the Second World War. It remains to add that the total production of all the Burmese fields in 1940 was 270,897,782 gallons of oil, together with 11,269,626 gallons of petrol from natural gas. Burma was invaded by the Japanese armies in January 1942 and by the middle of the year the whole country was overrun by them. The wells of all the fields were denied to the enemy, the larger ones plugged with cement and scrap iron, the smaller ones rendered as useless as possible, the power-stations destroyed and the refineries in the neighbourhood of Rangoon severely damaged. Later, the major fields were the scenes of severe fighting and suffered further injuries by bombing and shelling, as well as from Japanese attempts to injure the oilsands as much as possible when the fortunes of war turned against them. After the end of the war in 1945, the rehabilitation of the oil industry was begun, but subsequently progress was greatly handicapped by widespread internal rebellion and unrest which it would be out of place to attempt to follow here. Burma became an independent State in 1948, and by 1950 it was possible, by means of inland water transport convoys under armed escort, to supply northern Burma with the products of a small refinery unit operating on the oilfields. In the state of security then existing, however, the main oil pipeline to Rangoon could not be repaired and for this reason the rebuilding of the main refinery at Syriam could not be completed. Dr Ba Thi of the Burma Geological Department kindly informs us that the production of crude oil in Burma for the years 1949, 1950 and 1951 was 8,671,148, 18,625,979 and 30,055,292 gallons. In November 1951, it was announced that the British Government had offered to lend the Burmese Government a sum of £2,500,000, towards a capital contribution of £5 millions which the Burmese Government were to invest in a joint oil venture with the three British oil companies operating in Burma, the new company to have a capital of £15 millions. Negotiations in connexion with this joint venture to operate the oil-producing and refining industry of Burma are reported to have been concluded with the signing of an agreement in Rangoon on 12 January 1954, under which, it is stated, the Burmese Government immediately acquires a 33 per cent interest in a new concern to be called the Burma Oil Company (1954) Ltd. But at the time of writing the state of the country continues to preclude the prospecting operations on which the long-term future of the industry depends.

OILFIELDS OF ASSAM

The Assam-Arakan geological province to which these oilfields belong stretches for 800 miles from the head of the Brahmaputra valley south-westwards through part of the highlands of central Assam into the Surma valley, thence southwards to the Bay of Bengal near Chittagong and so on to the Arakan coast of Lower Burma. The Tertiary rocks composing it consist in the main of great thicknesses of almost unfossiliferous, monotonous successions of impure sandstones, shales and clays. On the whole it is a deeply dissected region of high relief, heavy rainfall, almost impenetrable jungle and thick soil caps, which render the work of the geological surveyor particularly arduous and difficult.

The outlines of its stratigraphy and structure were due to the pioneering work of F. R. Mallet, Sir Edwin Pascoe, Sir Henry Hayden and other officers of the Geological Survey of India, but the details as they are known today are due to the labours of the geologists of the Assam and Burmah Oil Companies, and especially to the work of P. Evans and H. M. Sale.

The rocks themselves range in age from the Eocene to the Pliocene and are separable into six main divisions. At the bottom is Mallet's Disang Series, a very great thickness, perhaps 5,000 to 10,000 feet of almost unfossiliferous shales, slates and phyllites, best exposed in the Naga Hills and Manipur: near the plains occasional occurrences of foraminifera have shown that the Disang Series includes beds of Eocene age, but farther into the hills it may contain older strata. Equivalent to part of the Disang Series, occurring on the fringes of the Shillong Plateau and Mikir Hills, is the Jaintia Series some 3,000 feet thick, which includes fossiliferous limestones of Ranikot, Laki and Khirthar age. Both the Disang Series and the Jaintia Series are overlain by the Barail Series, 15,000 feet thick, made up of sandstones and shales with, in Upper Assam, a number of coal seams, some of which are thick. This may be partly Upper Eocene, but is now believed to be largely of Oligocene age.

A great break follows the Barail Series, and from comparison with conditions in north-western India and in Burma it is believed to have embraced much of late Oligocene time, and, in places, part of Lower Miocene time. Above this unconformity comes the Surma Series whose 13,000 feet of sandy shales, sandstones and mudstones are of Lower Miocene age. The Tipam Series, 12,000 feet thick, which follows, includes fairly coarse sandstones in the lower part and mottled clays in the upper part, and is of Middle Miocene age. Above another unconformity comes the Dupi Tila Series of sandstones and mottled clays, 10,000 feet thick, which is probably of Upper Miocene (Pontian) age. Finally above the Dupi Tila Series and separated from it by another unconformity are the soft sands and pebble beds of Mallet's Dihing Series which in places reaches a thickness of 11,000 feet, no doubt corresponding approximately with the Upper Siwaliks of north-western India and the upper part of the Irrawaddy Series of Burma. The thicknesses given for all these rock groups are maxima but they vary greatly from place to place; moreover, the subdivisions of each change markedly from one part of Assam to another, so much so that separate classifications have been adopted by oil geologists for the successions in Upper Assam, the north Cachar Hills, the Surma valley and Arakan. All that we have attempted to do here is to present a broad, general outline of a very heterogeneous system.

The whole of the Assam-Arakan Tertiary belt has undergone strong folding and long, anticlinal axes can sometimes be followed for many miles, the more sharply folded ones being associated with thrust faults. In the north-east, the thrusting has almost obliterated the anticlines and the general structure displays many nearly parallel thrust faults trending more or less north-east and south-west. The most north-westerly member of the whole series closely follows the boundary of the Naga Hills and the plains of the Brahmaputra river, and in places along it, though some anticlinal crests remain intact at the surface, they have usually proved to have been removed at depth by the thrusting. Further to the south-west and south, in the southern Naga Hills and through the Surma valley into the hills of Chittagong and Arakan, folding is more dominant than faulting and asymmetrical anticlines, separated by broader synclines, are more prevalent. In the south of Arakan the structure again becomes more complex.

Both oil and gas seepages are common: in Upper Assam oil shows occur in rocks ranging in age from the Disangs to the Tipam Series, but most frequently in the upper part of the Barail Series and the lower part of the Tipam Series. Occasionally coal seams saturated with oil have been found in the Barail Series. The gas seepages usually occur in *pungs*, an Assamese word denoting a swampy place in which salt water exudes from below. Away from Upper Assam and farther to the south-west, oil shows occur in the Barail and Surma Series, especially near the head of the Surma valley. Still farther south-west, between the Surma valley and Akyab, there are but few surface oil shows although numbers of occurrences of natural gas are known, especially about Chittagong. In the islands of Baronga, Ramree and Cheduba, both oil and gas seepages are fairly common. Submarine eruptions, sometimes of a very violent character, which occur from time to time off the Arakan coast, indicate the continuation of the petroliferous rocks below the waters of this part of the Bay of Bengal.

Much activity has been displayed in the search for oil-bearing structures in Assam and in the exploration of suitable ones by the drill, but the only areas which have yielded oil in commercial quantities are Digboi, in the Lakhimpur district of Upper Assam, and Badarpur, in the Surma valley, although small amounts have been found in the Makum-Namdang area of Lakhimpur and at Masimpur and Patharia in the Surma valley.

Early Drilling near Jaipur and Makum.   Oil drilling commenced in Assam in 1866 when four shallow wells, under 200 feet deep, were bored close to an oil seepage in the Coal Measures (the uppermost part of the Barail Series in Upper Assam), 3 or 4 miles southeast of Jaipur.   In 1867, three more shallow bores were made in rocks of the same age, near gas and oil seepages close to Makum, and small quantities of oil were obtained.   Nothing more appears to have been attempted until 1884, when the rights of the first lessees passed to the Assam Railways and Trading Company, a concern which bored several more holes at Makum between 1888 and 1895.   These were mostly about 500 feet deep, though one well attained a depth of over 1,000 feet and obtained sufficient oil to warrant the erection of a small refinery.   It is now known that the oilsands at Makum, within the reach of the drilling methods of those early days, all crop out at the surface.   The wells were shortlived, the prospects of increased output at any attainable depth were poor and attention was accordingly directed to Digboi.

Digboi.   Drilling commenced at Digboi in 1888, but it was not until 1892 that production commenced on the field.   In 1899 its control passed to the Assam Oil Co. Ltd, and at the beginning of the century output was still under one million gallons per annum. Over the years it slowly increased, and twenty years later was being steadily maintained at about 5 million gallons annually.   In 1921, the Burmah Oil Co. assumed technical control and in the next decade remarkable progress was made; by 1931, an output of over 53 million gallons had been reached, by 1936 this had increased to almost 65 millions; in 1944, over 82$\frac{1}{4}$ million gallons were obtained, and the annual average production for the five years ending 1950 was 65,521,230 gallons.   From 1892 to 1950 inclusive, a total of some 1,558 million gallons of oil have been taken from the Digboi field.   The crude oil is more or less saturated with solid paraffins of high melting point and it also contains considerable quantities of petrol; distilled in a refinery near the field, among its products are motor spirit, kerosene, jute batching oil, gas oil (high-speed Diesel oil), industrial Diesel oil, tea drier oil, furnace fuel oil, wax, lubricating oils and bitumen.   To conserve the oil resources, as little gas as possible is produced, and any gas remaining after the fuel requirements of both field and refinery are satisfied is returned underground.   As a final product the refinery produces about 1,200 tons of petroleum coke per month.   Digboi itself is in the Lakhimpur district, 16 miles north-east of Jaipur and about 7 miles north of Margherita.

Forty years ago, the oil-bearing area of the Digboi field was only known to cover an area of about 130 acres, about $\frac{3}{4}$ of a mile long

WESTERN PART OF DIGBOI OILFIELD, ASSAM

Assam Oil Co. Ltd.

and $\frac{1}{3}$ mile broad, and, in the words of Sir Edwin Pascoe, it was believed to lie ' on an anticlinal dome in all probability asymmetrical or overfolded towards the north-north-west '. Since then, according to E. V. Corps, its limits have been enormously extended along the strike of the fold, with resumption of production after the intervention of barren patches of ground, according to the interplay between the structure and the texture of the reservoir beds. It is now known to be a faulted anticline, the thrust underlying the whole structure possessing a high hade, so that although an anticlinal arch is apparent at the surface, at some distance down the thrust fault cuts across the axis of the fold, to run almost parallel to the beds on the southern flank. This feature sets definite limits to the downward extension of the oil pools and to the profitable limits of boring across the width of the fold itself. Thus, though a deep test at Digboi in 1931 revealed new oilsands below those then being drained, the thickness of the new group was curtailed by the occurrence of the overthrust at an unexpectedly shallow depth. Meanwhile, in 1930 a deep well in the Hansapung part of the field proved a large eastward extension of the deeper oil pools; later on additional extensions were discovered, especially by exploratory wells drilled during the war, when the output of Digboi was increased to meet the increased demands for petroleum products. Subsequently, further exploratory drilling both to the west and the east of the proved part of the field was disappointing, but between 1948 and 1952 several wells drilled still farther east have revealed the presence of useful additions to the reserves of this oilfield.

When Sir Edwin Pascoe was writing of Digboi in 1912, it was naturally supposed that the oil-bearing beds of the Digboi wells and the oilsands cropping out in the centre of the anticline could be correlated with the oil-bearing Coal Measures (Barails) of Jaipur and Makum. Later geological investigation has shown, however, that the oilsands of Digboi are in the Tipam Sandstone, which is the lower member of the Tipam Series, and that they are accordingly of approximately Middle Miocene age.

Badarpur. The oil seepages which occur near Badarpur, in the Cachar district, led to drilling by the Badarpur Tea Company and the registration of the Badarpur Oil Syndicate in 1912. In 1915 it was announced that the Syndicate had made an agreement with the Burmah Oil Co. Ltd. As described by G. W. Lepper, the field occupies a small dome with a steep, faulted, eastern flank, about a mile long with a maximum width of a quarter of a mile. Output commenced in 1917, reached a maximum of over 8 million gallons in 1920, dropped rapidly to half that amount, and gradually decreased to 55,867 gallons in 1933, when the field was abandoned after giving a total of 58,431,000 gallons. The oil was of a heavy, poor quality and accompanied by large quantities of water. In all 60 wells were drilled, but the decline in yield was rapid and was

usually accompanied by a great increase in the production of water.
The main output came from sands down to 1,400 feet; those at
lower levels proved to contain only very small amounts of oil.
The outcropping beds belong to the lowest division of the Surma
Series and the wells were drilled both into its rocks and into those
of the underlying Barails.

Other Areas. Many efforts have been made to find new oilfields:
in Upper Assam anticlinal structures, apparently suitable as far
as surface indications were concerned, have proved on boring in
one area after another to possess thrust faults of high enough hade
to render them worthless. In the Surma valley, where such
faulting is not so widespread, no success has yet attended the costly
prospecting that has been carried out.

Ten miles to the east of Badarpur lies the Masimpur anticline,
a closed structure of relatively large size with many gas and oil
seepages. The Burmah Oil Co. drilled its first well here to a depth
of 1,540 feet in 1918; since then over ninety shallow holes have
been drilled for structural information, and in addition eight holes
have been taken to between 1,000 and 4,000 feet, the deepest well
reaching 7,685 feet in 1931. Further drilling was planned, but
during the second world war all prospecting work both in Assam
and elsewhere was discontinued at the request of the Government
of India, in order that the available effort could be concentrated
on the known producing fields. Very difficult technical problems
have been encountered at Masimpur, and although a few shows
gave, over a period of several years, a small amount of oil (little
more than 50,000 gallons all told) no commercial production has
yet been proved. The sequence of test wells and bore holes drilled
for structural information has cost about $1\frac{1}{2}$ crores of rupees and
yet the anticline cannot be considered as finally proved and found
wanting. Its example is quoted in detail here to illustrate the time,
trouble and expenditure needed in the search for a new oilfield.

South of Badarpur, test wells on the Kanchanpur and Chhata-
chura anticlines have found no paying production. The Patharia
Hills anticline on the south-eastern edge of a wide alluvial area in
the Surma valley is a very pinched fold with almost vertical dips
on each flank. In the crestal area the fold is asymmetrical with a
steeply dipping and faulted western flank. Three wells have been
drilled, the deepest reaching 5,411 feet, but the only oil produced
was less than 250,000 gallons obtained at intervals about twenty
years ago from the first well drilled. This anticline lies on the
boundary between Assam and East Pakistan, and the sites of these
test wells are in Pakistan.

Geological prospecting, accompanied in some cases by
geophysical work, and in many instances taking advantage of the
aid offered by aerial photography, has covered all the remaining
more accessible parts of Assam but without revealing promising

structures. This geological work has also extended into Tripura, where structural conditions are somewhat less unpromising, but so far it has not been possible to test any of the Tripura anticlines by the drill.

In Upper Assam, renewed attempts to obtain oil from the Makum-Namdang lease have been made from time to time, but after a sequence of failures, during which 18 wells were drilled in different parts of the structure to depths of from a few hundred feet to over 5,000 feet, it was concluded that commercial production was not obtainable. The few wells which gave any showing of oil at all had a very rapid decline in yield and the lease was relinquished in 1950.

South-west of Digboi, in the Jaipur anticline, attempts to find oil continued at frequent intervals from 1920 to 1946, but the wells were all complete failures. Farther south-west test wells at Bandersulia, Tiru Hills, Barsilla and Nichuguard, all in the hills on the south-east side of the Assam Valley, have also proved unsuccessful. The anticlinal structures tested are cut off by thrust faulting, and in the comparatively small thickness of beds above the fault (whether Tipam Series, Surma Series or Barails), no productive sands have been found.

Early in 1953, the Assam Oil Company struck an oil-bearing formation at Nahorkatiya, 18 miles west of Digboi. The geophysical survey of the area, interrupted by the second world war, was resumed in 1951 and the test drilling started in May 1952. This well, Nahorkatiya No. 1, the deepest yet drilled in India, began a daily production of 20,000 gallons of crude oil from a depth of 11,715 feet in March 1954. A second well had then reached a depth of over 7,000 feet and a site had been selected for a third well. The oil will be piped to the refinery at Digboi through an eight-inch line laid alongside the road connecting Nahorkatiya with the older field.

PROSPECTS FOR PETROLEUM IN OTHER PARTS OF INDIA

Practically the whole of Peninsular India and the greater part of the Himalayas can be ruled out in any search for oil. Various parties, including those of the Geological Survey of India, have investigated the possibilities in Kutch and Saurashtra and have concluded that they are not promising. There are indications of oil and gas in the foot-hills of Jammu, Kashmir, extending on the one hand to the small fields of the Punjab and on the other to link up with the Tertiary foot-hills of the East Punjab, north-western Uttar Pradesh and Nepal. Gas seepages are known to occur in the Kangra district of the Punjab and in Nepal, where age-long pilgrimages have been made to the sacred fires for which they are responsible. Sufficient is known of the geology of the Himalayan foot-hills generally, however, to show that their structure is almost universally unsuitable for the accumulation of petroleum. At the same time, only large-scale geological surveys can show whether or not there may be some few areas where conditions are less unfavourable and which may accordingly be thought worth the final test of the drill.

A few gas seepages have been reported from the eastern coastal tracts of the Peninsula, in areas where rock exposures are not plentiful, and it is probable that the gas is marsh gas originating in the alluvium and having no connexion whatsoever with petroleum (see NATURAL GAS). As the thickness of marine sediments in the areas concerned is believed to be only small and as there is no evidence of well-marked folding, the prospects have not appeared sufficient to petroleum geologists to warrant either detailed geological mapping or geophysical surveys. In the western coastal strip, the limitation of marine sediments to a very small area also renders them unattractive.

Much of the large alluvial area of the Brahmaputra and Ganga has been surveyed by geophysical means; gravity surveys have been used for covering large tracts, and seismic surveys have been carried out in certain selected smaller areas; in West Bengal a magnetometric survey was made during 1951–2. Taken as a whole, the results of the geophysical work on the alluvial areas is reported to have been extremely disappointing.

CONDITIONS IN EAST PAKISTAN

A few oil and gas shows have been recorded from the southeastern part of East Pakistan (the Sylhet and Chittagong districts and the Chittagong Hill Tracts) but so far no oilfield has been found. The unsuccessful drilling at Patharia, on the boundary between the Sylhet district and Assam, has already been referred to. Near Chittagong a well-known gas show occurs on the Sitakund anticline, but drilling there about forty years ago failed to find oil and later structure drilling has revealed the complexities of the overthrusting on the western flank of this anticline. A test well on the neighbouring Patiya anticline was begun in 1952. Farther north, structure drilling and gravity surveys have been carried out near Sylhet, and a large part of the alluvial area of the Surma valley and the Ganga-Brahmaputra delta has been covered by geophysical prospecting, either by gravity or magnetic measurements.

In the preparation of these short accounts of the oilfields of Burma, East Pakistan and Assam, the authors have had the great advantage of the help and friendly criticism of Mr P. Evans, Chief Geologist of the Burmah Oil Co. Ltd. They also wish to express their gratitude to Mr E. S. Pinfold, Chief Geologist of the Attock Oil Co. Ltd, for the following authoritative account of the oilfields of West Pakistan which is reproduced here in his own words.

OIL-BEARING REGIONS OF WEST PAKISTAN
by
E. S. Pinfold, M.A., F.G.S.

Oil and bitumen have been known and used in West Pakistan from the beginnings of civilization; bitumen, probably from Baluchistan, was used as mortar in some of the buildings of Harappa and Mohenjodaro. The first attempt to develop oil production was made in 1870 when an American oil expert was invited by the Government of that time to report on oil prospects and to recommend a testing programme. There was a renewal of the search in 1890 and a little oil was obtained from shallow wells drilled near Jaba in the western Salt Range and at Chharat to the south of the Kala Chitta Hills; small amounts of this oil were utilized in the gas-works of Rawalpindi for many years.

The oil occurs in a narrow belt of Tertiary rocks in the outer foot-hills of the Himalayan, Baluchistan and Sind mountain ranges and the belt continues along the Makran coast into Iran. Oil seepages are numerous in the Rawalpindi, Attock, Jhelum and Shahpur districts to the east of the Indus, and in the Kohat, Dera Ismail Khan, Dera Ghazi Khan and Sibi districts across the river. No oil seepages are known in Lower Sind, but natural gas is evolved at several places: in Las Bela State and in the Makran, the flows of mud associated with some of the gas shows form mud volcanoes, and those at Chandragup at the mouth of the Hingol River are amongst the largest known.

Most of the region in which the oil shows occur was mapped by A. B. Wynne of the Geological Survey of India about the middle of the last century, and some of the anticlinal structures on which oilfields have since been found are clearly indicated on his maps.

With few exceptions, the oil and gas shows of West Pakistan occur in rocks of Middle or Lower Eocene age and these rocks are mostly marine sediments with some intercalations of beds laid down in fresh or brackish water conditions. The rock-salt deposits of the Kohat salt region are of Middle Eocene age and are closely associated with the oil seepages of that district. It is possible that the alternation of marine and brackish water conditions was responsible in part for the formation of the oil from the remains of marine organisms.

These Eocene beds are overlain with pronounced unconformity by a series of freshwater sandstones and shales, several thousands of feet in thickness, of Miocene, Pliocene and Pleistocene age, known as the Murree-Siwalik System. This formation is highly fossiliferous and has yielded a continuous record of terrestrial vertebrate life over these periods.

Finally, during the uplift of the Himalayan and associated mountain ranges, the region was subjected to compression and earth movement resulting in fold structures, some of which have served as areas of accumulation and reservoirs for oil, but the more favourable and open folds occur only in the outer foot-hills zone. Although seepages are numerous further into the hills, the folding there is usually too intense and the folds themselves too compressed or broken to hold useful oilfields—several test wells have been drilled near seepages in the closely folded foot-hills without successful results.

The four oilfields so far discovered are near the centre of the Potwar Plateau which lies between the Kala Chitta and Khaire Murat hill ranges on the north and the Salt Range on the south. Structurally the Potwar is a large synclinal basin occupied by a great thickness of Siwalik rocks. The principal axis of the basin coincides nearly with the valley of the Soan river and is known as the Soan syncline. The synclinal structure is interrupted on both flanks by strike faults and anticlinal folds, and it is on some of these anticlines that productive oilfields have been developed. In the order of their discovery these fields are Khaur, Dhulian, Joya Mair and Balkassar.

The Khaur and Dhulian dome structures are arranged *en échelon* along the first anticlinal fold north of the main syncline and 'parallel with it. The Joya Mair and Balkassar folds are interruptions to the south flank of the Soan Basin about twenty-five miles south of Khaur and Dhulian.

Khaur. The Khaur oilfield was discovered in 1915.[1] It occupies the summit of a long narrow anticline, the crest maximum of which lies 44 miles south-west of Rawalpindi. Murree rocks form an ellipse in the axis of the fold and are surrounded by ridges of Lower Siwalik sandstones. The crest of the fold is open, but dips steepen rapidly to 35° on the south flank and to 60° and 70° on the north. A strike fault runs parallel and close to the crest; this, like all other important faults of the region, is an overthrust, the north flank of the anticline overriding towards the crest.

The Khaur field differs from the others in that most of the oil produced from it has been from the freshwater sands of the Murree Series; production has been found in all the sands from the surface down to the Eocene limestones at over 5,000 feet. The oil is believed to have had its origin in these limestones and to have reached the overlying sandstones by migration. It has been suggested that migration took place along fault planes, but no close relation between faulting and oil occurrence has been recognized. On the other hand, there is no doubt but that the oil is contained in the fissures of the sandstones, and fissuring of both sandstone and shale beds may have played a major role in the upward migration of the oil.

Owing to the 1914–18 war, the pipeline to Rawalpindi and the refinery erected there were not completed until 1922, and it was

[1] The recognition that the Khaur anticline was a potential oilfield is due to the work of Mr Pinfold himself. J.C.B.

only then that the productive capacity of the field could be tested. Results were somewhat disappointing, for the production of a large number of shallow wells fell off very rapidly due to the drainage of the fissure system in each sand. The highly saline water which later accompanied the oil was under moderate to high pressure, and oil and water flowed at the surface during the early life of the field. New sands were tapped as drilling was carried to greater depths and each new sand caused a revival of production, though usually followed by a rapid decline.

Drilling to the Eocene limestones at over 5,000 feet proved extremely difficult and hazardous owing to the excessively high pressures (over 6,000 pounds per square inch) in the lower formations and the consequent heaving of the shale beds above the limestones. Some production has been obtained from the Eocene but not in the amounts hoped for, and it seems clear that much of the oil originally in the limestones has been lost by migration to the overlying Murree rocks.

Owing to the failure to obtain fresh production, the output of the field has now declined to a few barrels daily from a number of stripper wells. Its total production from the commencement of work in 1915 to date (October 1952) has been a little over 160 million gallons.

Recently another well has been drilled to the limestones, but its successful completion has been prevented by pressure troubles and heaving formations. A well formerly carried down some distance into the limestones struck heavy flows of brine containing much sulphuretted hydrogen.

Dhulian. The Dhulian field is on a more open dome structure eleven miles south-south-west of Khaur. It forms part of the same general uplift, with its axis parallel to the Khaur axis though aligned two miles to the south of it. Its gentler folding is reflected in the wide crestal ellipse of low dipping rocks; the outer flank dips being about 35° on the south and 30° on the north. There is a low westerly pitch as the fold merges into the Soan syncline.

The Dhulian crest is at a much higher stratigraphic level and is in Lower Siwalik rocks which causes the Eocene to lie approximately 2,000 feet deeper than at Khaur. All the light crude oil is contained in the Eocene limestones at depths of from 7,650 to over 8,000 feet. The Murree rocks a short distance above the Eocene have given a small production of a heavy crude known as 'black oil' which is thought to be seepage oil of Murree times. The absence of light crude from the Murree rocks, in contrast with the conditions at Khaur, may be due to reduced fissuring in the more open fold. A strike fault runs near the crest at the surface but hades northwards so that if it cuts the limestones, this must be north of the productive area. Another fault has been observed in the limestones in one well on the south-eastern edge of the field.

It was recognized from the outset that the Dhulian structure was a possible oilfield, and testing began shortly after the Khaur field reached its full development. The early drilling was done by cable tools and the first four wells had to be abandoned one after the other because of high-pressure water flows from the Siwalik and Murree sands. The fifth well was drilled by the rotary system and reached the Eocene in 1935. A good show of oil was obtained, but this well proved to be at the eastern edge of the field and production was therefore short-lived. In 1937, No. 7 well, known as the Coronation Well, came in as a large producer of high-grade oil.

The field was linked by pipeline with Khaur and Rawalpindi and production from Dhulian proved a valuable supplement to the declining production at Khaur. The field was operated at a high rate during the war years, and this may have hastened the appearance of salt water with the oil and caused a sharp decline of output from 1942 onwards. The total production of Dhulian from this level to date (October 1952) has been over 213 million gallons.

Recently, following small shows of oil at lower horizons in other fields, a well was carried down to test for deeper oil. A new productive zone was found in the Lower Eocene (Ranikot) limestone. This, like the upper horizon originally, is under very high reservoir pressure. Another well has obtained similar results and others are being taken in hand to deepen and so to test the size of the new oil pool.

Drilling difficulties at Dhulian have been much less than at Khaur, though large flows of very hot water under considerable pressure have to be drilled through and cemented off behind casing.

Unsuccessful test wells were drilled by the Attock Oil Company at Chharat, Ganda Kas and Bokra, in the northern foot-hills east of the Indus; at Chorlakki in the north-eastern corner of the Kohat district; and at Babai and Dalwatti on the Marwat Range on the eastern border of the Bannu district. Other unsuccessful tests were drilled by the Burmah Oil Company at Meyal, fifteen miles north-west of Dhulian, and at Khabakki on the Salt Range; another failure was drilled by the Whitehall Corporation at Jhatla, thirty miles south of Dhulian. The Attock Oil Company also drilled a test at Jhatla with negative results.

Notwithstanding these disappointments, prospecting was renewed with even greater activity during the later years of the war. Another test was made of the Meyal structure, this time by the Attock Oil Company, and one of the test wells was carried to over 10,000 feet but no show of oil was obtained. Another failure had to be recorded at Uchhri, thirty miles further to the north-west, where a test was abandoned at over 9,000 feet. Two structures in the south part of the Potwar were tested and these tests proved successful; these are now the oilfields of Joya Mair and Balkassar, 25 miles south-east of the Khaur and Dhulian fields.

Joya Mair. The Joya Mair structure was described as suitable for the retention of an oil pool by Dr D. N. Wadia, in the Records of the Geological Survey of India for 1929. He pointed out that, although the crest of the fold is tightly compressed at the surface, the flank dips are low and the fold might be expected to be more open at depth. All this received striking confirmation when the first well, put down in 1945, encountered oil at 6,900 feet in Eocene limestones dipping at only moderate angles. On a short test the well flowed at the rate of several thousand barrels daily (one barrel is equal to 40 Imperial gallons). The oil, however, is quite different in character from that of the Khaur and Dhulian fields, in that it is a very heavy (S.G.=0·950) black crude containing nearly 70 per cent asphalt. It is unique in that the middle fractions, the lubricating oils, are absent. Although quite fluid under reservoir conditions of high pressure and high temperature, the oil when exposed at the surface loses its dissolved gas and lighter fractions and becomes solid asphalt in the course of a few days.

Two wells have been drilled to the oil zone and are now in production.[1] A third well drilled further down the southern flank of the structure failed to get oil in the Eocene and was deepened to test lower formations. It penetrated Carboniferous and Cambrian rocks and ended, owing to mechanical difficulties, at 8,820 feet in the Saline Series of the Salt Range sequence. An unsuccessful deep test was drilled by the Burmah Oil Company on the northern flank of the Joya Mair structure.

The Joya Mair oil is transported to the Rawalpindi refinery in tank wagons fitted with special heating arrangements. It is refined in a separate plant, the main product being bitumen.

Balkassar. The Balkassar structure is situated ten miles west of Joya Mair, these two folds having much the same relations to each other as the Khaur and Dhulian folds. The surface crest at Balkassar is at a higher horizon than that at Joya Mair, though the steep dips in the higher part of the Joya Mair cross-section add to the depth to be drilled there and so lessen the differences in depth which would otherwise have occurred. The structure at Balkassar is very open, the dip in the limestones being only 1° to 3°. A belt of comparatively steep dips lies along the north-western flank of the structure. Due to the northerly thickening of the Murree-Siwalik formations, the crest maximum at depth lies about two miles to the south of its position at the surface.

The first well drilled by the Attock Oil Company in 1946 reached the Eocene limestones at 8,135 feet, and shows of oil were obtained in the Bhadrar beds, dolomites, limestones and shales, which lie above the main Nummulitic limestone, known as the Sakesar Limestone. The well was deepened and found flowing

[1] Production in 1948 was 6,831,920 gallons.
　　　　,,　　,, 1949　,,　5,991,920　　,, ·

production in this Sakesar Limestone, and it is from it that most of the 140 million gallons of oil obtained to date have been won. In 1951, a well drilled some distance north of the earlier wells got good production from the Bhadrar beds themselves.

The Burmah Oil Company obtained production from a well drilled south of the Attock Oil Company's lease, and the field is at present being worked as a unit by the two companies. A peculiarity about the Balkassar field is that, whereas in the three older fields the oil occurs in the highest part of the structure, at Balkassar the productive area is asymmetrically disposed, good wells being obtained on the northern flank of the fold, whilst wells further south have so far proved disappointing.

Prospecting work continues actively, though now by new subsidiary companies formed in accordance with the Rules and Regulations of the Mines Department of the Government of Pakistan. The Pakistan Oilfields Limited was formed to take over the prospecting rights of the Attock Oil Company. This company is at present (1952) drilling a deep test at Bains, thirty miles south-south-east of Rawalpindi, as well as a number of shallow structure tests at Karsal, four miles north of the Balkassar field, and at Dhariala in the centre of the Salt Range Plateau.

Pakistan Petroleum Limited was formed to take over the Burmah Oil Company's licensed areas and is drilling a deep test at Chak Naurang, ten miles east of the Joya Mair field, in addition to further wells in the southern part of Balkassar. Deep testing is also in progress in the Bugti Hills of Baluchistan.

In the course of this work a large field of natural gas has been discovered at Sui, 60 miles north-north-east of Sukkur. The structure is an open dome in Siwalik rocks, the gas occurring in the underlying Eocene. Although the extent of the field is yet unknown, gas has been proved in two wells five miles apart and it is believed that the deposit will be capable of supplying West Pakistan's fuel requirements for many years. (See NATURAL GAS.)

The deepest well yet drilled in Pakistan was at Lakhra in Lower Sind, and this test had to be abandoned at 12,666 feet when hot salt water was encountered under extremely high pressure and could not be controlled. Other test wells drilled earlier in or near Sind were at Khairpur, Drigh Road near Karachi and, in 1916, at Chandragup in Las Bela.

It is natural that the search for oil becomes increasingly difficult as more and more of the apparently favourable areas are tested. Every scientific aid is being used in the task, including air photography and all branches of geophysical prospecting. The search for oil demands not only scientific and technical skill, but also large capital resources. The amount expended in oil prospecting in Pakistan to date amounts to many crores of rupees, but still the search goes on.

PROSPECTS FOR THE FUTURE IN PAKISTAN

The general outlook for petroleum prospecting in West Pakistan has been ably summarized by Dr D. N. Wadia, who outlines the region concerned as the broad zone of Eocene-Miocene sediments which stretches from Lower Sind to the north-eastern Punjab, passing through Baluchistan and the North-West Frontier Province and thence, after crossing the Indus between Kalabagh and Kohat, continues along the foot-hills of Jammu to Kangra. Surface indications of both oil and gas are known at many places in it, some localities have been tested, others have been examined, many but superficially, others in greater detail, but great tracts of the region still await methodical investigation by petroleum geologists: indeed, the most widely spread expanse of Lower Tertiary rocks ranging from the Makran to Karachi and thence northwards to Kohat, in which the sinuous, folded, surface exposures have a width of from 100 to 250 miles, remains for the most part unexplored from this point of view. Shallow wells drilled at Khattan, in the Marri Territory, between 1884 and 1896, yielded 837,825 gallons of crude oil, but from that time onwards until the recent test in the Bugti Hills, mentioned by Mr Pinfold, no drilling has been carried out in eastern Baluchistan.

In the Kohat salt-bearing region, according to Dr E. R. Gee, ' the rock salt at several places contains traces of oil and it is not improbable that it forms a cap-rock overlying in places petroliferous limestones and shales of Lower Eocene age '. The Tertiary strata of the Potwar, from the Kala Chitta ranges in the north to the northern slopes of the Salt Range in the south, represent a broadening out and simplification of the compressed and complex structures of Kohat. Writing of the Soan Basin as a whole, Dr Wadia has given his opinion that ' more drilling and extensive search for structures, with the aid of geophysical means can be confidently expected to produce a few commercially productive fields in this part of the north-west Punjab '.

The Eocene and higher Tertiary rocks of the Dera Ghazi Khan district in the south-west of the Punjab are in direct continuation with those of the Bugti area of eastern Baluchistan, and suitable structures, if found either in the foot-hills or beneath the alluvium of this region, should afford favourable conditions for the accumulation of oil pools. Further north, in the Sherani country of the North-West Frontier Province, the oil seepages of the Takht-i-Sulaiman Range, near Moghal Kot, have been known for more than 110 years.

From the North-West Frontier district of Hazara, the Tertiary rocks continue along the foot-hills of the Himalayas to the

Sadiya Frontier Tract of Assam, except for a small break near Darjeeling. The geological history of this zone and the structural deformations it has undergone during the course of that history, combine together to make the chances of the occurrence of profitable petroliferous deposits within it extremely problematical.

It remains to mention that Lower Tertiary rocks are believed to underlie the recent deposits which stretch eastwards from the foot-hills of Sind, Baluchistan and the southern Punjab up to and beyond the Indus, but the location of structures under the thick alluvial blanket demands geophysical prospecting of a highly specialized kind. The abandonment of the test in such an area, at Lakhra, in the Dadu district of Lower Sind, 125 miles from Karachi, after it had reached a depth of 12,666 feet in January 1950, has already been referred to by Mr Pinfold.

The search for new oilfields in Pakistan will continue but it can only be scientifically prosecuted by organizations, as Mr Pinfold has already stated, having at their command not only skilled geological advisers and experienced technicians but also large capital resources.

The Trade in Petroleum and its Products

The production of petroleum in the former Indian Empire increased from an annual average of about 58 million gallons, worth less than a quarter of a million pounds sterling, at the beginning of the century, to one of 336,145,426 gallons, valued at £4,871,565, over the pre-war period 1934–8. To this amount Burma contributed 77·9, Assam 19·6 and the Punjab 2·5 per cent. The highest output was reached in 1938, with a production of 350,905,636 gallons, or roughly 1,381,000 tons, but as the world's total output of crude oil for that year was some 267 million tons, it is evident from a global point of view that the contribution of the Burmese and Indian fields is insignificant; indeed, for many years their combined output has consistently represented much below 1 per cent of the world's total. Yet to the regions concerned, these oilfields are of great importance.

The separation of Burma from India took place on 1 April 1937, and this event together with the overrunning of the country by the Japanese armies in 1942, the separation of Pakistan from India on 15 August 1947, and the general results of the second world war, have had far-reaching consequences for the oil business of the subcontinent. For the three years ending 1936, that is for the last pre-war period during which the Indian Empire existed as a single unit, India, which at that time included both Burma and Pakistan, consumed an annual average of 468,325,000 gallons of oil products, made up of kerosene, 46 per cent; fuel oil, 28 per cent; petrol, 19 per cent and lubricating and batching oils, 7 per cent. Over half of this amount (55 per cent) was made in her own refineries from home-produced crude oil, the remainder, consisting for the most part of kerosene (30 per cent) and fuel oil (60 per cent), being imported from abroad. The kerosene came from Russia, 67·5 per cent; Sumatra, 11·7 per cent; Iran, 10·7 per cent and Rumania, 5·2 per cent, with smaller quantities from Borneo, Java, the United States of America and elsewhere. Of the fuel oil 74·7 per cent was brought from Iran, 21·4 per cent from Borneo and the rest from other countries. Thus, for the 192½ million gallons of kerosene which undivided India required in addition to her own manufactures, she depended mainly on the Soviet Republics, Sumatra and Iran, while three-quarters of the imports of fuel oil, amounting to more than 375 million gallons, were derived from Iran.

Turning now to the three post-war years 1948 to 1950, although exact figures are not obtainable at the time of writing, the average annual consumption of oil products for India alone, that is to say without either Pakistan or Burma, was approximately 728 million gallons, an increase of more than 56 per cent over the consumption of the whole of the former Indian Empire in 1934–6. The rate of increase was a rapidly progressive one between 1948 and 1950, and if the consumption for 1950 alone is taken—850 million gallons—the increase over the earlier period of 1934–6 becomes over 81 per cent. There is, however, one most noteworthy difference to be observed: whereas in the pre-war period India supplied 55 per cent of her own oil requirements, this proportion dropped to under 10 per cent and was but 7 per cent in 1949, partly owing to her loss of the oilfields of Burma and Pakistan and partly to the big increase in consumption.

Imported oil products averaged some 685 million gallons per annum during 1948–50, of which fuel oil accounted for 42·5 per cent, kerosene 27 per cent, petrol 23·5 per cent and lubricating and batching oils 7 per cent. Great changes have also to be noted in the sources of these foreign oils: of the kerosene supplies in 1948 and 1949, 68·5 per cent came from Iran and 20 per cent from Bahrein Island in the Persian Gulf, while the same two regions contributed no less than 90 per cent of the petrol and 83 per cent of the imports of fuel oil. The lubricating and batching oils were bought as to 66 per cent of the total from the United States of America, followed by Iran with 24 per cent and the United Kingdom with 8·5 per cent.

Even before the separation of Burma and Pakistan oil exports of Indian origin had become insignificant, but the exports of paraffin wax were a most important article of commerce, averaging 48,014 tons, valued at Rs 2,01,00,886, over the three years 1934–8. Indian wax of this kind had a very wide distribution to most of the countries of the Commonwealth, to many parts of Europe, to both North and South America and to various Asiatic lands. Like the crude oils from most of the Burmese fields, the oils of the Digboi oilfield in Assam contain a high proportion of paraffin wax which still continues to be exported from this source of supply, the average quantity sent abroad from Indian ports for the two years 1948 and 1949 being 12,538 tons, valued at Rs 1,29,56,486; but about half of the Assam wax is exported through Chittagong in East Pakistan, the *total* average exports from Assam for the two years in question being about 25,000 tons.

The importation of oil products into India is increasing rapidly, their total cost rising from Rs 29 crores in 1948 to Rs 51 crores in 1949 and Rs 54 crores in 1950. No further argument is needed to strengthen the case for an intensified campaign of oil prospecting, particularly in Assam, to locate new structures as well as to investigate again some of the known ones, in the hope that new locations may yield production on anticlines already tested with negative results. India's dependence on imported fuels could be reduced to some extent by the manufacture of petrol from suitable coals of Bihar and elsewhere, a subject which is now under consideration.

As a result of discussions which took place in November and December 1951 between the Government of India and the Burmah-Shell group of companies and the Standard Vacuum Oil Company, agreement was reached on schemes under which two modern oil refineries would be erected near Bombay for the refining of imported Middle East crude oil. These refineries would be owned and operated by Indian companies and financed partly with Indian capital; the capacity of the Burmah-Shell group refinery would be 2 million tons and that of the Standard Vacuum refinery $1\frac{1}{2}$ million tons per annum. The Burmah-Shell scheme, it is stated, should lead to the investment in the oil-refining industry in India of about Rs 20 crores (one crore of rupees being equal to about £750,000) of sterling capital. The share of the Burmah Oil Co. Ltd in the

AVERAGE ANNUAL PRODUCTION OF PETROLEUM IN INDIA,
1900–38

PERIOD	AVERAGE ANNUAL PRODUCTION	AVERAGE ANNUAL VALUE	PROPORTION YIELDED BY		
			BURMA	ASSAM	PUNJAB
	gallons	£	%	%	%
1900–3	58,067,771	231,319*	97·6	2·4	..
1904–8	146,506,989	592,887*	98·0	2·0	..
1909–13	240,187,714	928,072*	98·2	1·8	..
1914–18	282,594,121	1,134,916*	97·4	2·5	0·1
1919–23	299,453,675	7,036,298	95·0	3·7	1·3
1924–8	290,321,036	6,268,229	88·9	7·7	3·4
1929–33	307,362,400	4,319,280	81·4	15·8	2·8
1934–8	336,145,420	4,871,565	77·9	19·6	2·5

* Value stated to be greatly underestimated.

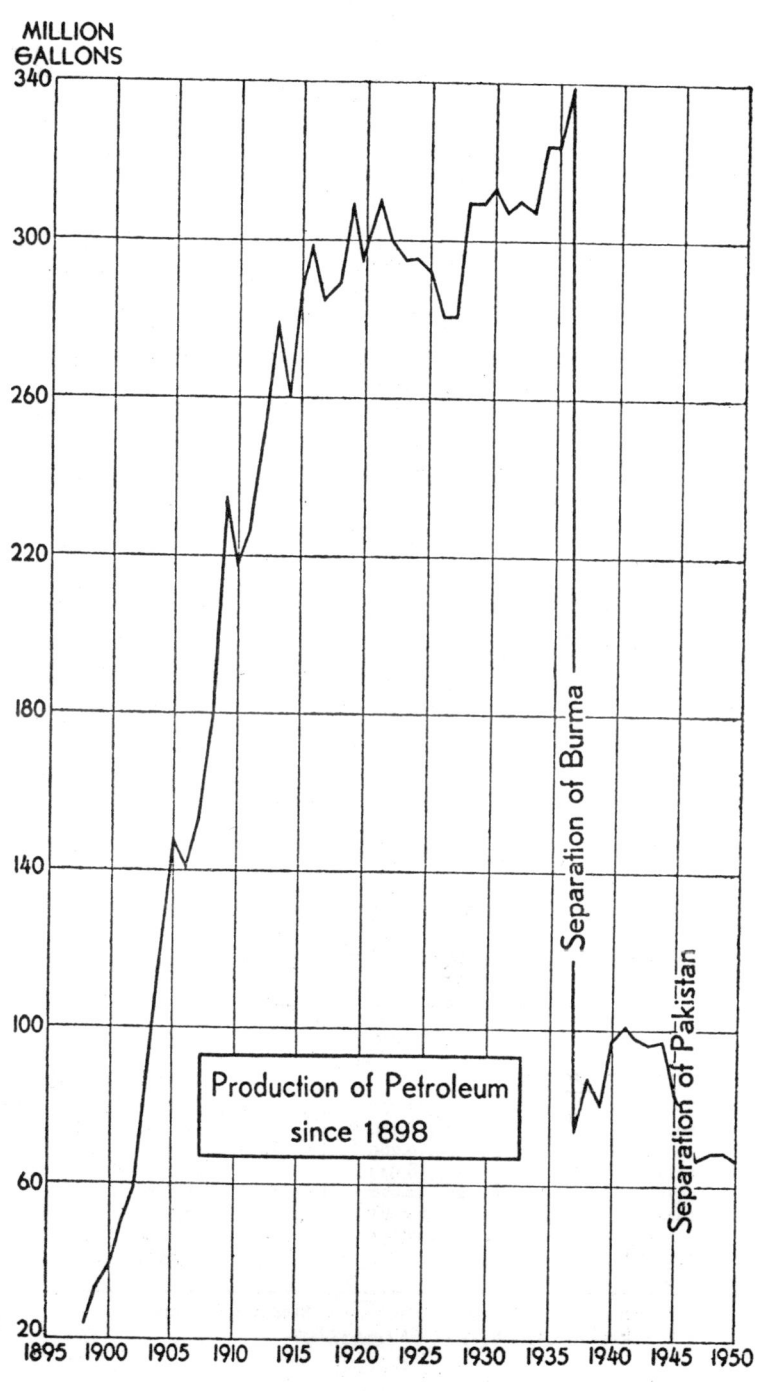

MILLION GALLONS

Production of Petroleum since 1898

Separation of Burma

Separation of Pakistan

provision of this capital is estimated at some £9 million. Another agreement following the general pattern of those of 1951 was signed in New Delhi on 28 March 1953. It provides for the establishment by the American Caltex Oil Company of a refinery at Visakhapatnam, Andhra, and involves an estimated expenditure of 15 million dollars. Desirable though these developments are, the greater part of the crude oil requirements of the new refineries will still have to be imported from abroad, unless and until new sources of supply are discovered in India, and it is to that imperative end that all available attention should be directed.

AVERAGE ANNUAL IMPORTS OF MINERAL OILS INTO INDIA
1900–38

Period	Average Annual Imports	Average Annual Value	Proportion Brought From				
			Russia	U.S.A.	Borneo*	Iran	Others
	gallons	£	%	%	%	%	%
1900–3 ..	85,463,994	2,314,801	74·6	18·9	..	..	6·5
1904–8 ..	73,624,177	1,944,175	31·6	32·5	..	..	35·7
1909–13 ..	89,329,698	2,451,987	7·2	53·2	18·0	0·27	21·31
1914–18 ..	89,747,579	2,748,990	0·4	54·8	23·3	9·2	12·3
1919–23 ..	117,241,203	5,514,977	..	40·0	19·2	32·4	8·4
1924–8 ..	194,518,757	6,999,856	..	34·8	17·0	38·2	10·0
1929–33‡ ..	228,315,287	7,164,512	11·0	15·7	14·1	41·7	17·5
1934–8†§ ..	236,340,516	4,431,120	14·3	0·5	17·7	45·0	22·5‖

* Includes Sumatra.
† Includes imports into Burma up to March 1937 only.
‡ Fiscal years.
§ Described as kerosene and fuel oils only.
‖ Includes 10·5 per cent from Burma.

AVERAGE ANNUAL EXPORTS OF INDIAN PETROLEUM AND PARAFFIN WAX, 1904–38

Period	Petroleum	Paraffin Wax
	gallons	tons
1904–8 ..	2,921,400	3,276
1909–13 ..	12,070,369	11,555
1914–18 ..	24,458,917	21,191
1919–23 ..	23,732,622	26,595
1924–8 ..	7,568,961	39,779
1929–33 ..	123,972	54,600
1934–8* ..	....	35,805†

* Includes exports from Burma up to March 1937 only.
† Valued at £1,128,729 or Rs 1,49,37,897.

OIL SHALES

Oil shales are shales or clays which on distillation yield petroleum of various grades, ' usually ranging ', according to one authority, ' from asphalt or paraffin through heavy lubricating and fuel oils to the lighter illuminating oils, kerosene, and to petrol and the petrol ethers '. The shales themselves contain no free oil but abound in vegetable remains, spores, grains of wax and resin. ' The oil-producing constituents are yellow bodies of microscopic dimensions which have been identified as pollen grains, algae and spores.' Many of these are of a secondary nature formed by the redeposition of resinous and cellulosic material. The richer varieties of oil shale can be ignited with a match and burn freely; indeed, the use of oil shale for fuel by Karen villagers of the Burma-Thailand frontier first directed attention to the rich deposits of that region.

OIL SHALES OF LOWER BURMA

Amherst District. The oil shales of the Kawkareik township, in the Amherst district of the Tenasserim division of Lower Burma, lie to the east of the Dawna range and close to the Thai frontier, indeed, two of the three basins in which they occur actually cross the border into Thailand. The deposits were described by Professor J. W. Gregory in 1923 and by G. de P. Cotter in 1924. Two of the areas are bisected by the Thaungyin river and, lying to the south and north of the frontier town of Myawaddy, are known as the Phalu and Mesauk-Methalaun-Melamat basins respectively, though it is possible that they join and form a continuous area across the frontier. The third is in the valley of the Mepale stream and derives its name from the village of Htichara.

The basins themselves are hollows in the older rocks which have been filled in by freshwater deposits of late Tertiary age, for the shales themselves contain the remains of fish and freshwater shells, together with the leaves of plants and ferns. They fall into two divisions, a lower one of sands and boulder beds and an upper one of shales with oil shales. In the Htichara basin, which is about 14 miles long and 9 miles broad, several quite rich seams of oil shale of varying thickness have been proved by boring to exist over a considerable area and down to a depth of 300 feet. The Mark Band seam is 6 to 7 feet thick and is stated to yield 15 to 20 per cent of crude oil. Five more seams containing smaller percentages of oil have been located above it. Samples of Htichara oil shale tested in the laboratories of the Geological Survey of India yielded between 9·78 and 16·20 gallons of crude oil per ton. The latter contained water, 13 per cent; light naphtha, 4 per cent; heavy naphtha, 3 per cent; kerosene 23 per cent; lubricating oil, 40 per cent; residue, 17 per cent. ' In the Htichara field ', writes Cotter, ' there appears to be a good supply of shale of a rich or fair average quality, so much in fact that it would be possible to obtain large quantities by open-casting.' Mining would be fairly simple; the strata dip gently, they appear to be fairly regular, the barren shales would form a good roof and floor, while the oil shales themselves would give solid, hard pillars. Originally bored by M. E. Moola and Sons Ltd, the Htichara deposits were afterwards leased to the Mepale (Burma) Oil Co. Ltd, and although an experimental retort was obtained for test distillations in 1932, large-scale exploitation had not commenced before the onset of the second world war.

OTHER OIL SHALE DEPOSITS

Oil shales have also been found in the Tertiary deposits which occupy the valley of the Theinkun stream, a branch of the Little Tenasserim river, in the Mergui district of Lower Burma, while other low-grade material is known to occur near Bonkun, in the Lenya valley of Mergui, and in that of the Great Tenasserim valley of the adjoining Tavoy district.

Low-grade oil shales have been noted by Cotter in association with the Salt Marl of the Punjab Salt Range, but they are not believed to possess any economic importance.

NATURAL GAS

Dissolved in the petroleum occurring in the pores of sands and limestones there is always some natural gas, consisting chiefly of methane, CH_4, with smaller amounts of other hydrocarbons; in many fields natural gas also forms a ' gas cap ' in the highest parts of the oil-bearing horizon. In the earliest days of the oil industry the importance of conserving this gas was not appreciated, but for many years past it has been realized that the pressure under which oil and gas exist in an underground sand, together with the amount of gas actually dissolved in the oil itself, are potent factors in the recovery of the oil, for it is in part the propulsive power of the gas, when the sand is tapped by the drill, which forces the oil to the well and helps to raise it there. Modern oilfield practice, therefore, permits as little of the gas to escape as possible, and aims at keeping the gas/oil ratio of the crude oil produced as low as circumstances permit. Gases escaping naturally, or pumped from oilsands, are also saturated with the vapours of highly volatile, liquid hydrocarbons in suspension which form a valuable source of gasoline when recovered in suitable plant. By 1931, over two million gallons of natural gasoline were being extracted annually from gases liberated on the Yenangyaung oilfield of Burma alone, and by 1939 installations on this and other fields in Burma were recovering such liquid hydrocarbons at the rate of over $11\frac{1}{4}$ million gallons per annum. The dry gas, stripped of its liquid contents, was used for fuel purposes and produced the electrical power which supplied the major oilfields with their energy. Any remaining surplus gas was returned to the underground reservoirs whence it came, to perform more useful work in repressuring the depleted sands and in bringing another load of gasoline to the surface.

The gas of the Digboi oilfield in Assam is used both for fuel and for repressuring the oilsands. As E. V. Corps has recorded, great attention is paid there to the gas/oil ratio, the producing conditions being varied to reduce the gas/oil ratio to the minimum attainable; wells which give high gas/oil ratios are closed in and not produced from until it is found that the oil can be taken at an acceptable gas/oil ratio. In the case of the Punjab, the Balkassar oil is associated with very little gas.

Besides the gas found in association with oil and coming from the same sands, there are other sands in various fields which contain gas alone and it is usually methane in a dry condition. The natural gas resources of Burma were fully described in a memoir of the Geological Survey of India, by Dr C. T. Barber, published in 1935. Two cases only can be mentioned here to indicate how great these resources are. On the Indaw oilfield alone there was available at that time a quantity of 12 million cubic feet daily and it could doubtless have been increased if necessary. Several wells on the Indaw field had already been abandoned on account of high gas pressure. Well No. 1 had been delivering gas steadily for 15 years with a very slight decline in yield and pressure and seemed likely to do so for years to come. At the other end of Burma, in the Thayetmyo district, searching for oil a well liberated gas at a depth of 2,525 feet, in quantities estimated at 39 million cubic feet in 24 hours. After escaping for eight months, the flow was brought under control with only a slight diminution of pressure. The gas liberated in this case represented the thermal equivalent of an oil well producing 5,000 barrels per day and it is now used to supply a cement works with its fuel. (See CEMENT).

A natural gas field of great extent has been recently proved in the southern part of the Bugti Tribal Area of Baluchistan some 60 miles north-north-east of Sukkur, a town on the Indus in Sind. The large open dome of Tertiary rocks in which it occurs was delineated many years ago on maps published by the Geological Survey of India but until 1952 it laid untested, when a well drilled in search of oil by the Pakistan Petroleum Company tapped its gas reservoirs. A second well five miles distant from the first one confirmed that these are of vast extent.

The Sui Gas Transmission Company has been incorporated in Pakistan to lay a pipeline, 350 miles in length, between the field and Karachi, at an estimated cost of £9 million. By March 1954 much of the equity capital had already been provided by investors in Pakistan, the Commonwealth Development Finance Corporation, the Pakistan Industrial Development Corporation and the

Burmah Oil Company. The magnitude of this concern is a measure of the belief of its sponsors in the capacity and probable length of life of the field itself.

There are many possibilities in the chemical utilization of methane and its associated hydrocarbons as a starting-point in the synthesis of a host of organic chemicals, including dyestuffs, solvents and anaesthetics. In some countries the natural gases are piped for great distances to industrial centres for heating, domestic and power purposes; in the United States of America they have been found to carry small amounts of helium, a light, non-inflammable gas which is extracted on a commercial scale and used for filling airships and other purposes.

In India natural gas has been tapped at Jagatia and Gogha in Saurashtra and at Baroda. It is believed to be derived from Upper Tertiary strata which rest on an underlying platform of Deccan Trap and which thicken towards the Gulf of Cambay. Dr P. K. Ghosh states that the Gogha gas sand lies at a depth of 812 feet below the surface and is 35 feet thick. A sample of the Gogha natural gas, analysed by H. E. Watson, contained 0.8 per cent of helium. Further exploratory drilling is essential before any conclusions can be drawn as to the extent of this occurrence.

Natural gas in smaller quantities is sometimes met with in sinking tube-wells for water in alluvial districts, and such occurrences have been reported from Saharmul, in the Mymensingh district of East Bengal, and from Thetkala, in the Pegu district of Lower Burma. In these and similar instances, the marsh gas was probably formed by the decomposition of vegetable debris in the local deltaic deposits. Three or four other occurrences have recently come to the notice of the Geological Survey of India from deltaic, alluvial deposits in the East Godavari and Krishna districts of Andhra and the Tanjore district of Madras. Samples of the gas from Tatipaka, in the first-named, and from Neypattur, in the last-named district, contained 70.4 and 69.1 per cent of saturated hydrocarbons and 1.0 and 0.5 per cent of unsaturated hydrocarbons, respectively. It is important to observe that though gas supplies from such sources may serve as fuel on a small scale for heating or for gas engines, it is delusive to regard them as certain indications of the presence of underground supplies of petroleum.

PART II

THE METALS AND THEIR ORES

CHAPTER II

THE PRECIOUS METALS

GOLD

PLINY, in A.D. 77, referred to the country of the Nareae, now identified with the Nairs of Malabar, as containing many mines of gold and silver, and there can be no doubt that gold mining in India dates from prehistoric times. Owing to the absence of references in the medieval Mohammedan records, however, some authorities believe that the greatest activity took place before A.D. 1000. The occurrence of alluvial gold in the southern portion of the Malabar district has received attention from the year 1793 onwards, and in 1831 Nicholson discovered the remains of numerous old workings in the south-east Wynaad, the highlands which lie between the Nilgiri plateau and the low country of Malabar proper. The region was prospected from about 1875 onwards but, although occasional discoveries of very rich pockets were made, the results on the whole were very poor. In spite of this no fewer than 33 companies were floated between 1879 and 1881, with an aggregate capital of over £4,000,000. The total quantity of gold produced appears to have been about 600 oz. and mining operations ceased in 1893. Investigations by Sir Henry Hayden and Dr F. H. Hatch, in 1899, of the veins near Devala and Pandalur gave average gold contents of under 2 dwt to the ton.

A re-examination of the veins in the same neighbourhood, however, by Dr H. Crookshank of the Geological Survey of India, in 1939-40, led him to believe that though small they still merit further attention. The failure of the earlier ventures is, in his opinion, not to be attributed entirely to low-grade ore, for bad financial management, metallurgical troubles, the low price of gold, the lack of mining labour, and the difficulties usually associated with pioneer efforts in an isolated, malarious region, also contributed to the collapse of gold mining in the Wynaad. During the last war, a company known as Nilambur Mines Ltd commenced operations, primarily with the object of exploiting the auriferous pyrite of the veins as a source of sulphur, but the importation of supplies from the United States in 1944 frustrated the plan and left the Company with the problem of proving the reserves of a low-grade, refractory, gold-bearing ore.

An examination of the Alpha and Harewood mines of this company was made by D. Kerr-Cross, Mining Engineer to the

Geological Survey of India, in 1951, which showed that the ore on No. 9 level of the Alpha mine averages less than 2 per cent sulphur and 2 dwt of gold per ton. There are however, some payable sections, totalling about 13,000 tons, averaging 2.91 per cent sulphur and 2.85 dwt of gold per ton, which might be worked at a small profit. The bottom level (No. 11), where almost 1,000 feet of driving had been done, was not examined due to ground collapse near the adit entrance. In the Harewood mine, the lode is of limited extent along both strike and dip. There is one payable length of about 100 feet but this is not expected to persist far below the bottom No. 5 level.

The gold of southern India and of Chota Nagpur is derived from quartz veins which traverse the rocks of the Dharwar System, consisting principally of hornblende, chlorite and mica schists, argillites and phyllites, quartzites and quartz schists, boulder beds and pebbly conglomerates, together with epidiorites and other intrusive masses of dioritic and basaltic character. They are found in long, isolated, more or less parallel bands and outlying patches in the gneisses, granites and charnockites forming the main mass of the Archaean complex. The vein quartz occurs in two forms, either as a dark blue or deep grey, semi-translucent variety, bearing marks of the intense strains to which it has been subjected, and usually associated with the hornblende schists, or an opaque, milky white kind often found traversing chloritic schists, and perhaps connected with the intrusion of basic dykes which are common in the system and of later age. While both varieties may be auriferous, the former kind more often carries gold in the south, while the reverse is commoner further north. This, however, is not an invariable rule; white veins have been found among the hornblende schists of the south and may be gold-bearing. In the case of the Kolar goldfield, now to be briefly described, some geologists trace a connexion between the auriferous veins and the hornblende schists, while others regard them as the end-product, the hydro-thermal stage of the Champion Granite, formed by quartz-bearing solutions emanating from the cooling magma, filling the fractures in the schists and in some instances replacing their walls by quartz.

The Kolar goldfield is in the district of the same name in eastern Mysore, about 125 miles west of Madras, and lies on a plateau 2,800 feet above sea level. Warren, in 1802, first directed attention to it after seeing shallow mining in eluvial deposits from which fragmentary quartz was extracted, crushed, and the gold recovered by washing and amalgamation. In earlier times, as later exploration proved, shafts had been sunk into the solid quartz, reaching a depth of 300 feet. Modern history dates from 1871, when Lavelle obtained the first concession and commenced a shaft on what is now the Ooregum Company's block. Between 1878 and 1882 various companies were formed to undertake gold mining, but by the end of 1884 most of them had exhausted their resources, and it was only a final effort on the part of the Mysore Company which in that year disclosed rich ore in the pillars of an ancient mine. From that time the history of the field, under the capable technical direction of Messrs John Taylor & Sons, has been one of practically uninterrupted success. The narrow belt of Dharwar schists on which the goldfield lies can be followed for about 50 miles from north to south, but the productive portion is confined to a length of about 4½ miles, on which are situated from north to south the Balaghat, Nundydroog, Ooregum, Champion Reef and Mysore mines, though the Nundydroog Company acquired the property of the Balaghat concern in 1932. From the commencement of operations until the end of March 1951 the total quantity of gold won amounted to 21,842,902 oz., valued at Rs 169·61 crores, while dividends paid to the end of March 1951 totalled Rs 37·82 crores. The royalties and taxes (including Gold Duty) paid by all the mines to the Government of Mysore to 31 March 1951 amounted to Rs 23·81 crores.

There are in all about thirty veins on the Kolar field, averaging 3 to 4 feet in width, though markedly lenticular, swelling and contracting at irregular intervals in both strike and dip. With few exceptions they are parallel to the foliation of the schists and are in fact the filled-in fissures which have opened along their lines of greatest weakness. They strike approximately north and south and in most cases dip westwards at 40° to 50°, steepening to almost vertical at great depths. Practically the whole of the gold, however, has come from one vein of this more or less parallel series and it is known as the Champion Reef. Its quartz is bluish-grey, clean and glassy, made up of large, irregularly locked grains with innumerable minute vesicles distributed throughout it, and its gold content is generally invisible to the naked eye. In places the vein bulges into large quartz bodies and in others splits into smaller veinlets. Characteristic of it are sharp folds, pitching at about 45° to the north, with thickened masses of quartz developed at the top and bottom of the folds and forming valuable sources of ore. The gold values are distributed in well-defined shoots, increase in ' fineness ' with depth and, according to Prior, are of later date than the quartz itself and than the large north-north-west, south-south-east faults which cross the field. Tourmaline is a very common accessory mineral; chloritoid is frequently seen; galena, arsenopyrite, pyrrhotite, pyrite, chalcopyrite, ilmenite, magnetite and scheelite have all been found with the gold. In the Oriental Lode there is no galena, its place being taken by small amounts of zinc blende and tellurides. Frequently associated with the quartz veins are thin, half-inch bands of pale green pyroxene in irregularly shaped crystals, often intergrown with calcite and partly altered to actinolite. In cases where the veins split into thin veinlets, these pyroxene bands increase until they form the chief constituent of the vein. The average grade of ore treated in the Kolar field during the 15 months ending 31 March 1951 contained 6·62 dwt of gold per ton.

The deepest point reached in the Champion Reef mine was 9,233 feet in December 1951. Development is carried out by means of levels at vertical distances of 100 to 150 feet, and the total footage of the underground workings to date exceeds 600 miles. The gold content of the quartz is remarkably persistent with depth, and although individual ore shoots may come to an end, new ones are found to take their places. At the 33rd level it was found that the Mysore North fault had entered the Champion Reef property from the adjoining Mysore mine, with the result that the ore shoot of the Main Reef on its southern edge was cut out between the 33rd and 58th levels. The orebody gradually diminished along its strike and was ultimately lost in a major pegmatite zone. But below this again, two more ore shoots were found on either side of the fault. The northern one, termed the Central Ore Shoot, commenced from the 61st level, whereas the southern one, termed the Glen Ore Shoot, was discovered on the 68th horizon; its northern edge follows roughly the southern fringe of the fault, and its southern portion has isolated shoots of ore which are displaying a tendency to merge with the main orebody. The Glen Ore Shoot is indeed a unique occurrence of great magnitude covering an area of over 56 acres. Fluctuations of gold distribution in the lode channel are marked but the average for the main orebody is approximately 14·9 dwt over a stoping width of 66 inches. Up to June 1950, it had been successfully developed for a depth of 2,500 feet, with increasing lengths of economic values along its strike, the maximum being 1,300 feet at the 76th horizon.

The Ooregum mine, with a vertical depth of 9,876 feet in June 1953, was at that time the deepest mine in the world. Its main orebody laid near the southern boundary of the property and continued beyond it into the adjoining Champion Reef mine. The sequence of deep mining operations necessary to extract it so restricted output that the Ooregum Mining Co. Ltd had to cease working about the middle of 1953, when its rights were transferred to the Champion Reef Gold Mines of India (KGF) Ltd, who are at present mining in the area. At these great depths rock bursts have become a serious hazard, compelling the use of packed crib sets and heavy masonry walls in the stopes to resist the ground pressures. Rock temperatures of the order of 140°F. at 9,000 feet have necessitated the introduction of air-conditioning plant at all the mines of the field. In the Nundydroog mine a strong pyritic vein was intersected in 1949 about 2,000 feet to the west of the Main Reef on the 48th level. It had been mined in the past from the surface to a depth of 700 or 800 feet, where the workings had been abandoned. It is up to 25 feet in width with a steep varying westerly dip and an average grade of 5 to 6 dwt of gold per ton. It has since been developed down to the 62nd level, or more than 5,000 feet vertically below the surface.

Kolar gold-bearing quartz is not refractory and yields its valuable contents to a simple combination of blanket concentration, amalgamation and cyaniding. Recovery averages over 98 per cent and the bars produced contain approximately 925 parts of fine gold and 70 parts per 1,000 of silver. Refining is carried out in the Bombay mint and the products—gold with 995 parts per 1,000 and fine silver—are sold in India.

As and from 6 May 1949, the control of the mining companies was transferred from London to Mysore, under the management of John Taylor & Sons (India) Ltd, and for the first time in their history, the companies held their annual general meetings in Mysore in 1949. The peak of production, 616,758 oz. of gold, was attained in 1905; it fell below half a million ounces in 1919 and has declined more or less continuously since then. The graph on page 128, although it includes the all-India gold production, of which Kolar forms the only significant part, illustrates this fall. For the five years ending 1938, the annual average was 326,188 oz.; for the next five-yearly period ending 1943, 280,408 oz. and for the quinquennium 1944 to 1948, 167,921 oz. In 1949 and 1950 the average was 175,258 oz., being 97 per cent of the total production of Indian gold, valued at Rs 5,45,43,140. These records need no explanation: they tell their own story of the gradual approach of an inevitable end of the abstraction of gold from those veins on the Kolar field which have been worked for so many years. At the same time, that end is not yet; given a sympathetic administration, freedom from acute labour troubles and the maintenance of the high standard of mining technique for which the field has long been renowned, it can be safely assumed that Kolar will continue to be an important producer for some years to come.

Kolar itself is one of the model mining towns of the world with a population of 134,000. The mines as a whole find employment for 189 Europeans and 23,700 Indians, of whom 14,870 work underground. The ore reserves of the individual mines on 31 March 1951 are given below:

ORE RESERVES OF THE KOLAR GOLDFIELD ON 31 MARCH 1951

Mine	Tons	Average Grade dwt per ton	Probable Reserves of Low-grade Ore Tons
Mysore	261,200	12·35	208,900
Champion Reef ..	527,409	11·47	66,384
Ooregum	155,026	9·15	57,870
Nundydroog	322,570	10·06	272,086

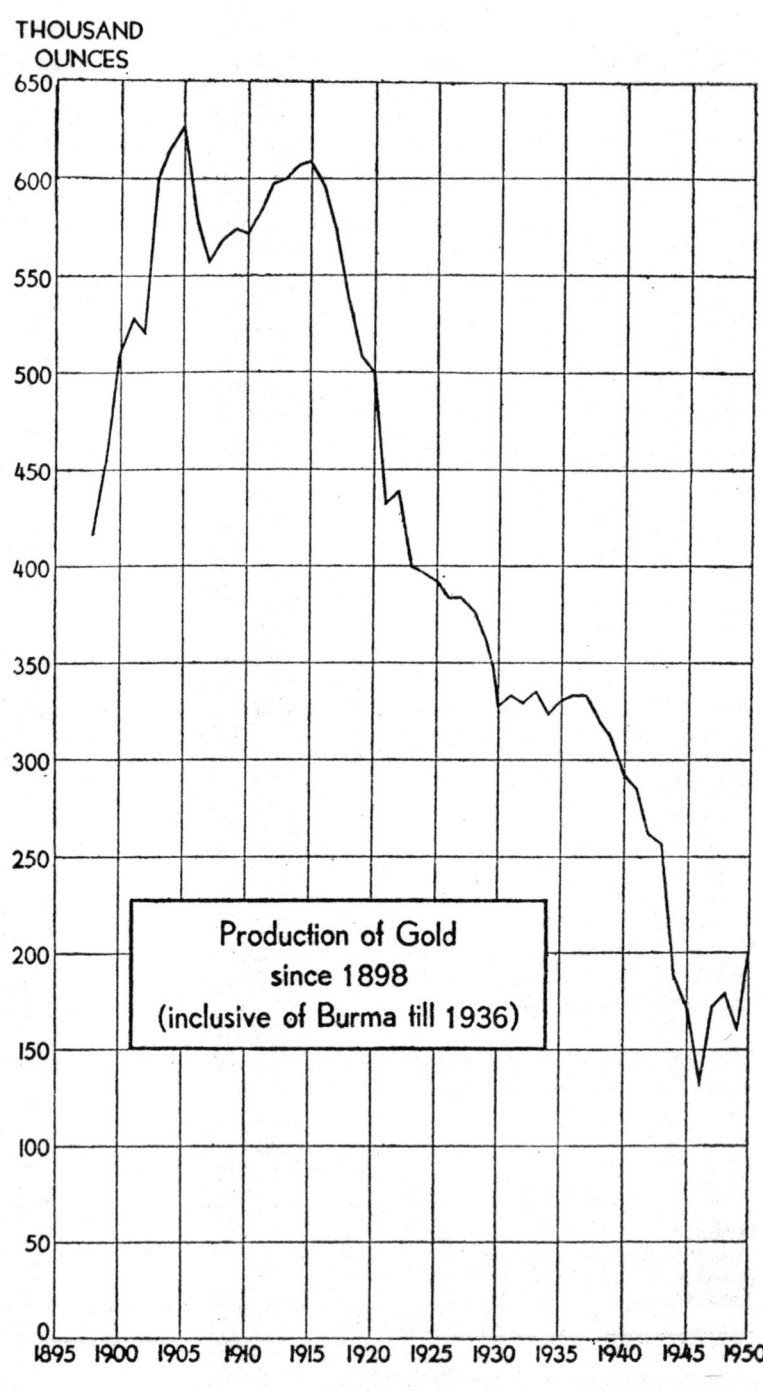

THOUSAND
OUNCES

Production of Gold
since 1898
(inclusive of Burma till 1936)

Hundreds of old gold workings have been found scattered over the surface of the Dharwar rocks in Mysore, but it is said that in the majority of instances they do not indicate the existence of valuable deposits beneath them. Equally disappointing has been the investigation of the numerous quartz veins which traverse the schists and crop out at the surface. Smeeth and Iyengar summed the matter up in the following statement: 'We may take it as an almost universal rule that outcropping veins are valueless.' After pointing out that it is possible that some zones of low-grade ore may be found of sufficient extent and under conditions favourable enough for cheap treatment to permit of their being worked, these writers conclude by saying: 'We cannot shut our eyes to the fact that the hopes based on the success of the Kolar mines and on the existence of numerous old workings have dwindled very seriously with the progress of survey work and deep prospecting.' It would be premature to assume, however, that this statement represents the last word on the subject. It now seems certain that the Kolar veins are closely associated in genetic relationship with the final phases of the Champion granite or gneissic intrusions, but to what extent this mother rock, its pegmatites and quartz veins, exist outside Mysore, the Bellary district (formerly of Madras) and the Dharwar district of Bombay is quite unknown. In both these districts there are quartz veins probably identical in age and character with those of Kolar, and a little gold has already been found in the northern part of the Chitaldrug belt. In the Gadag area of the Dharwar district, blue, diaphanous quartz veins, similar to those of the Kolar field occur, but, on the authority of Sir Edwin Pascoe, a former Director of the Geological Survey of India, it is quite unknown to what extent they are gold-bearing as they have been very little prospected.

Numerous old gold mines are scattered about in various parts of the Raichur Doab and the Surapur taluk of the Gulbarga district of Hyderabad. On an irregular area of Dharwar rocks which stretches through Maski, from the vicinity of the Tungabhadra river to the Krishna, they reach the unusual depth of 640 feet below the surface, bearing witness to the skill of an ancient race of miners about whom both history and tradition are silent. Near the old workings groups of mortars of large and small sizes are to be found in which the gold-bearing ore was crushed. 'They are to be seen in abundance at Topuldodi,' writes Captain L. Munn, at one time Mining Engineer to the Government of Hyderabad, and he continues: 'At Wondalli there are large saucer-like hollows, made in the trappoid rock, in which the ore was pounded by means of granite crushers of great size. These crushers must have been brought from a great distance, and from their enormous sizes it is evident that they were not worked by hand, but by means of some sort of framework which afforded leverage.'

The modern search for gold in Hyderabad dates back to 1886, when the Hyderabad (Deccan) Co. conducted prospecting operations over a period of twelve years, 1887 to 1899. More than three hundred old workings were discovered in parts of Hutti, Wondalli, Maski, Topuldodi, and Budhini in the Raichur Doab, as well as in the Manglur field in the Surapur taluk of Gulbarga. Most of these are stated to have received some attention, but it is important to note that only a few of them were bottomed. Realizing that diffused operations of this sort were a heavy drain on its resources, the Hyderabad (Deccan) Co. formed subsidiary concerns to undertake development work. These were:—(1) The Wondalli (Deccan) Gold Mining Co. Ltd which began work at Wondalli about 1895, but ceased in 1900. Its most productive year was 1899, when 18,970 tons of quartz were crushed for a return of 7,822 oz. of gold. The yield of gold from Hyderabad from 1898 to 1900, amounting to £54,310, was almost exclusively the produce of this mine. (2) The Hutti (Nizam's) Gold Mines Ltd started crushing with 10 heads of stamps (later increased to 30 heads) in 1903 and ceased in 1920, after the mine had reached a depth of 3,500 feet and gold worth £1,010,757 had been extracted. (3) The Topuldodi Gold Mines Ltd commenced mining in the vicinity of Topuldodi and Chincherki in 1905 and ceased operations in 1908. Its only recorded production was worth £8,319 in 1908.

Another company, the Deccan Gold Fields Development Co. Ltd, was formed in 1905 with the object of examining all the old workings left untouched by earlier prospecting operations. It is said to have paid particular attention to the Manglur field, but its activities came to an end with the outbreak of the first world war in 1914. With the exception of revision surveys by the Hyderabad Geological Department which resulted in the discovery of a new area near Hunkuni, in the Deodrug taluk, where a long line of old workings was partially opened up, nothing further was done until the Hyderabad Government financed a programme of detailed prospecting in the Manglur, Hutti and Maski areas, conducted by John Taylor & Sons, who commenced their explorations in 1937. In the Hutti area it was found that more or less continuous ancient workings exist on various veins over a total length of 11,000 feet of which only 3,100 feet had been explored underground by the former Hutti Company. In addition to the Main Mine, the old Village Reef and Oakley's mines were unwatered, developed and resampled so that by 1942, when work was temporarily suspended owing to the war, ore reserves totalling 229,536 tons, averaging 4·62 dwt of gold per ton, had been proved. The Hyderabad Gold Mines Co. Ltd was formed in 1948 with an authorized capital of Rs 1 crore and a pilot plant commenced crushing in September of that year. It was replaced by the main mill in November 1949, to which a cyanidation plant was added in August 1950 for the recovery of gold from the tailings. The present mill has a capacity of 150 tons a day but it is proposed to double this in the near future in order to increase production and reduce working costs.   From 1948 to 1951 inclusive 20,336 fine oz. of gold, valued at Rs 70,98,290 had been recovered. The ore reserves at the end of September 1951 were estimated to be 128,502 tons of an average value of 5·32 dwt and excluding some 80,000 tons of prospective ore of an average grade of 5·34 dwt of gold per ton. It is noteworthy that besides the single vein previously known in the Village Mine, at least two new ones containing gold in profitable quantities have been found.

Some geologists believe that an extension of the Kolar field may possibly be found in that part of the Chittoor district of Andhra which lies to the south-east of Kolar; in any case it has been proved that the autoclastic conglomerates of the Kolar field occur again near Bisanattam where, in addition, a tongue of Champion granite-gneiss projects into hornblende schists of Dharwar age. Between 1894 and 1902 quartz veins in this vicinity were opened up to a depth of over 750 feet by the Mysore Reefs Kangundi Gold Mining Co. Ltd, and approximately 10,000 tons of ore were crushed and amalgamated with a recovery, it is said, of about 6,000 oz. of gold. Several further ventures have been made here during the past 30 years, the latest being by the South Kolar Gold Mines Ltd of Bombay, who between 1945 and 1948 partially reconditioned the old shaft, dewatered the mine to the 320-foot level and sampled the exposed vein. This is said to be in hornblende schist, to average 22 inches in width, to strike north-north-west and south-south-east, to dip westerly and to carry an average value of 5·19 dwt of gold. Some mining was done between July 1949 and June 1950, when operations ceased through lack of capital after recovery of a small amount of gold. Small amounts of scheelite (calcium tungstate, $CaWO_4$) and of cassiterite, the oxide of tin, SnO_2, have been detected in the old dumps at Kangundi. The auriferous quartz veins, according to S. Krishnaswamy, branch off and peter out into detached stringers and veins as traced southwards. The gold content is generally very low, seldom exceeding 2 dwt per ton.

Of the many old workings in Mysore, only the Bellara mine in Tumkur district was being developed by the Government of the State, under a ten-year scheme to remove all the gold-bearing quartz obtainable before the locality is submerged by the Lakkavalli reservoir, and till 1953–4, 5,447 *tolas* of crude sponge gold, valued at Rs 5,53,407, had been obtained before its closure.

In 1874, R. Bruce Foote found an auriferous quartz vein near Dambal, Dharwar district, Bombay, on the great belt of Dharwar rocks, known as the Dambal-Chiknayakanhalli band, which stretches from the southern part of Bombay State into southern Mysore. The area contains abundant ancient workings and was prospected between 1902 and 1904 by the Dharwar Reefs Gold Mining Co. Ltd, who started crushing in 1907, their ore coming from a mine near Kabligatti. In that year 4,916 oz. of gold were obtained and in 1908 the output increased to 7,242 oz.; but it then began to decline, and the mine, together with others that were under development in the neighbourhood, was closed in 1911. The Kabligatti vein system has been followed southwards for 8 miles into Sangli, and a parallel series occurs near Hosur, about 3½ miles to the west. These were also under development in 1906 both by the Dharwar Reefs Company and by other concerns, but none of them ever reached the producing stage. Auriferous quartz veins are very numerous in this region, but they are individually of no great extent or thickness; belonging to two separate series, an older of blue, diaphanous quartz, associated with the metamorphosed igneous rocks, and a younger of ferruginous, white quartz veins, associated at Kabligatti with carbonaceous phyllites, they finally dispel the older idea that the gold is confined exclusively to blue quartz veins of the Kolar type. The ancient workings, which in places reached a depth of 300 feet, are restricted to two veins of white quartz, though actually both varieties may be gold-bearing. It should be stressed that although the veins of Kolar and some of the other goldfields are genetic associates of the Champion granite-gneiss, gold has also been found in veins of later periods, some of them perhaps post-Archaean. The total recorded production of the Dharwar field was worth £80,209.

A belt of Dharwar schists stretching north and south through the Anantapur district of Andhra, known as the Penukonda belt, contains several large quartz veins associated with chloritic and hornblendic schists. The occurrence of old workings near Ramgiri led in 1905 to the formation of the Anantapur Gold Field Ltd, and in 1908 to that of the North Anantapur and Jibutil Gold Mines Companies, with mines of the same names. At the former a depth of 1,150 feet was reached by 1924, when operations ceased after yielding gold to the value of £782,023.

The Chota Nagpur division of Bihar is traversed from east to west by a series of argillites, phyllites, talc and mica schists of Dharwar age which enclose quartz veins of both types mentioned earlier, but here the gold is found, as a rule, in the opaque white and younger veins. Many altered basic intrusives related to epidiorites occur in the gold-bearing areas. Both veins and old workings are very numerous, and small quantities of alluvial gold occur in most of the streams, where its extraction on a small scale by the tribesfolk of Singhbhum is still carried on. Following the discovery of rich ground in the Sonapet valley in 1888, in 1890 a gold boom, centred on this region, occurred in Calcutta, and thirty-two companies, with a total capital of nearly £1,000,000, were formed, but by the end of 1892 only two of them remained in existence. Later investigations by J. M. Maclaren proved that the gravels are too low in gold to be worked profitably. Various localities are known in which auriferous veins occur, but in this case again, assay results have been uniformly poor, though favourable territory for further prospecting is believed to exist. The distribution of the gold-bearing veins of Singhbhum suggests, according to J. A. Dunn, a relationship with the late basic intrusive phase of the Dalma volcanic rocks. The discovery of old workings near Kundrukocha, in Dhalbhum, close to the Mayurbhanj border, on a series of veins of blue-grey quartz in Dharwarian phyllites, led to the formation of the Dhalbhum Gold & Minerals Prospecting Co. Ltd, which recovered 6,034 oz., valued at £26,839, between the years 1915 and 1920. All but 250 oz. of this total came from one pocket at Porojarna. According to Sir Lewis Fermor, the richer veins average only about 4 dwt to the ton, though the Porojarna shoot averaged about 20 dwt. The Kundrukocha mines have been leased to E. O. Murray and one of them is again being worked intermittently.

Certain auriferous quartz veins which occur in quartzites, phyllites and quartz schists and are traceable for about three-quarters of a mile at Lawa in Manbhum, have been investigated recently by the Lawa Gold Mines Ltd. The gold content is said to average 7 dwt per ton and to be associated with copper ores and tellurides. Further occurrences of gold-bearing quartz veins are known at Ichagar, Burndih and Maysara, in the neighbourhood of Lawa. At the last-named locality, where rich ore pockets are sometimes found, according to D. K. Chandra, a Company entitled Maysara Development Ltd was engaged in prospecting work.

Dr J. A. Dunn believed that no gold deposits have as yet been found in southern Chota Nagpur which offer scope for the activities of mining companies with large capital, adding, however, that there are opportunities for individual prospectors and even for small syndicates. New veins may still be discovered, particularly in the schist zone underlying the lavas of the Iron Ore Series, and prospecting should be concentrated on the so-called blue quartz veins.

The gold occurrences of the Mingin Hills in Upper Burma, though of no commercial value, as far as is known at present, are of interest in that they furnish an example of the occurrence of the metal entirely different from that found in the Dharwarian rocks of the Indian peninsula. The hills which lie between the Mu and Meza streams, both tributaries of the Irrawaddy, are, according to F. Noetling, formed of eruptive volcanic rocks. Five localities are known on the eastern flanks where veins containing auriferous pyrites occur, and three others where the mineral has been mined by the Burmese from volcanic ash. One of the veins was mined near Kyaukpazat between 1898 and 1903, when the pay shoot was lost and the enterprise abandoned. This vein averaged 3½ feet in width, 240 feet in length and was followed down to a depth of 420 feet. It was occasionally clean but more often well mineralized, carrying 5 per cent of chalcopyrite, pyrite, galena, franklinite and small amounts of altaite, the telluride of lead. The country rocks were tuffs and breccias of andesitic facies and Tertiary age, intruded in places by quartz diorites. The total production from the Kyaukpazat mine was probably worth between £19,000 and £20,000.

Alluvial gold is found in the sands of many rivers in India, Pakistan and Burma, in fact, as La Touche points out, there is hardly a province of the former Indian Empire in which its recovery from river sands is not, or has not been, practised by the inhabitants, though the quantity which appears in the official returns from such sources is insignificant and the statistics are known to be incomplete. In the case of rivers draining the Indo-Gangetic plain, including the valley of the Brahmaputra in Assam, the metal is derived not only from rocks which were its original home, but for the most part from others into which it was introduced along with the transported material of which they are composed. The regular recovery of a few ounces used to be reported annually from the Singhbhum district of Bihar; from the Katha and Upper Chindwin districts of Burma; from Kashmir, where washing is carried on along the Indus valley in Gilgit and Baltistan; from the Punjab, where it is practised in the Attock, Ambala and Jhelum districts, and from the Garhwal and Bijnor districts of Uttar Pradesh. The alluvial miner in these and other regions is, as often as not, a cultivator who adds to his meagre income by indulging in the speculative pastime of gold-washing when the crops do not demand his immediate attention. The small quantities of the precious metal so obtained in most cases probably find their way direct to the local goldsmith to be turned into jewellery, and in so doing short-circuit the path to the revenue collector's office.

Dr J. M. Maclaren, who made a searching investigation of the whole matter, concluded that in few countries is alluvial gold more widely distributed than it is in India, which in this case includes both Pakistan and Burma, and in few countries does it show less tendency to aggregation under the influence of running water. He pointed out that wherever streams drain areas of ancient schistose rocks and possess the proper gradients for the deposition of gravel, they carry small amounts of gold. Such conditions apply in many parts of Mysore, Madras, Bombay, Hyderabad, Madhya Bharat and Chota Nagpur, and to these we may add Upper Burma, Tenasserim and the Shan States, Chitral, parts of the upper Indus valley and certain tributaries of the Brahmaputra in Upper Assam; 'but in no case,' wrote Maclaren, 'so far as is yet known, are the gravels sufficiently rich to warrant European examination, though they may in many cases afford a few weeks' employment during the cold weather to the local washer, who is content to work for a return of $1\frac{1}{2}$ to 2 pence per day'. Maclaren's own investigations in the richest streams of Chota Nagpur proved that the alluvial ground contained on the average about 1 to $1\frac{1}{2}$ grains of gold per cubic yard, and that the six inches or so of the bottom gravel, which under normal circumstances would naturally be the richest, yielded not more than 2 grains per cubic yard. Maclaren's work was done in 1903 and in the intervening years nothing has been discovered to lead to any modification of his opinions. Discussing them in 1942, after his own extensive surveys in Singhbhum, Dr J. A. Dunn wrote: 'Washing for alluvial gold is likely to continue as an intermittent occupation of the villagers in certain localities. There is little probability that alluvial deposits will be found such as would pay a company to sluice on modern methods. The values quoted by Maclaren of 1 to 2 grains of gold per cubic yard in the Sonapet valley would be payable under certain conditions of topography, rainfall and depth of alluvium. But in the Sonapet valley the thin alluvium with rocky outcrops is not conducive to sluicing on a large scale with low costs, and any attempt to do so must be condemned at once.' It must be recognized that the seasonal changes from the low waters of the dry weather to the raging floods of the rains, which characterize rivers subject to the periodic variations of a monsoon climate, do not bring about the tranquil conditions necessary for the accumulation of thick gold-bearing gravel deposits.

Gold-washing thrived at one time in those parts of Jashpur, Madhya Pradesh, which lie south of Latitude 22°39', within the drainage areas of the Ib river and its tributaries the Maini and Sonajori; old workings in the gravels are very numerous and small-scale work still persists. Recent investigations have shown that the values are found mainly in those gravels which lie on a gneissic bed rock and under alluvium which may range up to 30 feet in thickness. This gravel itself is up to 10 feet in thickness and carries an average gold content of 2 grains per cubic yard, but the available reserves total little more than one quarter of a million cubic yards and are scattered in patches up and down the banks of several streams. The gold has been traced to quartz veins traversing the gneissose granite country rock and random samples yielded up to 16 dwt per ton.

Similar deposits are still being worked in the Koraput district of Orissa, particularly in the Kolab river below its junction with the Rongpani; in the Rongpani itself as well as in its tributaries the Jan and Dharan *gedda*, and in the Garia *nadi* where it debouches from the hills near Doraguda. The yields are said to average 1 to 3 grains per cubic yard. Other similar operations continue in the alluvium of the Brahmani river in Bonai and Bamra and in the bed of the Sona *nadi* in Kharsawan. The alluvium of certain streams in Khairagarh and Kanker, Madhya Pradesh, is known to be auriferous, while a few ounces are still recovered every year from the Sona *nadi*, near Kalagarh, in Garhwal, Uttar Pradesh.

The sparsely distributed alluvial gold of several of the Himalayan rivers and their tributaries, not only in Garhwal, but also in Kumaun, the Kangra valley, the Simla Hills, the Punjab and the North-West Frontier Province of Pakistan, is still won on a small scale, as, for instance, on the Indus around and above Attock, on the Soan in the Potwar, and on the Teria Panjkora and Swat tributaries in the north-western part of the North-West Frontier Province. The Bunhar and Kahan, tributaries of the Jhelum river, also contain alluvial gold. Certain of the acid volcanic rocks north of Injan Dheri in the Mardan district contain small quantities of gold; tuffaceous rhyolites collected by A. L. Coulson in this vicinity yielded 0·3 to 4·3 dwt per ton. These rocks may be the source of the alluvial gold of the Kabul river and its tributary the Kalpani *nala* which have been the scene of washing operations in past years. Gold-washing has been carried on in Chitral from time immemorial as a State monopoly, the workers performing their task in return for the small estates they enjoy and never exerting themselves to any great extent. During the summer the Chitral river is in flood and in the winter the water is too cold to allow work to be done; the working season therefore only extends from mid-September to the end of November in the autumn, and from mid-March to the end of May in the spring. The only tributaries of the Chitral river which carry gold are the Reshun, Kuragh and Roman *gols*, and although washing operations are prosecuted for some considerable distance upstream towards Mastuj, they are concentrated mainly downstream, between Drosh and the Afghan border. Usually, attention is confined to the recent deposits, but in some places, according to Habib Rahman of the Geological Survey of Pakistan, as in the neighbourhood of Dammar Nisar, older gravels lying 15 to 20 feet above the present level of the river are worked.

The pioneers of gold dredging in Burma were W. R. Moore and J. Terndrup, through whose enterprise a company known as the Burma Gold Dredging Co. Ltd was formed which carried on operations in the upper reaches of the Irrawaddy and about the confluence of the N'mai Hka and the Mali Hka, in the Myitkyina district, between 1903 and 1918. The average value of the gravels was about 3 grains per cubic yard, and a total of 56,624 oz. of gold, worth £217,381, was recovered, together with small quantities of platinum and its sister metals. The dredges were eventually removed to the Tavoy district and helped in the successful inauguration of the tin dredging industry there. The Mandalay Gold Dredging Co. Ltd obtained a large concession in the Lower Chindwin river between Minsin and Homalin, but the dredger sent there in 1905 was wrecked on the way and the undertaking abandoned. In 1905, a dredger erected on the Namma river, a tributary of the Salween in the Northern Shan States, where preliminary exploration is alleged to have proved the existence of approximately 40 million cubic yards of gravel, with an average value of 5·43 grains of gold per cubic yard, was found unable to perform its task owing to the cementation of the ground by calcium carbonate.

Many localities where indigenous gold-washing is, or has been, carried on, in the Chindwin, Katha and Myitkyina districts are listed in the writings of H. S. Bion, H. L. Chhibber and E. L. G. Clegg, and to these V. P. Sondhi has added others mainly in the Southern Shan States. The richest occurrences are perhaps those of the Uyu valley, a tributary of the Chindwin, which it enters near Homalin, but they are said to be so intermixed with barren sands and gravels that systematic large-scale operations would not be profitable. New occurrences described by V. P. Sondhi include an almost constant band of gold-bearing gravel, three feet in thickness, at the base of river deposits in parts of the Panglang valley, worked in the past by Chinese miners from pits sunk through its alluvial covering; the presence of gold in streams draining areas occupied by Chaung Magyi rocks between the Salween valley and Kengtung, and the auriferous gravel and boulder terraces in many of the valleys between Kengtung and the Thai border. In the Mong Hpayak, Monglen and Hawngluk valleys, the gravels are generally buried under 5 to 10 feet of barren overburden. The gravels of a number of streams draining the northern side of the Mogok massif, as well as those of other tributaries of the Shweli river in Mongmit, are also known to carry gold. While much still remains to be done, such systematic prospecting of the gold-bearing alluvial deposits of Burma as has been undertaken in the past has proved that, in most cases, they are too lean to hold out hopes of successful dredging. It is possible, however, that better ground remains to be discovered, especially in the upper branches of the Irrawaddy and Chindwin and their tributaries.

No attempt is made here to discuss the intricate ebb and flow of the import and export trades in gold bullion and coins into and out of India in pre-independence days: it must suffice to repeat the official opinion that at the present time India is just self-sufficient as regards her own requirements of gold, which are mostly for ornaments, and that, as a consequence, some measure of control was essential for conservation purposes. Before the last war gold was exported in huge quantities, the annual average amount for the five years ending 1938 being 3,725,383 oz., valued at Rs 34,34,94,121, against imports of 115,110 oz., valued at Rs 1,14,52,579. This led to the introduction of controls to regulate the outward flow of the precious metal. For the three years ending 1946, exports averaged 25,291 oz., worth Rs 42,95,358, and by 1948 no gold was leaving the country. Imports for the same three years averaged 66,098 oz., valued at Rs 1,30,71,678.

SILVER

More than half of the world's silver, which in the period 1934-8 averaged some 241½ million ounces yearly, is said to be won not from silver mines, but as a by-product from argentiferous lead, zinc and copper ores, and although many of the lead ores which have been found in small quantities at numerous localities in India,

Pakistan and Burma have proved to be silver-bearing, not one of them has yet proved of any economic importance, with the single exception of those of Bawdwin in the Shan States (see LEAD).

The silver minerals in the Bawdwin ore are not visible to the naked eye, but by microscopic study J. A. Dunn demonstrated the presence of pyrargyrite at all depths in the mine, either alone or replacing tetrahedrite, boulangerite and bournonite. Pyrargyrite, or Ruby Silver Ore, is a sulphantimonite of silver, $3Ag_2S.Sb_2S_3$, and contains $59 \cdot 8$ per cent of the metal; tetrahedrite, a sulphantimonite of copper, $4Cu_2S.Sb_2S_3$; boulangerite, a sulphantimonite of lead, $5PbS.2Sb_2S_3$; and bournonite, a sulphantimonite of both lead and copper, $2PbS.Cu_2S.Sb_2S_3$. Some of the silver is also present in solid solution in the galena of the Bawdwin ores. As a rough indication of the amount of silver present in the ore, it may be taken that the general mixture of galena and zinc blende as mined contains approximately 1 oz. of silver for every unit per cent of lead. Taken over a number of years an average of 1 oz. of silver was obtained for every $1 \cdot 1$ per cent of lead.

It is instructive to trace the passage of the silver in its progress from the mine to the refinery, for the treatment of the run-of-mine ore in the milling and flotation processes resulted in an increased percentage of silver in some of the products and a smaller quantity in others. For instance, in one pre-war year, the ore delivered to the mill from the mine contained:

Silver $20 \cdot 5$ oz.; Lead $24 \cdot 93$ per cent; Zinc $12 \cdot 76$ per cent. In the next table the composition of some of the products made in the mill at Nam Tu from this ore is shown: all of them, with the exception of the zinc concentrates exported to Europe for treatment, were smelted on the spot.

COMPOSITIONS OF MILLED PRODUCTS OF ORE FROM BAWDWIN

PRODUCT			ASSAY VALUE			
			Silver	Lead	Zinc	Copper
			oz.	%	%	%
Coarse Concentrate	..	..	$45 \cdot 86$	$65 \cdot 03$	$9 \cdot 10$	$0 \cdot 33$
Float Concentrate	..	..	$40 \cdot 24$	$70 \cdot 18$	$7 \cdot 32$	$0 \cdot 50$
Copper Concentrate	..	..	$135 \cdot 70$	$34 \cdot 77$	$13 \cdot 06$	$9 \cdot 85$
Iron Concentrate	..	..	$11 \cdot 52$	$14 \cdot 41$	$12 \cdot 15$	$0 \cdot 57$
Zinc Concentrate	..	..	$9 \cdot 02$	$6 \cdot 01$	$51 \cdot 66$	..

The assay figures demonstrate how the silver is associated with the lead and copper rather than with the zinc, as indeed is only to be expected from the mineralogical constitution of the ores. A series of average assay values of some varieties of hard lead and of the copper matte produced by smelting these concentrates is given below.

COMPOSITIONS OF SOME SMELTER PRODUCTS MADE FROM BAWDWIN ORE

SOURCE	Silver	Lead	Copper
	oz.	%	%
Hard Lead from Ore	68·13	96·92	. . . .
Hard Lead from Copper Concentrates	301·67	94·88	. . . .
Hard Lead from Iron Concentrates. .	72·05	94·84	. . . .
High-Grade Copper Matte	82·29	27·72	43·67

The silver was finally recovered from the hard lead in the refinery where the Parkes' process was in use. Statistics of silver production at Nam Tu from 1909 to 1940 are summarized in the table below. As the ore reserves at Bawdwin at the time of the Japanese invasion in 1942 totalled over three million tons with a silver content of over 15 oz. per ton, it is evident that large quantities will be forthcoming when mining operations resume their former activities. The processing of surface ore stocks during the year ended 30 June 1952 yielded a total of 231,670 ounces of refined silver. The reopening of the mine is described under LEAD, page 162.

PRODUCTION OF REFINED SILVER AT NAM TU, 1909-40

PERIOD	QUANTITY	VALUE
	oz.	£
1909–13	399,715	46,460
1914–18	4,831,504	679,222
1919–23	17,639,125	3,189,110
1924–8	28,632,070	3,766,634
1929–33	32,288,126	2,718,282
1934–8	29,669,932	2,906,625
1939–40	11,920,000	1,143,783
TOTAL . .	125,380,472	14,450,116

This total of more than 125 million ounces does not represent all the silver yielded by the mine, for varying small amounts remained in the zinc concentrates which were doubtless recovered in the countries to which they were sold; moreover, the copper matte which was exported for refining also contained a great deal. In the 162,241 tons of matte, valued at £3,790,113, produced from 1924 until the end of 1940, it is calculated that there were approximately 12½ million ounces of silver, for its average content only once fell below 60 oz. per ton, attained a maximum of over 93 oz., and usually ranged between 70 and 80 oz. per ton. It should not be forgotten that the Chinese mined this ore deposit for its silver content alone for centuries, and the vast quantities of cupellation slags which they left behind were some measure of the large amounts of the metal which they recovered. Though primarily a lead-zinc-copper sulphide orebody, it is easy to understand how it obtained its Burmese name of *baw dwin*, or 'silver mine'. The maximum silver production, as far as European mining is concerned, was attained in 1928, with 7,404,728 oz., which were worth £890,004. In later years somewhat smaller amounts were extracted, as a natural result of the deliberate reduction of the throughput of lead ore. India was the natural market for the Burmese silver, but in 1932, for the first time in its history, the Burma Corporation failed to dispose of its silver in India, whereupon the monthly production was shipped to England for sale in the open markets of the world. Production of refined silver from accumulated ore stocks commenced once more at Nam Tu in 1948, and from that time until the end of 1951, 381,093 oz. had been recovered.

The gold from the Kolar field of Mysore nearly always contains some silver which is recovered in the course of refining operations, and small quantities of similar origin were obtained from the Anantapur goldfield during its active life. The available statistics of the silver derived from these sources are summarized in the following table :

SILVER RECOVERED FROM INDIAN GOLD REFINING, 1915–50

PERIOD			ANANTAPUR GOLDFIELD		KOLAR GOLDFIELD	
			oz.	£	oz.	£
1915–18	..	..	4,324	607	....	....
1919–23	..	..	2,895	531	124,940*	22,589
1924–8	..	..	478**	47	109,781	14,060
1929–33	..	..	....	....	112,212	11,576
1934–8	..	..	....	....	122,250	13,221
1939–43	..	..	....	....	107,683	16,514
1944–8	..	..	....	....	63,434	18,917
1949–50	..	..	....	....	26,951	9,048

* For four years only. Returns commenced in 1920.
** For four years only. No production in 1928.

The lead and zinc concentrates from Zawar in Udaipur, Rajasthan, contain respectively more than 24 and 5 oz. of silver per ton. The recovery of the silver commenced at the lead smelter of the Metal Corporation of India at Tundoo in the Jharia coalfield in February 1954, and up to June 1954, 63,348 fine ounces of silver had been produced.

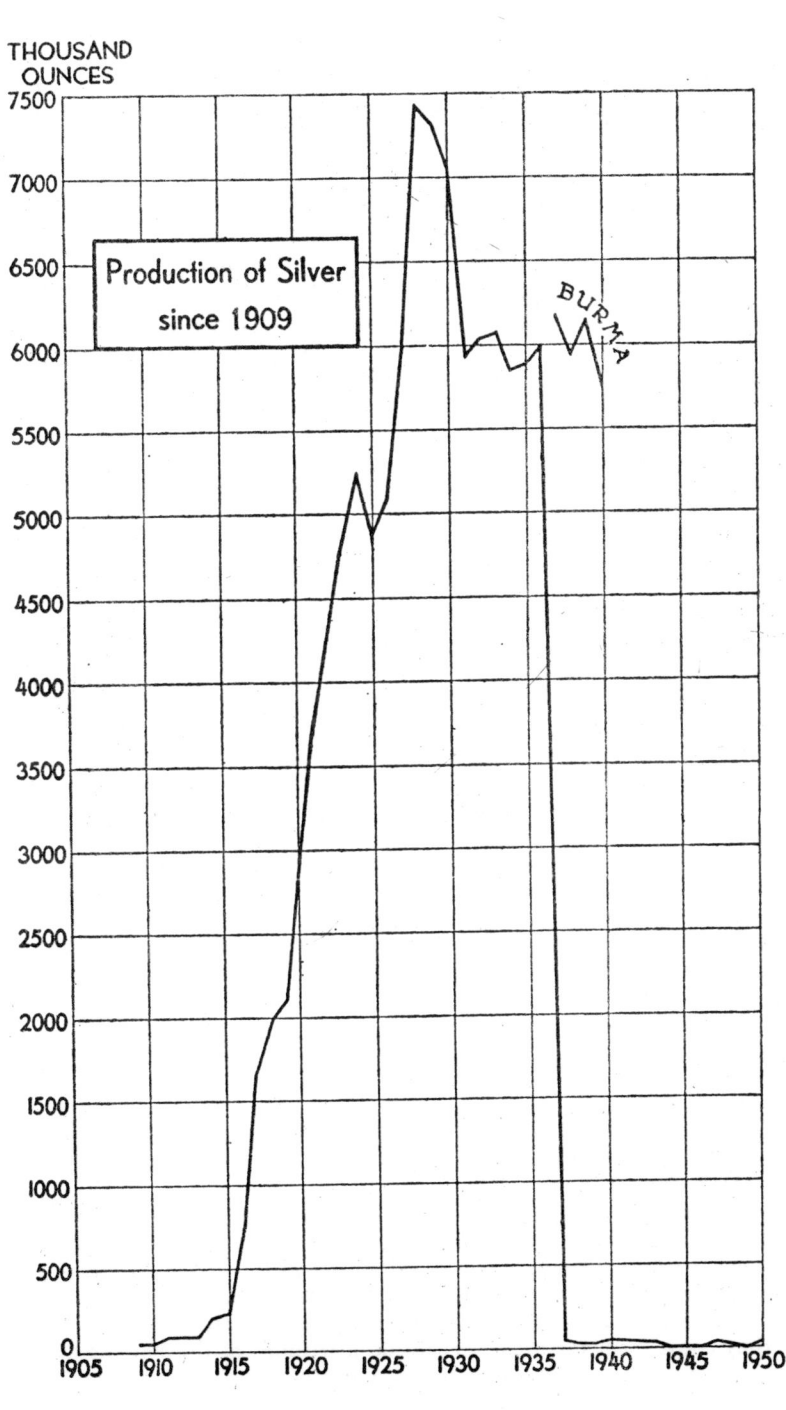

THOUSAND
OUNCES

Production of Silver
since 1909

BURMA

India imports large quantities of silver bullion, the average quantity for the two years 1949 and 1950 being 103,531 oz., valued at Rs 4,29,597.

METALS OF THE PLATINUM GROUP

Platinum, Palladium, Rhodium, Iridium, Osmium, Ruthenium

Platinum, which occurs naturally in the metallic form, is almost always associated with varying quantities of the related elements palladium, rhodium, iridium, osmium and ruthenium. Iridosmine, or osmiridium, is a natural alloy of iridium and osmium in variable amounts, and small percentages of the other members of the group are also usually present in it. In 1831, James Prinsep proved that a button of white metal, which had been sent to the Asiatic Society of Bengal, was an alloy containing 25 per cent of platinum and 40 per cent of iridosmine, the remainder consisting of gold, iron, arsenic and lead. The specimen came from Ava, in Burma, then, as now, an independent country, and Major Burney, the first British Resident at the Burmese Court, later explained how it was obtained with the gold dust from streams entering the Chindwin river from the west, near Kanni. Captain Hannay, in 1857, stated that platinum occurs in appreciable quantity in the auriferous sands of the Hukawng valley, and H. S. Bion, who examined the gold-bearing alluvial deposits of the Chindwin and its tributary the Uyu in 1912, reported that platinum with osmiridium was detected in almost every locality, but in very small amounts, its mode of occurrence being the same as that of the gold. In 1927, H. L. Chhibber investigated alluvial gold workings in another portion of the Uyu valley in the Myitkyina district, and found small quantities of platinum as a constant associate of the gold. It was carefully removed from the gold concentrates by the local washers and then thrown away.

Platinum and iridosmine then are characteristic associates of the alluvial gold of the rivers in the north of Burma, and it is not surprising therefore to find that ' platinum ' was recovered regularly by the Burma Gold Dredging Co. Ltd during its treatment of the gravels of the Irrawaddy and its branches in the Myitkyina district, between 1903 and 1918. The records are probably incomplete, but they show a recovery of 219 oz., valued at £1,332, between 1911 and 1914.

It is more than a coincidence that platinum and iridosmine were identified by Mallet in 1882, accompanying gold in concentrates from the sands of the Noa Dihing river of Assam, for this river drains the opposite flanks of the Patkoi range, indeed, the distribution of the occurrences generally leads to the suspicion that they come from the great serpentine intrusions of the Patkois and

Arakan Yomas. The iridosmine from the Noa Dihing valley probably belongs to the osmium-rich variety known as siserskite. Sperrylite, platinum diarsenide, $PtAs_2$, the only known native compound of the element, has been detected in heavy sand concentrates from some of the tributaries of the Irrawaddy in Myitkyina district, Burma.

The examination of a number of samples of Indian stream gold, stored in the Geological Survey Museum in Calcutta, proved the presence of platinum in specimens from streams in Singhbhum, Manbhum and in the Brahmini river in Orissa, and led Mallet to conclude: 'It seems not improbable that platinum is somewhat widely diffused in the southern part of Chota Nagpur, and perhaps throughout a larger area. But the specimens do not in themselves give ground for believing that it occurs in more than minute quantity. It is, however, possible that the gold washers may sometimes find grains sufficiently large to attract their attention, and that they reject them as useless.' Amongst the specimens containing platinum was one from the Gurma river near Dhadka, in Manbhum, and many years later E. O. Murray obtained silvery grains of platinum from much the same locality while panning for gold, the identification of the metal being confirmed later in the Geological Survey laboratory. J. A. Dunn thought that the origin of this platinum is possibly connected with the basic intrusives which crop out in the schists north of the Dalma lavas.

Traces of platinum have been reported in bauxite from Dhangaon, Jabalpur district, Madhya Pradesh, and in bauxitic mud residues from Tungar Hill, Bassein, Bombay.

Apart from the uses of platinum and palladium in jewellery and for other decorative purposes, all the members of the group possess properties which make them of great value in many branches of industry. Such properties include their high melting-points, freedom from attack by most chemicals, high strength at elevated temperatures, resistance to electrical spark erosion, colour, reflectivity and catalytic activity. Platinum provides the chemist with both laboratory and works utensils; for large-scale operations platinum-clad or lined equipment is available. Alone, or alloyed with other members of the group, it is the catalytic agent for the conversion of sulphur-dioxide into the trioxide, in the manufacture of sulphuric acid; in the production of high-octane petrol and other petroleum products; in the production of nitric acid by the oxidation of ammonia, a process in which gauzes made of platinum-rhodium alloys are employed, and, with palladium, in many hydrogenation operations. The electro-chemical industry uses platinum anodes in the preparation of hydrogen peroxide and other highly oxidized substances, and anodes of platinum-iridium alloys in electro-plating and the recovery of metals from waste solutions. For the commercial manufacture of glass fibres platinum nozzles, being resistant to the attack of molten glass, are essential. In the production of rayon, or artificial silk, the viscose solution is forced through tiny holes in a spinneret immediately before its coagulation into thread. These holes must be of extremely accurate dimensions and must retain their size and shape in constant use, entailing great resistance to both wear and corrosion; gold-platinum and platinum-rhodium alloys are therefore widely used. In the electrical trades, alloys of platinum with one or more of its sister elements, or with tungsten in some cases, have many applications, including contact points in magnetos, coils, sparking-plugs, telephone and other relays; in resistance thermometers, thermocouples for measuring high temperatures, furnace heating elements to operate at temperatures up to 1600° C. and so forth.

Palladium, like platinum, has both ornamental and useful applications and is now available in many prefabricated forms for personal adornment and decorative purposes, including foil beaten in the same manner as gold. Apart from the alloys already mentioned, there are others in which it plays an important part, particularly those employed in dental metallurgy for various fittings and clips. Owing to its remarkable power of adsorbing gases, palladium is an excellent catalyst for hydrogenation and dehydrogenation processes. In a spongy form it possesses the unusual property of adsorbing about 900 times its own volume of hydrogen and for this reason may be employed in the purification of this gas for special purposes.

Iridium is employed mainly as a hardener for alloys of the softer platinum-palladium group, particularly in the alloys used by the electrical industry, and in the manufacture of hypodermic needles, dental plates and surgical instruments, as well as in many forms of chemical apparatus. While the hardness of native platinum may vary between 4 and 4½ on the Mohs' scale, that of the natural alloy of iridium and osmium ranges between 6 and 7.

Osmium is the heaviest of all the metals and, with a melting point of 2700° C., the most refractory member of the platinum group, while its hardness is only exceeded by that of iridium. Iridosmine is widely employed in the tips of gold fountain-pen nibs on account of its qualities of hardness and resistance to ink corrosion. Similar alloys are used for bearings in watches and compasses and in the contact points of electrical devices.

Rhodium is a lustrous white metal which is said to be as malleable and ductile as silver. It is almost insoluble in all acids and has a higher melting point than either platinum or palladium— 1995° C., compared with 1733° C. and 1555° C. respectively—and it possesses a more efficient reflecting surface than chromium; thus, apart from its utility in catalysts and alloys it is plated on to mirrors for searchlights and lamps, on to silverware to prevent tarnishing, and on to special electrical contacts and components to give them hard and resistant coverings. To the decorative alloys of platinum it imparts a brilliant surface after polishing.

Ruthenium, the rarest member of the group, occurs in iridosmine, but as a rule only to the extent of 4 or 5 per cent. It is described as white, hard and brittle, and next to osmium as the most infusible metal of the group. It is employed entirely as a hardening element in platinum and palladium-base alloys.

The metals of the platinum group are both rare and costly. Forty years ago the cost of platinum was a little less than that of gold, but by 1920, owing to its introduction into jewellery, it brought seven or eight times the price of gold. In later years, owing to increased production in Canada and elsewhere, the prices of platinum and its relatives decreased greatly. In the second edition of this book, published in 1936, the prevailing prices for August, 1935, are given as platinum £7 per oz., iridium between £9 and £10 per oz.; palladium, the cheapest metal of the group, about £4 and osmium between £7 and £9 per oz. By 1950 they had shared in the spectacular rises in the market value of most metals and, on the London market, platinum was then quoted at £27 per oz., or over twice the prevailing price of gold; palladium at £7 to £10 per oz.; rhodium at £40; iridium at £55; and osmium at £70 per oz.; while ruthenium was obtainable at about the same cost as platinum.

The world's production of the platinum metals in 1948 is estimated to have been about 532,000 oz., to which Russia is thought to have contributed some 125,000 oz., while Canada gave 121,404 oz. of platinum and 108,343 oz. of the related metals, and South Africa 68,923 oz. of platinum and 5,520 oz. of osmiridium. By 1950 the South African output had increased to a total of 256,385 oz. and that of Canada to 269,442 oz.

The Canadian production is a by-product from the smelting of the Sudbury nickel-copper ores, in which the platinum metals and gold are present only to the extent of roughly two parts per million parts of ore, but, because of the large tonnage of ore dealt with, the actual output of these precious metals is very considerable. The sludges and residues which contain them are dealt with at the refinery of the Mond Nickel Co. Ltd at Acton, England. Most of the primary platinum deposits, including those of Canada, the Bushveldt in South Africa and the Urals region of Russia, are genetically associated with basic and ultrabasic rocks of the gabbro and peridotite families. Osmiridium is also a by-product of gold mining in the Transvaal. From the primary deposits, secondary ones of an alluvial, placer character are formed and have been worked on a large scale in the Urals, Colombia, Ethiopia, Alaska, Sierra Leone and elsewhere. All Indian ultrabasic rocks, especially the occurrences of dunite and similar types found in the neighbourhood of chromite deposits, and the eluvial and placer deposits derived from them, should be prospected for platinum, bearing in mind the fact that it was not a metal in which the miners of former times had any particular interest.

CHAPTER III

THE MORE IMPORTANT NON-FERROUS METALS

COPPER

The copper ores of peninsular India, as V. Ball first pointed out, occur both in the older crystalline rocks and in several of the younger groups, as, for example, in those of Cuddapah, Bijawar and Aravalli age. In extra-peninsular India they are found for the most part in highly metamorphosed rocks, the precise age-relationships of which are not in all cases clear as yet. The commonest ore is the sulphide of copper and iron, copper pyrites or chalcopyrite, $Cu_2S.Fe_2S_3$, but near the outcrops it is usually altered into the green basic carbonate, malachite, $2CuO.CO_2.H_2O$, or the blue basic carbonate, azurite, $3CuO.2CO_2.H_2O$. As a general rule, to which, however, there are some notable exceptions, Indian copper ores are not found in true lodes, but are either sparsely disseminated, or are locally concentrated in more or less extensive bunches or nests in the enclosing rocks; occasionally, cracks and small fissures have been filled with infiltrated ore and thus resemble true lodes.

Copper-bearing minerals have been reported from practically every State in India; from Baluchistan, the North-West Frontier region and the Punjab, in Pakistan; from the Shan States and the districts of Myitkyina, the Lower Chindwin, Salween, Amherst, Tavoy and Mergui in Burma: in both the peninsular and extra-peninsular regions of India, there are old copper mines of great antiquity whose histories are completely lost. Copper ores were smelted in prehistoric times and may have supplied the needs of the country for many later centuries, but in the days of the early European contacts with India, the mining and smelting of copper ores fell to quite a small scale, and fifty or sixty years ago was only carried on in the most petty manner. In the great majority of cases, the miners were unable to cope with the water which flooded their workings once they attained any noteworthy depth, and, in spite of the fact that labour costs must have been small, the metal which was turned out by the indigenous smelters could not be sold at competitive prices in the home markets against metal imported from abroad. Only the larger occurrences of copper ores can be dealt with here.

In the Singhbhum district of Bihar, a copper-bearing belt delineated by many ancient workings, and some 80 miles in length, commences at Duarparam, on the Bamini river, in the Kera Estate, Singhbhum, and strikes in an easterly direction through Kharsawan and Seraikela into Dhalbhum, where it curves to the south-east through Rakha Mines and Mosaboni, ending to the south-east at Baharagora. The whole region took part in the great mountain-building, fold movements of Archaean times which resulted not only in well-defined geo-anticlines and synclines, but in the over-turning towards the south of the close isoclinal folds which already filled in the broader structures. Then followed the culminating event, the development of a vast zone of overthrust along the southern limb of the central geo-anticline, which had formed the axis of this Archaean range. The rocks to the north, already completely metamorphosed, were thrust bodily against the less altered ones to the south, and along the whole length of the over-thrust shearing was both close and complete. At the same time, extensive intrusions of soda-granite and granophyre were taking place, tongues of which, caught up in the thrust zone, were sheared as completely as the enclosing schists and in places entirely mylon-itized. Two other shear zones indicate parallel lines of movement but do not concern us here. This tectonic history is important, for the movements which it records are the factors that have con-trolled the distribution of the later ore deposits of Singhbhum, and the copper belt for most of its length follows the main zone of over-thrust across the country, while the lead ore deposits of Dhadka, in Manbhum, are probably related to a smaller overthrust further north.

The mineralization of the copper belt is genetically connected with the intrusion of the soda-granite, and its first stage was the formation of apatite-magnetite veins along the fissure planes. The deposition of the sulphide minerals which have formed the copper lodes followed as a second phase, both sets of minerals being re-garded by J. A. Dunn as high-temperature liquations from the same residual soda-granite magma, relief of pressure rather than falling temperature being the controlling agency in the process. In most parts of the belt the copper-bearing minerals are too widely disseminated to reward exploitation in any notable degree, but this does not hold for the important section between Rajdah and Badia. At the Rakha Mines and at Mosaboni, both of which are within this particular section of the belt, the ore channels are best described as sheeted zones, containing one or more veins of solid sulphides together with mineralization of the sheared country rock of both walls. The solid ore may vary from a few inches to several feet in thickness, thinning out or tailing off when continued along the strike direction, to be followed by other occurrences more or less en échelon. The width of the mineralized side walls varies greatly; at the Rakha mines the lode channel contains values across an average width of 5 feet; at Mosaboni the average width is greater than this, and exceptionally has reached a width of 30 feet. At

Mosaboni the country rock is granite, altered to chlorite-biotite-quartz schist along the lode-channel; at the Rakha mines it is quartz schist changed into chlorite-sericite-quartz schist as it approaches the mineralized zone.   The main sulphides are chalcopyrite and pyrrhotite, the magnetic sulphide of iron; the subordinate ore minerals are pyrite, pentlandite (the sulphide of iron and nickel, $2FeS.NiS$), violarite (another sulphide of iron and nickel $(NiFe)_3S_4$), and millerite, nickel sulphide (NiS).   The gangue includes quartz, chlorite, biotite, tourmaline, magnetite and apatite.   At the surface the sulphides have been oxidized, and in the dumps left by the ancient miners malachite, azurite, chrysocolla (a hydrated silicate of copper), cuprite (the red, cuprous oxide, Cu_2O), native copper, and, occasionally, chalcocite (cuprous sulphide, Cu_2S) are to be found.   There are no zones of enrichment, and the products of supergene alteration give place gradually to normal primary sulphides, usually within much less than 200 feet in depth.

The first allusion to the copper ores of Singhbhum appears in a paper by W. Jones, dated 1829, but it was not until 1854, when J. C. Haughton described the old workings of Kharsawan, in the Journal of the Asiatic Society of Bengal, that their existence was definitely established.   About this time, Emil Stoehr was commissioned to examine the deposits on behalf of two Calcutta firms, and his report led to the formation of the first Singhbhum Copper Company in 1857.   It commenced operations in Seraikela, at Namdup and Jamjora, and though it obtained good ore was so burdened by excessive royalties payable to the Rajas of Seraikela and Dhalbhum, by an expensive establishment of Saxon miners and English smelters, by the erection of costly smelting plant and by other premature and excessive expenditure, that it is not surprising that it was dissolved in 1859.   A second concern, the Hindostan (Singhbhum) Copper Company, started mining at Rajdoha in 1862, but by 1864 had shared the fate of the earlier one.   Valentine Ball's classical memoir on the Singhbhum region appeared in 1881, but it was not until 1891, with the formation of the Rajdoha Mining Company, that any further underground exploration was attempted.   This company opened up a lode at Rakha but further work seems to have been prevented owing to lack of funds.   About 1903, Sir Thomas Holland visited the copper belt and, impressed by its potentialities, as well as by the unsatisfactory state of definite knowledge concerning them, arranged for more detailed investigation.   During the years 1906-8, selected localities were systematically drilled by the Geological Survey of India, in a successful campaign which directed renewed attention to the belt and laid the foundations of its modern industrial development.   The Cape Copper Company bought the Rakha mines of the Rajdoha Mining Company in 1908, developed them actively, proved large ore reserves, erected a milling plant and commenced production in 1914.   Smelting commenced in 1918 and continued until March

1923, when work ceased owing to financial difficulties, after the production of 180,095 tons of ore, valued at £224,702, from which 3,550 tons of copper, worth £319,381, had been made.

Between 1911 and 1918, the Cape Copper Company had done a little prospecting at Mosaboni, Laukesra and Surda, localities lying eight to ten miles to the south-south-east of Rakha, on the continuation of the belt in that direction, and in 1920, the Cordoba Copper Company, under the management of John Taylor & Sons, took an option on the Mosaboni area of some 20 square miles from the Cape Copper Company. This option was exercised in 1924, after the Main and Western Lodes at Mosaboni had been developed to a depth of 500 feet, and the existence of considerable ore reserves proved. In 1924, the Indian Copper Corporation of today came into existence as a reconstruction of the Cordoba Copper Company. During this period other prospecting ventures were made in the Sideshur-Kandadih area by the North Anantapur Gold Mines Ltd, who partially developed a copper lode at Chapri, an area which had been already bored between 1918 and 1920 by Messrs Tata Sons Ltd in partnership with Gillanders, Arbuthnot and Co. Again, the Ooregum Gold Mining Co. Ltd sank shafts and discovered a lode at Galudih in Kharsawan.

The existing leases of the Indian Copper Corporation Ltd extend over an area of some 24,089 acres and include the producing mines of Mosaboni, Badia and Dhobani; the two former are connected underground while Dhobani lies somewhat further to the west. Its single lode, which is in epidiorite, was reported to be approaching exhaustion in 1950. By October 1953 the Dhobani mine had been closed owing to lack of profitable ore and in the Badia mine at that time there was little evidence that the ore-shoots of the upper levels were continuing to the deeper ones. At the Mosaboni mine, however, some of the ore-shoots have continued downwards though on a diminishing scale, but this tendency had been counterbalanced by the discovery of a new lode, termed the North Badia, which was then persisting downwards in a more satisfactory manner. A circular shaft of 16 feet internal diameter was then being sunk some 3,500 feet out on the hanging wall side to intersect the lode at No. 18 level, and to continue to No. 20 level, a vertical depth of 2,250 feet. It will provide improved ventilation and give better hoisting facilities, allow development in depth and so determine the continuation of the deposits. In this connexion further secondary sinking will eventually be necessary below the 20th level. Two roughly parallel lodes have been worked at Mosaboni, dipping east at approximately 30° to 35° from the horizontal; they have been developed north and south for a total distance of three miles, and by the end of 1950 to a depth of 2,000 feet. The reserves at that time totalled 3,087,195 short tons, with an average copper content of 2·51 per cent. The ore is conveyed by an aerial ropeway for a distance of about 6 miles to Maubhander, near Ghatsila, where the concentration plant, smelter, refinery and rolling mills of the Corporation are situated. Until 1950, practically all the copper produced was alloyed with zinc and converted into brass, or ' yellow metal ' (62 per cent copper with 38 per cent zinc), which was rolled into sheets and marketed entirely in India, the first sheet to be made having been rolled in 1930. In 1950, however, owing to the scarcity and cost of zinc, it was decided to substitute as far as possible the rolling of copper sheet. The Government of India also placed an order with the Corporation for refined copper ingots, to be supplied at the rate of 200 tons per month during the year 1951. Between 1925 and 1950, 6,788,283 tons of ore were raised, mainly from the Mosaboni mine, of an estimated value of Rs 11,91,18,492, or £8,933,886 approximately. From this ore, over the same period, 124,498 tons of refined copper, averaging about 99·5 per cent copper, were made, to be alloyed with zinc and turned into yellow-metal sheets and circles for the Indian trade. The quantity of refined copper produced in the five years ending 1948 averaged 5,967 tons per annum, compared with 6,235 and 6,510 tons during the five-yearly periods ending 1943 and 1938, respectively. The corresponding figures for the brass made from it were 8,185, 8,523 and 9,817 tons. The averages for the two years ending 1950 were 6,502 tons of copper and 8,980 tons of brass.

Chalcopyrite occurs with the lead-silver-zinc sulphides in certain parts of the great ore deposits at Bawdwin, in the Shan States of Burma, particularly at the northern end of the Chinaman orebody and in the Shan, Meingtha and Chin lodes. The copper is recovered in the course of metallurgical operations at Nam Tu and used to be exported to Europe in the form of matte, which, in addition to some 40 to 44 per cent of copper, contained from 25 to 30 per cent of lead and 70 to 80 oz. of silver to the ton. This material was first produced in 1924, and from that time until 1940, 162,241 tons, valued at £3,790,113, had been shipped. It is estimated to have contained 68,510 tons of copper. Production commenced again in 1948 and from that year to the end of 1951, 302 tons of copper matte had been recovered.

The extensive old workings at Baragunda, Hazaribagh district, Bihar, where copper pyrites occurs in lenticular stringers and disseminations in schists and quartzites, have been the scene of various later, unsuccessful ventures. In 1888, the Bengal Baragunda Copper Company produced 218 tons of refined metal here, but J. A. Dunn, in 1942, considered the deposit to be too small and of too low a grade to be worth reopening.

In Madhya Pradesh copper ores occur near Sleemanabad and Niwar, Jabalpur district, as well as in Narsinghpur, 80 miles to the north, on the same strike. The veins at Sleemanabad are in dolomitic limestone, from 6 inches to 3 feet in width, and contain chalcopyrite, tetrahedrite (the sulphantimonite of copper, $4Cu_2S$.

Sb_2S_3), galena, pyrite and magnetite, with small gold and silver values. They were prospected in 1904-8 and again in 1937, but full information about their size and extent is lacking.

In Andhra there are extensive old workings near Garimanipenta, in Nellore district, which have yielded a few tons of ore in recent years, but which have not yet been systematically investigated in depth. The Chitaldrug district of Mysore has also yielded small quantities of ore from a felsite which cuts the Jogimaradi Trap at Ingladhai.

Copper mining probably persisted longer in Rajasthan than in any other part of the Peninsula. Old workings near Khetri, Babai and Singhana in Jaipur are almost continuous for 15 miles, in the upper part of a zone of slates and schists of Ajabgarh age, and are now in a ruinous, waterlogged condition. Nevertheless, A. M. Heron, a former Director of the Geological Survey of India, believes that ore still exists in sufficient quantity to justify reopening and drainage, while proper prospecting offers possibilities of a large, low-grade undertaking. Cobalt minerals are associated with the copper ores at Babai. J. P. David has more recently described the principal ore as chalcopyrite, occurring in slate as 'irregular stringers and disseminated fine grains, sometimes continuous and always lenticular'. Three average samples of such ore from Barkera contained 0·95, 2·10, and 11·8 per cent of copper, respectively, with traces of cobalt in the third. Another series from Akhwali, near Bagor Fort, contained 2·0, 3·3, 3·5, 5·2, and 12·8 per cent of copper respectively, with traces of cobalt and silver. The oxidized ores, malachite and azurite, are associated with larger quantities of silver, usually 3 or 4 oz. per ton of ore. The old workings at Daribo, in Alwar, were re-examined recently, and the grade of ore found in them is stated to have been good enough to warrant further exploration. Much the same remark applies in the case of certain deposits which lie across the south-western boundary of Rajasthan, at Zari and Kalikui, in Chota Udaipur, Bombay, and from which 6 tons of malachite were obtained in 1948.

There are many occurrences of copper ores in the outer ranges of the Himalayas at intervals from Sikkim in the east to Kashmir in the west. In Sikkim, they were worked extensively in the past by Nepalese miners and were prospected by Burn & Co. of Calcutta, whose operations, however, were suspended during the first world war (1914-18) and never resumed. According to Sir Lewis Fermor, who visited the region in 1911, the more important of a number of orebodies are at Bhotang, 44 miles from Siliguri on the Gangtok road, and Dikchu, about 7 miles to the north of Gangtok, within a mile of the Gangtok-Lachen road, and 75 miles from Siliguri. At the latter place, a clearly defined lode had been opened up along its strike for 200 feet, and proved to have a width of 3 feet, bearing 6·14 per cent copper. The mineralization here is confined to a belt of highly crystalline mica schists with associated gneisses, which form a boundary zone between the Daling Series and the Sikkim Gneiss. At Bhotang there are two parallel but disturbed ore bands about 3 and 2½ feet thick respectively, separated by some 10 feet of slates, and their content of copper is said to be somewhat higher than that of the Dikchu lode. Later sampling by D. Kerr-Cross revealed that the Dikchu lode as exposed in the adit is of rather higher grade than at Bhotang, but it is in a very isolated locality and extremely difficult of access. These ore bands are interbedded replacement deposits in comparatively unaltered Daling slates. In both cases the chief ore mineral is chalcopyrite and the commonest associated sulphide is pyrrhotite, but galena and sphalerite (zinc blende) are also common, especially at Bhotang. The rarer associates are compounds of bismuth, antimony and tellurium. The telluride of bismuth, tetradymite, Bi_2Te_3, has been recognized in specimens of copper ore from Sikkim, together with linnaeite, a sulphide of cobalt, Co_3S_4. Other deposits of similar, interbedded, replacement types occur in the Rhotak valley, at Sirbong, Pachikhani, Pakyong and elsewhere in Sikkim.

To the south of Sikkim, in the Darjeeling district of West Bengal, disseminations of copper minerals in slates and schists of the Daling Series have been mined in the past by primitive methods at several places. Perhaps the most promising of these is at Komai, on the left bank of the Mo Chu, where lenses of rich ore, 2 to 4 feet in width, occur in slates. Little is known of the copper ores of Nepal, beyond the fact that they are associated with the ores of cobalt and nickel, and have been worked on a small scale as at Sikpasorkhani and elsewhere. To the west of Nepal, and in the Almora district of Uttar Pradesh, there are old copper workings near Dewal Thal and elsewhere, but as far as surface indications go they are not particularly promising. Further west still, in Garhwal, there are ancient copper mines at Pokhri and at Dhanpur. J. B. Auden, who visited Pokhri in 1939, was of the opinion that there are probably two lodes in schistose quartzites and chlorite phyllites, forming part of the Garhwal Series in the Chamoli tectonic window, the southern lode having a footwall of sideritic limestone. According to G. N. Dutt, the dolomites and quartzites of the Garhwal Window Series contain a mineralized zone, marked by the presence of the ores of copper and lead, which extends over 60 miles between the Bhagirathi valley in Tehri Garhwal and Dhanpur in Garhwal district, but its economic potentialities have still to be determined. Continuing to the north-westwards, old copper mines have been reported from the Simla Hills, near Solan, as well as from a number of places in the Kulu area. Near Sungam in the Kangra district, small parcels of ore have been obtained from quartz veins traversing Cambrian schist, but very little is known either of this or the other occurrences. Copper-bearing minerals have been found at numerous places in Kashmir and Jammu, and they were mined, in some instances, in times long past, either from lodes with a quartz gangue which are found in Palaeozoic slates, or from veins which follow planes of brecciation in the Great Limestone. Perhaps the two more important deposits are those of Shumahal, near Hapatnar, in the Kashmir valley, and Gainti, in the Riasi district. At the former locality a slaty band is impregnated with a multiplicity of small veins and lenticular bodies of quartz with chalcopyrite, oxidized at the surface to malachite, azurite and cuprite. At Gainti, chalcopyrite and malachite are distributed along fracture lines in a particular zone in the Great Limestone Series. Where tested, the ore averaged 2·6 to 2·7 per cent of copper. Referring to the copper deposits of Kashmir, C. S. Middlemiss wrote: 'Working them under modern conditions will depend on the opening up of the country by communication lines, on the co-ordination of related industries and on the utilization of by-products.'

In the Punjab of Pakistan, nodules of copper pyrites occur in beds of variegated clay, associated with the Speckled Sandstone of the Salt Range, and especially on the scarp above Katha, in the Shahpur district. From the North-West Frontier Province come reports of ' showings ' of ore in Chitral, Waziristan and the Mohmand territory: in 1949, S. Tayyab Ali found a vein of chalcopyrite, $3\frac{1}{2}$ to $4\frac{1}{2}$ feet thick, intimately mixed with quartz and pyrite, near Imirdin in the Lutkho valley. Copper ores were at one time smelted at Jalai Robat, in the Chagai district of Baluchistan, where large heaps of slag still exist. Low-grade ores have been reported from quartz veins in the Kojak-Amran range of the Quetta-Pishin district, and as disseminations in the Tertiary syenites of western Baluchistan.

India's imports of copper and brass for the pre-war period 1934-8 averaged 37,281 tons per annum, valued at Rs 2,30,99,723 (£1,732,479), compared with 34,670 tons and £2,276,872 in the quinquennium ending 1932-3. These figures are by no means exceptional, for in earlier years still such imports often cost the country £2¾ million and exceptionally more than £3½ million per annum. Two-thirds of the pre-war imports were derived from the United Kingdom and Germany and these supplies ceased on the outbreak of hostilities. Thus, over the war period, 1939-43, imports fell to 19,569 tons, valued at Rs 1,93,73,473 (£1,453,010). To overcome shortages and meet internal munitions' demands, a second copper refinery was erected in India in 1940, where, up to 1943, some 17,000 tons of refined copper were made on Government account, from imported Rhodesian blister copper, part of which entered into the composition of the 13 separate varieties of brasses which were then made in the country for special purposes. During the first post-war year, 1946, imports of brass and copper jumped to 65,777 tons, valued at Rs 7,21,32,282 (£5,409,916), and included in this total are nearly 29,000 tons of high-grade copper destined for the manufacture of electrical cables and wires in India.   In 1950, 41,851 tons of wrought and unwrought copper alone, valued at over Rs 9 crores, were imported.   In spite of the fact that there is a tendency for aluminium to replace brass in the manufacture of the traditional Indian cooking and household utensils, the consumption of copper must increase to keep pace with general industrial development.

To meet this existing and growing demand there is an internal, yearly out-turn of but 6,000 to 6,500 tons of copper.   If the country is to be independent of external supplies, which may become precarious in times of war, more home production is essential, and it can be met, at least in part, by extending mining operations in the Singhbhum belt.   It is perfectly true that the metallic contents of this belt are unusually scattered, but it is not generally realized that it has not been fully prospected.   Disseminated as its copper contents are, the actual amount of copper ores within the belt as a whole place it, as J. A. Dunn remarked, amongst the world's greatest mineralized zones, and it is extremely unlikely that the lodes now under exploitation at Mosaboni and Badia are the only profitable ones to be found throughout its entire length.   Dunn believed that the lodes in the south-east, in a compact area to the north-west of Baharagora, which have never received any attention, deserve proper investigation, and in his writings various locations are mentioned which offer scope for further work.   Amongst others, the whole zone of schists forming the centre of the Surda ridge, honeycombed as it is with ancient workings, should be systematically sampled with a view to mining on a large scale by open-cast methods.

The copper ore deposits of Rajasthan and of Sikkim have promising possibilities, but in both instances expensive exploratory work is needed, especially in the former case.   Little is to be gained by surface examinations alone, or, for that matter, from opening up ancient workings unless they are to be extended, for the old miners of past generations were adepts in removing every scrap of visible ore from them.   Depths unattainable by them must be reached and explored, either by drilling, or, better still, by mining and drainage, before any proper evaluation is possible.   Experience in the successful search for other minerals under similar conditions proves that this demands both time and capital.   Such undertakings are not for the individual or for small syndicates; they are more properly ventures to be financed and technically controlled by the State, or by large-scale enterprise.   It is as well to recall here that all the early attempts to mine copper ores in Singhbhum were profitless failures, until the Geological Survey of India carried out a diamond drilling campaign along the copper belt during the years 1906-8, and, in so doing, redirected private enterprise into what has since become a well-established mining and metallurgical industry.

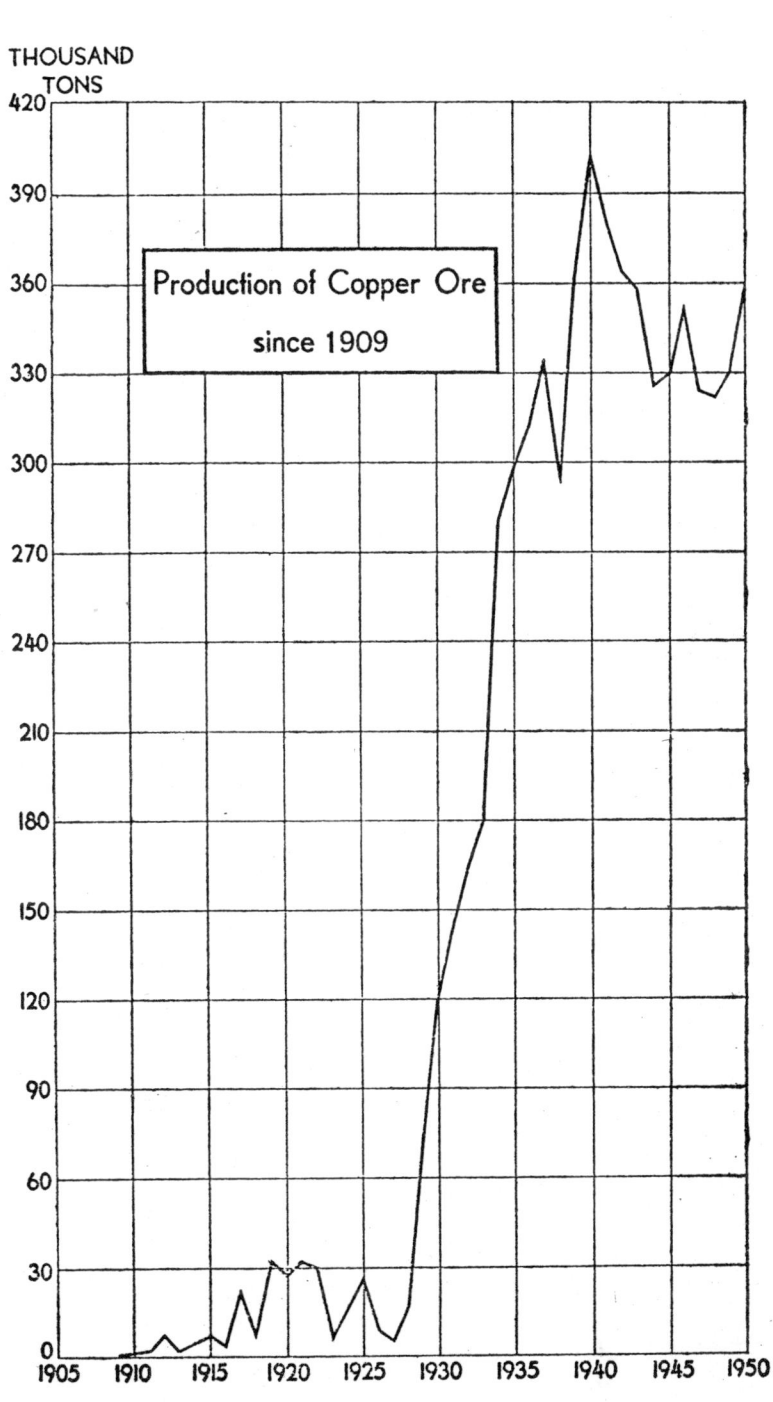

THOUSAND
TONS

Production of Copper Ore

since 1909

LEAD

Although galena, the sulphide of lead, sometimes accompanied by the carbonate, cerrusite, $PbCO_8$, has been found at many places in India and Pakistan, and although at some of these it was mined on a small scale to supply local needs in times past, the vast majority of these occurrences are of mineralogical interest only and far too limited in extent to offer hope of profitable exploitation. Reference has already been made under COPPER to the lead ore deposits of the Dhadka neighbourhood, in Manbhum, Bihar, but prospecting operations in 1904 and 1905 proved them to be but sporadic and superficial and no continuous lode was found. A re-examination by A. K. Dey in 1934-5 confirmed this conclusion. On many occasions after 1850 until the early years of the present century, various deposits scattered across Bihar were opened up by syndicates and companies without any success. 'It is perhaps possible that in some cases the capital available was too limited,' writes J. A. Dunn, 'but the author is of the opinion that failure was entirely due to the absence of any deposits of reasonable size.' A thorough trial of a deposit at Beldi, in Manbhum, was made by Messrs Mackinnon Mackenzie & Co. in 1904-5. The ore obtained was railed to Howrah and smelted in a small furnace at Shalimar, but after yielding $91\frac{1}{2}$ tons of lead, 4,716 oz. of silver and 86 grains of gold, the deposit petered out in depth. In the absence of new discoveries, therefore, lead mining is unlikely to be established in Bihar, and unfortunately, the outlook in most of the other States is, at present, equally unpromising; many of the known deposits have been re-examined in recent years and the reports on them have concluded monotonously with the words 'of no economic value'. During 1951-2 lumps of galena were found in a field at Metri some 25 miles north-west of Bellary in Mysore by workmen engaged in the collection of *kankar*. The occurrence was opened to a depth of 15 feet and about 15 tons of galena, assaying $82 \cdot 53$ per cent lead, $12 \cdot 77$ per cent sulphur and $2 \cdot 71$ oz. silver, were recovered, but no vein had been met with when prospecting was abandoned owing to lack of funds. Of extra-peninsular occurrences, E. R. Gee considered that the galena-bearing lodes of the Kulu area and particularly those near Jhari, Saugthan, Uchich, and Khanor Khud, which in some cases also carry copper minerals as well as gold and silver values, are deserving of detailed investigation. He also mentions the galena occurrences of the Great Limestone of Riasi, in southern Kashmir, and states that, though they have been explored, the results were not available, except for $1 \cdot 5$ tons of galena reported to have been produced in Kistwar in the district of Doda, Kashmir. Full details of all the known lead ore localities are obtainable from the published summaries of the mineral resources of the various States and from the *Directory of the Economic Minerals of Pakistan* (1950).

In the ancient mines of Zawar, Udaipur, Rajasthan, reopened by the Geological Survey of India during the last war, there is an exception to this depressing record, for here mixed ores of lead and zinc are being won by the Metal Corporation of India Ltd who, since 1945, have raised 30,978 tons of ore and smelted them at their Tundoo works, on the Jharia coalfield, for a return of 1,464 tons of 99·9 per cent lead, valued at Rs 17,88,734. For the year 1951, a further 859 tons of metallic lead, valued at Rs 15,00,000, have to be added to this total. A description of the mines is to be found under ZINC.

With this introduction, the story of the lead, silver and zinc industries of the former Indian Empire centres entirely around the history of the discovery of the great ore deposit of Bawdwin, in the Shan States of Burma, and of the expansion of mining and metallurgical enterprise there. This mine, unique of its kind in the world, was originally opened by the Chinese, perhaps in the early part of the fourteenth century, and it supplied large quantities of silver to their exchequer until its abandonment in the middle of the nineteenth century, on account of deep drainage difficulties and the outbreak of the Mohammedan revolt in Yunnan. The vast heaps of rich lead slags, left after the silver had been extracted from the ores, attracted attention in the early days of the present century, and from 1909 onwards yielded large tonnages of metallic lead until they were exhausted. European exploitation dates from 1902, but, as is so often the case, the early ventures were not encouraging, until exploration below the level of the old workings resulted in the discovery of the Chinaman orebody in 1912. In 1919, the Burma Mines Ltd was acquired by the Burma Corporation Ltd, which had its headquarters in Rangoon. The capital of the Corporation was Rs 18,00,00,000, in Rs 10 shares, of which 1,35,41,689 were issued, and in May 1935 the capital was changed to Rs 18,00,00,000 divided into 2,00,00,000 shares of Rs 9 each.

In the neighbourhood of Bawdwin, a series of rhyolitic tuffs, lava flows and breccias, with coarse felspathic grits, of early Palaeozoic age, has been intensely crushed and disturbed by overthrust faulting. Within this shear zone, intimately connected with the faulting, lies a well-marked ore channel, at least 8,000 feet long and 400 to 500 feet wide, and within this ore channel again, so far as it has been developed, three major orebodies, once united, but now separated by post-mineralization cross-faulting, have been found. They are of approximately equal length, with the Chinaman orebody in the centre; the Shan lode, from which it was torn and thrown approximately 700 feet to the south-west by the Yunnan fault, lies to the north, while the Maingtha lode, at its other end, has been moved 1,200 feet to the south-east by the Hsenwi fault. The ores themselves have been deposited from solutions which, there is some reason to suppose, originated from a deep underlying

granite magma and, finding easy passage through the shear planes
of the intensely crushed overthrust zone, metasomatically replaced
the minerals of the congenial rhyolitic tuffs.   The typical ore is
a fine-grained, intimate mixture of galena and sphalerite with chalcopyrite in places; it is frequently banded and often shows signs
of crushing.   The rarer ore minerals include pyrite, arsenopyrite,
löllingite, gersdorffite, cubanite, tetrahedrite, bournonite, boulangerite and pyrargyrite.   In the shallow oxidation zone, near the
surface, cerussite, anglesite, pyromorphite, melaconite, chalcocite,
native copper, malachite, azurite, calamine, massicot, goslarite and
brochantite have been found.   The central orebody—the Chinaman—is a huge, lenticular replacement, averaging about 50 feet
in width with a maximum of some 140 feet of solid lead-zinc sulphides.   It has been developed for over 1,000 feet and to a depth
of more than 1,200 feet, where the mineralized zone ceases at the
base of the rhyolitic tuffs.   The Shan lode averages about 20 feet
in thickness and is characterized by its high copper values at certain
levels.   The Maingtha lode, discovered in 1929, is also about 20
feet thick, and whilst its upper portion above No. 6 level is lead-
zinc-copper ore, similar to that of the Chinaman orebody but with
lead and zinc values lower and copper values higher, and about
the same silver ratio, below that horizon copper ore is found with
very little lead or zinc, but with profitable values of nickel and
cobalt, apparently in a definite ratio of nickel 2 : cobalt 1, though
even here, the silver ratio remains the same as in the rest of the ore.
To the north of the Bawdwin fault (the most important of the pre-
mineralization disturbances of the area), and some 2,000 feet from
it, there is a flat-dipping vein of chalcopyrite in rhyolite, known as
the Chin lode.

The major axis of the orebody as a whole has a general pitch
to the north.   In the Chinaman and Shan lodes the dip is high
to the west with a tendency to turn over in the lower levels, whereas
in the Maingtha section it is to the east.   For the most part the
hanging wall is well-defined and regular, but the foot wall is ill-
defined with no clean boundary: mineralization becomes sparser
in this direction and often continues considerable distances before
barren rock is reached.   As the values gradually decrease, the
mining limit of the stopes is arbitrarily fixed by what is considered
to be payable ore at the time.   For some years it was defined as
ore containing not less than 20 per cent combined lead and zinc,
and, if lowered, will add considerably to the reserves of low-grade
ore.   On both sides of the solid ore-core, but more generally towards the east, thin parallel bands of ore occur in the mineralized
tuffs of the ore channel, but these branch veins unite, as a rule,
with the solid ore in depth.   In the following table the changes in
the distribution of the silver, lead, zinc and copper contents of the
three main orebodies are shown as their depth from the surface
increases.

ASSAY VALUES OF BAWDWIN ORES AT VARIOUS DEPTHS

OREBODY AND LEVEL	SILVER OZ.	LEAD %	ZINC %	COPPER %	SILVER RATIO	
					to LEAD	to ALL METALS
Chinaman No. 2	19·4	24·1	20·9	0·10	1 - 1·24	1 - 2·32
,, No. 4	31·7	31·8	22·8	0·70	1 - 1·03	1 - 1·70
,, No. 6	23·0	28·1	14·2	0·50	1 - 1·22	1 - 1·85
,, No. 9	14·6	23·0	9·1	0·30	1 - 1·58	1 - 2·22
Maingtha No. 2	13·3	15·4	11·4	1·23	1 - 1·16	1 - 2·11
,, No. 4	18·3	24·0	12·7	1·31	1 - 1·31	1 - 2·08
,, No. 6	13·9	17·4	6·4	1·60	1 - 1·25	1 - 1·83
,, No. 9	5·0	7·3	1·4	3·50	1 - 1·46	1 - 2·44
Shan No. 2	13·3	24·6	6·8	0·70	1 - 1·85	1 - 2·41
,, No. 4	23·7	14·8	10·2	8·20	1 - 0·62	1 - 1·40
,, No. 6	19·1	21·0	13·1	2·20	1 - 1·10	1 - 1·90
,, No. 9	21·3	30·3	10·0	0·35	1 - 1·42	1 - 1·90

'For all practical purposes,' wrote E. L. G. Clegg, a former Director of the Geological Survey of India, ' the mine is now fully developed. In depth the mineralized zone ceases at the base of the Bawdwin rhyolite series, as was originally predicted by Coggin Brown.'

The main way into the mine is by Tiger Tunnel, 7,250 feet long, 653 feet below the zero level at Bawdwin and corresponding to the sixth level of the mine. It is masonry-lined, double-tracked from the portal to Marmion's shaft and is the chief haulage and drainage level; all ore, as mined, is raised or lowered to it, to be trammed out by electric locomotives to the storage bins at Tiger Camp. Marmion's shaft is sunk from the surface at Bawdwin, through the country rock on the west of the Shan orebody, and is 1,741 feet deep, with 14 levels at intervals of 120 to 150 feet.

The mine is connected with the smelter at Nam Tu, 13 miles distant, and with the Burma Railways at Nam Yao, 547 miles from Rangoon, by the Corporation's own railway, 45 miles in length. The milling and flotation plant had a capacity of 800 to 1,000 tons per day, and there were five blast furnaces with their attached roasters, as well as the refinery in which the silver was separated from the lead. Hydro-electric power was obtained from the Corporation's plant at the Mansam falls on the Nam Yao river.

In the following table the total quantity of lead extracted from the Bawdwin ores in Burma, from the commencement of operations in 1909 up to the end of 1941, is shown.

These figures include antimonial lead, the average annual production of which for 1934-8 was 1,269 tons. The highest annual production was attained in 1929, with 80,233 tons of metallic lead.

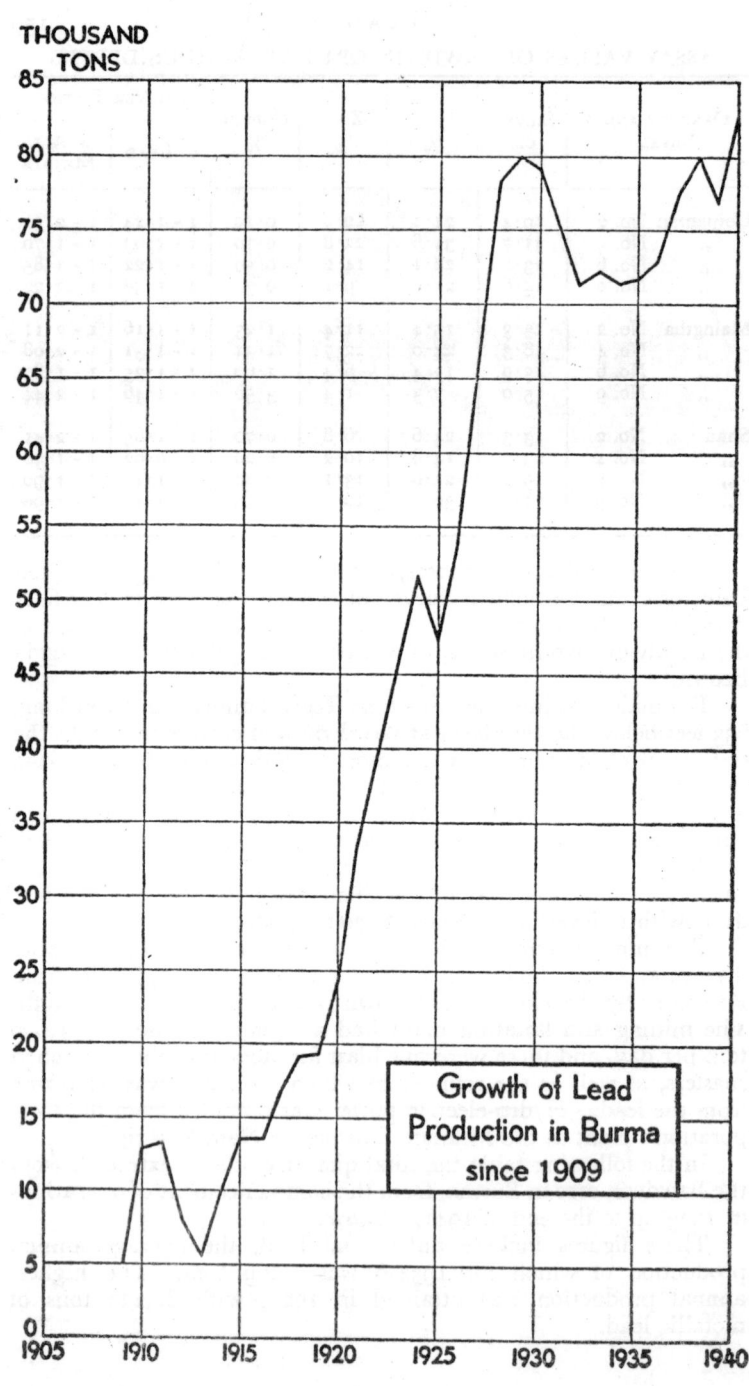

Growth of Lead
Production in Burma
since 1909

PRODUCTION OF LEAD AT NAM TU, 1909-41

Period	Total Tonnage	Sterling Value
1909–13	45,550	632,505
1914–18	73,817	1,792,345
1919–23	161,902	4,405,718
1924–8	297,715	8,340,471
1929–33	377,995	5,887,169
1934–8	374,780	6,218,633
1939–41	229,895	3,715,342 *
Total ..	1,561,654 tons	£30,992,183

* Value for 1941 is estimated.

The following table shows the ore position at the Bawdwin Mine on 1 July 1939, the last detailed figures available to the authors: at that time the total ore reserves amounted to 3,610,803 tons containing 17·7 oz. of silver, 23 per cent of lead, 13·8 per cent of zinc and 0·92 per cent of copper. They also included approximately 280,000 tons of copper ore. In 1942, the year of the Japanese invasion, the reserves were 3,130,199 tons with 15·1 oz. of silver, 19·5 per cent of lead, 12·1 per cent of zinc and 0·84 per cent of copper.

ORE POSITION AT THE BAWDWIN MINE ON 1 JULY 1939

	Tons	Average Assay Values			
		Silver oz.	Lead %	Zinc %	Copper %
Chinaman Orebody ..	6,897,859	21·1	25·0	16·1	0·40
Shan, etc., Lodes ..	2,454,270	17·8	21·5	10·7	2·09
Maingtha Lode	1,617,121	13·0	15·2	9·0	1·97
Chin Lode	20,500	1·9	nil	0·5	8·41
Total (Proved & Probable)	10,989,750	19·1	22·7	13·8	1·05
Excess tonnage * ..	286,417	8·9	13·3	3·8	nil
	11,276,167	18·9	22·5	13·6	1·02
Extracted	7,668,222	19·4	22·3	13·5	1·07
Reserve in Mine ..	3,607,945	17·7	23·0	13·8	0·92
Ore Stocks	2,858	14·1	19·0	10·5	0·65
Total Ore Reserves ..	3,610,803	17·7	23·0	13·8	0·92

* Excess tonnage is from completed stopes.

Disturbed conditions in Burma following the war have hindered the large-scale resumption of base metal production at Nam Tu, but towards the end of 1948 it became possible to dispatch fuel supplies there again, and with them to commence smelting accumulated ore stocks and to send the finished metal to Rangoon for sale. The production in 1948 was 264 tons of lead, which increased to 846 tons in 1949. It was stated in November 1951 that no forecast could be made as to when production from newly mined ore could be restarted, as this depended on security conditions in Burma and on the restoration of adequate, through, railway traffic between Rangoon and Nam Tu. At the same time the sale of the undertaking was announced to a new Company, to be known as Burma Corporation (1951) Ltd, in exchange for 3,159,730 fully paid shares of Rs 10 each in that concern. The Government of the Union of Burma have also agreed to subscribe by instalments in cash, at par, for 3,159,730 shares of Rs 10 each, in the capital of Burma Corporation (1951) Ltd, thus obtaining an equal participation in that Company. It can only be hoped that by this means the whole industry will be rehabilitated and brought once again to its full productive capacity and, further, that the association of the State with it will soon lead to the development of similar mineral deposits in other parts of the Union.

During the year ended 30 June 1952, the available labour force was increased from 497 to 1,058 men, employed solely on repairs and preparation for the resumption of mining, the initial target being 8,000 tons of ore per month, for which a force of 1,600 is required. Rehabilitation of the Man-sang Falls hydro-electric power station was in progress, and during the year sales of products obtained from the processing of surface stocks amounted to 4,798 tons of refined lead, 231,670 oz. of refined silver and 3,251 tons of other products. The remaining surface stocks were estimated to yield ultimately 1,400 tons of refined lead, 180,000 oz. of refined silver and some quantity of other products.

A small indigenous lead industry existed in Mawson, one of the minor States in the Myelat division of the Southern Shan States, from the fourteenth century until it was extinguished on the annexation of Upper Burma by the British, in 1886. Several more or less parallel ore-bearing zones occur in the local Plateau Limestone, and in older rocks of Ordovician age, which are traceable by means of old workings and slag heaps. The Shan miners obtained the lead ores mainly from clay-filled cracks and fissures in the limestones, but extensive modern exploration has, up to the present time, only succeeded in locating two small orebodies. One of these was developed at Bawzaing by a European company, where the probable ore reserves at the end of 1930 were stated to be 185,400 tons, containing 7 per cent of lead with 13 oz. of silver. The mine was closed in that year and has not been reopened. For the five years ending 1928 a total of 25,440 tons of lead ore and slags, valued at £27,940, were produced in the Southern Shan States, compared with 434 tons for the previous period of equal duration. During the years 1935 to 1937, 9,542 tons of ancient lead slags were collected and exported.

The amount of lead imported annually into India is normally between 7,500 and 8,000 tons, but for the three years 1949 to 1951 the annual average increased to 10,004 tons, valued at Rs 1·6 crores approximately.

ZINC

Ancient zinc mines, reputed to have been discovered in the fourteenth century and to have been closed during the great famine of 1812-13, exist near Zawar, 15 miles due south of Udaipur, Rajasthan. The old workings all lie within a radius of 3 miles of Zawar; the principal ones, according to A. M. Heron, stretching for about three-quarters of a mile, to form a vast open-cast in brecciated limestone of Aravalli age, averaging 80 feet in width and 40 feet in depth, with irregular, cavernous excavations of unknown extent in its bottom. No traces of the ore-bearing minerals were visible at the surface, but the clinker which still filled the old retorts from which the ore was distilled, and which are still to be found in countless numbers in the vicinity, contained varying quantities of zinc and lead.

During the last war, owing to the shortage of lead and zinc in India as a result of the loss of Burma, the Government decided to reopen the Zawar mines under the direction of the Geological Survey of India, and five adits were driven into selected sites in the Mochia Magra ridge, but, as it became evident that no supplies of lead or zinc could be obtained from this source during the war, the Government sold back the mining rights to the Mewar State for about one quarter the cost of the development work. In 1945, the State leased the area to the Metal Corporation of India Ltd, which by the end of 1950 had raised 31,812 tons of ore. From this, 4,358 tons of hand-dressed lead concentrates were obtained, railed to the Corporation's works at Tundoo, near Katrasgarh, in the Jharia coalfield of Bihar, and smelted for a return of 1,464 tons of 99·9 per cent lead, valued at Rs 17,88,734. A flotation plant was installed in May 1950 which separated 655 tons of zinc concentrates during the year, analysing 48·76 per cent zinc, 4·23 per cent lead and 0·21 per cent cadmium. The zinc concentrates are shipped abroad for reduction, on the understanding that half their metallic contents are returned to India. It is the present aim of the Corporation to crush 175 to 200 tons of mine ore daily, and this is estimated to yield some 15 tons of lead concentrates and 25 to 30 tons of zinc concentrates per diem.

During the year 1951, the output of zinc concentrates from the flotation plant was increased to 2,110 tons, averaging zinc 49·85 per cent, lead 5·10 per cent and sulphur 28·7 per cent. At the same time 1,783 tons of lead concentrates were produced, averaging lead 72·5 and zinc 7·04 per cent as far as the flotation product was concerned, but this tonnage also included a quantity of hand-dressed lead concentrate assaying lead 45·48 and zinc 12·14 per cent, as distinct from the flotation product.   The smelter at Katrasgarh treated 1,770 tons of lead concentrates for a return of 859 tons of metallic lead, valued at Rs 15 lakhs.   Of the zinc concentrates 1,965 tons, valued at Rs 6,50,000 (c.i.f. destination), were exported for treatment.   Plans are in hand to increase the mill throughput to 500 tons daily.   The principal ores are zinc blende and galena, associated with pyrite and some other sulphides, as disseminations and replacement bodies in dolomitic limestones, interbedded with phyllites and quartzites in a pitching overfold.   In the existing workings at Mochia Magra, which occupy but a small portion of the mineralized zone, D. Kerr-Cross, in March 1949, estimated a reserve of 442,000 tons of ore, averaging 11·58 per cent lead and 10·51 per cent zinc, within a depth of 50 feet, over a width of 120 inches for a length of 1,329 feet.   The mineralization appears to be extensive beyond these limits.   The mineralized zone found later is said to be from 85 to 100 feet in width and, according to B. Srikantan and M. R. Subramanyam, it extends downwards beyond a depth of 130 feet below the level of the 6th adit.   At the end of 1951, the ore reserves were stated to be of the order of 700,000 tons with lead 5·25 per cent and zinc 7·25 per cent, with 2 million tons of second-grade ore assaying lead 1·9 per cent and zinc 3·8 per cent and a probable reserve of 8 million tons of low-grade material containing a minimum of 3 per cent metal.   Geological research has already shown that the rocks in which the orebodies occur may be expected to continue downwards to considerable depths without much change, and as the mineralization has taken place through a series of cleavage planes, formed in the course of widespread regional metamorphism, there is no theoretical reason why it should die out in depth though the character of the minerals in the lodes themselves may change gradually.   The area mined by the ancients was much more extensive than the small section so far developed, and until the ridge running south from the old city of Zawar, the hills about Zamarmala, the hills known as Sonria and Rupria west of the Tiri river, as well as Balria Hill east of that river, have been fully examined, the full possibilities of the district cannot be said to be known.

The zinc ore deposits in dolomite at Darabi, Jammu, Kashmir, contain but meagre reserves of a few thousand tons of blende, while little is yet known of the deposits near Tiplin in Nepal.

The Burma Corporation Ltd used to produce large quantities of zinc concentrates from its milling plant at Nam Tu. It has been stated under LEAD that the ores of the Bawdwin mine are intimate intergrowths of argentiferous galena and zinc blende with small

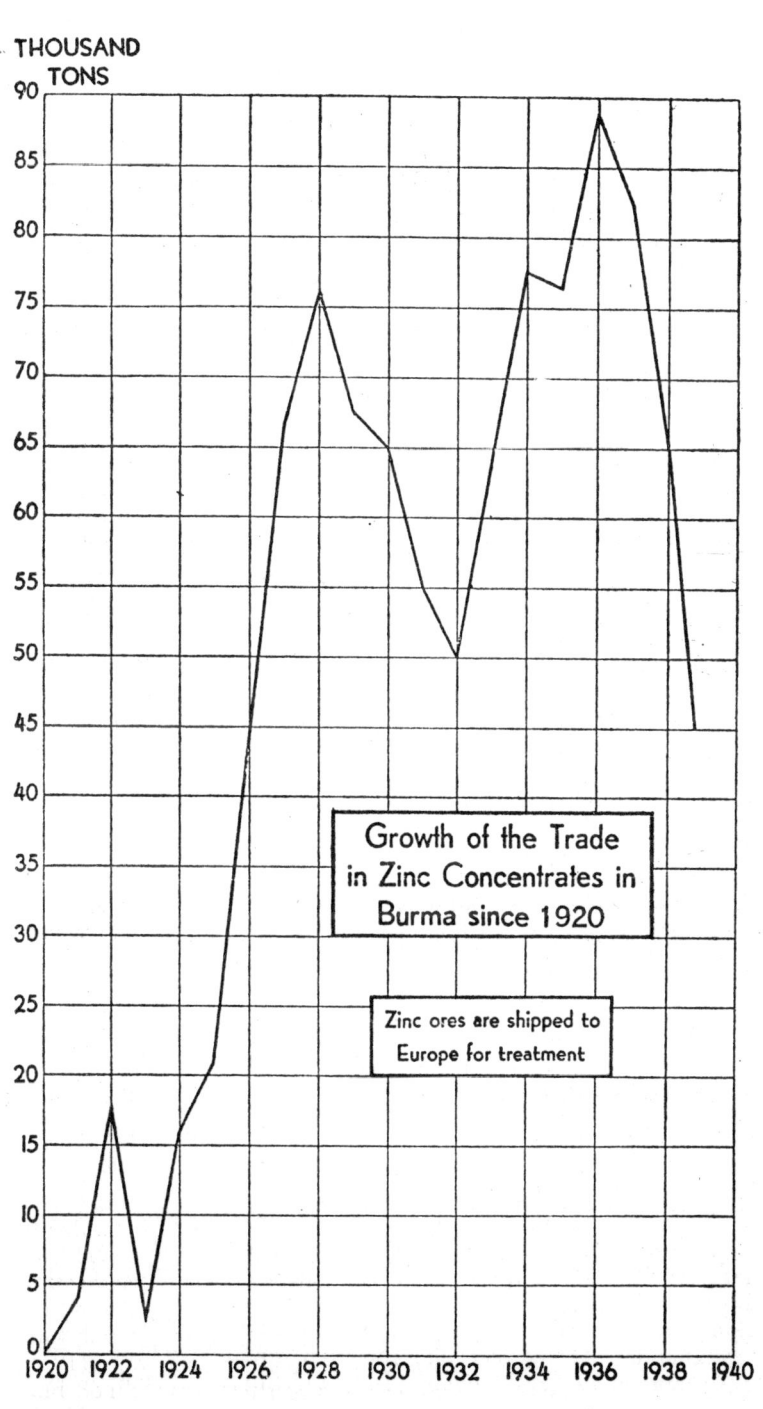

THOUSAND TONS

Growth of the Trade
in Zinc Concentrates in
Burma since 1920

Zinc ores are shipped to
Europe for treatment

quantities of chalcopyrite, and the reserves of ore still known to be in the mine in 1941, amounting to no less than 3,130,200 tons, are estimated to contain 12·1 per cent of zinc. As the table shows, a total of 985,963 tons of zinc concentrates, averaging over 50 per cent of zinc and valued at £4,853,971, had been produced between 1914 and 1940. Regarding the distribution of the zinc contents in the Chinaman orebody at Bawdwin, while the values remained fairly constant around 20·5 per cent zinc, down to and including No. 4 level, with some tendency for them to predominate over the lead content on the foot wall, below this horizon the zinc values of the mixed sulphides exhibit a progressive decrease from level to level, until they form only 9·1 per cent of the ore at the bottom of the mine.

In the following table the total quantities of zinc concentrates produced or exported by the Burma Corporation Ltd are arranged in periods of five years.

ZINC CONCENTRATES, PRODUCED OR EXPORTED, 1914-40

PERIOD		TOTAL TONNAGE	STERLING VALUE
1914–18*	..	11,974	27,274
1919–23†	..	24,198	122,435
1924–8‡ ..	..	206,702	1,881,727
1929–33‡	..	273,426	1,072,523
1934–8‡ ..	..	358,531	1,427,234
1939–40‡ §	..	111,132	322,778
TOTAL	..	985,963 tons	£4,853,971

* Three years only. No exports in 1917 and 1918.
† Exports.   ‡ Production.   § Two years only.
These concentrates averaged about 51 per cent zinc, 6 per cent lead and 9 oz. silver.

The peak year of output was in 1935 when 78,590 tons, valued at Rs 37,99,358 (£284,951), were produced, although the 73,552 tons turned out in 1937 had a considerably higher value, the actual figures being Rs 54,40,421 (£408,031). There have been times in the history of the mine when the production of zinc concentrates became unprofitable, owing to the low prices ruling for spelter, and was continued only because of contractual obligations and of the spread it afforded for transport and fixed charges.

These zinc concentrates were shipped almost entirely to Belgium until 1939, though Germany also received a share of them. Later, they were transferred to Australia until the Japanese armies overran Burma. A proposal to smelt the concentrates at Jamshedpur, and to recover their sulphur contents in the form of sulphuric acid, was abandoned some years ago, though it would have been of great advantage to the development of India's chemical and metallurgical industries at the time and is worth the serious consideration of both countries in the future. Another proposal to recover metallic zinc in the Toungoo district of Burma, by means of hydro-electric power generated on the Yunzalin river, shared the same fate.

India consumes large quantities of zinc, particularly for the manufacture of brass and other alloys, and for the galvanizing of corrugated steel sheets and numerous other iron and steel products. The metal is also used alone as the cylinder container of dry batteries for electric torches and for many forms of zinc die-castings. The oxide of the metal is a valuable pigment in the paint and colour trade, the sulphide is a constituent of lithopone, and there are many other important industrial applications of various zinc compounds. The imports of metallic zinc alone into India have increased threefold in the past fifteen years, and now exceed 33,000 tons per annum. Thus, in 1950, they totalled 33,440 tons and cost Rs 5,23,02,223, while the average for the three years 1949 to 1951 was 29,080 tons, valued at Rs 5·09 crores. The revival of Rajasthan's ancient zinc mining and smelting industry is thus a matter of urgent national consequence worthy of all the encouragement and assistance that the Republic can supply. The first action needed is further intensive development of the Zawar deposits, for until much larger reserves of the better grades of ore are proved than those known at the end of 1951, plans for the establishment of a zinc reduction plant in India, entirely dependent on the supply of such ores, can only be regarded as premature.

TIN

The oxide of tin, cassiterite, has been found at a number of places in the Hazaribagh, Ranchi and Gaya districts of Bihar, but none of the occurrences appear to possess economic importance, though as long ago as 1849 tin ore was being smelted in village iron furnaces at Purgo, in the Palganj estate near Parasnath. According to Sir Lewis Fermor, there is here a thin layer of cassiterite granulite, up to 6 inches thick and containing 30 to 50 per cent of the tin ore, in a much thicker band of microcline granite which itself contains scattered grains of cassiterite. Mallet described an attempt made about 1867 to work this deposit and states that the ore formed three or four lenticular beds in gneiss, seldom more than a foot or two across, but in places reaching a width of 13 feet. The lateral extension was about 60 feet, nearly parallel to the foliation of the gneiss. The beds were followed to a depth of some 60 feet, in an inclined shaft, before work was stopped by decreasing values and flooding. Another venture was made in 1891-2, when an inclined shaft was sunk on the ore band to a depth of 614 feet, but below 568 feet the ore band had disappeared. It had ranged in thickness from 6 to 18 inches and a sample from a full section of the working, consisting of 15 inches of ore band and the remainder wall rock with disseminated tinstone, yielded 1·87 per cent of tin. Other samples assayed 2·1 to 6·2 per cent of the metal. The mine was eventually abandoned through lack of funds. The occurrence was examined again in 1909-10 and the surface portion worked with the production of 6 cwt of tin, in the two years 1909 and 1910; a further 14 cwt were made in 1915. The prospects of reopening this tin mine are not encouraging. The other three occurrences of cassiterite in Hazaribagh are of scientific interest only: a few crystals have been found in a lens of granite enclosed in mica schists at Simratanri, small grains occur in a· dyke of lepidolite granite at Pihra and, again, in a granulite at Chappatand. The mineral has also been reported from a pegmatite intrusive into granulite, near Silli, Ranchi district; from Dhanras Pahar, in the Deo Raj estate of Gaya district, and in a vein associated with wolfram, a few miles north of Chhakarband in the same district, where it is said to be present to the extent of 1·5 per cent. Recently there has been an output of 7 tons of cassiterite from pegmatite in the hills to the north of Paharsingh in Ranchi district. Outside Bihar, cassiterite has been found, but again only in insignificant amounts, in a tourmaline pegmatite at Hosainpur, Palanpur, Bombay, where it is associated with gadolinite, a silicate of beryllium, yttrium and iron, and in alluvial deposits of streams draining the northern part of the Kapatgod range, near Dambal, Dharwar, Bombay. There are no recorded instances of the occurrence of tin ore in Pakistan.

The earliest reference to the occurrence of tin in Burma was made by Ralph Fitch in 1599, who remarked that on his journey from Pegu to Malacca, he passed by 'many of the ports of Pegu, as Martauan [Martaban] and the Iland of Taui [Tavoy], from whence commeth great store of tinne, which serueth all India'. The cassiterite deposits of Burma have indeed been worked from a remote antiquity, especially in the lower part of the Tenasserim division. The granitic mountain ranges of Lower Burma are but the northern continuation of the same rocks which have yielded the rich tin ore deposits of Malaya and of western Thailand. The region in which the Burmese ores occur corresponds with that described in the case of TUNGSTEN, for wolfram and cassiterite are most intimately associated and of identical origin.

The tin- and wolfram-bearing localities of the Mergui district, in the extreme south, lie in the Palaw and Palauk, the Mergui and Tenasserim and the Bokpyin and Victoria Point townships, of the north, central and southern portions respectively. The tin mines are situated principally on the mainland, in two parallel mineralized zones, but another belt traverses Lampi and adjoining islands in the Mergui archipelago. The ore zones are more or less parallel to, and genetically connected with, the granitic intrusions, and generally lie at or near their junctions with the sedimentary rocks of the Mergui Series. The tin ore occurs as a constituent of decomposed granite and greisen, associated with tourmaline and muscovite; in quartz veins, up to ten feet thick, with wolfram and one or more members of a sulphide suite of minerals; and in narrow quartz veinlets and stringers forming stockworks in rocks of the Mergui Series. Surface ore-deposits of both eluvial and alluvial origin are common, but while wolfram and cassiterite occur in the former, the tin ore is found alone in the latter, as it is resistant to the processes of disintegration and decay which remove the wolfram before it reaches the true water-sorted alluvials. All the known occurrences were listed by the late Rao Bahadur Setu Rama Rao in 1930, who also indicated the more promising areas which then remained to be prospected. By 1939, there were 219 separate mines producing tin ore in the Mergui district, in addition to 34 which were yielding mixed tin and wolfram concentrates. The vast majority of them were small Chinese-leased concessions from which a few tons of ore were won by ground sluicing in the rainy season, and only 9 of the whole total gave over 50 tons per annum. The more important areas lay around Palaw, Yamon, Theindaw, Thabawleik, Khechaung and Karathuri. Before the occupation of Burma by the Japanese in 1942, modern tin dredging was carried on by the Tavoy Tin Dredging Co. Ltd at Theindaw, from 1936; the Thabawleik Tin Dredging Co. Ltd at Thabawleik, from 1928; the Lenya Mining Co. Ltd at Yemon, from 1939, and the Tavoy Tin Dredging Co. Ltd at Karathuri, from 1938. The Thabawleik dredge alone had already, at times, produced over 600 tons of concentrates per annum; after the war it commenced operating again in 1947. The tabulation of tin ore statistics was commenced by the Geological Survey of India in 1898, and from that time until the end of 1939 the Mergui district had given a total of 22,311 tons of tin ore, averaging about 72 per cent of tin. In addition to this, between the years 1910 and 1922, 1,187 tons of metallic tin were made in small Chinese furnaces and exported. The maximum annual output was reached in 1939, when 2,017 tons of concentrates were won.

North of Mergui lies the Tavoy district where geological conditions are much the same as those prevailing in Mergui. Granite intruded into a series of sedimentary rocks forms the cores of its mountain ranges; quartz veins and pegmatites carrying wolfram and cassiterite and more rarely molybdenite, bismuthinite and bismuth, together with a large variety of sulphides, cut through them both. These minerals occur also in the eluvial deposits of the hill slopes, where ore-bearing veins are undergoing degradation, and in the coarse, unsorted debris at the heads of the flatter valleys. Cassiterite is found too in the water-sorted alluvial deposits, the gravels and sands of the lower portions of the streams, both of Recent and sub-Recent ages. Though Tavoy is primarily a wolfram-producing district, there are places within its densely forested 5,308 square miles which are richer in cassiterite than others, and it is from these and from the gradual extension of dredging operations that increased production has been and will be obtained. The Tavoy Tin Dredging Co. Ltd, the earlier activities of which were briefly outlined in the second edition of this book, continued later to operate three dredges in the Taungthonlon area where there are wide placer deposits, old river terraces and shallow leads of earlier stream channels containing tinstone. Another dredge of the same concern worked in the tideway of the Heinze Basin, on the northern coast of the district, and in 1939 won 571 tons of concentrates from the sea bed. Following the Japanese evacuation, two of its dredges in Tavoy and one in Mergui had been reconstructed by 1949. On the flats to the south of the Heinze Basin, the dredge of the Heinze Burma Tin Co. Ltd was installed, while yet another was recovering the tin ore from the alluvial deposits of the Khamaunghla valley.

Amongst important mines producing mixed concentrates were Hermyingyi, where over 60 different veins have been exploited; Kanbauk, with an important vein series and thick detrital and alluvial deposits of considerable extent; and Hpolon Taung, where the Anglo-Burma Tin Co. Ltd works rich horizons occurring in unusually thick deposits of sands, gravels and boulders, by hydraulic methods. In addition to these and other properties, well equipped with plant both for vein and hydraulic mining, there are in Tavoy many areas still worked by ancestral Chinese methods. The Tavoy field will always remain predominantly a wolfram-producing one: thus, of a total of 203 concessions in 1939, 93 yielded wolfram, 76 gave mixed concentrates and 34 tin ore. Between the years 1898 and 1939, the tin ore production of the Tavoy district was 42,249 tons, the maximum annual total being 3,360 tons in 1939. During the years 1912 and 1913, 128 tons of metallic tin were also exported from the district.

Small quantities of tin ore have also been won, since 1916, in the Amherst and Thaton districts, and in the Yamethin district of Upper Burma, since 1936, the total outputs recorded being 618, 381 and 118 tons, respectively. The geological surveys of these districts have not been completed, but metamorphic aureoles are known to exist around the intrusions of the local granites, of the same age as those of the Tavoy and Mergui districts further south, carrying tourmaline and veins of tourmaline micro-pegmatite which in places bear quartz stringers with cassiterite. The occurrences in Thaton lie at the ends of the wolfram-bearing areas of the Zingyeik range. In Amherst, alluvial ore has been won on Belugyun Island, at the mouth of the Salween river, and from both eastern and western flanks of the Seludaung range. The mountainous tracts of both these large districts are covered with dense forests and are very inaccessible, as there are no communications except primitive tracks, away from the larger rivers and their plains. Until they have been geologically mapped and prospected,

Brown & Dey, *India's Mineral Wealth, facing p. 170*

DREDGING FOR TIN ORE IN THE TAVOY DISTRICT, BURMA

it is premature to rule them out as potential tin-mining regions of little value. In Yamethin too, the mines lie in the forested mountains along the steep scarps of the Shan plateau, mainly around Hmanpyataung, and such rough tracks as do exist are due to the efforts of the mining community itself. This region borders the dry zone of Burma, and water for mining and concentration purposes is often difficult to obtain.

The output of the Southern Shan States is derived almost entirely from the important Mawchi mine in Karenni, where biotite granite has invaded a series of clay slates, fine-grained sandstones and grits, calcareous mudstones and limestones. The veins, about 64 of which are known, are mainly under 4 feet in width, productive in both granite and sedimentary rocks, and composed of quartz with cassiterite, wolfram, scheelite, tourmaline, pyrite, arsenopyrite, and a little chalcopyrite and galena. Outcropping on a steep mountainside they have been developed by adits at varying elevations. A self-acting ropeway, over a mile long, connects the mine with the mill 1,339 feet below, and with a capacity of 160,000 tons of ore per annum. A road, some 80 miles in length, constructed by Mawchi Mines Ltd, connects with the Burma Railways at Toungoo. The ore reserves at the end of 1938 were 712,540 tons carrying 3·02 per cent mixed concentrates which in that year assayed 38·39 per cent tin and 32·20 per cent wolfram. The total recorded output between 1904 and 1939, inclusive, was 24,991 tons of tin concentrates. Prospecting licenses were held over three more areas in Karenni. The post-war development of this exceptionally good mineral deposit has been prevented by armed conflict between the Burmese and Karen peoples. When these cease, granted the benefits of a sympathetic administration, the future of Mawchi is assured, and it will make once more its large and valuable contribution to the tin and tungsten mining industries of Burma for many years to come.

Production figures of Burmese tin ore commence in the period 1898-1903, with an average annual output of 82 tons, and the next period, 1904-8, registered little change with 83 tons yearly. This rose to an annual average of 124 tons over the quinquennium 1909-13, and thereafter the growth of the industry is apparent from the figures in the following table and from the graph on page 172.

No reliable statistics of production are available for the post-war period until 1947, when 1,270 tons of tin concentrates and 1,220 tons of mixed tin and wolfram concentrates were produced. The corresponding figures for 1948 and 1949, which we owe to the courtesy of Dr Ba Thi of the Burma Geological Department, were as follows:—Tin Concentrates 1,768 and 1,188 tons: Mixed Concentrates 2,122 and 1,469 tons. In 1950 and 1951 the output of tin ore was 1,816 and 1,295 tons and of mixed tin and wolfram concentrates 901 and 1,207 tons, for the respective years. The disturbed conditions in the tin mining areas since Burma became an

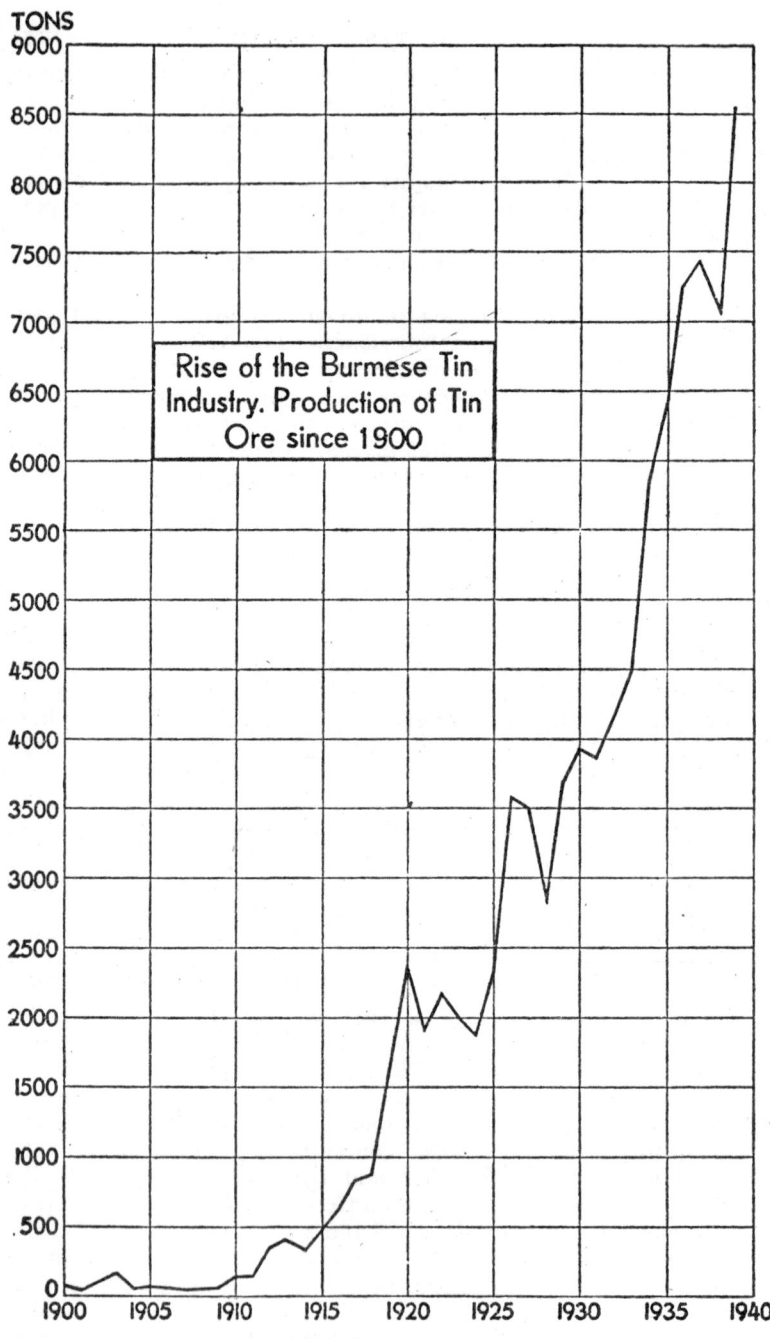

TONS

Rise of the Burmese Tin Industry. Production of Tin Ore since 1900

AVERAGE ANNUAL OUTPUT OF TIN CONCENTRATES IN BURMA,
1914–39

YEAR	CONCENTRATES Tons	TIN METAL IN CONCENTRATES Tons (estimated)
1914–18	650	455
1919–23	2,051	1,436
1924–8	2,817	1,972
1929–33	4,040	2,828
1934–8	6,824	4,777
1939	8,520	5,964

independent republic in 1948 have hindered the rehabilitation of the industry and as late as September 1951 it was reported that mining was at a standstill in some districts.

Between 1914 and 1939, the average annual value of the tin concentrates produced in Burma rose from approximately Rs 7 lakhs to over Rs 99 lakhs. During the same period, 1914-39, the average annual market price of metallic tin ranged between £118 (in 1931) and £329 per ton (in 1918). In 1939 it was £226 per ton. Ten years later, 1949 closed with the price of tin around £600 per ton, and by the end of 1950 this had risen to £1,290 per ton, as stockpile buying developed in the metal markets and shortages increased due to large-scale purchases by Governments and private consumers in excess of their normal requirements.

In the early years of the present century India's imports of unwrought tin in the form of blocks, ingots, bars and slabs, averaged about 1,500 tons per annum. The changes since then up to 1943 are shown in the table, and later figures are of little use as guides to normal times, owing to disturbances caused to the trade by the war and its aftermath.

AVERAGE ANNUAL IMPORTS AND CONSUMPTION OF METALLIC TIN IN INDIA, 1924–43

PERIOD	IMPORTS Tons	VALUE Rs	CONSUMPTION Tons
1924–8 ..	2,716	95,35,073	2,573
1929–33 ..	2,450	56,01,000	2,410
1934–8 ..	2,429	70,18,672	2,342
1939–43 ..	2,440	78,07,868	2,366

Ninety-seven per cent of this imported metal came from the smelters in the Straits Settlements.

Amongst the alloys of tin imported into India from abroad are the solders, used in a great many industries for joining metallic surfaces, and the anti-friction and bearing alloys, employed widely in all kinds of machinery. For the five years ending 1937-8 the average annual imports of solder amounted to 258 tons, valued at Rs 4,55,528, while those of the anti-friction metals for the same period were 153 tons, valued at Rs 2,47,289. The Panel Committee was of the opinion that about 4,000 tons of tin in all its forms would be consumed in India during the first five post-war years. The only tin produced in India at present is secondary metal, recovered in small quantities, together with the oxide, from tin-plate scrap in the detinning plant of Messrs Montana Ltd, Bombay, which commenced operations in 1942. In this connexion it is as well to point out that the familiar ' tins ', in which foodstuffs of all kinds, tobacco, paints, petrol, paraffin and so forth, are packed, are mild steel containers, coated with a thin layer of tin to preserve them from rust, and that only about $1\frac{1}{2}$ per cent of the weight of an empty ' tin can ' is made of metallic tin.

Of an average annual world production, during the five years 1934-8, of 161,119 tons of tin, calculated in terms of the metal contained in the concentrated ore, Malaya with 33·5 per cent, Indonesia with 16·8, Thailand with 7·8 and Burma with 2·9 per cent, were together responsible for 61 per cent of the total. In addition to these countries, Bolivia added a further 15·1 per cent, China 6·5, Nigeria 4·9, the Belgian Congo 3·4 and Australia 2·0 per cent, with a number of other countries contributing smaller quantities still.

With the exception of Bolivia and China (in part), probably over 70 per cent of the world's tin production was won from alluvial and detrital deposits. As regards Burma, where much tin ore is a by-product of wolfram mining, approximately 44 per cent of the 1939 output came from true alluvial deposits, and of this 61 per cent was obtained by dredging and the remainder by gravel pumping and ground sluicing.

The established tin fields of the world are today more than capable of meeting normal peace-time demands, indeed, before the second world war, international schemes of voluntary output restriction were applied to maintain a profitable price for the ore. In support of this policy the Government of Burma stopped the issue of prospecting licenses for tin ore for a period commencing in 1935. The later effects of the Japanese invasion and of the unsettled conditions following it are too apparent to need comment. Under all these circumstances it is not surprising that Burmese tin mining shows so little progress. The Government of Burma has suggested that the tin companies operating in Lower Burma should combine and enter into a joint venture with the Government, but by the end of 1953 only exploratory discussions of the proposal had taken place.

A time is approaching, however, when the easily worked surface and sub-surface deposits of Indonesia and Malaya (where no less than 76 dredges, 518 gravel pumps and 23 hydraulic plants were operating in 1949), will show signs of inevitable exhaustion. It is then that Mergui and other parts of Burma will receive attention commensurate with the great extent of their tin-bearing rocks and their weathered products. In the meantime, as the late E. L. G. Clegg wrote in 1940, ' the fundamental necessity of the tin (and wolfram) areas in Burma is undoubtedly the improvement of their roads and tracks '.

CHAPTER IV

FERROUS AND OTHER RELATED METALS

IRON

THE approximate time of the commencement of iron manufacture in India is unknown, but at the time of Alexander's invasion (326 B.C.), the armed nations of northern India were as familiar with iron and steel as the Greeks themselves. The famous pillar at the Kutb, near Delhi, is of solid wrought iron of an excellent type, 23 feet 8 inches in length, 16½ inches in diameter at the base and 12 inches below the capital. It weighs over 6 tons and bears the epitaph, in Sanskrit, of King Chandragupta II, composed in or about A.D. 415. The manufacture of *wootz,* an Indian steel, anticipated the principle of the cementation process by many centuries, and this material was probably exported to western lands from before the Christian era, to be worked into the ' Damascus ' swords of medieval times. Until it practically succumbed, in comparatively recent years, before the competition of imported metal, the indigenous iron industry was both widespread and prosperous and there is hardly a single district from the extreme south of India to the Himalayas, or from the Shan States in the east of Burma to Baluchistan in the west of Pakistan, with the exception of the alluvial plains of the great rivers, in which ancient iron slags have not been found. It does not follow, however, that ores suitable either in quantity or quality for the needs of a modern blast furnace plant exist in all these places.

Failure attended every early attempt to graft European methods on to the local processes and to smelt iron ores on a large scale in India. In 1830, the Indian Steel, Iron & Chrome Co. was established by J. M. Heath with its works at Porto Novo in South Arcot district, Madras, where ores from the Salem district were smelted. These works were subsequently carried on by the Porto Novo Steel & Iron Co. and the East Indian Iron Co., additional furnaces being erected at Tiruvannamalai in North Arcot, at Beypur in Malabar in 1833, and at Palampatti in the Salem district in 1853. Pig iron from the Porto Novo works was shipped to steel-makers in Sheffield, and a large quantity of it was used in the construction of the Britannia tubular and Menai bridges in the United Kingdom. These concerns never paid a dividend, steadily lost their funds and finally closed down about 1867.

In Bengal the story begins with the grant by the East India Company to Messrs Farquhar & Motte, in 1778, of an exclusive right to manufacture iron within the Company's territories, a privilege which they enjoyed in the Birbhum district, in all probability using local methods, until they relinquished their grant in 1795. In 1839 Messrs Jessop & Co. conducted inconclusive experiments with Burdwan ore. In 1855, Messrs Mackay & Co. started on a small scale at Mahomed Bazaar, also in the Birbhum district, and their desultory operations were abandoned in 1875 after final experiments by Messrs Burn & Co. had proved them unprofitable. In the meantime the Kumaun Iron Works Co. Ltd had been formed in 1862, amalgamating plants which had been erected at Dechauri and at Khurpa Tal, in the Naini Tal district of Uttar Pradesh, in 1857. After many vicissitudes this enterprise failed as the others had done. Yet another attempt made in 1862, at Barwai in Indore, under the direction of a Swedish metallurgist, met with no better success. In all these undertakings charcoal was the fuel used, or proposed, and it was not until 1875 that advantage was taken of coke made from Indian coal. In that year a private company built two furnaces at Kulti, near Barakar, on the Raniganj coalfield, each capable of producing 20 tons of pig iron per day, but owing to insufficiency of capital it ceased operations in 1879, after making 12,700 tons of pig iron. In 1882 this plant was taken over by the Government and one furnace was restarted in 1884, continuing until 1889 when the works were resold to the Bengal Iron & Steel Co. Ltd, the predecessors of the Bengal Iron Co. Ltd, registered in 1919. The plant was entirely remodelled and the Company soon established iron smelting in India on permanent foundations, though a steel plant added in 1903 was shut down in 1905. Later developments include the formation of the Tata Iron & Steel Co. Ltd, the two original furnaces of which were 'blown in' in 1911 and 1912, at Jamshedpur, 154 miles west of Calcutta; the inauguration of the Indian Iron & Steel Co.'s furnaces at Burnpore, near Asansol, on the Raniganj coalfield in 1922; the completion of the Mysore Government's charcoal iron scheme at Bhadravati, near Shimoga, in 1933; and the amalgamation of the Bengal Iron Co. Ltd with the Indian Iron and Steel Co. Ltd, with works at Kulti and Hirapur, near Asansol, in 1936.

IRON ORE DEPOSITS OF BIHAR AND ORISSA

At the beginning of the present century the annual production of iron ore in India averaged about 65,000 tons; by the period 1939 to 1943 this average had risen to more than 3,000,000 tons per annum. The total amount of iron ore raised in India up to the end of 1950 was 70,658,400 tons, and of this amount no less than 67,778,000 tons, or 96 per cent, came from the mines of Bihar and Orissa; indeed, in recent years, more than 98 per cent of the ore supply has been drawn from these two States alone. The distribution of this and the remaining tonnage over the past 50 years is

shown in 5-yearly periods in the table on p. 192. As far as the
Bihar and Orissa output is concerned, Singhbhum, in Bihar, where
mining started in 1904, has contributed 47 per cent to the total;
Mayurbhanj, in Orissa, which began to produce in 1911, 42 per
cent, and Keonjhar, also in Orissa, the latest comer to the list, in
1927, 11 per cent approximately.

One of the pioneer geologists of Bengal, Pramatha Nath Bose
(1855-1934), the first Indian to be appointed to the graded staff of
the Geological Survey of India, discovered the haematite deposits
of Gurumaishini and other places in Mayurbhanj in 1904, while
R. Saubolle, a prospector of Martin & Co., Calcutta, found those
of Pansira Buru and Buda Buru, in Singhbhum, in 1907, for the
ores that had been worked earlier in that region were the magnetites of the ultrabasic magnesian rocks in the neighbourhood of
Kalimati near Tatanagar railway station. Later work by various
geologists revealed that in a region lying from 150 to 200 miles
west of Calcutta, within parts of Singhbhum, Keonjhar, Bonai and
Mayurbhanj, there exists one of the major iron ore fields of the
world in which enormous tonnages of rich ore are readily available.
It occurs usually at or near the tops of hill ranges, the most important of which runs from near Rontha in Bonai in a north-north-
easterly direction, rising 1,500 feet above the surrounding plains,
for about 30 miles: along practically the whole of this length, with
a few negligible breaks, high-grade haematite, averaging over 60
per cent of iron, is found. Smaller ranges roughly parallel to the
main one also contain good ore. In 1934, H. C. Jones estimated
the minimum quantity of ore with not less than 60 per cent iron,
then known, at 2,701,000,000 tons, distributed as follows in the
various areas—Singhbhum 1,047, Bonai (now in Sundargarh district)
648, Keonjhar 988 and Mayurbhanj 18 millions of tons.

In the Hirapur hills, some 5 or 6 miles west of Umarkot, in the
Koraput district of Orissa, there is a minimum quantity of 10
million tons of haematite averaging perhaps 60 per cent of iron and
0·3 per cent phosphoric oxide (P_2O_5), and ranging up to 62·7 per
cent iron, according to A. M. N. Ghosh. In 1939-40 B. C. Roy
examined the widely scattered lateritic deposits of Sambalpur,
ten of which he concluded contained 50 million tons of ore with
55 to 60 per cent of iron and 0·31 per cent of phosphorus; the
largest of these, on the Nalibassa hill, has about 15 million tons of
ore. A large deposit of haematite was discovered recently on the
Tomaka Range in the Sukinda area of the Cuttack district, Orissa,
by G. P. Rath. A representative sample of the surface ore
contained 68·7 per cent iron, 0·016 per cent phosphorus and under
0·01 per cent sulphur. The total reserves are said to be of the
order of 27 million tons of various grades. The deposit is now
being worked for export.

Further investigation by Dr M. S. Krishnan soon increased the
Keonjhar reserves to 1,483,250,000 tons. Later revaluations here and

elsewhere, as a result of further geological surveys and the evidence brought to light as mining operations have extended, enable the Geological Survey of India today to compute the probable total amount of high-grade iron ore available in Bihar and Orissa as approximately 8,000,000,000 tons, most of which can be won by open-cast methods. Moreover, there is perhaps double that quantity of lower-grade workable ore, to say nothing of vast tonnages of banded haematite, quartzite and ferruginous laterites containing around 30 per cent of iron. Mining operations have also shown that the solid haematite gives place to an unconsolidated or powdery variety at different depths.

The Iron Ore Series consists of conglomerates, purple sandstones and limestones, overlain by ferruginous shales and banded haematite quartzites with the iron orebodies, followed in their turn by another thick, shaly group with epidiorites and ash beds. The whole Series is of Archaean age and forms the uppermost of the two unconformable groups into which the Dharwarian rocks of Singhbhum have been divided.

Many theories have been advanced to account for these vast iron ore deposits but the one most generally put forward and accepted by H. C. Jones, F. G. Percival and Dr M. S. Krishnan is that originally their iron contents were marine, chemical precipitates, probably from solutions carried into the sea through the leaching of adjacent land masses. From them in the long course of geological time, the banded haematite quartzites and the haematite jaspers were formed, which many observers consider to be the mother rock of the ores. There is much field evidence tending to prove that the ores themselves arose through the replacement of the silica of the haematite quartzites by hydrated ferric oxide which later became converted into haematite. The removal of the silica and the replacement processes were brought about by the action of descending meteoric waters, and in those locations where the replacement has not been completed, broken, slumped, crumbly, porous, slabby and powdery ores exist.

M. V. Wazalwar[1] and others, however, take another view and believe that the shales are chiefly responsible for the formation of the iron orebodies and for that matter for the manganese ores of Keonjhar and Bonai as well. They hold that the original iron and manganese contents of the shales were unevenly distributed, possibly along certain well-defined zones, stating that the shales themselves have been found to pass laterally into banded magnetite quartzites as well as into banded manganese ore varieties. The quartzite masses in the shales, they think, are of a secondary character and seem to have been formed by percolating solutions in the zone of oxidation. At a later stage, the leaching out of silica and the enrichment of iron, as a result in large degree of colloidal

[1] Personal communication.

reactions, led to the building up of the orebodies. They also adduce evidence of the genesis of oxidic ores through an intermediate hydroxide stage aided locally by the comparatively high temperatures brought about by the intrusion of basic dykes, granites, pegmatites and quartz veins into the shales. 'The formation of the iron orebodies was on a much grander scale than that of the manganese ore deposits, which tend rather to occur as both large and small, irregular, segregated masses.

Dr J. A. Dunn (1935) divided the Iron Ore Series as follows:

5. Dalma series of volcanic flows.
4. Tuffs, lava flows, shales, phyllites and mica schists, quartzites and conglomerates.
3. Shales, phyllites and mica schists.
2. Limestones.
1. Sandstone conglomerates.

The iron ores and associated banded haematite quartzites occur in Zone 4. Dunn rejected the theory of their sedimentary origin and argued that they were formed by the secondary silicification of material now represented by ferruginous, chloritic or carbon shales or phyllites, many of which were tuffs in the first instance. He thought that this silicification was in part contemporaneous with the deposition of the beds themselves and resulted from thermal activities which accompanied the formation of the volcanic series. The iron, according to Dunn's views, was derived partly from the oxidation of the tuffs and flows *in situ* and partly represents a wash from them. Later solutions are believed to have rearranged the ferruginous contents with the production of the massive iron ores.

The haematites vary much in their physical qualities, and massive, laminated, micaceous, powdery, lateritic and brecciated kinds occur. The iron content is usually about 64 per cent, phosphorus ranges normally from 0·03 to 0·08, but may be as high as 0·15 per cent, sulphur is usually below 0·03 per cent. The chief characteristics of these ores are their high iron, low sulphur and titanium, and variable phosphorus contents.

IRON ORE MINING IN SINGHBHUM AND KEONJHAR

The Indian Iron & Steel Co. Ltd, the successors in title of the Bengal Iron Co. Ltd, has been exploiting since 1938 the deposits of Pansira Buru and Buda Buru in Singhbhum, 12 and 8 miles respectively south-east of Manharpur station on the Eastern Railway, to which they were connected by a light line about 1911. An aerial ropeway, carrying 40 tons per hour, transports the ore from the top of Pansira Buru to the storage bins at its foot, whence it is discharged automatically into the railway wagons. A gravity incline, with a capacity of 60 tons per hour, brings ore down from a spur of Buda Buru to the railway at its foot. The total quantity of ore available at Pansira Buru was originally estimated at nearly

10 million tons and at Buda Buru at 150 million tons. In both localities it is a high-grade haematite with the following average composition:

Iron	..	64·0 per cent	Magnesia	..	0·18 per cent
Silica	..	2·10 ,, ,,	Manganese oxide.	0·05 ,, ,,
Lime	..	0·15 ,, ,,	Sulphur ..	..	0·002 ,, ,,
Alumina	..	1·25 ,, ,,	Phosphorus	..	0·05 ,, ,,

The Gua mines of the same concern are also in Singhbhum, near the termination of a branch line of the Eastern Railway, ore dispatches having commenced with its completion in 1923. At present about 2,500 tons of ore are moved daily, by three self-acting inclines, to the head of a ropeway which delivers it to the railway.

The ores of the Bagia Buru range, which runs parallel to the Bara Jamda-Barabil branch of the Eastern Railway, have been quarried by the United Steel Corporation of Asia Ltd, a company managed by Messrs Bird & Co. Ltd, since 1923. These workings are in Keonjhar and yield haematite containing 58 to 60 per cent of iron. This concern, having at present no plant of its own, sells its ore to other smelters and at one time exported a substantial tonnage outside India. Manganiferous iron ores, containing between 30 and 35 per cent of manganese and about 20 per cent of iron in the form of limonite, are also obtained in the same vicinity and are sold to iron manufacturers in India.

The Noamundi mine of the Tata Iron & Steel Co. Ltd is also in Singhbhum, though its orebodies actually extend into Keonjhar. It is connected to the Amda-Gua extension of the Eastern Railway, to which two aerial ropeways deliver ore to the bins at Noamundi station. Discovered by R. Saubolle and C. R. N. Aiyengar, independently, in 1917, it consists chiefly of two parallel ridges, each about 2½ miles long and ½ mile wide at the north, becoming much broader at the south, and was described in detail by F. G. Percival (1931). He classified its ores into two grades, the first of which includes the massive and laminated haematites as well as the lateritic ones, while the second embraces the powdery and soft, shaly ores. The reserves of the former were estimated at 140 million tons and of the latter at 88 million tons. Dispatches commenced in 1926, while the bulk of the ore handled today is of the laminated type and averages about 60 per cent iron, 4 per cent silica and 5 per cent alumina. The soft powdery ores, both here and elsewhere, are of no immediate interest, for though they are rich in iron and could be sintered economically, they are not likely to be used while supplies of hard ore are so readily available for the blast furnaces.

Singhbhum and Keonjhar together supplied over 57 per cent of all the iron ore smelted in India up to the end of 1946, the former exceeding an annual output of one million tons in 1927 and, with varying fluctuations, reaching a peak of 1,800,574 tons in 1941, falling again to 974,805 tons in 1946, and averaging 1,406,823 tons yearly over the decade 1937 to 1946. Keonjhar passed the half million ton mark with 507,133 tons in 1944 and its average for the same decade was 401,531 tons per annum.

IRON ORE MINING IN MAYURBHANJ

Over twelve deposits of high-grade iron ore occur in the more accessible parts of Mayurbhanj, and three of them—Gorumahisani, Sulaipat (Okampad) and Badampahar—have been developed by the Tata Company. They are all joined to the Eastern Railway by a branch line about 56 miles in length. The ores are of the same types as those of Singhbhum and interbedded with them are haematite quartzites and shales. Gorumahisani is a hill mass with three separate peaks, the highest of which rises 3,000 feet above sea level. Estimated to contain 9,800,000 tons of ore by E. Curnow in 1914-15, it has actually yielded over 13 million tons, while later discoveries of rich material both *in situ* and as detritus have so augmented the reserves that at the end of 1946 they still amounted to some 19 million tons. An average of 20 analyses of detrital ore shows iron 61·46, phosphorus 0·048, sulphur 0·036, silica 3·34 per cent. The average composition of ten samples of solid ore shows iron 64·33, phosphorus 0·075, sulphur 0·021 and silica 1·64 per cent.

Okampad and Sulaipat (2,535 feet) are prominent peaks, a mile apart and some 12 miles south-south-west of Gorumahisani. The railway reached the neighbourhood in 1922 and a tram line connects the mine with it. The main orebody, again associated with banded haematite quartzites, lies at the crest of the hill and, with an outlier, was estimated by Curnow to contain 2,270,000 tons. On the removal of the rich ' float ' ore, however, further ore bands were discovered, so that although approximately 3,186,000 tons had been removed, the remaining reserves at the end of 1946 amounted to 850,000 tons. The Sulaipat ore is low in phosphorus and one of the finest in quality.

The Badampahar deposit occupies the 2,706-foot peak of the same name in the Sulaipat-Badampahar range, 8½ miles south-west of the Sulaipat mine. Its reserves, according to Jones, were about 7 million tons in 1928, but in 1940 further discoveries of large orebodies greatly increased them, so that by 1944 they were still of the order of 44 million tons. Dispatches up to December 1946 totalled 7,416,000 tons. A yellow ore, long neglected because of its poor appearance, is now mined; its bulk analysis shows iron 66·6, silica 0·72, alumina 0·42, phosphorus 0·062, sulphur 0·15, combined water 2·40 per cent and, like many of these ores, no titanium. The yellow colour may be due to the presence of ' limonite ' and the ore seems to be a product of replacement of a basic igneous rock. A small, isolated mass of magnetite also exists, but the greater bulk of the Badampahar ore is haematite which, while not so high in iron content as the varieties from Gorumahisani or Sulaipat, is highly valued by the smelters on account of its more porous character. A representative sample, quoted by Jones, had a composition of iron 57·60, manganese 0·52, silica 5·60, alumina 5·02, phosphorus 0·074 per cent; the average composition of the ore as mined in 1945–6 was iron 55·60, silica 7·39 and alumina 2·88 per cent. Work was commenced at both the Sulaipat and Badampahar mines in 1922.

The output of iron ore from Mayurbhanj, responsible for over 42·5 per cent of the total won from Bihar and Orissa up to the end of 1946, approached closely to 1 million tons per annum by 1924 and passed that figure by 1926. It then declined on the whole over a series of years, only to rise again later, so that the annual average for the decade ending 1946 reached 950,615 tons.

Smaller Deposits of the Ores of Iron

The enormous ore deposits of southern Singhbhum completely overshadow smaller ones of a similar character in various parts of Chota Nagpur which cannot be mined in competition with them. Others of different characters, both here and elsewhere, may find their special uses, as was indeed the case with the magnetites of Kudada and Patharghara, now exhausted, but worked at one time for the manufacture of high-phosphorus foundry pig iron. Similar magnetite ores occur on Gore Pahar, in Palamau, where Auden has estimated reserves of about 350,000 tons; at Sua, near Daltonganj, where A. K. Dey discovered another deposit, and near Sankhamur in Pallahara, Orissa, where B. C. Gupta found lenses of manganiferous magnetite. Analyses of the Gore Pahar ore show ferric oxide 69·23 to 72·66, ferrous oxide 21·60 to 22·50, silica 1·40 to 5·54, titania 0·50 to 1·60, alumina 0·50 to 1·10 and phosphorus pentoxide 0·02 to 0·03 per cent. The titanium- and vanadium-bearing iron ores are described separately under Titanium and Vanadium and it remains to mention the lenticles and nodules of a softer, limonitic, clay-ironstone character found in the Damuda Valley coalfields which served as a source of iron in the early days, and for which demand may arise again, for their use, after suitable treatment, in the desulphurizing processes of coking plants and gas-works.

Iron Ore Deposits of Madhya Pradesh

The iron ores of Madhya Pradesh are not systematically worked at present, though they have been drawn upon, as, for example, in 1923 and 1924, when for various accidental reasons, the mines of the companies operating in Singhbhum were unable to furnish regular supplies for their furnaces.

In the Chanda district at least ten separate deposits have been located, forming well-developed beds of haematite, sometimes with magnetite, associated with banded haematite quartzites of Dharwarian age. The two best known are at Lohara, described by Hughes in 1873 and by P. N. Dutta in 1910, and Pipalgaon (Hughes 1873). The former crops out in a hill nearly half a mile long, 200 yards wide and 120 feet high, and has been traced for a further 2½ miles. Regarding it Hughes wrote as follows: ' The view presented by such a mass of almost pure specular iron it does not fall to the lot of many men to see surpassed and those who possess the opportunity of visiting this place ought to do so, and carry away with them the remembrance of having looked upon one of the marvels of the Indian mineral world.' The Pipalgaon deposit he described as: 'An excessively fine mass of red haematite resembling that which occurs at Lohara if not having the same composition.'

The available quantities and compositions of the ores of these two, and of two further localities, Asola and Dewalgaon, as proved by V. R. R. Khedker in 1946, are shown in the following table:

ANALYSES OF CHANDA IRON ORES

	Reserves tons	COMPOSITION								
		SiO_2	Al_2O_3	Fe_2O_3	FeO	P	S	TiO_2	Total	Fe
Lohara ..	21 million	1·44	1·52	91·36	5·38	0·02	0·12	nil	99·84	68·04
Pipalgaon ..	300,000	1·56	1·07	82·37	14·12	0·09	0·10	nil	99·90	69·02
Asola ..	400,000	8·26	2·48	81·22	7·90	0·08	0·11	nil	100·00	62·91
Dewalgaon ..	250,000	2·90	2·24	85·35	9·33	0·02	0·14	nil	99·90	66·90

The ores of the Drug district were briefly described by Bose in 1887 and he noted that the most extensive deposits occurred in the Dhalli-Lohara *zemindari*. This region was investigated by C. M. Weld for the Tata Company in 1914. The iron ores resist the action of denudation and rise in hillocks above the level of the surrounding country. The ridge which includes the Dhalli and Rajhara hills extends for about 20 miles and attains heights of 400 feet above the plains. The ores are associated with phyllites and are often of the quartz-iron ore schist type, while the purer varieties form lenticular bodies at two horizons; those in the lower band being from 2,000 to 3,000 feet in length and 100 feet or so in thickness but the others in the upper band are comparatively smaller. The limited mass of haematite forming the crest of Rajhara Hill itself was proved by core-boring to contain 7½ million tons of ore with about 67·5 per cent of iron and a phosphorus content just below the Bessemer limit. More recent work has demonstrated that this is just a small portion of the reserves available here, for the western portion of Rajhara Hill is now known to contain a further 37½ million tons, while additional amounts of 24, 25 and 20 million tons are believed to be available near Jharandalli, Kondekasa and to the south-east of the latter place, respectively. The composition of the Rajhara ores is shown by the following analyses, the average of 64 samples:

ANALYSES OF RAJHARA IRON ORES

	IRON	PHOS-PHORUS	SULPHUR	SILICA	MANGANESE
Surface ore	66·35	0·058	0·108	1·44	0·151
Core ore	68·56	0·064	0·071	0·71	0·175

It has long been known that extensions of these ore deposits were to be found in Kanker and Bastar, to the south of Drug, and to P. N. Bose again goes the credit of noting two extensive deposits in the Antagarh *tahsil* of Bastar, over 50 years ago. It is only within recent years, however, that their magnitude and quality have been realized. H. Crookshank reported in 1938 that there are cliffs of iron ore, up to 500 feet in height, in the Bailadila Range of Bastar, capable of yielding at least 610 million tons of first-class ore with over 68 per cent iron, 0·096 per cent phosphorus and 0·042 per cent sulphur. Later work by A. M. Heron and D. K. Chatterjee increased these reserves to 3,600 million tons. Again, on the crest of the Rowghat, there are, according to D. K. Chatterjee, 740 million tons of haematite, with some limonite, within a depth of 150 feet of the surface. An average analysis of 34 samples from this area gave iron 64, phosphorus 0·08, and silica 1·76 per cent. The largest individual deposit on the south-west of the ridge contains some 500 million tons, the average of ten analyses of which showed iron 65·86, phosphorus 0·05, and silica 1·04 per cent. In some of these deposits the ores are soft and porous and, at times, limonitic.

In Kanker, Bastar district, K. K. Dutta and P. K. Chatterjee have found about 6 million tons of massive haematite with over 64 per cent of iron and practically no phosphorus, on the Ari *dungri*, near Parrekoro. A further 20 million tons of detrital, micaceous and specular haematite, in plates and slabs up to 4 feet across, is available, within a depth of 5 feet, around the base of the Ari *dungri*.

IRON ORES OF MYSORE

The ores of iron are widely distributed in Mysore but the only ones under exploitation are those of the Bababudan Hills, in the Chikmagalur district, originally described by Smeeth and Iyengar, as well as certain others including Sandur, Hospet and Ramagiri, which accrued to the State after its merger with the Bellary district in 1953. The crest of the Bababudan horseshoe-shaped chain of hills is formed almost entirely of banded quartz-iron ore rocks, largely haematite with some magnetite. The ores themselves, according to Smeeth, are either desilicified portions of these rocks or metasomatic replacements of quartz and silicates resulting in the formation of rich haematitic and limonitic mixtures, particularly on the more gentle slopes and undulations. Sampat Iyengar regarded the more or less banded and porous limonite-haematite ores as depositions of iron compounds removed in solution by meteoric waters from portions of the desilicified ferruginous quartz-zites. No estimates appear to have been made of the total ore reserves of these fields, though Smeeth gives figures for certain independent occurrences which are now superseded by the recent investigations of J. P. David. In the ridge and scarp of the Dupa-dagiri section of the Kemmangandi field he has proved the presence of 20 million tons of ore, averaging 54 per cent iron, 7 per cent alumina, 3 per cent silica and 0·10 per cent phosphorus, after making an allowance of 50 per cent in the total for rejections on account of lateritic impurities. The ores of the Kalhattigiri section are, according to David, of inferior quality to those of Kemman-gandi, and the reserves of workable ore therein are unlikely to exceed 10 million tons. Formerly, only ores averaging about 60 per cent iron were won for the Mysore Iron Works at Bhadravati, but today material ranging between 55 per cent and 60 per cent iron is supplied to them.

At Kemmangandi the ore is transported from the ridge to the base of the hill by a mono-cable ropeway, erected in 1924, and thence by tramway to the Bhadravati works, 23 miles away. A bi-cable ropeway, three miles long, is under construction, the upper terminus of which, 3,000 feet above its lower end, is in tramway connexion with the scarp and Dupadagiri sections. Mining commenced in 1923, and up to the end of 1946 787,256 tons of ore had been removed. Output varies with the demand for charcoal iron, and over the decade 1937 to 1946 averaged 37,157 tons per annum.

In Sandur, rich haematites derived from haematite quartzites are found as cappings, 100 to 200 feet thick, in association with manganese ores. These have been investigated by M. S. Venkat-ram who estimates that they contain a total of about 130 million tons, within 50 to 80 feet of the surface, in the following areas:

Donimalai	25,600,000 tons	Kanavehalli Range.	500,000 tons
Devadari Range ..	15,000,000 ,,	Ramandrug ..	30,300,000 ,,
Kumaraswami-Kammadheruvu.	25,400,000 ,,	Timmappanagudi.	32,800,000 ,,

In the extension of the Sandur ranges into Hospet taluk, there are, according to M. Krishna Murthy, about 6 million tons of haematite with iron content ranging between 60 and 65 per cent. The ores vary from soft to hard, massive, steel grey types and usually contain over 60 per cent of iron. About 2 million tons of iron ore of much the same quality are available in the Copper Mountain to the south-west of Bellary.

No account of the iron ores of Mysore would be complete without a brief reference to the discontinuous bands of ferruginous quartzites, and the magnetite-quartz rocks derived from them, which stretch from the south-western corner of the Bangalore district, across Tumkur into the Chitaldrug district. The magnetite-quartz rocks of the Maddur-Malavalli area of Mandya are amenable to magnetic concentration and yield products averaging 60 to 70 per cent of iron, with no more than traces of phosphorus, sulphur and titanium. B. P. Radhakrishna has estimated reserves of these rocks amounting to 41½ million tons, carrying an iron content of between 40 and 50 per cent. Similar ores, amounting to some 13 million tons, are said to be available in the Sargur area. In the Kunigal area of Tumkur there are probably a further 32 million tons to be found, but as garnet, hypersthene and amphibole are also present, they may prove of inferior quality. The Hiriyur area of Chitaldrug, Radhakrishna has computed, contains 55 million tons of brown haematite assaying 80 per cent of ferric oxide, with traces of sulphur and phosphorus, but a certain proportion of this consists of soft, powdery ore. In the Shimoga district too, which lies to the west of Chitaldrug, limonitic ores associated with manganese ores occur on the crest of Shankarguda. Analyses of these ores range up to 60 per cent of iron, but their high phosphorus content (0·1 per cent) precludes their utilization at present.

Iron Ores of Madras & Andhra

Iron ores are abundant enough in the Salem district of Madras to have led so astute a geologist as the late Sir Thomas Holland to declare that they are practically inexhaustible. For full details of their many occurrences in this and other districts of the State, the reader must be referred to the publications of the Geological Survey of India, and particularly to the writings of W. King and R. Bruce Foote, as only a selection from the recent investigations can be mentioned briefly here.

N. K. N. Aiyengar examined a large number of magnetite-bearing quartzite bands in the Salem-Tiruchirapalli (Trichinopoly) region in 1947 and found them intercalated with mica and chlorite schists, garnetiferous amphibolites and gneisses of Dharwar age. He regards the magnetite as a metamorphic derivative of haematite which, with an amphibole of the iron-bearing grunerite group, occurs in these ores in small quantities. Holland had already suggested that the common occurrence of magnetite with the haematite represented a stage in the thermal metamorphism of haematitic quartzites. The reserves of the more conspicuous and richer bands are conservatively estimated at 305 million tons, with an iron content of 35 to 40 per cent and phosphorus 0·03 to 0·15 per cent, distributed as follows:

Kanjamalai	..	55,000,000 tons	Attur area ..	.. 12,000,000	tons
Godumalai	..	12,500,000 ,,	Tirthamalai	.. 48,000,000	,,
Perumamalai	..	10,000,000 ,,	Rasipur-Namakkal.	34,000,000	,,
Chitteri and			Kollaimalai	.. 67,000,000	,,
Tainanda Hills	..	55,000,000 ,,	Pachchaimalai	.. 11,000,000	,,

A comprehensive report on these iron ores by Dr M. S. Krishnan and N. K. N. Aiyengar has been published by the Government of Madras. The magnetite at the foot of the Kanjamalai near Virapandi station in Salem is said to exhibit polarity.

In the Nidle, Konaje and Yenakal reserved forests and in the hills east of Kirnadka and Ajana of the Puttur taluk of South Kanara, S. Krishnaswamy and B. R. C. Iyengar have found ferruginous quartzites locally giving rise to lateritic iron ores containing over 50 per cent of iron. Lying near the coast these deposits are favourably situated for export purposes, but their extent, depth and reserves still need determination.

Several occurrences of good haematite, partly specular in character, have been developed along a fault plane which cuts across the basal Cuddapah rocks, and trends in an east to west direction, through Veldurti and Ramallakota in the Kurnool district, Andhra. These deposits were the subject of a detailed report by Dr M. S. Krishnan and M. S. Balasundaram, published by the Government of Madras, and contain some 4 million tons of ore within a depth of 100 feet from the surface, with an iron content ranging between 48 and 65 per cent and sulphur and phosphorus between 0·008 and 0·01 per cent, respectively. As far as existing knowledge goes the only other deposits in Andhra worthy of mention are those of the Copper Mountain in the Rayadrug taluk of Anantapur district where, according to M. Krishna Murthy, haematite of the order of 500,000 tons with over 60 per cent iron is available and the occurrences of Chabali, Pagadalapalle and Rajampet in Cuddapah, assumed to be capable of yielding some 300,000 tons, of which about one quarter may carry an iron content of 60 per cent or more. In the Chittoor district there is a band of iron ore, with up to 48 per cent of iron, near Sirsanambedu, which extends in a south-westerly direction into Nellore district. Detrital ore lying within three feet of the surface is being worked at present north of Jaggayyapeta in Krishna district and in the adjacent parts of Hyderabad, but the total reserves may not exceed 1½ million tons with 60 per cent or more iron content and up to 0·05 per cent phosphorus. Veins of magnetite in acid charnockites reported from near Bhimavaram, Yelleswaram, etc., in the Agency Tracts of the East Godavari district are apparently too small in extent to be of value.

Iron Ores of Hyderabad

The iron ores of Hyderabad occur in bands made up of crumpled, alternating layers of haematite (or magnetite) and quartz, $\frac{1}{8}$ to $\frac{1}{4}$ inch thick, the two minerals being present in approximately equal amounts. They are, in fact, typical banded haematite quartzites of Dharwarian age with an average iron content of about 40 per cent. As a general rule the bands run in straight lines and may be up to 3 or 4 miles long; their average thickness is about 50 feet, and their maximum thickness in the Chityal hills of the Adilabad district is 160 feet. They generally possess high dips and are often vertical, though in the Amberpet hills of the Karimnagar district, an exceptionally low dip of 22° upwards has been measured. Massive unlaminated iron ore without quartz is rare in Hyderabad; for example, in the whole of the Godavari river section at Chityal, with its total of 160 feet of ironstones, only one layer of solid ore up to 6 inches in thickness is known and it is only traceable for a few yards. Six main deposits have been mapped, each of which contains over five million tons of ore down to plains' level: Chityal, Kalleda-Dasturabad and Rebanpalli in Adilabad; Chandoli (Amberpet) in Karimnagar; Singareni in Warangal, and Kushtagi in Raichur district. There are innumerable smaller orebodies, according to Dr A. M. Heron, from whose account this note is summarized. These iron ores belong to a group common enough in many other parts of India, from which only low-grade, siliceous ores are obtainable without some form of mechanical concentration, and it is obvious that they compare unfavourably with the rich, high-grade ores now used by Indian iron smelters.

No account of the iron ores of Hyderabad would be complete without a reference to Konasamudram (east of Nizamabad), one of the localities where the steel was made from which the Damascus blades of the Middle Ages were fashioned. It was still being made and sold to Persian traders in 1820 when H. W. Voysey visited the place. A light brown, ferruginous lateritic ore from Tadpalli (Tadpolli) was the chief raw material, but the merits of the steel depended not on this, but on the metallurgical knowledge involved in the carburization and heat treatment of the iron smelted from it.

Other Iron Ore Deposits

It is known that there are deposits of haematite near Ratnagiri, in Bombay, and also in Goa. The reserves are said to be of the order of 10 million tons but no reliable estimates are available. The ores are believed to owe their origin to the removal of silica from ferruginous quartzites of Dharwar age. An agreement was announced in October 1951 between a mining company in Portuguese territory and the Konkan Mining Company of Japan, whereby the latter was to install on the former's mine, complete mechanical equipment designed for a maximum daily production of 2,000 tons of iron ore. This is stated to have involved a capital outlay of Rs 1½ crores, some Rs 75 lakhs of which was advanced to the Konkan Company as a loan by the Export and Import Bank of Japan and repayment for which is to be made by means of a *pro rata* export of ore to Japan. The open-cast mine of Sirigao, 32 miles inland from the port of Marmagao, now fully mechanized by Japanese engineers, was formally opened by the Governor-General of Portuguese India on 13 October 1953. The ore is delivered by chutes from storage bins at the mine direct into barges for water transport to Marmagao, whence it is exported.

Near Narnaul in Patiala, P. N. Bose in 1905 discovered bands of magnetite-haematite ores associated with ferruginous quartzites and granitoid gneisses. Later investigations have revealed reserves of the order of 5 million tons to a depth of 300 feet. Samples contained iron $57 \cdot 4$, alumina $4 \cdot 8$, silica $9 \cdot 3$, phosphorus $0 \cdot 43$ and sulphur $0 \cdot 15$ per cent.

Extensive deposits of magnetite with haematite occur as bands in quartzites in the Chichot subdivision of Mandi, Himachal Pradesh, but as G. Kohli has observed, there are no prospects of these being exploited as long as the high-grade ores of the country are available.

Low-grade, siliceous iron ores, in the form of banded haematite and magnetite quartzites, are common enough in the Dharwars and similar schistose rocks in Peninsular India to make newly recorded finds of little immediate economic concern. This also applies in the case of the ferruginous laterites which, although they often furnished ores for the small local furnaces in times past, are not utilized by the ironmaster of today. The lengthy lists of the iron ore occurrences of practically every State cannot be summarized here, but the interested reader will find them in La Touche's *Annotated Index of Minerals of Economic Value*, and in the *Annual General Reports* of the Directors of the Geological Survey of India, which have appeared since the publication of that work in 1918.

No deposits of high-grade iron ores comparable in any way with those of Peninsular India occur in either Pakistan or Burma, though the low-grade ferruginous laterites of the Salt Range Jurassic sequence, or the similar material at the base of the Eocene in Baluchistan and elsewhere, were worked for small-scale local consumption in the past in some localities. A survey made in 1952 revealed that the Mianwali, Sargodha and Attock districts of West Punjab have workable deposits of iron ore containing about 40 per cent iron.[1]

---

[1] In the North-West Frontier Province, iron ores are known to occur in the Panjkora valley; a large deposit of magnetite has been reported recently from Gowai in Chitral, where haematite also exists in quantity between Sanoghar and Mastey; a band of good, earthy haematite, 5 or 6 feet thick, was noted by Middlemiss on Sorban Hill in Hazara; while in Waziristan, local deposits of haematite and concretionary limonite occur in the Eocene or Mesozoic sedimentary strata.

The Pakistan Industrial Development Corporation has recently concluded an agreement with Krupps for the setting up of a pilot steel plant with an annual capacity of 50,000 tons of iron ingots in 1957, and later another plant capable of producing 300,000 tons of steel yearly at Kot Addu, West Punjab, where a big power station is to be installed by laying a pipe line from Sui to Addu.

The iron ore deposits of Burma are mainly of a lateritic character and are widely distributed throughout the country, forming the basis of the indigenous industry in the times of the Burmese Kings. None of them, so far as is known, offers any prospect of successful large-scale exploitation, especially in the absence of coking coals in the country. For special purposes they have their uses, as instanced by their role in the reduction of the lead ores of Bawdwin, and are obtainable in suitable grades from irregular beds capriciously distributed at the base of the red earths of the Shan Plateau.

It remains to add that manganiferous iron ores are quarried in India for blending purposes; that the nodules of clay ironstone found in the shales of some of the coalfields were for many years used as a source of iron by the Bengal Iron Co. Ltd; that the Travancore titaniferous iron sands are exported in very large amounts as a source of titanium compounds; that in the vanadiferous ores of Bihar and Orissa, the country possesses a potential source of that valuable metal; that certain varieties of massive haematite from Badampahar in Singhbhum and Sandur in Bellary have been found suitable for the production of hydrogen by the water-gas method adopted by the Fertilizer Works at Alwaye in Travancore, though high Indian railway freights make it more profitable to import Spanish ores for the purpose; and that various oxidized ores, often of a lateritic nature, furnish most of the natural red, brown and yellow pigments of the land.

The latest available estimates of the reserves of the major iron ore deposits of India are as follows:

IRON ORE RESERVES

| STATE | DISTRICT | TONNAGE | | IRON CONTENT |
		ESTIMATED	PROBABLE	
Bihar ..	Singhbhum	1,047,000,000	8,000,000,000	Mostly 60 – 68% Fe
Orissa ..	Keonjhar, Sundargarh	2,131,000,000		
	Mayurbhanj, Cuttack	91,000,000		
	Sambalpur, Koraput..	60,000,000		55 – 63% Fe
Madhya Pradesh..	Drug, Chanda, Bastar	4,482,000,000		60 – 68% Fe
Madras ..	Salem-Tiruchirapalli..	305,000,000	1,000,000,000	35 – 40% Fe
Mysore ..	Chikmagalur	30,000,000		50 – 60% Fe
	Bellary	138,000,000	300,000,000	45 – 65% Fe
Andhra ..	Anantapur, Kurnool, Cuddapah and Krishna	6,000,000		45 – 65% Fe
	TOTAL ..	8,290,000,000		

The vast quantities of workable, though somewhat lower-grade, ores of Singhbhum are not taken into account in the computation.

PRODUCTION OF IRON ORE IN INDIA, 1900–50

Period	Bihar and Orissa	Bengal	Burma	Madhya Pradesh	Mysore	Others	Total Tonnage	Total Value (Rs)	Average Annual Tonnage
1900–3	....	252,111	..	..	..	14,400*	266,511	5,81,775	66,628
1904–8	....	383,431†	..	10,949	..	13,134	407,514	10,32,690	81,502
1909–13	1,282,392	95,274	59,998	13,058	..	4,564	1,455,286	22,14,330	291,057
1914–18	2,001,643	3,447‡	106,532	37,379	..	747	2,149,748	26,11,590	429,949
1919–23	3,257,233	..	200,014	35,793	16,669§	757	3,510,466	77,67,619	702,093
1924–8	8,025,628	..	294,595	72,222	158,692	776	8,551,913	2,36,87,815	1,710,382
1929–33	8,619,115	..	124,337	3,983	135,388	10,943§§	8,893,766	2,19,47,239	1,778,745
1934–8	12,199,389	..	116,807	3,212	173,037	....	12,492,445	1,98,56,516	2,498,489
1939–43	15,096,356	..	..	2,287	236,867¶	2,970	15,338,480	2,75,94,530	3,067,696
1944–8	11,629,963	..	..	2,963	184,244	1,382	11,818,552	3,64,38,862	2,363,710
1949–50	5,666,426	..	..	1,624	92,166	13,500¶¶	5,773,716	2,80,34,353	2,886,858
Total	67,778,145	734,263	902,283	183,470	997,063	63,173	70,658,397	17,17,67,319**	.....

* Estimated.
† 286,347 tons from Bengal and 97,084 tons from districts which later became part of Bihar and Orissa.
‡ Ceased in 1915.   § Started in 1923.
¶ Includes 14,441 tons from Sandur in 1939 and 1940.
§§ All from Madras.
¶¶ From Bombay.
** Rs 17,17,67,319 = £12,882,547 @ Rs 1 = 1s. 6d.

THE MANUFACTURE OF IRON AND STEEL

Fifty years ago, about 1900, the average annual production of pig iron in India was approximately 35,000 tons, which came entirely from the works of the Bengal Iron & Steel Co. Ltd. For the five years ending 1950, it averaged 1,532,000 tons in round figures. The manufacture of steel commenced in 1912 and by 1941 had increased to over 1,000,000 tons per annum. Of the grand total of 41,716,412 tons of pig iron made during the present century, 63 per cent was produced by the Tata Iron & Steel Co. Ltd, 30 per cent by the Indian Iron & Steel Co. Ltd, 5·7 per cent by the Bengal Iron Co. Ltd or its predecessors, before its amalgamation with the Indian Iron & Steel Co. Ltd in 1936, and 1·3 per cent by the Mysore Iron Works. Of the grand total of 20,142,893 tons of steel, the Tata concern made 86·3 per cent, the Steel Corporation of Bengal 11·4 per cent, and the Mysore Works 2·3 per cent. Details of the growth of the industries are tabulated in the tables on pp. 199 and 201.

The Indian Iron & Steel Co. Ltd. The early history of the Bengal Iron Co. Ltd has already been mentioned; after various changes of fortune it went into voluntary liquidation in 1936 and was amalgamated with the Indian Iron & Steel Co. Ltd, a company, registered in 1918, which had commenced to smelt iron ores from its own mines at Gua, in Singhbhum, in two 500-ton blast furnaces in November 1922, at Burnpore, near Asansol, 132 miles north-west of Calcutta. The works of the combined concern are at Kulti, the original home of the Bengal Iron Co., and at Hirapur. At Kulti there are now two mechanically charged blast furnaces with a capacity of a quarter of a million tons of pig iron per annum. Coal is carbonized on the spot in four batteries of 132 by-product ovens with an annual out-turn of 200,000 tons of coke, 2,000 tons of ammonium sulphate, 6,500 tons of tar and 300,000 gallons of crude benzol.

The Company has inherited the long-time specialization of the Bengal Iron Co. in the manufacture of cast iron products and large foundries adjoin the blast furnaces, comprising pipe, railway sleeper and general castings sections. A spun-pipe foundry, added in 1945, has an annual capacity of 20,000 tons of cast iron pressure pipes, from 3 to 12 inches in diameter. The combined capacity of all the foundries is about 70,000 tons of finished products of British and Indian Standard specifications. Recent new developments include a heavy pipe factory to turn out 20,000 tons per annum, additional mechanized foundries, and a department for the manufacture of small and medium-sized castings in non-ferrous metals, with a capacity of 400 tons per annum.

The Hirapur works have two 800-ton modern blast furnaces, employing the tunnel system for the conveyance of fuel, and 75-ton ladles which convey the molten metal to two double-strand pig

machines, or to the pig-casting beds as the case may be, while all
the finished metal is handled by magnets. The by-product coking
installation comprises two batteries, each of 80 Simon-Carvé, hori-
zontal-flue, waste-heat ovens, with a daily output of 1,000 tons of
coke; another battery of 40 compound ovens of under-jet type, by
the same makers, which add a further 450 tons of coke to the daily
out-turn, and additional compound ovens, installed in 1939, and
again in 1947, bringing the total coking capacity to approximately
44,000 tons per month. For the recovery of ammonium sulphate,
along with the other usual by-products, a contact sulphuric acid
plant, capable of making 60 tons of 77 per cent acid daily, has been
installed. The Company owns large reserves of coking coal in
areas adjacent to the works, though at the present time it derives
its supplies from its own collieries at Ramnagar in the Raniganj,
and Noonidih, Jitput and Chasnalla in the Jharia field. The
composition of some typical products is given below.

ANALYSES OF IRONS MADE BY THE INDIAN IRON & STEEL CO. LTD

Foundry Standard	Silicon %	Manganese %	Phosphorus* %	Sulphur %
No. 1 ..	2.75 to 3.25	1.00 to 1.50	0.20 to 0.30	0.030
No. 2 ..	2.25 to 2.75	ditto	ditto	0.035
No. 3 ..	1.75 to 2.25	ditto	ditto	0.040
No. 4 ..	1.50 to 1.75	ditto	ditto	0.050

* Irons with phosphorus contents up to 1.5 per cent are made as required.

The Indian Iron & Steel Co. Ltd and the Steel Corporation of
Bengal have extensions in progress with a contemplated out-turn
of 800,000 tons of steel ingots per annum. In October 1952 the
principle of the amalgamation of the two concerns was approved
and negotiations were continued with the Government of India
and the World Bank for finance for an expansion programme
estimated to cost Rs 31 crores (about £24 million); in the same
year the two concerns were merged into a single company.

The Tata Iron & Steel Co. Ltd. The works of this Company,
which was founded in 1907 by the enterprise of Jamshedji Nusser-
vanji Tata, are at Tatanagar, then the small village of Kalimati
and now a modern industrial town, covering an area of 25 square
miles and lying on the Bengal-Nagpur section of the Eastern
Railway, 154 miles west of Calcutta, about 115 miles south of the
Jharia coalfield and 45 miles north of the iron ore field of Mayurbhanj and 70 miles north-east of the Singhbhum deposits. Supplies
of limestone and dolomite are drawn from quarries at Birmitrapur and
Panposh in Gangpur, 117 and 110 miles from the works, respectively.

The original plant had two blast furnaces capable of making 250 tons of pig iron a day, which were ' blown in ' in November 1911 and September 1912 respectively, and four open-hearth steel furnaces each of 40 tons capacity.   Today there are five blast furnaces with daily capacities of 550, 900, 800, 800 and 1,000 tons, able to deliver some 1,100,000 tons of basic pig iron per annum as well as 15,000 tons of ferro-manganese.   The gases from the blast furnaces, before being used in the stoves or under the boilers, are cleaned by modern methods, including a Lodge-Cottrell installation dealing with 15 million cubic feet per hour.

The first coking plant consisted of 180 Evance Coppee non-recovery ovens which were gradually replaced by Koppers, Wilputte and Simon-Carvé types.   Today there are three batteries of the last-named, carbonizing 1,300 to 1,400 tons of coal daily. In 1951, the last battery of Wilputte ovens was dismantled and is being replaced by a fourth battery of Simon-Carvés.   Over the years 1944 to 1946, the coke production from three Simon-Carvés and one Wilputte battery averaged 847,000 tons together with 37,000 tons of tar and 13,000 tons of ammonium sulphate.   A contact sulphuric acid plant produces some 50 tons of 98 per cent acid per day, used for the fixation of the ammonia content of the coke oven gases, for the pickling of steel sheets prior to galvanizing, and in the benzol-toluene plant which provides about $1\frac{1}{4}$ million gallons of these hydrocarbons annually.

The Company manufactures steel by a number of separate processes.   In its No. 1 shop there are eight basic, open-hearth furnaces, three of 70 tons, two of 90 tons, and three of 130 tons capacity.   The average annual production from these is about 350,000 tons of steel.   The Duplex system of steel manufacture, a combination of the acid Bessemer and basic open-hearth processes, is followed in shop No. 2.   The plant comprises three 25-ton acid-lined Bessemer convertors which receive the molten metal from the blast furnaces, after storage in a hot mixer; their semi-finished, blown product is transferred to three tilting basic open-hearth furnaces, one of 250 tons and two of 200 tons capacity each, for finishing the steel to predetermined composition.   The annual production of the Duplex plant is about 650,000 tons per annum. For the manufacture of acid steel, specified for the wheels, tyres and axles of railway rolling stock, etc., the Triplex process is adopted in Shop No. 3, where metal from the blast furnaces is blown in acid-lined Bessemer convertors to remove silicon, manganese and carbon as desired, and then charged into a basic open-hearth furnace to be dephosphorized.   The dephosphorized steel is then transferred to an acid open-hearth furnace in which the heat is finished.   Steel is also made in this shop by the Duplex process or scrap-carbon process.   The average annual production since 1942 has been about 42,000 long tons of acid steel, in addition to 16,000 tons of basic steel.   There are two 5-ton capacity Héroult-type electric

arc furnaces in Shop No. 1 which are used mainly for the manufacture of special and alloy steels, the average annual output being
about 15,000 tons. The manufacture of high-quality alloy, tool
and special steels was commenced in 1943 when a separate Tool
Steel Plant was inaugurated.   It contains one ½-ton high-frequency
induction furnace and ancillary equipment.   Two smaller furnaces
of the same type used for research purposes are installed in the
Research Laboratory.

The rolling mills of the Tata Company are equipped to turn
out finished steel products covering practically the whole range of
standard requirements.   In the blooming mills the steel ingots
from the soaking pits are reduced into blooms and slabs.   The
blooms are then rolled in the continuous sheet, bar and billet mill
into sheet bars, tin bars, sleeper bars, billets and so forth, or in the
rail and structural mills into rails, beams, angles, channels, etc.
The slabs are rolled in the plate mill into steel plates from ⅛ inch
to 3 inches in thickness and to a maximum width of about 7 feet.
The various types of bars proceed to their respective finishing mills,
and the billets to the Morgan merchant mill, or to other bar mills,
to emerge as light structural materials, light rails, fish plates, etc.
The sheet mills turn the sheet bars into black sheets of many sizes
and gauges, both of ordinary commercial qualities and of special
products such as deep drawing sheets, panel plates and high-silicon
sheets for the electrical industry; the average annual production
of sheets alone amounts to 150,000 tons.   Corrugated sheets, either
black or galvanized, are produced on rotary machines, and the
galvanizing of the black sheets, after pickling in dilute sulphuric
acid, is done by the 'hot-dip' process. Pressed steel railway
sleepers are made in a separate plant from sleeper bars rolled in
the sheet, bar and billet mill. A wheel, tyre and axle plant was
installed in 1941 and produces approximately 20,000 tons of such
products annually. The Company also makes from its own steel
in a separate factory a great variety of agricultural implements and
tools such as pick and felling axes, mattocks, crowbars, chisels,
powrahs, etc.

Amongst the special steels made are two types of low-alloy high-
strength materials, known by their trade names of Tiscrom and
Tiscor; the former is a high-tensile structural steel of which over
17,000 tons were used in the construction of the new Howrah bridge
over the Hooghly at Calcutta.   The second is a chromium-copper-
silicon-phosphorus steel employed in structural work where great
strength and corrosion-resistance, coupled with a reduction in
weight, are required. Special steels made to meet urgent demands
during the last war, or civilian needs since then, include high-speed
tool and shock-resisting steels, material for punches and dies and
armour-piercing shells, stainless steel for surgical instruments,
magnet steels and high-silicon sheets for electrical machinery, as
well as the coinage die steels for the Indian mints. To meet

war-time demands, the Tata Company made over 20,000 tons of bullet-proof plates and other ordnance steels. It also produced such alloys as ferro-tungsten, ferro-vanadium and silico-manganese from Indian raw materials.

The Company has its own plant for the manufacture of magnesia, chrome and other refractories as well as a welding electrode-making plant. Its control and research laboratories are equipped with up-to-date scientific appliances, not only for routine work, but for the investigation of all problems bearing on the production and processing of the ferrous metals and their alloys. A Technical Institute was inaugurated in 1921, for the theoretical and practical training in metallurgy, engineering, etc., of the supervisors and technicians employed in the works.

Many other industries have established themselves in and around Jamshedpur, including The Tinplate Company of India Ltd, The Indian Steel & Wire Products Ltd, The Indian Cable Co. Ltd, The Agricultural Implements Co. Ltd, and The Tata Engineering & Locomotive Co. Ltd.

A scheme was introduced by the Steel Company in 1933, whereby the employees share a percentage of the profits earned, and by this means labour is associated with the shareholders to the advantage of both. The bonus paid under the scheme for the year 1950-1 exceeded Rs 1 crore.

The present rated capacity of the steel works is about 750,000 tons of finished steel per annum, but the Company has undertaken a programme of expansion and modernization at an estimated cost of Rs 33 crores which will increase the capacity of the plant to 930,000 tons of finished steel per annum. In September 1951, the Company announced its decision to proceed with the manufacture of tubes in association with Messrs Stewarts & Lloyds Ltd, for which purpose, besides the tube mill, a special strip mill for the supply of the necessary skelp will be erected.

In the preparation of this note we have to acknowledge the generous assistance of Mr Phiroz Kutar, General Manager of The Tata Iron & Steel Company Ltd.

Analyses of various basic and foundry grades of pig iron produced by the Tata Company are given on the following page.

The Mysore Iron and Steel Works. The Mysore Government's Iron and Steel Works, where operations were commenced in January 1923, are at Bhadravati, 11 miles east of Shimoga, and consisted originally of a single blast furnace with a capacity of about 60 tons of pig iron daily, together with a wood distillation plant in which the charcoal used as fuel was made and the by-products— wood alcohol, calcium acetate and wood tar—recovered. The main source of the ore supply then, as now, was the Kemmangundi field in the Bababudan Hills, 26 miles to the south; limestone came from Bhandigudda, 13½ miles to the east; the wood supplies from

ANALYSES OF IRONS MADE BY THE TATA IRON & STEEL CO. LTD

GRADE	COMPOSITION			
	Silicon %	Manganese %	Phosphorus %	Sulphur %
Standard Quality (1)	2·75/3·25	1·0/1·5	under 0·40	under 0·035
(2)	2·25/2·75	1·0/1·5	ditto	,, 0·05
(3)	1·75/2·25	1·0/1·5	ditto	,, ,,
(4)	1·50/1·75	1·0/1·5	ditto	,, ,,
(5)	1·25/1·50	1·0/1·5	under 0·35	,, ,,
(6)	1·00/1·25	1·0/1·5	ditto	,, ,,
(7)	1·00 & less	1·0/1·5	ditto	,, ,,
Low Manganese Foundry (1)	2·75/3·25	0·5/1·0	under 0·40	,, 0·035
(2)	2·25/2·75	0·5/1·0	ditto	,, 0·05
(3)	1·75/2·25	0·5/1·0	ditto	,, ,,
(4)	1·50/1·75	0·5/1·0	ditto	,, ,,
(4X)	1·25/1·50	0·5/1·0	under 0·35	,, ,,
Low Manganese Basic Special	1·00/1·25	0·5/1·0	ditto	,, ,,
Low Manganese Basic	1·00 & less	0·5/1·0	ditto	,, ,,
High Manganese Basic	1·00 & less	1·5/1·75	ditto	,, ,,

the adjoining forests. A steel plant consisting of a Siemens-Martin, open-hearth furnace of 25 tons capacity, and a rolling mill designed to finish 20,000 tons of steel per annum, commenced production in 1936, while additional plant was added in 1950.

It has recently been decided, after consultation with Norwegian specialists, to introduce electrical smelting using power from the Jog Falls. Two furnaces, each to produce 100 to 110 tons of iron daily, are contemplated, and these are intended to raise output from 25,000 tons to nearly 100,000 tons per annum. The blast furnace will continue to function but will use coke in place of charcoal.

Two electric furnaces with a daily capacity of 6 or 7 tons were installed at Mysore City during the last war for the manufacture of ferro-silicon, which was supplied to other users in India as required. It is now proposed to make ferro-silicon in a new and larger unit at Bhadravati, and to devote the furnaces at Mysore City to the production of ferro-chrome and similar alloys.

ANALYSES OF MYSORE PIG IRONS

GRADES	Silicon per cent	COMPOSITION
High-Silicon	2·51 to 3·00	
Silicon	2·01 to 2·50	In all these grades the content—
I	1·66 to 2·00	of manganese varies from 0·50 to 1·00 %
II	1·26 to 1·65	of phosphorus is about 0·10 %
III	0·81 to 1·25	of sulphur is less than 0·02 %
IV	0·51 to 0·80	of total carbon is about 3·7 to 4·20 %
V	below 0·50	of combined carbon is about 0·3 to 0·7 %.

The Steel Corporation of Bengal. The Steel Corporation of Bengal Ltd was formed in 1937, with a capital of Rs 5 crores, under the managing agency of Burn & Co. Ltd, Calcutta, to manufacture steel billets, sections, rails, sheets and related products from the pig iron produced at the Hirapur works of the Indian Iron & Steel Co. Ltd. The works of the Corporation are at Napuria, close to those of the Company, and they share common water, electricity and gas supplies. The first steel ingot was cast here in November, 1939. The steel plant comprises both convertor and basic open-hearth smelting shops. The mill contains a 40-inch blooming mill, 34-inch and 18-inch section mills, with the usual ancillary equipment-maintenance shops, test house, convertor bottom house and laboratory. The capacity of the plant is about 350,000 tons of finished steel annually.

PRODUCTION OF PIG IRON IN INDIA, 1900–50

	Bengal Iron Co.	Tata Iron & Steel Co.	Indian Iron & Steel Co.	Mysore Iron Works	TOTAL TONNAGE	Average Annual Tonnage
1900–3	140,000*	..	..	..	140,000	47,000†
1904–8	209,595*	..	..	..	209,595	41,919
1909–13	241,820*	231,925‡	..	..	473,745	94,749
1914–18	381,579	835,185	..	..	1,216,764	243,353
1919–23	491,473	1,355,333	77,525§	9,732§§	1,934,518	386,903
1924–8	481,218	2,847,641	1,430,525	87,651	4,847,035	969,407
1929–33	300,009	3,712,302	1,496,824	87,185	5,596,320	1,119,264
1934–8	125,850	4,512,040	2,742,005	93,382	7,473,277	1,494,655
1939–43	..	5,805,742	3,399,905	134,106	9,339,753	1,867,951
1944–8	..	4,887,263	2,256,622	107,101	7,250,986	1,450,197
1949–50	..	2,067,788	1,128,845	37,786	3,234,419	1,617,210
TOTAL	2,371,544	26,255,219	12,532,706	556,943	41,716,412	..

GRAND TOTAL OF PIG IRON=41,716,412 tons.

Bengal Iron Co.'s ..	..	percentage of total	5·7	per cent	
Tata Iron & Steel Co.'s ..		,,	,, ,,	63·0	,, ,,
Indian Iron & Steel Co.'s.		,,	,, ,,	30·0	,, ,,
Mysore Iron Works'	..	,,	,, ,,	1·3	,, ,,

NOTE :—The Bengal Iron Co. Ltd was amalgamated with the Indian Iron & Steel Co. Ltd in 1936.
* Production of Bengal Iron & Steel Co. Ltd.
† Approximate.
‡ Commenced December 1911.
§ Commenced in November 1922. Figures for 1923 only.
§§ Commenced in 1923.

Hindustan Steel Limited. The articles of association of this Indo-German Company were signed in Delhi on 21 December 1953 on

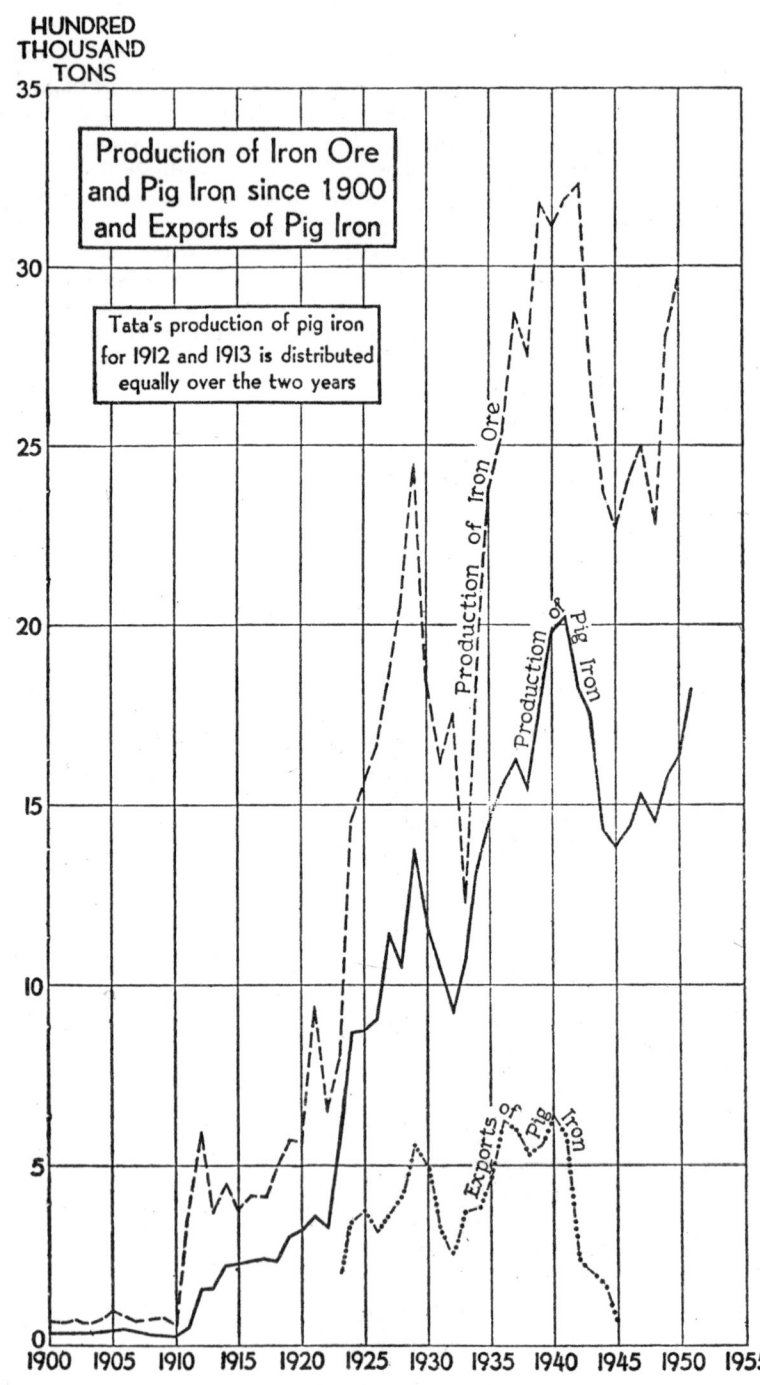

HUNDRED
THOUSAND
TONS

Production of Iron Ore
and Pig Iron since 1900
and Exports of Pig Iron

Tata's production of pig iron
for 1912 and 1913 is distributed
equally over the two years

Production of Iron Ore

Production of Pig Iron

Exports of Pig Iron

behalf of the Government of India and of the German combine of Krupps and Demag. The new company has an authorized capital of Rs 1,000 million and is to erect a steel plant with an annual capacity of 500,000 tons capable of expansion to 1,000,000 tons, at an estimated capital cost of some Rs 71,25,00,000. A site for the plant has been selected at Rourkela in Sundargarh, Orissa and work is expected to commence shortly.

An Indo-Russian agreement for the construction of a steel plant with a capacity of one million tons per annum near Bhilai, Madhya Pradesh, was signed in New Delhi, on 2 February 1955. A British group has offered to erect a third steel plant.

PRODUCTION OF STEEL IN INDIA, 1911-50

	Tata Iron & Steel Co.	Steel Corporation of Bengal	Mysore Iron Works	TOTAL TONNAGE	Average Annual Tonnage
1911–13 ..	63,154*	..	..	63,154	31,577
1914–18 ..	479,930†	..	..	479,930	95,986
1919–23 ..	864,280*	..	..	864,280	172,858
1924–8 ..	1,593,993†	..	..	1,593,993	318,798
1929–33 ..	2,212,854†	..	..	2,212,854	442,531
1934–8 ..	3,243,512	..	40,663‡	3,284,175	656,835
1939–43 ..	3,906,069	803,660 §	129,993	4,839,722	967,944
1944–8 ..	3,573,165	1,099,960	148,901	4,822,026	964,405
1949–50 ..	1,441,840	488,651	52,247	1,982,738	991,369
TOTAL ..	17,378,818	2,392,271	371,804	20,142,893	..

GRAND TOTAL OF STEEL = 20,142,893 tons.

Tata Iron & Steel Co.'s ..	..	percentage of total steel	86·3
Steel Corporation of Bengal's	..	,, ,, ,, ,,	11·4
Mysore Iron Works'	..	,, ,, ,, ,,	2·3

* Ingots.   ‡ Commenced in 1936.
† Steel including rails.   § Commenced in 1940.

THE TRADE IN IRON AND STEEL

During the five years following the first world war, 1919-23, the whole of the Indian Empire of those days imported pig and other forms of crude, metallic iron at the rate of about 31,000 tons yearly, an amount almost identical with that of a still earlier decade. Since those times imports of raw iron have gradually shrunk into insignificance, and the few hundred tons which still appear in the Customs Returns probably represent special varieties imported for particular purposes. While this change was taking place India became an exporter of metallic iron, and even before the first world war had shipped her own homemade product to Burma, the Straits

Settlements, Ceylon, Java, Manchuria, China, Japan, Australia, New Zealand, the Pacific Coast of the United States and South America. As a matter of historical importance it should be recorded that during the first world war the export of both iron and steel from India was prohibited by the Government of the day, and the whole output of steel rails taken for use in the campaigns in Mesopotamia, East Africa, Palestine and even as far away as Greece. Shell steel was supplied to the Indian munitions factories, and both the iron-producing companies then in existence made ferro-manganese on a large scale. Post-war conditions interfered for some years with the resumption of the export trade in pig iron on its former scale, but it slowly recovered and averaged some 379,000 tons per annum over the decade ending 1933, and rose to over half a million tons (519,850) yearly in the next quinquennium, 1934-8. The years of the second world war witnessed a decline to an annual average of 442,600 tons over the years 1939-43, followed by an exceedingly steep drop to 85,468 tons, the average for the three years 1944-6, while the average for the two years 1948 and 1949 was but 49,383 tons. The record year was in 1940 when 627,099 tons of pig iron were shipped abroad. Of the grand total of 8,860,166 tons of pig iron, valued at Rs 37,07,01,336, exported during the 23 years 1924-46, 48·1 per cent went to Japan, 32·2 per cent to the United Kingdom, 11·5 per cent to the United States of America and the remaining 8·2 per cent to many other lands, including China and Germany.

As the details given in the table opposite demonstrate, India still imports vast quantities of capital goods in the form of iron and steel pillars, girders, bridge work, bolts and nuts, nails, hoops, strips and fencing materials as well as railway track materials and fittings, to say nothing of machinery of all descriptions and consumer goods such as cutlery and hardware. In the pre-war quinquennium, 1934-8, these cost the country about Rs 21 crores annually, excluding what was spent on railway plant and rolling stock. Over the seven years 1939-45, the total value of such imports was still over Rs 17 crores, and on the conclusion of the war the figures rose to considerably more than Rs 35 crores in 1946. Taking fabricated iron and steel articles alone, and leaving out of consideration all forms of machinery, hardware and cutlery, 273,852 tons were imported annually over the five years 1934-8; contraction during the war was inevitable and severe, but by 1949 such imports were back to 179,000 tons and in 1950 had risen to 317,000 tons, valued at Rs 16 crores. This expenditure, as Dr M. S. Krishnan has written, ' can be eliminated only by immediately putting into effect a large expansion programme of the iron and steel industry'. The Five-Year Plan announced in July 1951 envisages an increase in steel production from the present annual total of some 1,005,000 tons to 1,315,000 tons by 1955-6. Whether this will then satisfy internal demands remains to be seen. It is

AVERAGE ANNUAL IMPORTS OF IRON AND STEEL, 1914-46

		1914–18	1919–23	1924–8	1929–33	1934–8	1939–45	1946
Cutlery and hardware ..	Rs	3,54,20,070	7,00,57,822	5,68,41,372	3,96,06,660	3,37,62,058	1,91,26,417	4,13,13,418
Machinery and millwork ..	Rs	5,40,11,565	22,31,18,902	16,84,91,502	15,55,51,821	14,85,08,811	13,37,08,070	29,51,95,783
Railway plant and stock ..	Rs	5,42,29,755	14,31,94,046	6,74,70,501	....	....	....	....
Iron bars, pig iron, etc. ..	Rs	47,64,090	71,92,301	26,09,415	9,70,093	4,94,565	1,93,493	1,46,086
	Tons	23,425	31,120	16,678	7,098	3,581	880	345
Iron or steel beams, etc. ..	Rs	8,29,67,164	16,91,52,163	17,17,19,344	8,57,72,791	66,97,442	33,35,404	55,34,150
	Tons	300,473	443,629	795,102	457,635	37,317	7,810	6,035
Steel angles, bars, etc. ..	Rs	1,47,32,760	3,87,59,033	2,64,00,149	1,47,22,708	1,01,24,099	67,29,800	60,89,964
	Tons	74,143	163,143	242,958	136,312	80,525	34,989	17,367
Iron or steel bolts, etc. ..	Rs	....	....	....	....	1,01,95,562	81,87,283	47,48,220
	Tons	....	....	....	....	56,020	22,904	11,144
TOTAL ..	Rs	24,61,25,404	65,14,74,267	49,35,32,283	29,66,24,073	20,91,82,537	17,12,80,467	35,30,27,621

NOTES :—
' Iron or steel beams, etc.,' includes channels, sheets, pillars, nails and rivets.
' Steel angles, bars, etc.,' includes tees, springs, ingots and blooms.
' Iron or steel bolts, etc.,' includes nuts, hoops, strips and fencing materials.
Imports of fabricated iron and steel, excepting machinery, hardware and cutlery, had risen to 179,000 tons in 1949 and 317,000 tons, valued at over Rs 16 crores, in 1950. Their value in 1951 was more than Rs 20 crores.

neither a large amount judged by the fact that ' steel forms the skeleton framework within the body of modern civilization ', nor by its equivalent of 1,336,040 metric tons, compared with the 1950 production of other steel-making nations as expressed in metric tons as follows: the United States 87·7, the Soviet Union 27·6, the United Kingdom 16·6, Western Germany 12·1, France 8·7, Belgium and Luxembourg 6·2 and Japan 3·8 millions. As far as natural resources are concerned, India with her immense deposits of iron ore and manganese (which is just as essential in making steel as limestone or coke), can expand her ferrous industries in any direction considered desirable. These resources are far greater than those of any other Asiatic country. A great and rapidly growing home market exists for steel products of every description. Her geographical position gives easy accessibility to the markets round the Indian and Pacific Oceans. Her ironmasters, steel-founders and technicians are men of great metallurgical skill and commercial ability. All these things presage expansion in the future.

MANGANESE

The world's production of manganese ores averaged about 4,850,000 tons per annum over the five years 1934-8 and in normal times the demand for the ore rises and falls with the fortunes of the iron and steel industry, in which about 90 per cent of the output is consumed; a further 5 per cent is used for non-ferrous alloys and the remainder for chemical purposes. The world's output of steel expanded from about 13 million tons per annum in 1890 to over 132,000,000 tons in 1937, and over the same term of years the annual yield of manganese ores increased from less than half a million tons to more than six million tons, a march of progress in which India's manganese ore deposits played no inconsiderable part.

Employed to some extent in the manufacture of pig iron, the element is used chiefly in the form of ferro-manganese and spiegel-eisen as a purifying agent in deoxidizing, desulphurizing and re-carbonizing steel, and, having performed these indispensable functions, most, but not all of it, passes into the waste slags. For these purposes it is essential and has no substitute. To the genius of J. M. Heath, a servant of the East India Company who resigned his appointment to develop the iron and steel industry in south India, are due those earliest successful experiments with manganese which, in the words of an American authority, completely revolutionized the steel industry of England and through it of the whole world. Practically all steels contain manganese, usually ranging around 0·5 per cent; high-tensile structural steel may contain from 1·3 to 1·6 per cent, and rail steel from 0·9 to 1·2 per cent. Sir Lewis Fermor has stated recently that for every ton of steel produced some 60 lb. of high-grade manganese ore are necessary.

Manganese steels with 12 or 13 per cent of the metal, besides being practically non-magnetic, are exceedingly hard and tough, qualities which account for their uses in many types of mining, milling, dredging and digging machinery, such as rock crushers, buckets and tumblers, excavators and railway and tramroad points and crossings, as well as in light armour for aircraft and such articles as steel helmets. Manganese also enters into the composition of a number of alloy steels containing chromium, nickel and molybdenum. The alloys of manganese and copper serve many useful purposes, as for example in turbine blades, which contain 4 or 5 per cent of the metal. 'Manganese bronze' is a high-grade brass, toughened and strengthened with 3 or 4 per cent of manganese, which resists corrosion and is used in marine engineering for ship propellors as well as in the chemical and brewing industries. Another alloy of copper, with 8 to 12 per cent of manganese and 4 per cent of nickel, is drawn into wires for electrical resistances. The commercial manganese-aluminium alloys contain from 0·5 to 3 per cent of manganese; one type with 1·25 per cent manganese is used in the manufacture of aircraft tanks, hollow ware and the bodywork of transport vehicles; another with 4 per cent copper, 0·5 per cent magnesium and 0·5 per cent manganese has been largely used in the construction of many types of aircraft, especially when clad with a coating of pure aluminium.

The peroxide ores of manganese are the starting-point in the manufacture of the metal itself by the aluminothermic process, and some of the Indian ores of this type yield a satisfactory commercial grade of metal without recourse to wet chemical methods. Their chief use, however, is in the make-up of dry batteries and cells of the Leclanché type, in which they act as depolarizers. They can be employed in the manufacture of bromine and iodine, certain organic chemicals, as well as the disinfectants sodium and potassium permanganate and sodium manganate. Manganese ores have been in use in India from very early times for colouring glasses and enamels green, violet, brown and black, and they are still employed throughout the world both as decolorizing and as tinting agents. In the former case the right proportion of manganese neutralizes the green colour due to ferrous salts (see under GLASS SANDS); in the latter they impart purple, chocolate, grey and black colours to the bodies or the glazes of bricks, tiles and pottery wares. Certain organic compounds of manganese are widely used in the paint, oil and varnish industries as drying agents of vegetable oils. Finally, the sulphate and acetate of manganese are valuable fertilizers, especially for neutral soils and for alkaline soils which are deficient in available manganese.

HISTORY OF THE INDUSTRY

The Indian manganese industry dates from 1891, when a syndicate was formed to open up the Kodur deposits of the Srikakulam

MAP IX

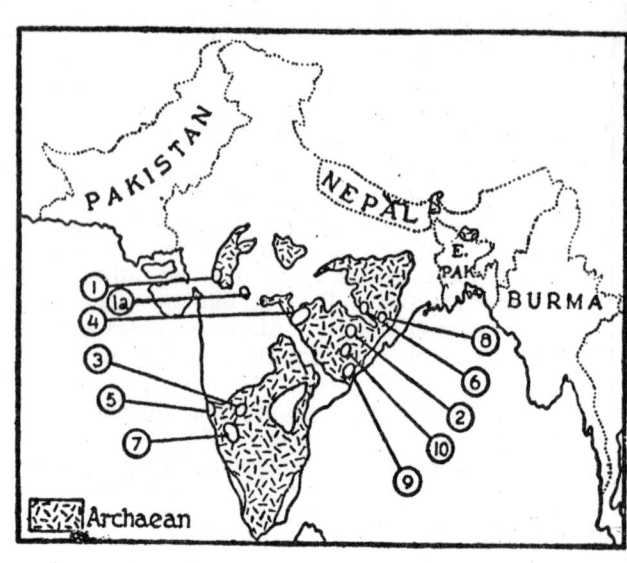

MANGANESE
ORE-BEARING
AREAS

Archaean

Miles

Scale of insets

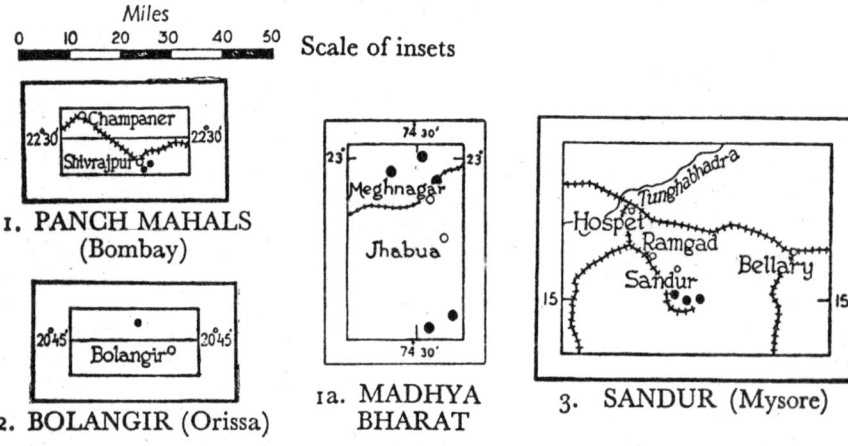

1. PANCH MAHALS
(Bombay)

2. BOLANGIR (Orissa)

1a. MADHYA
BHARAT

3. SANDUR (Mysore)

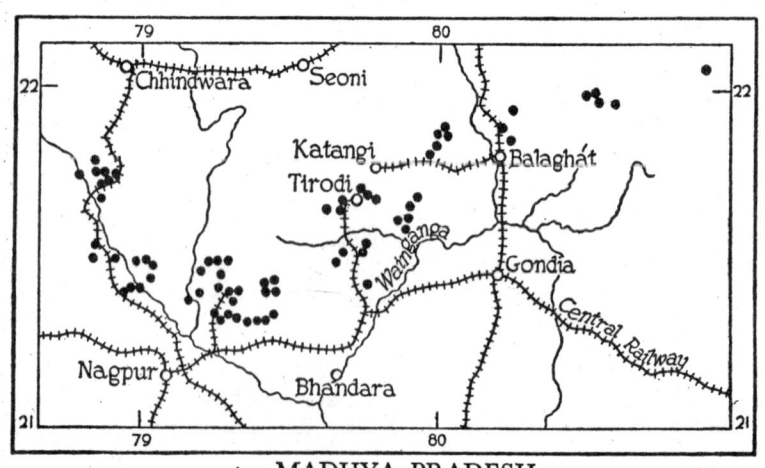

4. MADHYA PRADESH

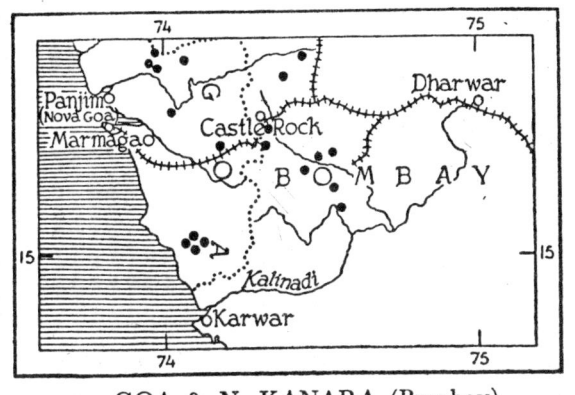

5. GOA & N. KANARA (Bombay)

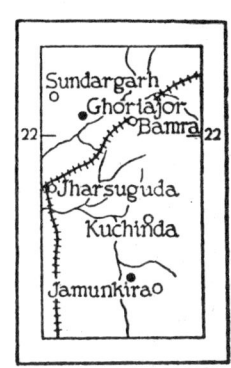

6. GANGPUR
BAMRA (Orissa)

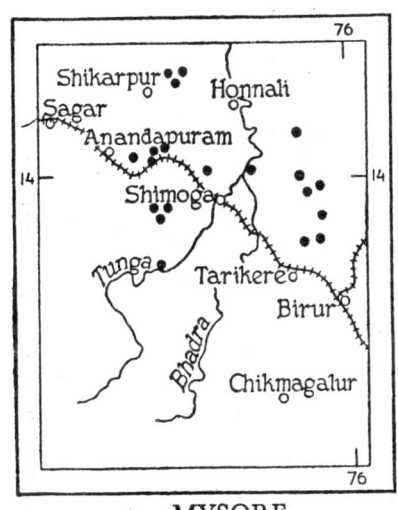

7. MYSORE

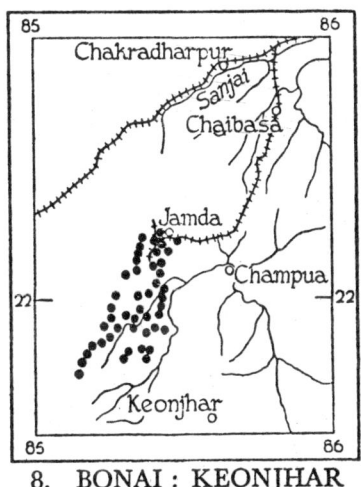

8. BONAI : KEONJHAR
(Orissa) & SINGHBHUM
(Bihar)

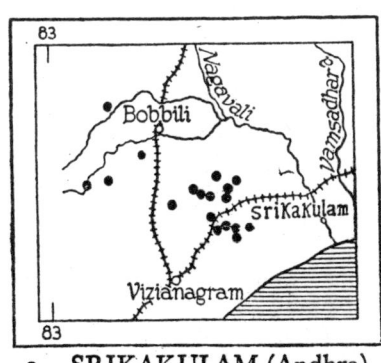

9. SRIKAKULAM (Andhra)

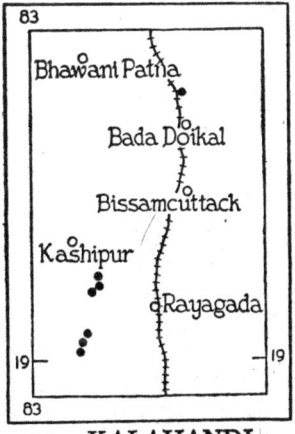

10. KALAHANDI :
RAYAGADA (Orissa)

district of Andhra; while in 1894, the Vizianagram Mining Co. Ltd was formed. Little prospecting seems to have been necessary in those early days, for in 1885 W. King of the Geological Survey of India had found psilomelane, a valuable ore of manganese, used on a large scale as road metal to the north of Vizianagram. The Central Provinces Prospecting Syndicate commenced work on the previously known Mansar deposit, in the Nagpur district, in 1899; in 1901 on the great Balaghat orebody, and in 1903 at Chikhla and Kurmura in Bhandara: in 1908 it became a limited company with about 20 mines in various parts of Madhya Pradesh. It has had a most successful career and changed its name into the Central Provinces Manganese Ore Co. Ltd in 1924. In 1904, the Central India Manganese Co. Ltd was formed to continue the work of earlier concessionaires on several deposits in the Nagpur district, and in 1905 extended its operations into Bhandara. The Central Indian Mining Co. Ltd was incorporated in 1903, with mines at Kodegaon and later at Kachi Dhana, Sitapar and Gowari Warhona in Chhindwara. Several other firms and individuals commenced work on a smaller scale in Madhya Pradesh between 1903 and 1906.

The first prospecting licence in Madhya Bharat was granted over the Kajlidongri deposit, in Jhabua, to Messrs Kiddle, Reeve & Co. of Bombay, in 1902. Development commenced to the south of Chaibasa, Singhbhum, in what was then Bengal but is now Bihar, in 1904, and was later continued by the Madhu Lal Doogar Syndicate. The Shivrajpur Syndicate was working in the Panch Mahals of Bombay in 1905 and the Bamankua Mining Syndicate in 1907. The earliest prospecting licences in Mysore were granted in 1904, and the Mysore Manganese Co. Ltd was registered in 1906, with rights in the Shimoga district. The Peninsular Minerals Company of Mysore Ltd was formed in 1906, with its mines in the Tumkur and Chitaldrug districts, and the Shimoga Manganese Co. Ltd in 1907. In addition to most of the companies mentioned the following have been at work within more recent times:

Andhra : Seth Shreeram Durgaprasad & Fatechand Narsingdas, P. O. Chipurupalli, Srikakulam (successor to the Vizianagram Mining Co. Ltd); Gourisankar Mining Co., Chipurupalli, Srikakulam.

Bihar : The Indian Iron & Steel Co. Ltd, Calcutta; N. V. Rathor, Chaibasa, Singhbhum; Mangilal Rangta, Chaibasa, Singhbhum.

Bombay: The Kanara Mining Co. Ltd, Bombay; Lalbhai P. Patel, Bombay; Shivrajpur Syndicate Ltd, Bombay.

Madhya Bharat : T. S. Poddar, Meghnagar, Jhabua.

Madhya Pradesh: B. P. Byramjee & Co., Nagpur; Madhya Pradesh Mines Ltd (formerly Bansilal Abirchand Mining Syndicate), Nagpur; F. X. Rebellow, Nagpur; S. Abideen, Nagpur; J. D'Costa, Nagpur; Shamji Naranji, Ramtek, Nagpur; Cheniram Jesraj, Nagpur; Oke Brothers, Nagpur; Diwanchand Jiwar,

Nagpur; G. H. Rawell & Sons, Ramakona, Chhindwara; A. P. Trivedi, Balaghat; Seth Gopikisan Agarwal, Tumsar; Seth Shreeram, Tumsar.

Mysore: Mysore Iron & Steel Works, Bhadravati; R. K. Mining Industries, Chitaldrug; The Sandur Manganese & Iron Ores Ltd (successor to the General Sandur Mining Co. Ltd), Sandur, Bellary.

Orissa: Tata Iron & Steel Co. Ltd, Jamshedpur, Bihar; The Orissa Minerals Development Co. Ltd, Calcutta; Serajuddin & Co., Keonjhargarh; Government of Orissa; M. A. Tulloch, Bara-Jamda, Singhbhum; The Aryan Mining & Trading Corpn. Ltd, Calcutta; S. Lal, Mosaboni Mines, Singhbhum; The Jeypore Mining Syndicate, Rayagada, Koraput.

Goa: The Goa Mining Co., Marmagao.

INDIAN MANGANESE ORE DEPOSITS

Manganese ore deposits have been mined in many parts of the Indian Peninsula, the most important being in Madhya Pradesh. Sir Lewis Fermor divided them into three groups: (1) deposits interbedded with Archaean rocks, including the gondites: (2) deposits associated with the kodurites, and (3) lateritoid deposits or surface enrichments of a lateritic character, some of which are now known to merge downwards into more or less dispersed replacement deposits. Members of the first group, which have supplied by far the greater proportion of the ore, occur in Bihar, Orissa, Madhya Bharat, Madhya Pradesh, Bombay and Mysore; those strictly associated with gondites being confined to the Balaghat, Bhandara, Nagpur and Chhindwara districts of Madhya Pradesh, Jhabua in Madhya Bharat, Narukot in Gujerat and Gangpur in Orissa. From 29 mines of this type no less than 15,152,619 tons of ore had been removed up to 1938. The second group occurs only near the eastern coast in the Srikakulam district of Andhra, in Ganjam and in Koraput, Orissa, but it is of comparatively little importance. Examples of the third group can be found in almost any locality where the other two occur, normally overlying them; at the same time many of these surface deposits are emplaced above rocks which contain but small quantities of manganese. From deposits of this type ore has been won in the Singhbhum district of Bihar; Keonjhar, Bonai and Bolangir-Patna in Orissa; the North Kanara and Belgaum districts of Bombay; Sandur taluk in the Bellary district and the Chitaldrug, Chikmagalur, Shimoga and Tumkur districts of Mysore. Many other occurrences of manganese ore are known elsewhere, though they are more of scientific interest than of economic importance.

The typical Indian manganese ore of commerce is a mixture of two minerals, braunite and psilomelane, of variable grain size but normally hard and fine, but there are other important minerals including hollandite, jacobsite, sitaparite and pyrolusite. The exact chemical constitution of some of these minerals is still uncertain, but psilomelane, the most abundant of all Indian manganese minerals, and, with braunite, forming probably at least 90 per cent of the exported product, includes both psilomelane proper, a manganate of manganese and barium with essential water, and cryptomelane, a manganate of manganese and potassium. It is probable that both components are present in the Indian mineral usually termed 'psilomelane' and its content of metallic manganese may be as low as 45 per cent or as high as 60 per cent. Braunite is a twin compound of the oxide and silicate of manganese, $3Mn_2O_3.MnSiO_3$, often with part of the manganese in the oxide replaced by iron. After psilomelane it is the most abundant of the manganese ores of India, with 52 to 58 per cent of manganese and from 1 to 10 per cent of iron. Hollandite is another manganate of manganese, iron and barium, closely approaching psilomelane in composition, but differing from it in being, as a rule, anhydrous. It contains from 45 to 56 per cent of manganese and 3 to 7 per cent of iron. Jacobsite is a member of the spinel group of minerals with the chemical formula $(Fe.Mn.Mg)O.(Fe.Mn)_2O_3$, which when intergrown with hausmannite, the oxide of manganese Mn_3O_4 (manganese 72 per cent), forms the ore known in India as vredenburgite. Sitaparite, another Indian speciality, is thought by some mineralogists to be a relative of bixbyite, $MnO_2.FeO$, with lime; others give its formula as $(Mn.Fe)_2O_3$ with CaO, containing 44·09 per cent of manganese and 19·32 per cent of iron. Pyrolusite is the dioxide of manganese usually with a little water; it is sometimes pseudomorphous after manganite, $Mn_2O_3.H_2O$, but with the atomic structure of polianite, another dioxide, and it contains 63·2 per cent of manganese.

The bedded manganese ores of India, like those of Brazil, the Gold Coast and South Africa which are of similar Archaean age, were originally sediments, some of which contained varying proportions of manganese. As a result of regional movements, and profound metamorphism intensified in some cases by the contact effects of later intrusions, the primary sands and clays were changed into quartzites, phyllites, and mica schists: the purer manganese-bearing sediments into crystalline manganese ores and the mixtures into the distinctive rocks to which Fermor gave the name of 'gondites'. True gondite is a rock made up of the manganese garnet, spessartite and quartz, but spessartite rock itself, rhodonite rock and rhodonite-quartz rocks are also common; rhodonite being the silicate of manganese $MnSiO_3$. Since their discovery in India gondites have been identified in both the Gold Coast and Brazilian manganese ore deposits and, apart from giving clues to the origin of the ores, they are important because as a result of surface oxidation changes they can give rise to deposits of manganese ores.

OPENING UP A MANGANESE ORE DEPOSIT

In Madhya Pradesh particularly, but to some extent elsewhere, the primeval sediments were rich enough to form manganese ores of the braunite-sitaparite-hollandite type, possibly with pyrolusite, on metamorphism, while some of them, intruded by pegmatites, have recrystallized as braunite; the jacobsite-hausmannite types of ore may have had a similar origin. Under the prolonged action of weathering, acting downwards to considerable depths, the manganese minerals mentioned have been largely altered to psilo-melane-pyrolusite mixtures while the silicates of the gondites themselves have yielded psilomelane, pyrolusite and possibly braunite. These are not theoretical speculations, for the various stages in the transformations are often clearly visible, and the orebodies, well bedded as they are to the prevailing rock strike, can be seen passing into fresh representatives of the gondite series.

In the Nagpur-Balaghat region the orebodies form lenticular masses and bands intercalated in quartzites, schists and gneisses, often disposed along the same line, as, for instance, in the Nagpur district where they stretch from Dumri Kalan to Khandala, a distance of twelve miles, and include the valuable deposits of Beldongri, Lohdongri, Kacharwali and Waregaon. They frequently attain huge dimensions. Thus the Balaghat deposit is 1¾ miles long, another at Manegaon, in Nagpur, 1½ miles long, while the band running through Jamrapani, Tirodi and Ponia, in Balaghat, is exposed more or less continuously for six miles. Equally impressive are the large amounts of ore yielded by some of these single deposits and particularly by Tirodi, Balaghat, Chikkla (in Bandhara), Kandri, Mansar (in Nagpur) and Kachhi Dhana (in Chhindwara), which by the end of 1938 had given 2,219,921, 1,881,594, 1,158,416, 1,376,726, 1,099,465 and 922,214 tons respectively. Many of them originally formed small hills which favoured exploitation by the simpler forms of quarrying, indeed, most of the ore is still won by open-cast methods, ranging from shallow surface workings to deep quarries, and at only four localities has it yet been necessary to adopt underground methods: these are at Kandri and Mansar in Nagpur, Bharwali in Balaghat and at Shivrajpur, in the Panch Mahals of Bombay. Diamond drilling at the Balaghat mine in 1949 and 1950 has proved that orebodies of these types extend to considerable depths, and contain ores of excellent quality to these depths in sufficient quantities to maintain outputs for very many years to come. Gondite ores generally are of the first grade with a manganese content of over 48 per cent, together with moderate quantities of second-grade material containing 45 to 48 per cent of the metal.

The manganese ores of the second group are associated with the kodurites, a name given by Fermor to a series of rocks, found in the Srikakulam district of Andhra and in Orissa, associated with other crystalline Archaeans, and ranging from ultra-acid types such as quartz-orthoclase rock at one end of the series to ultrabasic varieties at the other. Typical kodurite, the basic member of the series, is composed of potash feldspar, spandite (a garnet intermediate in composition between the manganese garnet, spessartite, and the calcium-iron garnet, andradite) and apatite. The exact origin of these rocks is doubtful and varied opinions about them have been advanced by Fermor, P. Sampat Iyengar, Dunn and others, but whatever it may have been, they have been greatly altered since their formation, with the production of lithomarges, manganese ores and secondary products such as chert, ochres and wad. Their orebodies are commonly extremely irregular, but occasionally, as at Garbham in Srikakulam, possess a well-developed dip and strike. Some of them are of great size; Garbham itself was the largest, with a length of 1,600 feet and a width of 167 feet at its thickest section, 100 feet of this being ore and the remainder lithomarge and wad; between 1896 and 1938 it gave 1,010,561 tons of ore. The Kodur deposit of this group, with an output of 417,711 tons between 1892 and 1938, has the distinction of being the first to be mined in India. The ores generally are for the most part psilomelane with subordinate pyrolusite, braunite and manganmagnetite ($(Fe.Mn) O.Fe_2O_3$), though at Garividi the mixed jacobsite-hausmannite, known as vredenburgite, occurs. They are, as a rule, second- and third-grade ores characterized by high iron and phosphorus contents and comparatively little silica.

The lateritoid deposits are secondary surface replacements, often found on rocks of Dharwar age, resembling laterite in their irregular structures, their radiating, botryoidal and stalactitic-like habits easily betraying their origin. They invariably contain high percentages of iron and often grade through ferruginous manganese ores and manganiferous iron ores into iron ores proper. Their manganese minerals are pyrolusite, psilomelane, wad (soft amorphous mixtures of impure oxides of manganese, passing into psilomelane) and, more rarely, pseudo-manganite ($Mn_2O_3.H_2O$), passing into pyrolusite: their iron contents take the forms of limonite and earthy haematite. The chemical characteristics of ores of this group are high iron, low manganese, low silica and often very low phosphorus contents, and they are usually classified as second-grade manganese ores and third-grade ferruginous manganese ores. They have been won for the most part in Bellary district, once part of Madras but now in Mysore, where on one property alone, that formerly of the General Sandur Mining Co. Ltd, A. K. Dey has estimated there are still about 800,000 tons available.

Of the replacement or segregation deposits, which often underlie such irregular lateritoid deposits, those of Dhubna and Jampani, in Keonjhar, are good examples. Here, lenticular bodies and pockets of ore, up to 400 feet in length and 10 to 20 feet in thickness, containing reserves of about half a million tons, have been formed at the junction of shales with haematitic iron ores. The lower grade ores of the Liligumma *zemindari* of Kalahandi, on the other hand, are associated with khondalites and hypersthene-bearing rocks, but in the Kashipur area there may be about 100,000 tons of better quality material. Thin veins and small lenses of psilomelane occur in a shear zone in steeply dipping Cumbum shales near Janapalacheruvu in the Kurnool district of Andhra. The manganese ores of Goa occur as pockets in manganiferous, ferruginous shales enriched by lateritization and recalling similar deposits in the Jamda area of Singhbhum. A fair proportion of the ores from the Sanguem district are of chemical grade with low phosphorus and silica contents. In the Bardez, Sanguem and other districts of western Goa, manganese ores associated with high-grade iron ores are mined from thick laterite formations. Over the years 1947 to 1949, 17,261 tons of manganese ores were won in Goa. Several small scattered occurrences of manganese ores are known in the adjoining districts of Bombay, varying in the amount of their reserves from about 10,000 to 120,000 tons.[1]

At Hopong, in the Southern Shan States of Burma, 3,000 tons of ores of a pyrolusitic character were won by the Japanese during the occupation, and a further 3,000 tons approximately were produced in 1950. One orebody is about 200 feet in length with a width of 50 feet or so of good ore and appears to be surrounded by material with a much higher iron content, and then by soft, manganiferous earth containing some limestone and traces of rhodochrosite. Other occurrences probably exist in the same neighbourhood and seem to be related in origin to the residual iron ore deposits of the *terra rossa* of the Shan States.

Indian ores containing over 48 per cent of manganese are classified in the first grade, those containing between 45 and 48 per cent in the second grade, and ores with less than 45 per cent as third-grade material. In Bihar, however, this system is not adopted and all ore with less than 48 per cent manganese is either sold at second-grade prices, or marketed on its analysis. Some qualities ranging down to 32 per cent of manganese and up to 17 per cent of iron are disposed of as manganese-iron ores to the iron and steel manufacturers. Analyses of typical ores as shipped in 1946 are given in the table on p. 214.

THE INDIAN MANGANESE ORE TRADE

India's chief competitors in the manganese ore trade of the world for many years were Russia and Brazil, but entering the business in 1891, she had displaced Russia from the leading position by 1907, with a production of 902,291 tons, and continued to maintain her lead until 1912, when the relative positions of the

[1] In West Pakistan, four small deposits of low-grade manganese ore, containing a total estimated quantity of some 500,000 tons, have been located recently in the States of Las Bela and Kalat, according to the ECAFE Report, 1953.

two countries were reversed. The first world war (1914-18) paralysed the Russian industry and affected the Indian one to some extent, while Brazil and the United States greatly improved theirs, though insufficiently to oust India from the premier position which she had regained in 1916. During this period, 1914 to 1918, the average annual output was 577,457 tons, but exports were limited by shipping shortages so that by 1919 over 300,000 tons of ore were stocked in the country. It was about this time that a number of new competitors appeared, particularly Egypt, Cuba and the Gold Coast, the ore from the last being in part first-grade quality with 51 to 52 per cent manganese.

ANALYSES OF INDIAN MANGANESE ORES

MINE	Mn	Fe	SiO$_2$	P	MnO$_2$	REMARKS
MADHYA PRADESH						
Balaghat ..	51·0	7·0	6·5	0·10	55·0	Mine ore
,, ..	48·5	8·0	5·5	0·06	45·0	Boulder ore
Bhandara ..	50·5	7·5	8·0	0·16	28·0	Mine ore
,, ..	49·5	7·5	7·0	0·08	34·0	Boulder ore
Dongri ..	51·25	6·5	3·5	0·275	75·0	Run of Mine ore
,, ..	59·0	1·0 max.	1·0 max.	0·29	90·0	Low ferruginous per-oxide ore
,, ..	58·5	2·75 max.	2·0 max.	0·32	88·5	Standard peroxide ore
BOMBAY						
Shivrajpur ..	48–50	4–5	6–8	0·23–0·26	..	First-grade ore
,, ..	46–47	5–7	9–11	0·24–0·28	..	Second-grade ore
,, ..	43–44	6–8	12–14	0·24–0·27	..	Third-grade ore
ORISSA						
Keonjhar ..	49·0	8·56	4·40	0·135	..	First-grade ore
,, ..	45·8	8·18	5·25	0·165	..	Second-grade ore
,, ..	40·0	13·80	5·70	0·047	..	Third-grade ore
,, ..	..	0·16	0·40	..	91·96	Manganese dioxide ore, First-grade
,, ..	..	0·91	0·95	..	88·0	Manganese dioxide ore, Second-grade
MYSORE						
Sandur ..	40·2	16·40	1–2	0·02	56·5	Low-grade ore

Analyses kindly supplied by the following Companies : the Central Provinces Manganese Ore Co. Ltd, the Shivrajpur Syndicate Ltd, Bird & Co. Ltd, and the General Sandur Mining Co. Ltd.

In the first quinquennium following World War I, that is to say over the years 1919 to 1923, India maintained her lead with average annual exports of 624,635 tons, compared with Brazil's 297,497 tons and Russia's 170,000 tons, while Egypt and the Gold

Coast followed closely in the fourth and fifth places. Improvement continued over the next five-yearly period, 1924 to 1928, with an annual average production of 953,037 tons and a peak of 1,129,353 tons in 1927, but the Russian industry was recovering its lost ground, rising to an average of 730,279 tons, while Brazil fell away to 263,675 tons and the Gold Coast occupied the fourth place with 352,232 tons.

The years 1929 to 1933 were particularly remarkable, for from the world's highest recorded output of 3,598,343 tons in 1929, production slumped to 1,218,879 tons in 1932, the lowest figure for many years. The results were disastrous. The Indian annual average dropped 41·4 per cent to 558,596 tons, the Brazilian by 50 per cent to 127,175 tons, the Gold Coast fell to 279,947 tons, but Russia continued to recover and finally displaced India from her leading position. It was during this period too, that South Africa, another formidable competitor of India, entered the world's markets. By 1932 the collapse of the trade had reduced the level of Indian production to that of 37 years earlier and while the output in 1933 (218,307 tons) was a little over one fifth that of the peak year of 1927 (1,129,353 tons), its value (£123,171) was about one twenty-second part of the same (£2,703,068). It is not surprising that a number of mines were closed down and some companies forced into liquidation.

Prosperity returned in the next period, 1934-8, when India's annual average tonnage increased to 776,151 tons, with a new peak of production of 1,051,954 tons in 1937 and exports of 1,151,834 tons in that year, a record not only for India but for the world. Notable too was the rapid rise of the new port of Visakhapatnam (Vizagapatam), which from 1935 took the lead as an exporting harbour and was followed by Calcutta, Marmagao and Bombay.

The effects of the second world war were not strikingly marked over the years 1939 to 1943, the annual average tonnage remaining much the same at 771,471 tons, but thereafter, shipping difficulties and shortage of rail transport became acute so that output for the three years ending 1946 averaged only 278,160 tons. An improvement was registered in 1947 and 1948 and the quinquennium closed with an annual average of 362,277 tons.

The years 1949 and 1950 were prosperous ones again, as the rearmament projects of the Atlantic Powers, with their concomitant demands for greater supplies of steel, as well as stock-piling operations particularly in the United States of America, gained momentum. As a result there was an increase of almost 23 per cent from a production of 525,876 tons in 1948 to 645,825 tons in 1949, followed by a further expansion of nearly 40 per cent to 901,609 tons in 1950 and to a new record of 1,283,929 tons in 1951.

Of the 16,252,000 tons of manganese ore shipped from 1895 to 1931, but excluding the exports from Marmagao, in Portuguese India, the destinations of which are not known, exactly 40 per cent went to the United Kingdom, 21·3 per cent to Belgium, 17·16 per cent to France and 15·38 per cent to the United States of America. The countries taking smaller quantities included: Holland 2·11 per cent, Italy 1·16, Germany 1·39 and Japan 0·71 per cent. Between the years 1932 and 1946, a further 7,727,000 tons went to foreign lands, and of this quantity the United States received 37·9 per cent, the United Kingdom 24·4, Japan 15·1, France 10·7, Belgium 6·4, Italy 1·6, Germany 0·7 and other countries 3·2 per cent. In these figures the shipments from Marmagao are included from 1942 onwards. Exports to enemy countries ceased with the second world war, and the most noteworthy features of the war period were the decline in exports to the United Kingdom and their increase to the United States, a feature of the trade which still continues, for of the 1,601,450 tons exported in the three years 1948-50 inclusive, just two-thirds was destined for the United States and approximately one-third to the United Kingdom and other countries. During their brief occupation of Burma, the Japanese are said to have mined some 3,000 tons of manganese ore from a surface deposit in the Hopong State of the Southern Shan States, but little is known at present of the nature of this occurrence.

Madhya Pradesh is by far the most important producing region and was responsible for no less than 69 per cent of the total Indian production of 31,685,758 tons up to the end of 1950; Madras including Andhra came next with 14·5 per cent and was followed by Bihar and Orissa with 7·8, Bombay with 5·4, Mysore with 2·6 and Madhya Bharat (Central India) with 0·7 per cent of the total, respectively.

The prosperity of the export trade, apart from its ability to deliver manganese ores at the sea-ports at competitive market prices, which in India is largely a question of labour costs and railway freight charges, depends entirely on the world's demand for steel. There is no better illustration of this than the prevailing conditions of the great depression of 1929 to 1933; in 1929 the world's output of steel had reached 118 million tons, the highest figure recorded up to that time, and the world's output of manganese ores attained a record of 3,598,343 tons, to which India contributed 994,279 tons, or 27·6 per cent. By 1932, the world's steel production had dropped to 49·7 million tons and the world's output of manganese ores to 1,218,879 tons, of which India's share was 212,604 tons or 17·4 per cent. Over the same period the market price of manganese ore fell from 14·0 pence per unit in 1929, to 9½ pence per unit in 1932. In the same manner the improvement in the Indian trade which followed later was but a reflection of the revival in steel manufacture, itself accelerated

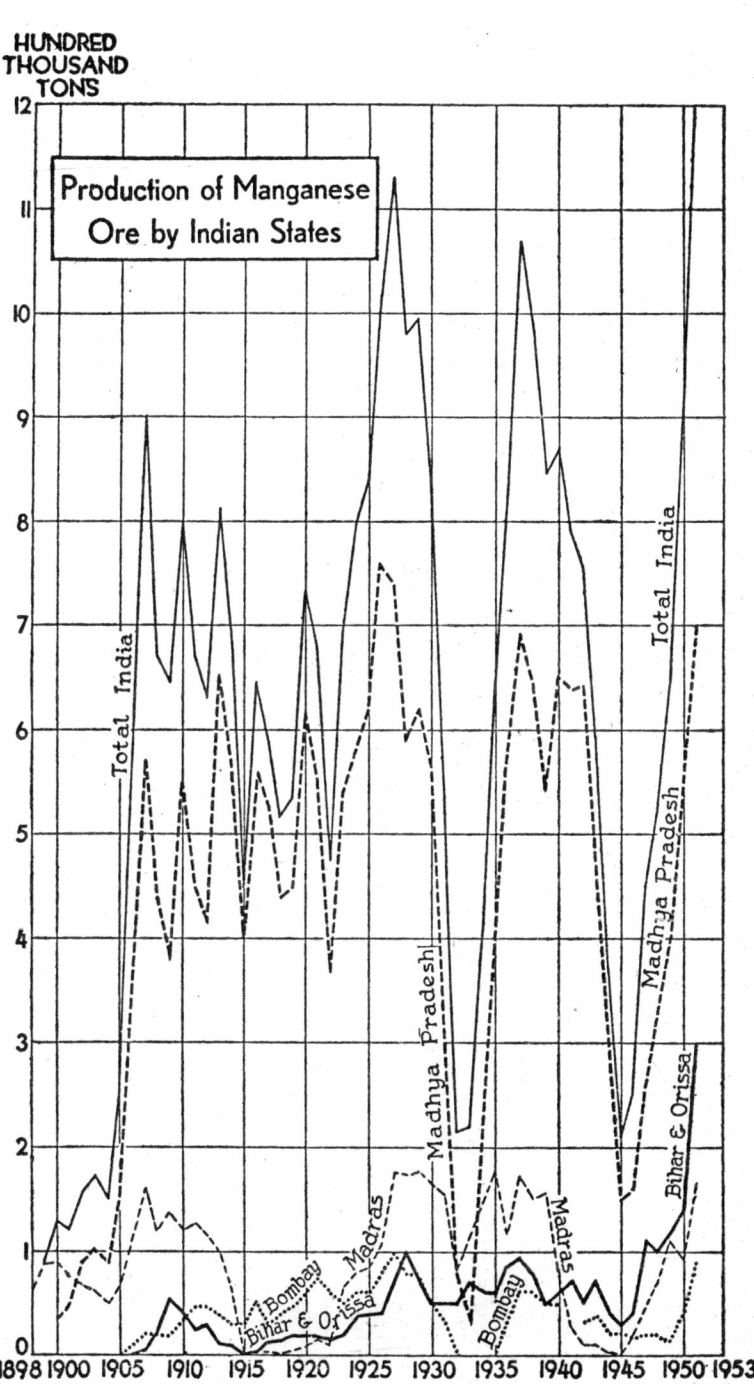

HUNDRED
THOUSAND
TONS

Production of Manganese
Ore by Indian States

PRODUCTION OF MANGANESE ORES IN INDIA, 1892–1950

PERIOD	BIHAR AND ORISSA§	BOMBAY	MADHYA BHARAT	MADHYA PRADESH	MADRAS (ANDHRA AND BELLARY DISTRICT)	MYSORE	TONNAGE TOTAL	EXPORT VALUES (f.o.b.) £	PERCENTAGE OF WORLD'S PRODUCTION
1892–8	..	..	..		225,346	..	225,346	233,845	....
1899–1903	..	..	6,800*	312,621**	384,378	..	703,799	873,175	....
1904–8	23,933***	54,213†	140,946	1,584,523	513,845	228,243††	2,545,718‡	3,386,595	50·6 (1908 only)
1909–13	160,558	178,360	42,773	2,442,424	598,468	141,401	3,563,984	4,227,025	40·7
1914–18	37,662	175,216	7,008	2,479,402	66,973	121,023	2,887,284	6,276,651	34·1
1919–23	102,267	286,475		2,527,011	98,910	108,513	3,123,176	9,473,413	44·1
1924–8	282,622	367,198	27,783	3,302,796	624,556	160,232	4,765,197	12,497,315	33·6
1929–33	290,613	160,304	..	1,582,666	698,962	60,435	2,792,980	3,761,413	::
1934–8	467,431	155,222	..	2,481,652	762,720	13,729	3,880,754	8,625,291	::
1939–43	463,990	165,640§§	..	2,943,723	280,696	3,308	3,857,357	8,071,809	::
1944–8	354,197	97,817¶	4,837	1,213,957	137,664	2,937	1,811,409	3,468,471	::
1949–50	308,388	66,708¶¶	2,833	938,075	207,127	5,623	1,528,754	9,304,039	::
TOTAL	2,491,661	1,707,153	232,980	21,808,850	4,599,655	845,444	31,685,758	70,199,042	....

GRAND TOTAL to end of 1950, 31,685,758 tons, valued at £70,199,042.

* Production commenced in Madhya Bharat in 1903.
**   „   „   „   Madhya Pradesh in 1900.
***   „   „   „   Bengal (later Bihar & Orissa) in 1906.
††   „   „   „   Bombay in 1905.
§§   „   „   „   Mysore in 1906.
‡ Includes 15 tons from the Pab Hills, Jhalawan, Pakistan.
§   „   the Eastern States from 1934.
§§   „   19 tons from Rajasthan.
¶   „   4,393 tons from Rajasthan.
¶¶   „   10,576 tons from Banswara, Rajasthan.

by the preparations for war, increased, then as now, by the purchases of reserves of minerals of munitions value which nations collect for use in emergencies.

The reserves of high-grade manganese ore in India have been conservatively estimated at 18 million tons, while lower-grade ores may amount to twice this quantity. In all probability appreciable increases will have to be made in these figures, as the diamond drilling campaign initiated of recent years in Madhya Pradesh is extended both there and elsewhere, not to mention the possibility of entirely new discoveries.

India's first concern is the conservation of sufficient supplies of high-grade ore to meet the demands of her own expanding iron and steel industry and steps have already been taken in this direction. For the year 1950, a target of 700,000 tons of high-grade ore was fixed as the official maximum quantity against which export licenses were issued, though the export of lower grades was permitted without limit. If requirements in the next few years are placed at 110,000 tons per annum, or double the pre-war consumption, there is more than enough for many years to come, but the more distant future must be borne in mind, as it is within the country's power to become a very large producer of steel. This is the problem which must ultimately decide how far it is desirable for India to compete in the world's market for manganese ores. Here, it can only be stated that India is extremely unlikely to suffer from a shortage, that external demand will always be keen when the world needs steel, and that there is no apparent reason why the industry should not surpass its former peaks of production, provided that the long-term planning authority of the State considers it politic for it to do so. Stricter attention should be paid in future to the introduction of modern concentration methods, to recover ore from low-grade materials and from the spoil heaps which have accumulated from the wasteful methods of the past. Finally, the most profitable possibilities lie in the production of ferro-manganese in India and its export in that form rather than as the raw ore. As Dr J. A. Dunn pointed out: 'With low manganese-ore production costs and low freight charges, India should be well able to compete in the ferro-manganese trade.'

FERRO-MANGANESE

Over forty years ago, in 1909, Sir Lewis Fermor wrote as follows: 'There seems to be room for a handsome profit in manufacturing ferro-manganese in India,' yet it was not until October 1915, and on account of the increase in its price caused by conditions during the first world war, that its manufacture was commenced by the Tata Iron & Steel Co. Ltd, and in November of the same year by the Bengal Iron Co. Ltd. The production of the alloy in India since that time is summarized below:

PRODUCTION OF FERRO-MANGANESE IN INDIA, 1915-50

Period	Total Tonnage	Period	Total Tonnage
1915–18 ..	20,347*	1934–8 ..	49,407
1919–23 ..	16,956	1939–43 ..	78,136‡
1924–8 ..	42,338	1944–8 ..	51,405
1929–33 ..	30,633†	1949–50 ..	31,515§

   * After satisfying the needs of the Indian steel industry a balance of 7,555 tons was exported to France, the United States of America, Italy and Natal.
   † Production of the Tata Iron & Steel Co. Ltd only.
   ‡ The year of peak production was 1941 with 31,563 tons.
   § Early in 1955, the Government of India authorized a Bombay firm to erect, with American collaboration, a ferro-manganese plant at Tumsar, to make 30,000 tons annually.

Very large quantities of ferro-manganese are made in other countries; the British consumption alone is at present about 400,000 tons per annum and likely to rise to half a million tons; by 1944 the United States was producing over 700,000 tons per annum, in addition to more than 165,000 tons of spiegeleisen and large amounts of silico-manganese. During the war years Germany made about 90,000 tons of 30 - 60 per cent Mn. ferro-manganese, and 41,000 tons of higher-grade material annually, as well as 408,000 tons of 14 - 30 per cent spiegeleisen, and 240,000 tons of the same alloy with 6 - 14 per cent of manganese, a yearly total of 779,000 tons.

The question is often asked why India does not manufacture ferro-manganese for these and other markets and the answer usually given is that her ores and cokes contain too much phosphorus. To be acceptable to the market, the phosphorus content of ferro-manganese should not exceed 0·1 per cent, although 0·3 per cent is often taken as the maximum limit. By the careful selection of suitable ores, which are obtainable from Madhya Pradesh and else-where, and a coke such as that yielded by coal from the Giridih coalfield, with its phosphorus content of 0·022 per cent, this difficulty could doubtless be overcome. After all, Indian iron and steel works make their own requirements by the normal blast-furnace methods, and will continue to do so in the years to come, when the output of the Jamshedpur plant alone is increased from its existing capacity to the 930,000 tons of steel per annum con-templated, when the extensions of the other steel works are in being, and when the projects for the national steel works come to fruition.

In addition to its production in the blast furnace, ferro-man-ganese is also made on a large scale in electrical arc furnaces, and it may well be that by this process the difficulty mentioned could be com-pletely overcome, though cheap electrical power would be essential.

Standard ferro-manganese contains about 80 per cent of metallic manganese and 5 to 7 per cent of carbon, the balance being mainly made up of iron; standard spiegeleisen contains about 20 per cent of manganese. Ferro-manganese made in the blast furnace may contain from 27 to 86 per cent of manganese and spiegeleisen from 5 to 30 per cent. The products of the electric furnace are richer and may contain up to 95 per cent of manganese. Other ferro-alloys of a similar nature made in the electric furnace are silico-manganese and silico-spiegel. Metallic manganese is used in the manufacture of alloys in which the presence of iron is undesirable, such as the manganese bronzes and certain copper-nickel-manganese alloys. It is also employed as a deoxidizer in non-ferrous metallurgical operations, and is made commercially by reducing its oxides, either by the aluminothermic process or by means of silicon, with or without silico-manganese. An American process depends on the electrolysis of manganese sulphate leached from low-grade ores, and any or all of these products may contain from 97 to over 99 per cent of the metal.

In addition to the quantities used in the production of ferrous alloys, manganese ores are also added to blast furnace charges in Indian iron works. The total amount consumed by the companies concerned for all these purposes up to the end of 1950 was 1,667,367 tons. In recent years this consumption has averaged about 10 per cent of their production—a fraction which it is believed will increase in the future. It may be added here that in addition to the quantities required by the iron and steel works, some 4,000 tons of manganese ores are used annually in India by glass manufacturers and makers of dry batteries.

NICKEL

Nickel occurs in small quantities in the lead-zinc-copper-silver ores of Bawdwin in the Shan States of Burma, and in the course of the smelting operations which were carried on at Nam Tu, until the invasion of Burma by the Japanese in 1942, it was recovered regularly in the form of a speiss. The mineral gersdorffite, a sulpharsenide of nickel, $NiAsS$, is the principal source of the element, for J. A. Dunn detected it under the microscope in almost every example from a collection of more than sixty specimens of lead-zinc ores from various parts of the great Bawdwin orebody. There are two varieties of gersdorffite, designated as *alpha* and *beta,* and the latter by loss of sulphur can graduate into chloanthite, the diarsenide of nickel, $NiAs_2$, which in its turn may graduate into smaltite, the corresponding diarsenide of cobalt, $CoAs_2$, by isomorphous intermixture.

Regular returns of speiss production commenced in 1927, and from that time until the end of 1940, 45,457 tons had been made, containing an estimated total of 13,223 tons of nickel, together with large quantities of cobalt, silver and copper. The speiss was shipped from Burma to Germany for treatment.

AVERAGE ANNUAL PRODUCTION OF NICKEL SPEISS AT NAM TU, 1927–40

PERIOD	TONS	VALUE	COMPOSITION			
			NICKEL	COPPER	COBALT	SILVER
		Rs	%	%	%	oz. per ton
1927–8 ..	1,982	3,55,747	24·72	15·56	*	32·89
1929–33 ..	3,211	8,19,023	27·98	11·64	*	30·06
1934–8 ..	4,032	13,04,918	30·44	9·28	5·85	19·07
1939–40 ..	2,638	12,61,182	30·91	8·23	7·97	14·83

* 3 to 4 per cent cobalt approximately.
N.B.—According to the Mines Department of the Government of Burma, 3,620 tons of nickel speiss, of unknown composition, were produced in 1951.

Nickel is a constituent of some importance in the copper ores of Singhbhum, Bihar, though the metal has not been recovered from them up to the present time. J. A. Dunn has stated that pyrrhotite, the magnetic sulphide of iron, is perhaps more abundant than chalcopyrite itself in these Singhbhum ores, and that it contains irregular, microscopic patches of both pentlandite and violarite, sulphides of nickel and iron with the formulae $(NiFe)S$ and $(NiFe)_3S_4$ respectively. Millerite, the sulphide of nickel, NiS, has also been identified.

Nickel ores are also known to occur in Nepal; thus a vein cropping out at Bhorle, near Nangre, has been traced for 2,500 feet and has been worked by the local inhabitants in places to a depth of about 100 feet. Its average nickel content, according to A. G. Jhingran, is about 2 per cent, present mainly in the form of the diarsenide, chloanthite, $NiAs_2$, associated with which are cobaltite, the sulpharsenide of cobalt, $CoAsS$, traces of zinc and some bismuth compounds.

The presence of both nickel and cobalt in the pyrrhotite of the Khetri deposits of Jaipur, Rajasthan, was proved by F. R. Mallet. The metal also occurs in the mixed sulphide ores (pyrrhotite, pyrite and chalcopyrite) of the Tovala taluk in Travancore; in the sulphides associated with the gold-bearing quartz veins of Kolar, Mysore and as a bloom on the serpentines of Pai Khel in Waziristan, Pakistan. In Kashmir, nickel-bearing minerals have been found at Ramsu, Buniar and Khaleni, as well as in the vicinity of the sapphire mines of Padar. Samples of copper ores from the Riasi *tahsil* contain up to 1·68 per cent of nickel.

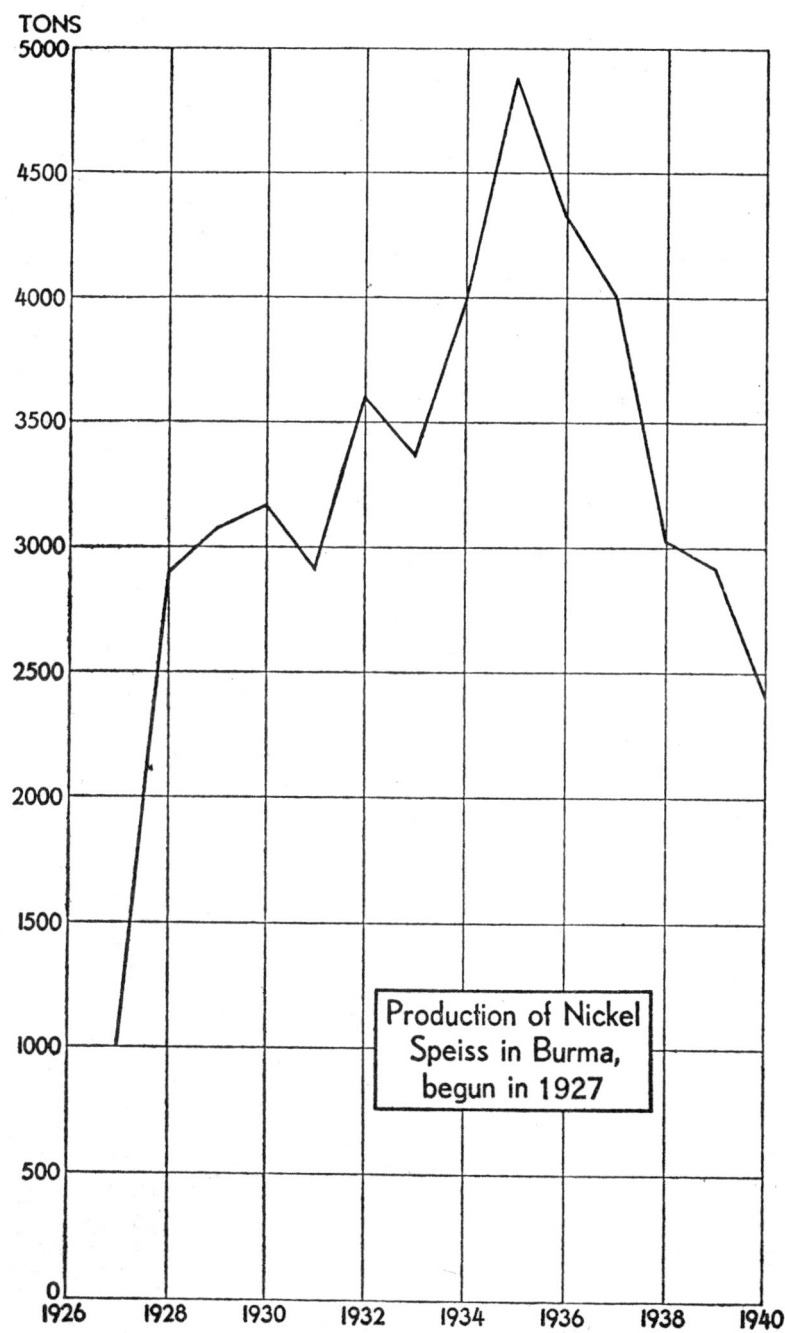

Production of Nickel
Speiss in Burma,
begun in 1927

The announcement of the discovery of large deposits of garnierite, a hydrated silicate of magnesium and nickel, in Singhbhum in 1934, has not been confirmed, but S. K. Borooah has described zaratite, a basic nickel carbonate, $NiCO_3 \cdot 2Ni(OH)_2 \cdot 4H_2O$, from the chromite deposits of Nuasahi in Keonjhar. It is a green earthy mineral found in the gangue and in the interspaces between the chromite grains themselves. This chromite contains 0·3 per cent of nickel and 0·6 per cent of cobalt.

Uses of Nickel

In 1948 the world's consumption of nickel, outside the Soviet Union, has been estimated at over 130,000 tons and in 1948 the world's production, allowing 25,000 tons for the Soviet Union, has been given as 149,000 tons though the data are admittedly incomplete. Some 60 per cent of the total consumption is said to be employed in the preparation of nickel alloy steels of various kinds while nickel plating is the second largest field of use, though nowadays generally as an undercoat to chromium. Pure nickel is to be found in the coinage of no less than thirty-six countries, including some of the coins of the Indian Republic. It is also used in the fabrication of vessels to withstand corrosion, either alone or as nickel-clad steel; to build up worn machinery parts by electrodeposition; in radio valves and in depth sounders.

Nickel improves the strength, toughness and hardness of steel, increasing its uniformity, reliability and resistance to fatigue, shock and wear. Taken at one time for the production of armour plate and armaments generally, it was widely regarded solely as a munitions metal until after the first world war; today the low-nickel steels with $\frac{1}{2}$ to 9 per cent of nickel find widespread uses in motor vehicles, locomotives, tractors, excavators, oil-well casings, aircraft and marine engines and indeed in machinery of almost every description. The stainless nickel steels with 2 to 26 per cent of nickel, including the well-known 18/8 variety (see Chromium), possess outstanding corrosion resistance and, finding applications in many industries, are one of the major outlets of the metal. Still higher percentages of nickel and chromium give the heat-resisting steels for furnace parts, mechanical stokers, diesel engine valves and so forth. The nickel-chromium alloys, such as one which contains 80 per cent of nickel and 20 per cent of chromium, have high scaling and electrical resistance, which accounts for their employment as heating elements of electrical furnaces, fires and domestic appliances. The 'Nimonic' alloys of the Mond Nickel Co. are nickel-chromium alloys with small amounts of other elements, which by reason of their resistance to high stresses, high temperatures, gas attack and creep are employed in jet aircraft and similar forms of power production. Their very superior strength at elevated temperatures makes them the strongest of the materials available for the blading of gas turbines. Another alloy, known as ' Inconel ', containing 80 per cent of nickel, 14 per cent of chromium and 6 per cent of iron, finds its chief applications in the food-processing and chemical industries.

Ferro-nickel alloys display wide variations in their magnetic and thermal properties, dependent on their content of nickel. The non-magnetic alloys, with 8 to 27 per cent of nickel, are useful materials for reducing losses in electrical generating plant, transformers and motors. The magnetic alloys, with 35 to 90 per cent of nickel, find their way into telegraph and telephone instruments, submarine cables and radio equipment; others by reason of their predictable behaviour on heating find a place in thermostats, circuit breakers, gas supply controls, overload devices as well as in air speed and altitude indicators. Certain special steels containing nickel, aluminium and cobalt possess twenty-five times the magnetic strength of carbon steel and are employed in loud speakers, small motors, radar instruments, telephone receivers and deaf aids. Nickel steel with 36 per cent of nickel, known as ' Invar ', expands and contracts only to a very minute extent with changes of temperature and is used in measuring tapes, chronometers, etc. Another alloy has much the same expansion as glass and can take the place of platinum for ' lead-in ' wires.

Nickel improves the strength, toughness and structure of grey cast iron, and such alloys are employed as beds for heavy machinery, cylinder blocks and heads; added to white cast iron, in amounts of 4 or 5 per cent, it imparts high wear-resistance and hardness, conferring at the same time an ability to withstand severe wear and abrasion, such as are met with in components of rock and ore crushers, grinding mills, ball mill linings, brake drums and metal rollers. This alloy is known as ' Ni-hard '. Other alloy irons combine the effects of nickel with those of chromium, molybdenum and other elements and are made to meet special requirements in mechanical engineering.

The nickel-copper alloys include ' Monel metal ', which contains about 68 per cent of nickel, 30 per cent of copper with a little iron, and is made directly from its ore without preliminary separation of its two chief ingredients. It resembles silver in appearance, is superior to bronze in durability, equals steel in strength, is amenable to both hot and cold working, resistant to chemical attack, and, consequently, has a very wide range of industrial applications—from house roofs and shop fronts to the parts of aircraft near the compass, for it is non-magnetic; from turbine blades and pump bodies to the canning equipment of food factories; from sinks and soda fountains to pulp and paper mills; from the pots and pans of the kitchen to the evaporators of the chemical factory and the finishing machines in dye works and laundries.

An alloy with 40 per cent nickel and 60 per cent copper has high electrical resistance which changes little with variations of temperature and accounts for its use in electrical apparatus. Another alloy, with about 30 per cent nickel and a small amount of iron in addition to the remaining copper, is a standard composition for the condenser tubes of naval vessels and large steamships and, indeed, for any other situation subject to the corrosive effects of rapidly moving sea-water carrying air bubbles in suspension. The addition of aluminium to the brass, and of iron to the cupronickel alloys formerly used for this purpose, has greatly lengthened the average life of these tubes, increased the steaming capacity of ships and the trustworthiness of their means of propulsion. These and related alloys find outlets in chemical, oil and power plants and are also used in munitions for bullet envelopes.

The 25 per cent nickel-copper alloy is a standard form of coinage in many countries, including India, and in Britain where, since 1946, it has replaced silver. Five per cent of nickel has been added to Indian silver coins since 1940. Other nickel alloys include ' nickel silver ', formerly known as ' German silver ', a series containing copper, nickel and zinc, with the nickel proportion ranging from about 5 to 30 per cent, and varying the colour from pale yellow to silvery white as the nickel increases. They are made into table-ware and decorative articles of many sorts as well as into flat springs for electrical contacts. ' Silver Plate ', or ' E.P.N.S.' as it is often branded, is nickel silver with an electro-deposited coating of pure silver. Nickel is also added to brasses and bronzes to improve their wearing properties; for instance, the Indian brass coinage of 1941 contains 1 per cent of nickel. High-nickel bronzes have their place in steam engineering for valves, pumps, shafts and bearings. The metal is also a component of many complex light alloys to which it gives added strength and hardness, so making them suitable for pistons, connecting rods and cylinder heads of aircraft and automobile engines and for the frames of motor vehicles.

Several salts of nickel are valued catalysts, especially for the conversion of liquid animal and vegetable oils into solid edible fats. Other applications are in the cracking of petroleum, the purification of coal gas, the synthesis of nitrates, ammonia and many organic compounds. The sulphate goes into the solutions of nickel-plating baths; the hydroxide into the positive plates of nickel-iron and nickel-cadmium storage batteries.

This is but a skeleton outline of a most versatile metal which now plays a part in most modern industries.

Consumption of Nickel in India

Over the years 1934-46 the mints at Bombay, Calcutta and Lahore, the last of which, now in Pakistan, commenced operating in 1943, consumed 1,991 tons of nickel, valued at Rs 88,25,637. As the metal was not available from external sources during the war period, 851 tons of cupro-nickel scrap, valued at Rs 12,99,493, and containing 20 per cent of nickel and 80 per cent of copper, were obtained from the Indian Ordnance Department for the Bombay mint.

Indian imports of German silver and articles made from it continued to grow until the war slowly strangled the trade. From an annual average of 906 tons, valued at Rs 14,36,362 for the five years ending 1932-3, they had risen to an average of 1,132 tons, valued at Rs 13,26,498, over the five years ending 1937-8. The next decade (1938-9 to 1947-8) started with still greater imports of 1,748 tons in its first year, but thereafter the decline was swift and practically ceased between 1942-3 and 1945-6. This decline was followed by a rapid recovery and the ten-yearly period closed with an annual average of 649 tons and Rs 6,95,012. The marked increase since then, totalling no less than 4,158 tons and Rs 1,93,59,420, for the two years ending 1949-50, may be due in part to the replacement of depleted stocks.

India possesses a source of nickel in the copper ores of Singhbhum, and it is unfortunate that no attempts are made to recover at least part of it to meet the country's demand for the cupro-nickel alloys. It is only fair to the copper smelters to point out, however, that the nickel content of Indian refined copper is said to be advantageous in the particular commercial uses for which it is made. It is true that the ore contains only 0·083 per cent of nickel, taking the only analysis available, which refers to ore won in 1934, but with an annual output of 350,000 tons of ore, this represents 290 tons of nickel every year. Indian refined copper is said to average 0·649 per cent nickel, and to account for only 13 per cent of the nickel originally present in the ore, according to Sir Lewis Fermor, the balance being lost in either the ore concentrating or smelting processes.

Over 90 per cent of the total nickel production of the world outside the Soviet Union is supplied by the nickeliferous sulphide ores of the Sudbury Basin in Ontario, Canada, where the ore reserves in 1949 totalled 236 million tons, containing 3·2 per cent nickel-copper, of which about one half is nickel. The ore deposits are closely associated with a body of norite and micropegmatite, outcropping as an oval ring 37 by 17 miles in diameter and 1 to 3·6 miles broad, and lie along or close to the outer margin of the norite. They consist of rock fragments cemented by the sulphides and partly replaced by them. Similar ores are mined at Petsamo, formerly in Finland but now in the Soviet Union. The nickel ores of New Caledonia are of the silicate type, as are those of the southern Urals, Greece, Brazil, Venezuela and the southern Celebes. Lateritic nickel ores have been mined on a small scale in Cuba.

COBALT

A complex ore of cobalt known as *sehta*, which contains the minerals cobaltite, the sulpharsenide of cobalt, CoAsS, and danaite, a cobalt-bearing variety of mispickel, the sulpharsenide of iron, FeAsS, occurs with copper and iron pyrites sparsely scattered in irregular strings, layers and lenticles through black slates, without any resemblance to a true lode, in the Babai copper mines of the Khetri area of Jaipur in Rajasthan. The country rock is mostly black slate, siliceous and splintery, with indefinite bands of quartzite of the Ajabgarh Series, in the Delhi System, and is intruded by amphibolites. The mines have been closed as far as copper is concerned for many years, and the extraction of *sehta* ceased about 1908. It used to be recovered by crushing the slate and panning the powder, the heavy concentrate so produced being sold to the Jaipur jewellers for the production of the beautiful blue glazes of their enamel work. Its place is now taken by a more expensive, but better quality, imported product containing cobalt.

Cobaltite is known to occur at several localities in western Nepal, including Tamgas and Samar Bhamar where, judging from the many abandoned pits and adits, now for the most part under water, extensive workings existed in the past. Samples from one adit averaged 5·85 per cent of cobalt. The places mentioned are 5 or 6 days' marches from the nearest railhead at Shohratganj (Shararatgarh). The occurrence of cobaltite with the nickel-bearing ores of Bhorle, in Nepal, is referred to under NICKEL. Linnaeite, a sulphide of cobalt, Co_3S_4, has been recognized in some of the copper ores of Sikkim.

Certain varieties of chromite from the Nausahi area of Keonjhar are reported to contain 0·6 per cent of cobalt and 0·3 per cent of nickel. The presence of both elements has been detected frequently in Indian manganese ores, while mammilary concretions probably best designated as wad, associated with the iron ores of Olatura, near Madanpur, Kalahandi, Orissa, contained 0·82 per cent of cobalt oxide, CoO. According to T. L. Walker, this cobaltiferous wad approaches the New Caledonian and Australian asbolites in composition, and while the sample assayed is not rich enough to be of any commercial value, it would not be surprising if an ore of such variable composition were locally richer than this particular sample, and in that case be rich enough to be worth exploiting.

The presence of cobalt in the mixed lead-zinc sulphide ores of Bawdwin, in the Shan States of Burma, was first noticed by the growth of thin, encrusting layers of pink erythrite on stacks of ore which had been left on the surface exposed to the action of the weather. This mineral, which is also known as cobalt bloom, is the hydrated arsenate of cobalt, $Co_3As_2O_8.8H_2O$, and an alteration product of the original sulpharsenides of the ore itself. During smelting operations the cobalt finds its way into the nickel speiss, the composition of which is given in the table on p. 222. As the Bawdwin mine was deepened, the cobalt content of the speiss gradually increased from 3 or 4 per cent in the early years (1927-33) to nearly 8 per cent in 1940, and it is calculated that from 1927, when shipments commenced, until 1940, they contained between 2,270 and 2,370 tons of metallic cobalt.

Cobalt enters into the composition of many ferrous and non-ferrous alloys; thus it is an important addition, in amounts of from 5 to 12 per cent, to high-speed steels based mainly on tungsten or molybdenum, or on both these elements, increasing their cutting efficiency at high temperatures. The permanent magnet steels, already referred to under NICKEL, and known under such names as 'Alnico', contain from 12 to 24 per cent of cobalt, 14 to 32 per cent of nickel, 8 to 12 per cent of aluminium, and, in some cases, 3 to 6 per cent of copper, as well as small additions of titanium, and owing to their very high coercive forces have replaced for many purposes the cobalt steels, which up to the time of their discovery were the best permanent magnet material available. Cobalt steels, apart from their uses in tool and magnet steels, have many other applications in situations where resistance to stresses, oxidation, corrosion at high temperatures and very low coefficients of expansion are needful, and are to be found in razor blades, surgical instruments, die steels, engine valves, glass-to-metal joints and seals, as well as in some parts of jet propulsion machinery. The largest single use of the metal today is in the cobalt-nickel-chromium base alloys required particularly for jet engines.

Cobalt is the chief binding metal or matrix used for cementing the carbide of tungsten, as well as those of molybdenum, titanium and tantalum, the sintered powders of which may contain up to 14 per cent of cobalt. Such materials are the hardest known products of metallurgy, surpassing the hardest steel in this respect and of great industrial utility as tips for many kinds of cutting and abrading tools.

The 'stellites', alloys of cobalt, chromium and tungsten, sometimes modified by the addition of other elements, have been mentioned under CHROMIUM. They may contain from 45 to more than 60 per cent of cobalt and furnish cutting tools superior in some respects to those made from high-speed steel, especially in their performance at elevated temperatures. Such alloys, in the form of welding rods, were in common use on the oilfields of Burma to build up the worn edges of drilling bits: by their means hard-wearing layers can be applied to any machine parts where they may be required.

Cobalt in small quantities increases the hardness and electrical conductivity of the copper-beryllium alloys. It has an important function as a catalyst in the Fischer-Tropsch process for the synthesis of liquid hydrocarbons from carbon-monoxide and hydrogen mixtures; the material used in the German plants during the last war for this purpose is stated to have consisted of cobalt 100, thoria 5, magnesia 8, and kieselguhr 200 parts. The metal has also been used as a catalytic desulphurizer of crude petroleum.

The ceramic industry absorbs much of the cobalt oxide of commerce to give the blue glazes of pottery and earthenware; glass and enamel makers also use it for similar purposes. Cobalt salts are, on the other hand, employed as decolorizing agents in potteries to counteract the slight yellow tinge caused by traces of iron compounds when most clays are fired, the complementary blue coloration neutralizing the yellow one, and yielding a pure white product. In the vitreous enamelling of iron and steel, small additions of cobalt oxide to the frits promote the adherence of the coatings to the metal bodies. Soluble cobalt compounds are added to nickel-plating baths to produce hard, smooth and bright surfaces on the finished articles, and so to lessen or eliminate later costly polishing operations. Certain organic compounds, such as the resinate and oleate of cobalt, are active driers of oils and superior in this respect to compounds of iron and manganese: by their use a number of semi-drying oils can be employed in the manufacture of paint in place of the more expensive linseed oil. They have further uses in the manufacture of waterproof textiles, printing inks, linoleum and other products. Other cobalt salts are employed in veterinary medicine and in the form of soil dressings on grazing lands as a preventive of deficiency diseases amongst sheep. The radioactive isotope known as cobalt 60, a product of the atomic pile, emits gamma rays of much the same energy as those from radium. It has a half-life of 5·3 years and is a substitute for radium both in therapeutics and in industrial radiography.

Thirty years ago the world's annual consumption of cobalt was about 750 tons; by 1939 it had reached 4,000 tons and in 1948 the estimated output of the producing countries, still expressed in terms of metallic cobalt, was about 5,900 tons. Practically the whole of this is obtained, just as it was in Burma, as a by-product from complex ores primarily smelted for other metals and principally for copper; thus the copper deposits of Katanga, in the Belgian Congo, and those of Northern Rhodesia, between them accounted for over 78 per cent of the total in 1948. If the copper ore deposits of Rajasthan, or of the Outer Himalayan belt in Sikkim, Nepal and elsewhere, eventually come to be worked on a large scale, it is likely that India will enter the list of cobalt-producing countries.

CHAPTER V

THE STEEL-HARDENING METALS

CHROMIUM

CHROMITE, the ore of chromium, has the ideal composition $FeCr_2O_4$ or $FeO.Cr_2O_3$, corresponding to 68 per cent of chromic oxide, but as part of its iron is often replaced by magnesium and some of its chromium by aluminium, the commercial ore seldom contains more than 50 per cent of chromic oxide, Cr_2O_3.

The mineral was first mined in Baluchistan in 1903, in Mysore in 1907 and in Singhbhum in 1909. It was not until 1937 that Seraikela of the Eastern States Agency, now part of Bihar, began to deliver chromite, to be followed by Keonjhar, now in Orissa, in 1943. The Krishna district of Andhra has made small contributions since 1941, and sample parcels have also been taken from Salem in Madras and from Ratnagiri in Bombay.

The Baluchistan ores, discovered by E. Vredenburg in 1901, occur sporadically as veins and irregular, magmatic segregations in serpentines formed by the alteration of saxonites (enstatite peridotites) of Cretaceous age. The chief mines are near Hindubagh, in the Zhob Valley, but production was extended to the adjoining Quetta-Pishin district in 1937. Similar intrusive, ultrabasic rocks have been found in Waziristan further to the north-east, and in Kalat to the south and certainly merit prospecting for chromite. The Baluchistan ore is of exceptional quality and as exported from Karachi often averages over 53 per cent chromic oxide.

Over 40 per cent of the grand total of India's chromite production has been mined or quarried from the Mysore and Hassan districts of Mysore, where the mineral was discovered by H. Slater in 1898. Veins, lenses and segregations of chromite, often associated with magnesite, occur in serpentinized ultrabasic rocks between Mysore City and Nanjangud, and have been exploited at a number of localities. The Sinduvalli mine of Mysore Chromite Ltd reached a depth of 600 feet and gave over 136,000 tons of high-grade ore, averaging 50 per cent chromic oxide, before becoming exhausted. Smaller deposits at Talur, Uradabur and Dodkatur yield low-grade ore (40 to 44 per cent Cr_2O_3), while several others which are not mined average about 30 per cent. Further low-grade deposits are known in the Chikmagalur, Shimoga and Chitaldrug districts. At Pensamudra, about three miles from Arsikere in the Hassan district, low-grade ores are mined and concentrated by

Mysore Chromite Ltd for the manufacture of sodium dichromate at Mysore, Bombay and Kanpur. There are many orebodies in this area, lenses and veins in talc-serpentine rocks, themselves altered enstatite-peridotites of the Nuggihalli schist belt which stretches for 35 miles from Jambur to Arsikere. They are mainly of low-grade quality but at Byrapur massive and friable high-grade ores are found, averaging 48 to 50 per cent chromic oxide. Worked extensively in the past for export, these are now reserved for ferrochrome manufacture at the Mysore Iron and Steel Works, and such small quantities as are removed at present supply refractory materials for use in these works. Mysore chromite in general, as exported from Marmagao in the past, contained from 40 to 48 per cent of chromic oxide.

The chromite deposits of Singhbhum, found by R. Saubolle in 1907, lie near Jojohatu, west of Chaibasa, in partly serpentinized saxonites, dunites and pyroxenites. Their lenticular veins, up to 3 feet in width and 100 feet in length, are not large, but they form a persistent ore-bearing horizon capable of yielding 4,000 to 5,000 tons of 50 per cent ore per annum for many years to come, according to Dr J. A. Dunn. Adjoining Singhbhum, the former state of Seraikela (now in Bihar) yielded a few hundred tons of low-grade chromite from the usual, highly altered, ultrabasic intrusive rocks, between 1937 and 1942.

In Orissa, large orebodies were discovered on the Baula Hills in Keonjhar in 1943. Here, lenticular, steeply dipping, echeloned lenses of ore, primary differentiates of an ultrabasic magma, have been intruded in successive stages so that several generations of chromite are recognizable; a coarse-grained early one, preceding a medium-grained intermediate stage, and a final fine-grained phase, both of which cut through the coarse ore in places. The massive hand-cobbed ore, as marketed, averages 52·4 per cent chromic oxide, according to S. K. Borooah, and thus compares favourably with Baluchistan chromite. The probable reserves to a depth of 50 feet are of the order of 200,000 tons, and up to February 1949 approximately 50,000 tons had been won. Further finds of chromite have been reported from localities close to Nausahi as well as from the adjoining Sukinda Estate, in the Cuttack district of Orissa. The chromite in Sukinda occurs along a quartzite-peridotite junction and as small patches in lateritized dunite. To the west, in Dhenkanal district, rich deposits capable of yielding at least 120,000 tons have been found along shear zones in peridotite south of Maruabil. The mineral also occurs in quartzite near Ghotringa, 12 miles north-west of Maruabil, and near Khantalsuan 10 miles further north-west.

About 11 miles south of Tiruchengodu, in the Salem district of Madras, chromite is associated with other minerals in parallel bands which have been traced for a distance of 12 miles in the local anorthite gneiss. By magnetic methods alone, concentrates can be obtained from these ores containing up to 40 per cent of chromic oxide and it is possible that they may prove useful for refractory purposes.

The chromite deposits of Kondapalle, Krishna district, Andhra, are in the form of lenses and pockets in partly serpentinized pyroxenites interbedded with charnockites, and their exploitation has assumed some importance since 1948, but they appear to be pinching out in depth. Low-grade deposits occur in serpentine near Kankanli, in Ratnagiri, and Vagda, in Savantwadi, Bombay. The mineral has been found at many other places in India, Pakistan and Burma and only those larger deposits of actual or potential commercial importance at the time of writing can be mentioned here. Others certainly remain to be located, particularly in regions containing many outcrops of ultrabasic rocks such as Manipur and the Arakan Yoma.

The lustrous, silvery-looking, coating of chromium now plated on so many articles to protect them from rust and wear is familiar everywhere, but this use accounts only for insignificant amounts of chromite. Today, probably more than half of the world's production of some 1·5 million tons (excluding the Soviet Union) is consumed by the metallurgical industry, perhaps about 40 per cent for refractories and the remainder for chemical manufactures.

Chromium is the most widely used of all the steel-alloying elements because of its ability to impart additional strength, hardness and resistance to corrosion. By varying the quantity of chromium, by the addition of other elements with it, particularly nickel, tungsten, molybdenum, vanadium and manganese, and by suitable heat treatments, a bewildering variety of different steels are made, each with its distinctive properties and special applications. They range from the low-chromium steels with from 0·5 per cent to 4 or 5 per cent of the metal on the one hand, to alloys with little or no iron at all on the other. In the former group, often containing nickel and other elements as well, are some steels very widely used by the mechanical engineer, particularly for gears, ball and roller bearings, shafts, axles and connecting rods in all kinds of civil and military vehicles, in locomotives, tractors and excavators, as well as in armour-plate, projectiles and machinery subject to rough usage. In the latter group are the nickel-chromium alloys of the 80/20 class—the heating elements of electrical furnaces, fires and domestic appliances. Similar alloys are to be found in the vital parts of jet engines as they withstand high stresses, elevated temperatures, the attack of hot gases and are resistant to creep.

Between these extremes are many other important groups including the 'stainless' steels, with 12 per cent to 20 per cent of chromium; the 'rustless' irons with 2 per cent to 5 per cent of chromium; the high-speed tool steels with about 4 per cent of chromium; the corrosion-resisting steels of the 18 per cent chromium and 8 per cent nickel type, and the heat-resisting steels with some-what higher percentages of the same metals, extensively employed for furnace parts, diesel engine valves and so forth.

Other important chromium alloys include ' Inconel ' with 80 per cent nickel, 14 per cent chromium and 6 per cent iron, a favourite material for the manufacture of food-processing equip-ment, and the ' Stellites ' with 20 to 35 per cent of chromium, 50 to 65 per cent of cobalt, tungsten and other elements—extremely hard substances used for machine tools, abrasive facings, rock drills, etc.   Metallic chromium, of 99·0 to 99·5 per cent purity, is made on a large scale by the aluminothermic reduction of chromic oxide, itself prepared from sodium dichromate, a product obtained by roasting chromite with sodium carbonate and limestone.   For many purposes, the alloy ferrochromium with 60 to 70 per cent of chromium, made by reducing chromite with carbon in the electric furnace, is used.   High and low carbon varieties are marketed, the latter containing from 0·03 to 0·15 per cent carbon.

Chromite is an essential mineral for the iron and steel industry, and after being turned into bricks, shapes, plasters and cements is utilized in the construction and repair of steel furnaces.   These uses are more fully discussed under REFRACTORIES.

The chromates and dichromates of sodium and potassium, together with many other salts of the element such as chrome alum and chromium sulphate, are important industrial chemicals, partic-ularly in the tanning and dyeing trades.   Indian annual imports of the dichromates before 1939 were of the order of 1,000 tons per annum, but the war demand increased to some 6,000 tons per annum and led to the development of their manufacture in the country, so that by 1946, 13 factories with a total capacity of 5,075 tons per annum were in existence.   The chromate of lead furnishes several yellow pigments for the paint-maker; mixed with Prussian blue it yields various green pigments.   The basic lead chromate supplies the chrome reds.   The chromates of zinc and barium, like those of lead, are also employed extensively for colouring paints, linoleum, rubber and ceramics.   Chromic oxide, besides being a source of the pure metal, is a valuable green pigment, as are a number of hydrated oxides, obtainable in commerce under various names.   Chromic acid solutions are used in chromium plating, in the anodizing of aluminium and in the protection of magnesium base alloys.   Chromium plating is not entirely a matter of produc-ing a durable and decorative finish on articles in common use; thicker coatings are sometimes employed to resize machine parts, to increase the wear-resistance on tools and to line pump rods, engine cylinders and machine-gun barrels.   Chromium salts are also used in photography, in the manufacture of safety matches, in the bleaching of oils and fats, in some types of electrical batteries and as catalysts in the preparation of aviation petrol and methanol, an industrial alcohol.

From the commencement of chromite mining in 1903, up to the end of 1946, a grand total of 1,409,423 tons, of a reported value of Rs 2,27,56,593, had been produced. Of this amount 672,117 tons, or 47·6 per cent, were from Baluchistan; 575,325 tons, or 40·9 per cent, were from the Hassan and Mysore districts of Mysore; 139,109 tons, or 9·8 per cent, were from Singhbhum; 20,403 tons, or 1·4 per cent, from the Eastern States Agency (now parts of Orissa, Bihar, Madhya Pradesh, etc.), and the remainder from the Krishna district of Andhra and from Bombay. Over the 44 years involved India contributed 52·4 per cent and Pakistan 47·6 per cent to the grand total. For the five years ending 1946, the average annual tonnages were 24,071, valued at Rs 3,60,476, for Baluchistan; 6,581 tons, valued at Rs 1,85,430, for Mysore and 4,696 tons, valued at Rs 1,75,935, for Singhbhum. It is not surprising that output reached its record of 62,307 tons in 1937, for chromite ranks high in the list of minerals of strategic importance.

Since the separation of Pakistan in 1947, India has won a further 93,417 tons of chromite, valued at Rs 28,98,003, in the years 1947 to 1950 inclusive: of this quantity 39·8 per cent came from the Hassan and Mysore districts of Mysore, 36·7 per cent from Keonjhar, in Orissa, while the remainder was nearly equally divided between the Krishna district of Andhra with 11·8 per cent and Singhbhum with 11·7 per cent. In Pakistan during the same three years 72,404 tons were raised.

Only about 5,000 tons of the chromite mined annually in India used to remain in the country, the remainder being exported, though in 1949, export quotas were introduced to control this overseas trade. In the pre-war period 1934-8, Norway received most of India's chromite, followed by Germany, with the United Kingdom a close third. Norway with her abundant supplies of hydroelectric power doubtless used the ore for the production of highgrade ferro-chrome for sale to the steel-making countries.

The chief producing countries are the Soviet Union, Southern Rhodesia, Turkey, the Union of South Africa, New Caledonia, Cuba, Yugoslavia and Greece, and it is very noteworthy that all the major steel-making countries of the world are dependent on imported ores. In the pre-war quinquennium, the world's average annual production was approximately one million tons, to which India contributed 4·5 per cent and occupied the eighth position on the list.

India and Pakistan between them possess sufficient chromite reserves of the varying grades required by the consuming industries and will doubtless develop the manufacture of more finished products in all three branches—metallurgical, refractory and chemical—in due course. Earlier experiments in the manufacture of ferrochrome at Bangalore and Bhadravati were unfortunately abandoned in 1932, but during the last war the ordnance factories made their own requirements. As the Indian steel industry grows and the present output of special steels expands, the internal demand for chrome ores of both metallurgical and refractory grades will increase, and the country is fortunate in that, unlike most other large steel-producing countries, it has at hand more chromite than it needs. Chromite bricks and other chrome refractories are made at present by the Tata Iron and Steel Company and by Messrs Burn and Company, in sufficient quantities to satisfy home needs. The solution of the question of an external market for Indian-made high-grade low-carbon ferro-chrome rests almost entirely on the cost of electrical power. Without cheap power, a quality alloy of the type envisaged could not compete successfully with the existing European and American brands in foreign markets.

Finally, the pioneer work of P. I. A. Narayanan on the beneficiation of chromite ores should lead to the profitable working of lean ores, unmarketable in normal times. This is perhaps the most serious problem facing the chromite mining industry in India.

NIOBIUM (COLUMBIUM) AND TANTALUM

Columbite and tantalite, the niobate and tantalate of iron and manganese, respectively, $(FeMn)Nb_2O_6$ and $(FeMn)Ta_2O_6$, are hard, black, massive or orthorhombic minerals which pass by insensible gradations from normal columbite, the nearly pure niobate, at one end of an isomorphous series, to normal tantalite, the almost pure tantalate at the other; theoretically, the pure niobate of iron contains $82 \cdot 7$ per cent of niobium pentoxide (Nb_2O_5) and the corresponding tantalate $86 \cdot 1$ per cent of tantalum pentoxide (Ta_2O_5). As niobium is only about half the weight of tantalum, the specific gravity of the mineral changes with its chemical composition, becoming greater as the tantalum percentage increases, and ranging from $5 \cdot 1$ in columbite up to almost $8 \cdot 0$ in tantalite, thus affording a rough-and-ready means of determining quickly to which end of the series any particular specimen belongs. As a general rule, Indian ores are richer in niobium but some varieties with over 30 per cent of tantalum pentoxide have been sold as tantalum ores. The twin minerals have now been identified from over twenty localities in India, ranging from Mysore in the south to Kashmir in the north, of which only a selection can be referred to here.

Their earliest mention is in the Report of the Madras Museum for 1855, ferro-tantalite, an old name for tantalite, having been identified by E. Balfour from a specimen collected at Palni, in Madurai district. In 1894, Sir Thomas Holland found both columbite and tantalite in a pegmatite on Pananoa Hill, in the Monghyr district of Bihar, while about 1900 B. Jayaram reported its presence in a pegmatite near Masti, Bangalore district, Mysore. Crystals of columbite up to 14 lb. in weight, arranged in fan-like aggregates in the feldspar of pegmatite intruded into garnetiferous mica schists near Pichhli, Gaya district, Bihar, were described by G. H. Tipper in 1919. Similar occurrences to these are known in other pegmatites in various parts of Bihar and Mysore, as well as in the Nellore district of Andhra and Tiruchirapalli district of Madras.

In 1943, J. K. Soneji found columbite-tantalite crystals in his mica mine at Ugai, Kekri *tahsil,* Ajmer-Merwara; later W. N. Khan reported the same mineral in appreciable quantities in Mewar, where it was mined at Lakola, Soniana and Sangua in 1943, together with beryl from the same pegmatites. There are further occurrences in the Lohagal-Makewali area, at Qazipura, west of the Ajmer reservoir, and at Bir, eight miles south of Ajmer. In the parent pegmatites of Rajasthan the minerals are usually associated with pink or white albite, often of the clevelandite variety, greenish mica, quartz and beryl. H. Crookshank, with a wide experience of these rocks, believes that columbite is commonly present wherever beryl is found, but on account of its general outward resemblance to the relatively valueless ilmenite, which with magnetite is distributed sparingly in a great many pegmatites, it has escaped the notice of the beryl miners. It is to be looked for in the intergrowths of quartz-feldspar and small beryls, rather than with the large beryl crystals of the pegmatite cores.

Small parcels of 112 lb. and 100 lb. of columbite were won in Mysore in 1913 and in the Monghyr district of Bihar, respectively. The mines in Merwar yielded a total of 6,660 lb. in 1943, of which 1,555 lb. came from Sangua and the remainder from Lakola and Soniana. The ore from Sangua averaged 13·8 per cent Ta_2O_5 and 61·7 per cent Nb_2O_5; the Soniana ore 39·4 per cent Ta_2O_5 and 41·4 per cent Nb_2O_5; the Lakola ore 30·5 per cent Ta_2O_5 and 45·5 per cent Nb_2O_5. As the official statistics issued by the United States Bureau of Mines reveal that 21,600 lb. of niobium ore and 1,805 lb. of tantalum ore were imported from India into that country in 1943, it is evident that the Indian statistics are incomplete. Such as they are they show a further output of 1,019 lb. of columbite-tantalite in 1944. There can be little doubt that appreciable quantities could be obtained in Merwar provided prices were sufficiently attractive.

Other Indian minerals containing niobium and tantalum are samarskite, a niobate and tantalate of yttrium, and the cerium group of elements, uranium, iron and calcium, from Sankara, Nellore district, Andhra; sipylite, a niobate and tantalate of the rare earth elements and uranium, from Sankara and Razulapad, in Nellore; hatchettolite or endolite, the former being a variety of pyrochlore with uranium and the latter probably an altered pyrochlore, itself a niobate and titanate of the cerium elements and other bases with thorium, from Vayampati, Kadavur (Tiruchirapalli); aeschynite, a niobate and titanate of the cerium elements with thorium, and often containing uranium in addition, and euxenite, a niobate, tantalate and titanate of yttrium, cerium and uranium from the Erania taluk of Travancore. Other complex niobates, tantalates and titanates of the rare earth elements such as fergusonite, the niobate and tantalate of yttrium, and annerodite, the niobate of uranium and yttrium, occur in Ceylon, and as more or less similar geological conditions prevail in the adjacent parts of southern India, intensive prospecting would probably reveal them there too. They are all of pegmatitic origin and of more potential value for their uranium content than as ores of niobium or tantalum.

Tantalum is marketed in the form of powder, ingots, wire and strip, and by reason of its mechanical strength, hardness, ready workability, high melting point and resistance to corrosion by most chemicals, has many uses. Niobium (known as ' columbium ' in the United States of America) has similar properties, and mixed alloys termed ' ferro-columbium ' in commerce, which in reality contain all three metals, are made directly from columbite by the aluminothermic process.

Tantalum is employed in the manufacture of large high-vacuum valves for radio broadcasting and reception, for it has the additional property of absorbing gases when heated; its inertness renders it suitable for chemical works equipment, especially in acid absorption plants, valves and nozzles for water chlorination, linings for steel and copper pipes and so forth. It is employed in spinnerets for rayon fibres, in electrical rectifiers, in fountain-pen nibs and in surgical and dental instruments. It does not irritate living tissue and is used in plates for skull injuries as well as in pins, wires and screws in osteological operations. Tantalum carbide is one of the hardest substances known and is incorporated with tungsten carbide in tips for machine tools. The metal has been substituted for platinum for some purposes and its oxide enters into the formulae of some types of glasses for aircraft camera lenses.

The metal niobium has assumed importance as a fractional addition to steels of the stainless types in which it acts as a carbide stabilizer, prevents intergranular corrosion and increases resistance to excessive heat. ' It is therefore a vital constituent of heat-resisting steels for gas turbines and jet engines and an essential addition to electrodes for welding certain stainless steels,' writes Sir Charles Goodeve of the British Iron and Steel Research Association, adding that niobium is also a constituent of recently-developed permanent magnet alloys. ' Alternatives—such as titanium or tungsten—may be used for some purposes, but the demand for niobium, particularly for heat-resisting steels in gas turbines will most probably increase.'

Over the three years 1937-9 about 500 tons of columbite and 150 tons of tantalite were produced in the world as a whole. In 1948, the total combined production of both minerals was 1,773 tons, of which at least 1,100 tons were of columbite and the remainder mainly tantalite-columbite concentrates. Nigeria produces over 85 per cent of the world's columbite, mainly from gravels in which it is associated with cassiterite. It is a by-product of the Nigerian tin mines, and the bulk of the output (over 2,000 tons in 1944) has come from the re-treatment of old dumps. The exported ore averages 65 per cent Nb_2O_5 and 5 per cent Ta_2O_5 and nearly all of it is shipped to the United States of America. The Belgian Congo follows in the second place, with 143 tons of tantalite-columbite concentrates and 513 tons of mixed cassiterite-tantalite-columbite concentrates in 1948. Australia was for long the largest producer of tantalite but little is mined there at present. Other countries such as Brazil and South Rhodesia have given appreciable quantities in times of emergency. The high outputs from Nigeria cannot continue for long unless new deposits are found, while the increasing demand for niobium should mean stable markets and good prices for columbite in the future. It is in the light of these circumstances' that the development of India's resources of these scarce and valuable minerals should be viewed.

MOLYBDENUM

Molybdenite, the sulphide of molybdenum, MoS_2, contains 60 per cent of the metal and is a lustrous, lead-grey mineral usually found in small scales which, owing to its perfect basal cleavage, can be split into thin leaves by the finger-nail. It resembles some forms of graphite extremely closely and has probably often been overlooked by prospectors in Eastern lands on this account. It has been found at many places in India, including parts of Chota Nagpur and chiefly in the Hazaribagh district, as, for example, with the sulphides of lead, copper and zinc near Mahabagh, at Baragunda, and elsewhere. It occurs in a granite-gneiss at Cherrapunji, in the Khasi Hills of Assam, in pegmatite veins at Kumavaram and other places in the Godavari district of Andhra; under similar conditions near Karadikuttam and Kodaikanal Road station, in the Madurai district of Madras; associated with pyrrhotite at Mangamalai, Travancore and in the elaeolite syenites at Kishengarh, Rajasthan.

In Burma it is a constituent of some of the wolfram and cassiterite-bearing veins of the Indo-Malayan mountain ranges, as at Mekontaung in Yamethin, and Shwegyaung in Mong Pai, as well as at various localities in Tavoy and Mergui. At the wolfram mines of Sonsinpaya, Wagon North, Thingandon, Hermyingyi and Widnes in the Tavoy district, it is more abundant than elsewhere. An unusually large quartz vein in the Shinmataung section of the Widnes mine, 6 to 8 feet in width, contains a little wolfram, some pyrite and relatively large amounts of molybdenite. The mineral is also a rare accessory of the local granite but is commoner in pegmatites and greisens, in veins with wolfram or cassiterite, or both, or, again and very much more rarely, in quartz veins in which it is the sole metallic mineral, or perhaps accompanied with a little pyrite. It is found more frequently in veins traversing granite than in those penetrating sedimentary rocks, and it usually lies close to the walls, intergrown with the mica often present in such positions. Small specimen parcels of molybdenite have been shipped from Lower Burma from time to time, but the total output has been quite insignificant. As a result of primitive mining methods and the absence of suitable milling and concentrating machinery, these deposits have never received the attention which they deserve.

Molybdenum is prepared by the reduction of its oxide with hydrogen and is a silvery white metal with the high melting point of 2620°C. In the form of wire, rod and sheet it is widely employed in the manufacture of incandescent electric lamps, particularly as filament supports, and in wireless valves and electronic devices of many kinds; thus the heaters of radio receiving and transmitting valves may be of molybdenum-tungsten alloy. Other applications of the metal include contact points, electrodes, spot welder tips, thermo-couples and heating elements of electric furnaces. Its principal use, however, is in the steel industry as an alloying element, for added to steel in the form of ferro-molybdenum, molybdenum trioxide or calcium molybdate, in amounts usually ranging from under 1·0 to 1·5 per cent, it imparts strength, elasticity, resistance to shock and fatigue, and so enhances the effects of other additions such as nickel, chromium and vanadium. Such alloy steels have their special applications not only in structural materials but also in aircraft and motor vehicle engines, the reciprocating parts of locomotives, drilling machinery and so forth, besides being used for certain types of armour plate and projectiles. Molybdenum-bearing cast irons too, are tougher, stronger and more easily machined by reason of its addition. It is an important component of high-speed self-tempering machine tools used for cutting steels, and during the last war, owing to the scarcity of tungsten, molybdenum was widely employed as a substitute. With chromium and cobalt it enters into the composition of some varieties of the non-ferrous 'stellite' alloys which are also employed as cutting tools.

A number of molybdenum compounds find applications in the chemical and ceramic industries. Ammonium molybdate is the standard reagent for the analytical determination of phosphorus. In passing, it is to be noted that the rare element rhenium occurs chiefly in molybdenite ores.

The average annual world's production of molybdenum for the period 1934-8 was approximately 10,000 tons of which the United States supplied about 90 per cent, mostly from a single deposit at Climax, Colorado, where the grade averages about 0·5 per cent of the sulphide. In 1947 the world's total was over 21,500 tons, of which 93 per cent came from the United States with smaller amounts from Canada, Finland, Norway, Mexico and Chile.

TITANIUM

Ilmenite, a titanate of iron, $FeTiO_3$, with $31\cdot6$ per cent of titanium, is often referred to in the older Indian geological literature as titaniferous iron sand, titaniferous iron ore, titanoferrite, meccanite and iserine. It can be found in the concentrates of the sands of most Indian rivers traversing crystalline rocks, but the black sands of the Travancore coast are its sources of greatest importance. Here it is derived from the gneisses and associated pegmatites which build up most of southern Travancore, whence, with quartz, garnet, monazite, zircon, arizonite, sillimanite and rutile, it is carried by the rivers to the sea shore and concentrated into certain patches of sand lying along the beaches between Nindikarai, north of Quilon, on the west coast, to Cape Comorin and thence up the east coast to Lipurum, in Tirunelveli district, a distance of about 100 miles. Smaller patches of similar sands are also known on the beaches of Malabar, Ramanathapuram, Tanjore, Visakhapatnam and Ganjam and are being worked also at Malgund, north of Ratnagiri, Bombay. India's reserves of ilmenite in this form alone total between 300 and 350 millions of tons.

The Travancore sands are exploited at Manavalakurichi near Kolachel and at Kovilthatam, 8 miles north of Quilon, and, as won, contain 50 to 70 per cent of ilmenite, averaging about 55 per cent of titania (titanium dioxide, TiO_2), with monazite, zircon, garnet, rutile and sillimanite as by-products. Rutile, the natural dioxide, with 60 per cent of titanium, which forms from 1 to 4 per cent of the sand grains and some 2 per cent of similar deposits in Ceylon, has a much higher market value than ilmenite, owing to its special uses, higher metallic content and greater scarcity. It is recovered from the zircon fraction of the sand, in which it forms about 12 per cent of the total. Rutile is plentiful in the kyanite-bearing rocks of Lapsa Buru in Singhbhum, but has not yet been recovered commercially. Arizonite, which remains with the ilmenite, is another titanate of iron, $Fe_2O_3.3TiO_2$, with about 36 per cent of titanium.

Titanium-bearing magnetites occur in Singhbhum, Mayurbhanj, the Channapatna area of Mysore, and other places. Vanadiferous ores of this type described by J. A. Dunn and A. K. Dey from Singhbhum, for example, average $17\cdot47$ per cent of titania. Although various processes have been devised in some countries to produce pig iron and slags, usable as a source of titanium compounds, from such materials, the necessity does not arise in India with its vast resources of more tractable iron ores and of ilmenite.

A further potential large-scale source of titanium exists in Indian laterites and bauxites, the latter often containing upwards of 8 per cent titania, and forming a useful by-product of the aluminium industry of the future. Methods for its recovery have already been proposed by a number of Indian chemists.

Titanium is a silvery-white, light metal with a density of 4·5 (compared with 2·7 for aluminium and 7·8 for iron) and a melting point of 1795° C., compared with 1537° C. for iron. It is strong, hard and tough with great resistance to corrosion, combining, it is said, the properties of stainless steel with those of the strong aluminium alloys, and is now obtainable in limited quantities in a wide range of fabricated products. It is made commercially by various methods, including the reduction of its tetrachloride with magnesium, but its high cost of production severely restricts its use at present. When improved and cheaper methods of production have been invented, its applications in structural and mechanical engineering will expand rapidly. It is reported that a contract was signed on 10 August 1953 between the British Ministry of Materials and Imperial Chemical Industries Ltd under which this firm is to construct the first full-scale plant for the manufacture of metallic titanium in Britain and that production is to commence in 1955.

Ferro-titanium, used at one time to deoxidize steel made by the Bessemer process, is now employed to introduce titanium into foundry irons and into steels of miscellaneous types, particularly into the chromium-nickel, heat-resisting and stainless varieties, as well as for cleansing purposes into steels that are to be rolled into galvanized sheets or tinplates, or made into enamelled ware or stamped articles. By reason of one or other of its properties as a gas-removing, grain-refining, age-hardening or strengthening element, titanium is to be found in a number of nickel, nickel-cobalt and aluminium alloys, as well as in those used for the manufacture of permanent magnets.

Titanium carbide is extremely hard and is incorporated with the carbides of tungsten and other metals in tools for cutting steel, in dies and in abrasive wheels. The electric welding of steel, which has superseded riveting in many processes, necessitates the employment of rods coated with rutile or titanium dioxide to stabilize the arc and to improve fluxing.

Titanium compounds are employed in the manufacture of vitreous enamels for steel and cast-iron goods, in the production of honey-yellow underglazes for porcelain and in the ivory finish of artificial teeth. Titanium dioxide, either alone in amounts of 8 to 12 per cent, or with the addition of zinc oxide, produces the pleasing ' crystal ' glazes of porcelain. Other titanium salts have their applications in glass-making, while rutile and the magnesium· orthotitanates derived from it enter into the composition of electric condensers because of their high dielectric constants; further, the. titanates of barium and strontium are the predominating components of the ultra-high insulating ceramics.

Certain titanium salts are used as catalytic agents. Both titanous chloride and sulphate possess strong colour-reducing properties and are employed as stripping agents for wool, cotton, viscose and acetate textiles as well as for decolorizing paper, removing iron stains and bleaching discoloured whites in laundering; in sugar refining; in textile printing; for the removal of iron from sand to be used for making optical glass and as analytical reagents. Titanium phospho-oxalate and titanium potassium oxalate are fixing agents in the dyeing and staining of leather, and themselves yield fast, yellowish-brown shades on vegetable tanned leathers. The tetrachloride, a straw-coloured liquid, furnishes range-finding devices and obscuring smoke screens for land and sea operations in warfare, as well as the substance of ' sky-writing ' by aircraft in times of peace. Artificial rutile, a product of the electric furnace, is cut into synthetic gems.

Most of the world's production of ilmenite, however, is consumed in the manufacture of the titanium dioxide pigments, which by reason of their opacity, covering power, chemical inertness, low specific gravity, non-toxicity and cheapness are employed on an increasing scale in white paints, enamels and lacquers for indoor use. ' Titanium white ', as the dioxide is called, coprecipitated, or mixed with barium or calcium sulphate or with lithopone as extending agents, forms the basis of many paints both for interior and exterior decoration. The same material, with its high index of refraction, brightness, fine subdivision and ready dispersion, is widely used in the manufacture of the better grades of paper, as a delustrant of rayon fibre and as a white colouring for rubber compositions, printing inks, plastic articles, soaps and cosmetics.

The phenomenal expansion of ilmenite production in India, from 400 tons in 1912 to over 250,000 tons in 1938, is a measure of the rise and development of ' titanium white '. By the end of 1938, over 1 million tons of ilmenite concentrates had been shipped abroad from the Travancore beaches and this had risen to over 2 million tons by 1945, while the grand total production up to the end of 1950 was 3,203,625 tons, of a nominal value of Rs3,16,11,439. The average annual output for the five years ending 1948 was 189,655 tons valued at Rs 20,22,487. The commercial production of rutile from the Travancore sands commenced in 1939, and up to the end of 1950, 10,670 tons valued at Rs15,55,184 had been recovered. From 1945, the Travancore State assumed control of the deposits and the sale of the products derived from them: the four firms formerly engaged in the business—Travancore Minerals Ltd, Hopkins & Williams (Travancore) Ltd, F. X. Pereira & Sons Ltd, and The Associated Minerals Co. Ltd—now work as agents of the State. The manufacture of titanium dioxide pigments was commenced in India during the autumn of 1951, at the works of Travancore Titanium Products Ltd.

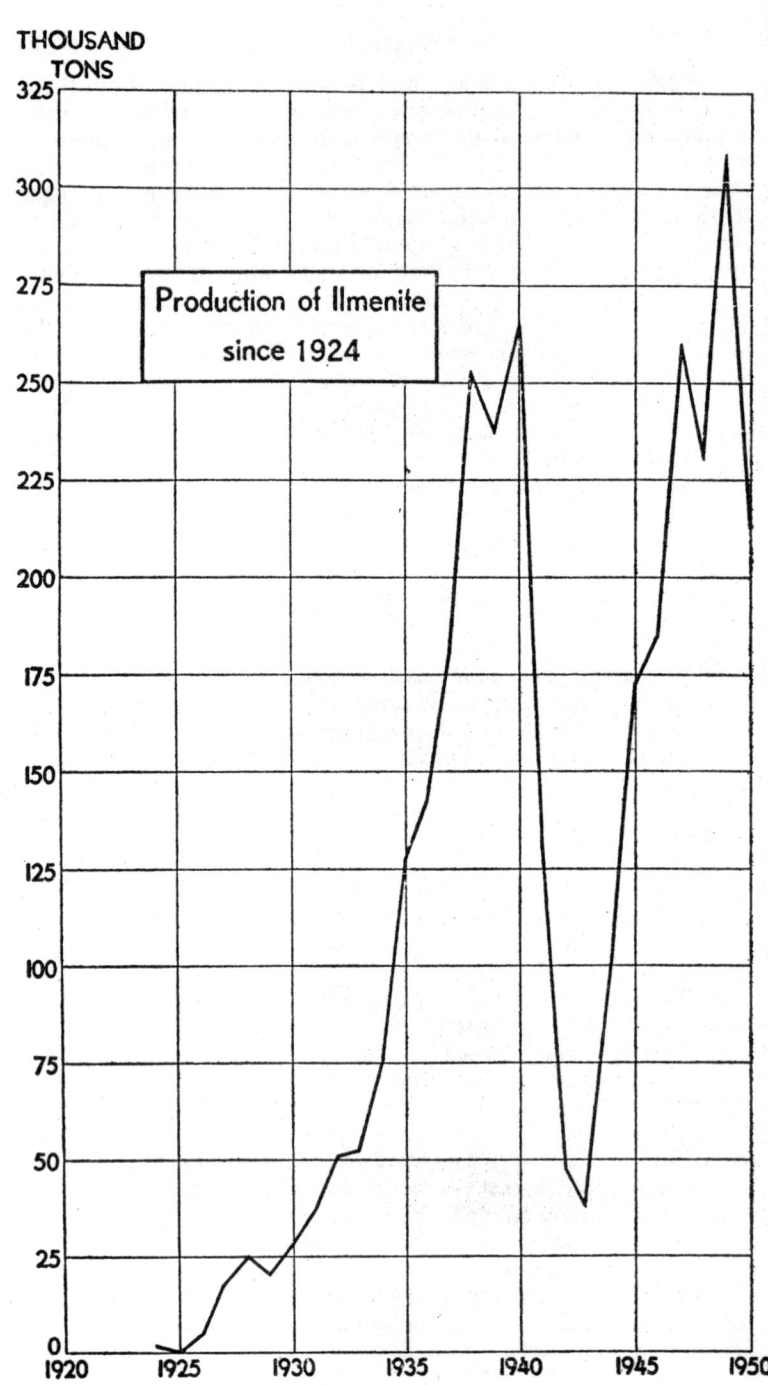

The world's annual average production of ilmenite for the five years ending 1938 was in the neighbourhood of 220,000 tons, and India alone was responsible for over 70 per cent of this, followed by Norway with 22 per cent, the remainder coming from Malaya (2·2 per cent), Senegal, Canada, Portugal, Egypt and Brazil. The whole of the Indian output was exported, mainly to the United States and the United Kingdom. The world's demand for ilmenite is increasing and is likely to continue to do so; at the same time, it is doubtful if India will retain so preponderating a position in the ilmenite trade of the future as she has occupied in the past, as competing sources of supply are developed. The output of ilmenite in the United States was under 5,000 tons a year in the period 1929 to 1938; war necessities compelled the opening-up of domestic resources, for ilmenite is not a rare mineral, so that today the U.S.A. heads the list, having produced 47 per cent of the world's total of 721,000 tons in 1948, against India's share of about 32 per cent.

TUNGSTEN

Wolfram, the chief ore of tungsten, is a mixture in any proportion of two minerals—ferberite, the tungstate of iron, $FeWO_4$, and hübnerite, the tungstate of manganese, $MnWO_4$; the former contains 70 per cent and the latter 76·6 per cent of tungstic oxide WO_3.

Tungsten is a hard, heavy, greyish-white element with the highest melting point, 3382° C., of all the metals as well as the highest recorded strength. Its most familiar use, when drawn into wire of extreme thinness, is in electric light bulbs, but apart from this it is an essential material in very many forms of electronic equipment, including X-ray tubes of all kinds; gas discharge, fluorescent and projector lamps; radar and television apparatus; radio transmitting and receiving valves; ionization gauges and cathode-ray tubes, particle accelerators and mercury rectifiers. Tungsten is also employed in spark-plugs, ignition and other contacts and tips, welding electrodes, glass-to-metal seals and crucibles. For most of these uses it has no satisfactory substitute, yet, taken all together, they make little impression on the consumption of wolfram.

By far the greater proportion of the tungsten manufactured, estimated at 85 per cent of the total, finds its way into ferrous alloys, much of it as ferro-tungsten; some 8 per cent is made into tungsten carbide, while electronics and miscellaneous uses account for the remaining 7 per cent. Just as tungsten filaments revolutionized electric lighting, for a tungsten filament lamp is four and a half times as efficient as a carbon filament one, so the high-speed tungsten steels changed the whole character of the metal-cutting business. A machine using a tungsten steel cutting tool can be run at five times the speed possible with one using a carbon steel tool; furthermore, the tungsten tool maintains its cutting power

up to red heat and is self-tempering. Tungsten is of vital importance in industry, especially in times of war or preparation for war,
and it has been truly stated that to deprive a nation of this metal
would cripple its military power and ruin its industrial life in times
of peace.

High-speed steels in common use contain 14 to 18 per cent of
tungsten, with 4 per cent of chromium and 1 to 3 per cent of vanadium, though there are many variations on this formula in some
of which molybdenum and cobalt also play a part.

Tungsten also enters into the composition of steels for armour
plate, gun barrels, armour-piercing shells, railway lines, car springs,
resistance wires, valves and valve seats of internal combustion
engines, dies for wire drawing, drilling, cutting and grinding tools,
knife and razor blades, hack saws, files and many other appliances.
It is also a component of the stellites, more fully described under
COBALT. Tungsten carbide is much harder than the hardest steels
and, with metallic cobalt as a binder or matrix, it is formed into
the tips of cutting tools which for some purposes are superior to the
high-speed steels. This and similar materials made from tungsten
and titanium carbides with cobalt, nickel or chromium, are also
used for tipping rock drills, wire-drawing dies, cutting glass and
porcelain and for general purposes where a super-hard substance
is required. The quantity of tungsten consumed by the chemical
industry is not large; cadmium tungstate is said to be used in preparing X-ray screens and sodium tungstate as a fire-proofing agent
for cloth.

India's known wolfram deposits are restricted in size and low
in grade; though capable of yielding a small production in emergencies they are not remunerative to mine in normal times. Thin
veins and stringers of quartz, interbedded with mica and tourmaline
schists of Dharwar age, at Agargaon, Nagpur district, Madhya
Pradesh, yielded about 6 tons of the mineral in the period 1907 to
1914, and a further 8 tons were won in 1916 from small quartz
veins in mica schists of the same age, at Kalimati, Singhbhum.
Quartz veins traversing phyllites and quartzites at Chenndapathar,
in the Bankura district of West Bengal, supplied 45 tons in the
period 1942-3, and recently small amounts of wolfram and scheelite
have been found by A. Hunday in a quartz vein north-north-west
of Porah *pahar*, about 14 miles further north. The wolfram-bearing
quartz-bodies in Aravalli schists at Jher and Palla, Ahmedabad
district, Bombay, have proved too lean for exploitation. Wolfram
has also been found at Kadavur and on the Ururakarad, in the
Tiruchirapalli district of Madras.

On Rawat Hill, near Degana, Jodhpur, Rajasthan, wolfram
occurs in veins and stockworks, with fluorite, biotite and small
quantities of pyrite, chalcopyrite and the phosphates triplite and
libethenite, penetrating both granite and Aravalli phyllites, into
which it is intrusive. Here, as elsewhere, it is also found in the

local eluvial deposits into which it has been shed by denudation. Discovered in 1913 by Suraj Prakash, these deposits yielded 208 tons during World War I (1914-18): idle for seven years, production was started again in 1926, but only 30½ tons had been won up to 1933. Another blank period followed, until the stimulation of the demands of World War II led to a re-opening of the old workings in 1937. In 1942, a concentrating mill was erected at Rawat and the average wolfram content of the veins estimated at 0·65 per cent. During the decade 1937 to 1946, 307 tons were produced, but by 1946, output had fallen to 3 tons per annum and then ceased.

Scheelite, the tungstate of calcium, occurs in the gold-bearing quartz veins of the Kangundi area, east of Bisanattam, in the Chittoor district of Andhra. Old mine dumps in this region assayed 0·25 per cent tungstic oxide (WO_3) and 0·04 per cent metallic tin.

In Burma, quartz veins containing wolfram have been found at intervals over a distance of 750 miles, from the Yengan and Mawnang States of the Shan States in the north, through the districts of Yamethin and the State of Karenni, to the Thaton, Amherst, Tavoy and Mergui districts in the far south. In all these localities the wolfram and cassiterite-bearing veins are most intimately associated with the intrusive biotite granite which forms the cores of the mountain ranges of the Indo-Malayan system, stretching further south still through western Siam to the Malay Peninsula. In Lower Burma the granite is intruded into a series of shales, slates, argillites and agglomerates with subordinate quartzites, limestones and conglomerates, probably of Carboniferous age, and known as the Mergui Series. Both wolfram and cassiterite occur very sparingly as accessory minerals in the granite. They are also found in pegmatite and aplite veins and in the greisen bands which traverse it. The mineral-bearing quartz veins, however, are of greater importance, and they are to be found either in the granite, or penetrating its contacts with the sedimentary rocks, or, again, enclosed within the latter themselves at no great distance from the granite. Under the influence of denudation the veins shed their metallic contents into the eluvial deposits of the hillsides, from which a great deal of wolfram and tinstone have been won. The latter mineral also finds its way into the true alluvial deposits of the river valleys, where it can be recovered by dredging. The ores were formed partly under conditions closely allied to strictly magmatic ones, and were also produced by processes in which gaseous agencies, including compounds of fluorine and sulphur, to some extent played a part, and in rare cases by hydrothermal reactions which followed as a consequence of the former ones.

Along the scarps of the Shan Plateau, in the east of the Yamethin district, there are three areas where both wolfram and cassiterite occur in quartz veins and pegmatites of a coarse-grained biotite granite and in the sedimentary rocks bordering its intrusion.   The Padaigyaung-Peinnedaik-Hmanpya area is the richest of the three and one of its mines used to produce over 200 tons of concentrate per annum.

Karenni possesses the very important Mawchi mine, with an average annual production for the four years ending 1939 of 2,390 tons of wolfram and 2,733 tons of tin ore.   Here, a large number of quartz veins, mostly under four feet in thickness, were mined both in the biotite granite and in the slates and argillites surrounding it.   The accessory minerals are scheelite, tourmaline, pyrite, arsenopyrite, chalcopyrite and galena.

The Thaton district has two separate producing areas, the first on the long granite ridge of Zingzeik, with thin but persistent wolfram-bearing pegmatites and quartz veins, some traceable for three miles, both in granite and in hardened sedimentary rocks; the second on the western flank of the Dawna Range, not far from the Thailand border, where, once more, the normal biotite granite carries many quartz veins of the usual type.   It is a richer area than the first-named, which possesses no great importance.

The leading wolfram deposits of the Mergui district are near Palauk in the north, and at Tagu in the valley of the Great Tenasserim river; here, as elsewhere, the veins are mined by underground methods during the dry season, but during the monsoon operations are largely confined to sluicing the eluvial deposits, both by the use of monitors and by hand methods, for the recovery of wolfram and tinstone, while the true alluvials of the valley bottoms are treated for their cassiterite contents.

The Tavoy district, with its area of 5,308 square miles, is by far the most important, and in 1939 there were over 190 producing concessions in it, compared with just over 100 in 1918.   Most of them are shallow workings operated by methods primitive in the extreme, but others are deep mines under efficient technical control and equipped with modern concentrating plant.   The largest mines are at Hermyingyi, Widnes, Kanbauk, Bwabwin, Byaukchaung, Pagaye, Wagon North and Paungdaw, and they are situated for the most part on or near the granite ranges which build up much of the district.

' The tungstate of iron, or wolfram sand,' wrote Dr Mason in his classical account of Tenasserim, published in 1849, ' much resembles tin and is found in most neighbourhoods where that ore is obtained.'   The mineral was completely overlooked, however, until 1908, when it was rediscovered by J. J. A. Page of the Geological Survey of India.   Mining commenced in 1910, and in 1911 an output of 1,300 tons made Burma the chief wolfram-producing country in the world at that time, a position she still occupied in 1914 when World War I found the British Empire dependent on Germany for its tungsten supplies.   The situation was successfully dealt with, and between 1914 and the end of the war in 1918,

17,642 tons of wolfram, valued at £2,323,000, were exported to meet the demands of the Allied Powers for this martial metal, and of this quantity, 14,000 tons came from the Tavoy field alone. In the meantime high prices spurred on production in other countries and by 1916 the United States of America and Bolivia had both outstripped Burma. By 1917 large quantities of wolfram were being shipped from China, which rapidly became the largest producer in the world. Stagnation followed the boom but revival came again as the world's armament industry began to accelerate its preparations for World War II, and the graph of production on page 250 demonstrates better than a verbal description can the changes that took place, particularly how output rose to its peak of 7,052 tons in 1939, to be followed once more by the inevitable decline, intensified in this case by Burma being overrun by invading Japanese armies in 1942. In the following table, statistics of production from 1914 to 1940 are summarized.

PRODUCTION OF WOLFRAM IN BURMA, 1914–40

Period	Average annual Production* Tons	Average annual Value Rs
1914–18 ..	3,473†	....
1919–23 ..	1,726‡	15,80,725
1924–8 ..	955	4,86,752
1929–33 ..	2,355	13,58,206
1934–8 ..	4,418	56,04,736
1939 ..	7,052	....
1940 ..	4,172	....

* Concentrates with 60% WO₃.
† Includes 143·9 tons from India.
‡ Includes 47 tons from India.

No reliable figures are available for the post-war period until 1947, when Burma produced 349 tons of wolfram concentrates and 1,220 tons of mixed wolfram and tin ore concentrates. From 1948 to 1951, inclusive, 1,386 tons of wolfram were won, as well as 2,108 tons of mixed tin and wolfram concentrates in 1950 and 1951. The rehabilitation of the industry has been hampered by disturbed political conditions since the country attained its independence in 1948.

Between the years 1937 and 1946, India, as distinct from Burma, produced a total of 353 tons of wolfram, valued at Rs 8,04,550, and of this quantity 88 per cent came from Jodhpur and the rest from Bengal.

World production of tungsten ore in 1939, in terms of 60 per cent WO₃ concentrates, was approximately 34,000 tons, to which China contributed 33·6 per cent, Burma 20·8 per cent, Portugal

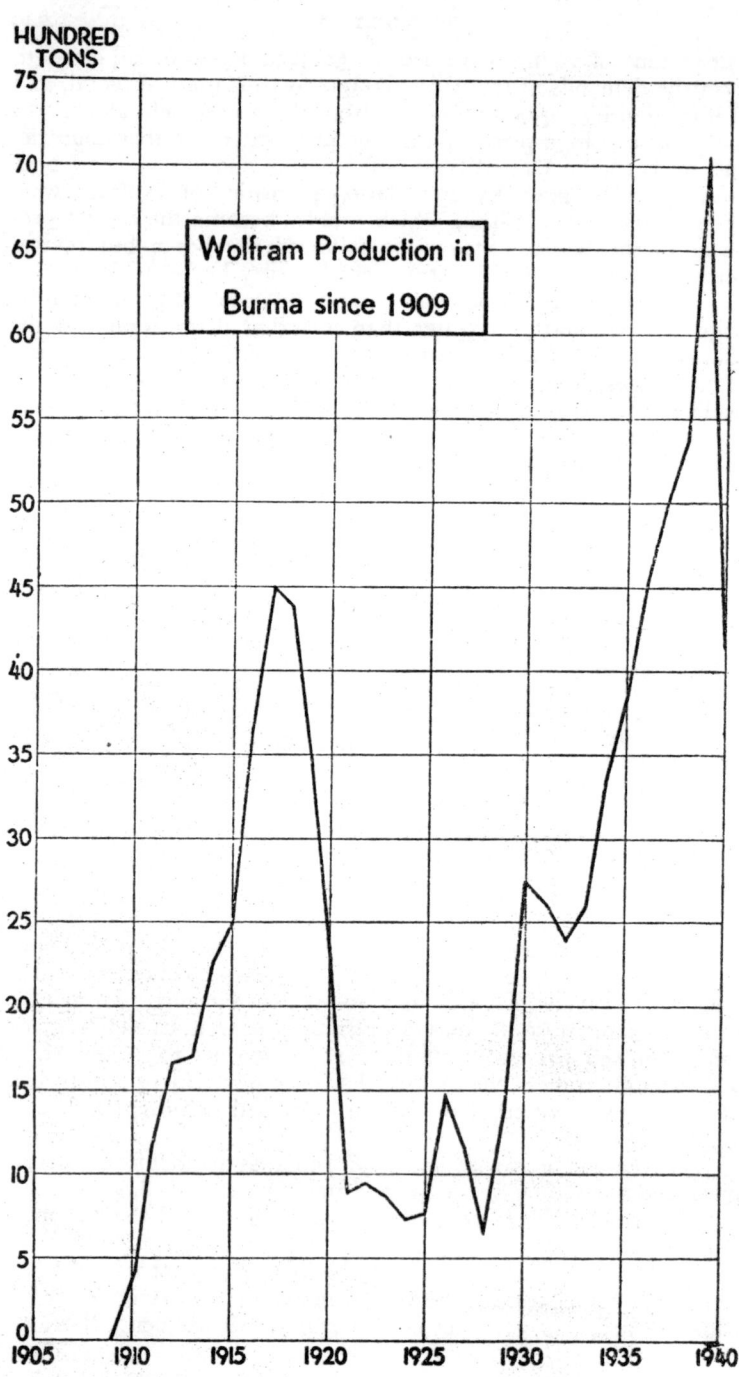

HUNDRED
TONS

Wolfram Production in
Burma since 1909

11·4 per cent, the United States 11·3 per cent, Bolivia 9·8, Argentina 3·9 and Australia 3·0 per cent. Incomplete returns for 1948 reveal a world's estimated production (again omitt..ng the Soviet Union) of some 26,500 tons, of which China was probably responsible for over 35 per cent, followed by the United States with 15 per cent, Portugal with about 10 per cent and then by Bolivia, Brazil and Australia, in the order named. The violent fluctuations of the demand for wolfram are well illustrated by the world's production figures for 1943, when over 56,000 tons were produced, compared with 1947, when less than 18,000 tons were recorded. Burma possesses great resources of tungsten ores, recoverable either independently, or as a by-product of tin mining, and it is hoped that the day is not distant when she will again enter the lists as a large producer of both these valuable mineral commodities.

VANADIUM

Vanadium is a soft, malleable, silver-white metal made by reducing its pentoxide with calcium but which at present has no industrial uses in its elementary form. The world's production of vanadium ores, reckoned in tons of the metal, averaged about 3,200 tons in the period 1939 to 1943, and had fallen to some 1,800 tons in 1950, though this takes no account of output in the Soviet Union or its satellite States. It is said that approximately 95 per cent of the total output is used in the alloying of steel and the remainder consumed for chemical purposes. The element is introduced into steel either in the form of the oxide, or as ferrovanadium, and even in very small amounts imparts strength and ductility, producing at the same time a finer-grained product more resistant to shock, fatigue and torsional strains besides acting as a powerful deoxidizing agent. Vanadium steels, which may also contain one or more of a number of other alloying metals such as chromium, nickel, manganese and molybdenum, serve a large variety of special purposes, especially in the construction of axles, springs and other parts of motor vehicles and railway rolling stock. They are also used for boiler plates and pressure vessels, rock crushers, armour plate, gun shields and ordnance, as well as for constructional steels. Vanadium is sometimes added to cast iron, and it is an important ingredient of many of the high-speed cutting and die steels.

Vanadium pentoxide is a widely used catalytic agent in the synthesis of ammonia, and in the manufacture of sulphuric acid is displacing the more expensive platinum in the contact process. Some of its salts have limited uses in the paint and glass industries, in the printing and dyeing of fabrics and in pharmacy.

Vanadium-bearing titaniferous magnetites with a percentage of the pentoxide (V_2O_5) varying from 0·8 to 3 per cent occur near the southern border of the Dhalbhum subdivision of Singhbhum

and extend into Mayurbhanj, the more important localities including Kumhardhubi and Dublabera. Similar ores have also been
found near Nuasahi in Keonjhar. According to J. A. Dunn and
A. K. Dey, they are in very close association with basic and ultrabasic rocks, sometimes altered to serpentines, more often to epidiorite, but, as a rule, little changed from the original basic gabbro
of which they are magmatic segregations. The vanadium is contained in a new mineral named coulsonite, a variety of magnetite,
$FeO.Fe_2O_3$, in which part of the ferric iron is replaced by vanadium,
giving the formula $FeO.(FeV)_2O_3$. Since its discovery in India,
this mineral has been found in Ontario, Canada and in New York
State of the United States of America.

A green mica distributed in a quartzite at Mahalgaon, Bhandara
district, Madhya Pradesh, contains 0·48 per cent of vanadium
oxide (V_2O_5) and 2·74 per cent of chromium oxide (Cr_2O_3):
according to S. K. Chatterjee it appears to be intermediate in composition and optical properties between fuchsite, the chromiferous
mica, and roscoelite, the vanadium-bearing mica. Such roscoelitic
micas also occur in the kyanite and sillimanite-bearing rocks of the
Bhandara district. Roscoelite, with 1·5 to 5 per cent vanadium,
has been used as a source of vanadium in the United States.

Vanadiferous magnetite with an average content of 0·56 per
cent of vanadium pentoxide (V_2O_5) and up to 0·85 per cent of
chromic oxide (Cr_2O_3), occurs to the north of Godasahi, Nilgiri,
Orissa, where, according to H. Nandi, about 200,000 tons are
available. A smaller occurrence with 1·08 per cent of the vanadium pentoxide and 1·27 per cent of the chromium oxide (Cr_2O_3),
is known at Rangamati, in the same area. Vanadiferous magnetite,
amounting to about 50,000 tons according to B. C. Gupta, occurs
as lenticular bands in the ultrabasics at Nausahi in Keonjhar district, also in Orissa. Two picked samples gave 0·92 and 1·84 per
cent of V_2O_5 on analysis.

The world's vanadium supplies are drawn for the most part
from the patronite (vanadium sulphide) deposits of Minasragra in
Peru, from the carnotite (hydrated vanadate of uranium and potassium) and roscoelite deposits of Colorado and Utah, from various
vanadates of lead found in the oxidized portions of the lead-zinc
ore deposits of Broken Hill, in Northern Rhodesia, and from similar
ores of the Otavi region of South-West Africa.

The ashes of certain coals, hydrocarbon oils and asphalts contain
comparatively large amounts of vanadium, which is profitably
recovered from the soot of furnaces burning such fuels. It has been
found in the ashes of lignite at Neyveli, South Arcot, Madras, and
reported (and denied) that the ash from the Varkala lignites of
Travancore contains 2 per cent of vanadium oxide.

The possibility of inaugurating a vanadium industry in India
depends on the successful development of a method of its recovery
from the titanium-bearing magnetites, but further investigation of

vanadium content of the green micas, of the ashes of Indian coals and oils, and of its occurrence in laterites, bauxites and blast-furnace slags, might lead to a modification of this view.

ZIRCONIUM

The two minerals baddeleyite (or brazilite), the natural oxide of zirconium (ZrO_2), and zircon, zirconium silicate ($ZrSiO_4$), with 60·2 per cent of the metal, compared with 74·0 per cent in the oxide, supply most of the world's requirements of zirconium and its compounds at the present time, requirements which have grown rapidly in recent years and are likely to expand. Baddeleyite was discovered in Ceylon, in the gem gravels of Ratnapura, but is only of economic importance in Brazil. Zircon is one of the commoner accessory minerals in all kinds of igneous rocks, but especially of granites, pegmatites and nepheline syenites. From the pegmatitic varieties of the latter group as well as from other sources come the brilliant, precious kinds of Ceylon and Burma, described under GEMS. The sand derived by the weathering of the zircon-containing rocks, after their lighter portions have been washed away, contains concentrations of the heavier, more resistant minerals such as zircon, monazite, rutile, ilmenite and garnet. Thus it comes about that zircon is obtained as a by-product in the winning of monazite and ilmenite from the fine, granular, black sands of the Travancore coast, in which it occurs to the extent of about 6 per cent. Zircon production commenced in 1922 and from that time until 1946, when the publication of further statistics ceased for strategic reasons, 38,094 tons, valued at Rs 14,61,000 approximately, had been won. For the same reasons it is not permissible to discuss the probable future of the industry here, except to add that large reserves of zircon exist, sufficient to meet any domestic demand that is likely to arise either now or in the distant future.

Zirconium is a soft, lustrous, greyish-white metal, produced either by the thermal dissociation of its tetraiodide, or by the reduction of its tetrachloride with magnesium, and is obtainable in commerce in the form of powder, sheet, wire or rods. It is very reactive with both nitrogen and oxygen and burns brightly when heated in the air, a property accounting for its use in flashlight powders, primings for explosives, and in the removal of traces of gases from vacuum devices of various kinds. The metal is said to have great resistance to the attack of alkalis and is used in parts of rayon-spinning machines. Alloys such as ferro-zirconium and zirconium-ferro-silicon are used to remove oxygen, nitrogen and non-metallic impurities generally from molten steel, and in so doing to give the finished product greater uniformity in composition and grain. Ferro-zirconium is made in the electric furnace by the reduction of mixtures of zircon and iron ore, or by the aluminothermic smelting of the mixed oxides. As an alloying addition to

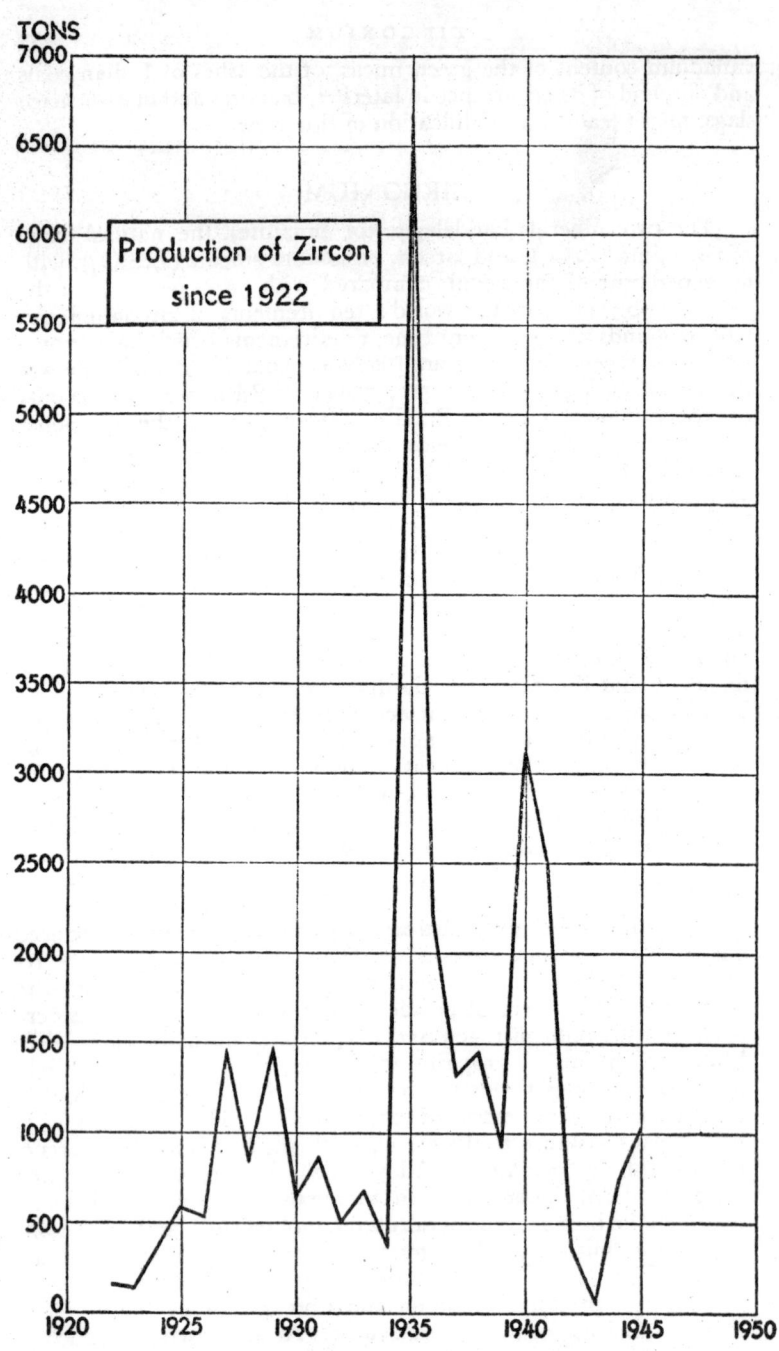

special steels, zirconium increases ductility and resistance to shock and fatigue; such steels have been employed in the manufacture of light armour-plate and projectiles. Fractional percentages of the metal added to the nickel-chromium alloys lengthen their operational lives in industrial and domestic heating apparatus. The strength of copper is very greatly increased by the addition of from 5 to 10 per cent of zirconium, and it forms hard alloys with nickel which have been used as cutting tools. Its alloys with magnesium are referred to under MAGNESIUM and CERIUM, the outstanding effects of the metal being evident in intensive grain refinement, improved corrosion resistance and better workability. A recent authority has stated that the zirconium-magnesium casting alloys are becoming increasingly popular both in the United Kingdom and abroad, and that virtually every new aircraft flown in England at the present time contains an appreciable number of zirconium alloy castings, either in its structural components or in its engines, or in both.

The rare element hafnium is a constant associate of zirconium in its natural compounds, their relationship having been compared to that existing between niobium and tantalum or between adjacent members of a rare earth series; belonging to the same group in the Periodic Classification, they possess similar chemical and physical properties, and the separation of hafnium from zirconium is a tedious process. This has a bearing on the potential use of zirconium in atomic energy developments, particularly as a sheathing metal for the natural uranium rods in nuclear reactors, or as a moderator. Sir John Cockcroft has stated that for these purposes zirconium with its low absorption capacity for neutrons must be free from the strongly absorbent hafnium.

The natural silicate zircon is stable to about 1800° C., when it dissociates into zirconia, one of the most refractory substances known, and a siliceous glass. It is being employed increasingly in a number of metallurgical processes further described under RE-FRACTORIES. Graded zircon sands, with the addition of a suitable bond, make useful cements for coating the surfaces of less resistant refractories. Zirconia is employed in the manufacture of special porcelains, such as those used for sparking-plugs, where its high dielectric strength and power to resist temperature changes under rigorous conditions are distinctive. It is also a component of some types of heat- and chemical-resisting glasses, and has other applications including its use as a white opacifier in vitreous enamels and ceramic glazes, where it is said to be replacing both tin and antimony compounds, as well as in white paints and lacquers. It is also incorporated into some forms of white rubber and leather as well as into polishing and toilet powders. A recent official American report classifies the existing industrial uses of zircon in that country as follows—refractories, 45 per cent; foundry facings, 19 per cent; porcelain enamels, 7 per cent; metals and alloys,

7 per cent; pottery, 7 per cent; electrical and chemical porcelain, 3 per cent; glass, 1 per cent; miscellaneous, 11 per cent.

Most of the world's zircon supply is at present derived from naturally concentrated beach sands, recalling those of Travancore, which are situated along the coast and its accompanying dunes between Coffs Harbour in New South Wales and Stradbroke Island in Queensland, Australia. From this source alone came almost 22,000 tons out of an estimated world's total of between 26,000 and 27,000 tons of zirconium minerals in 1948. The Australian consumption of zircon is small and by far the greater part of the production is exported. Brazil is the second largest source of supply and in 1948 gave about 3,500 tons to the world's markets, mainly of baddeleyite. Other producing countries include the United States of America, French West Africa, Egypt, Madagascar and Norway.

CHAPTER VI

THE LIGHT METALS

ALUMINIUM

ALUMINIUM, the silvery ductile metal with a density about one-third that of steel or brass, owes its industrial importance to its lightness and the ease with which it can be fabricated—rolled into sheets, strips, plates and sections; drawn into tubing and wire; forged, cast, extruded or powdered; joined, extended, spun or coloured after anodizing. It alloys readily with other elements, particularly copper, magnesium, silicon, manganese and zinc, forming both ' wrought ' and ' casting ' alloys, many of which are harder, stronger and tougher than the pure metal itself. It possesses marked corrosion resistance, high electrical and thermal conductivity and is a good reflector of light and radiant heat.

Though it is the most abundant metal in the crust of the earth, it is troublesome to separate from its natural compounds and sixty years ago was little more than a laboratory curiosity. By the end of the first world war in 1918, the world's production of the metal was only about 150,000 tons per annum; in 1937 this had risen to nearly half a million tons, in 1941 to almost one million tons, and in 1943 not far short of two million tons; in 1950 approximately one and a half million tons were made, excluding the production of the U.S.S.R. and her satellite countries. The expansion during the period of the second world war was in great measure due to martial demands from the aircraft industry, naval dockyards and ordnance factories.

The group of alloys of the duralumin type, which contain 3 or 4 per cent of copper and smaller quantities of magnesium and other metals, are used in vast quantities in the framework of aircraft. Threequarters of the frame weight and up to one half of the weight of engines and propellors of a modern aeroplane are said to be made up of aluminium alloys. Modified aluminium-silicon alloys are sand- and die-cast for engine mountings, cylinder blocks, pistons, gear boxes, crank cases and bearing housings for internal combustion engines. The wrought aluminium-magnesium alloys, with 2 to 7 per cent of magnesium and under 1 per cent of manganese, combine high strength with corrosion-resistance and are used in the construction of marine auxiliary vessels. During the last war other alloys were developed for aircraft armour, portable landing mats for air strips and troop shelters, while aluminium foil was used in large quantities to baffle enemy radar observations. Aluminium alloys today find increasing outlets in the construction of road and railway vehicles and their fittings, as well as in structural engineering of all kinds including that of prefabricated buildings and bridges.

Aluminium cable, reinforced by a steel core, is now a standard material for overhead electrical transmission lines, as in the case of the British National Grid. It also has advantages over lead as a sheathing for other cables in special positions and as flashings for roofs and walls. There are now few branches of human activity into which the metal does not enter; its multifarious uses range from mining equipment to domestic cooking utensils and household appliances, from bicycles to beer barrels, from corrugated roofing sheets to the 'silver paper' wrappings of food and confectionery, or to imitation gold ornaments fashioned from aluminium bronze.

Aluminium powder is a very powerful reducing agent and is the foundation of the alumino-thermic process for the production of metals, such as chromium and manganese, as well as special alloys such as ferro-niobium. The process is also used for the welding of rails and heavy steel sections. According to Dr G. P. Contractor, the use of aluminium is an almost universal practice in the manufacture of rimming steel. Paint made from aluminium powder is unusually durable and possesses both decorative and preservative qualities.

The principles of the processes used in the extraction of aluminium today are substantially the same as those discovered by C. W. Hall, a 22-year-old student, in 1886: the electrolysis of alumia (aluminium oxide), in a bath of molten cryolite. The ore bauxite was in the early days, and still remains, the essential raw material from which alumina is prepared. For the profitable operation of the process large amounts of electrical energy are required. Dr T. T. Read, Professor of Mining in Columbia University, recalls that it takes 25,000 kilowatt-hours of electrical energy to produce a ton of aluminium and since $1\frac{3}{4}$ pounds of coal are required to generate a kilowatt-hour in an average steam power plant, the equivalent of twenty times as much coal (without any by-product recovery) is required to make a ton of aluminium as a ton of iron. This is on the assumption that a ton of coal (in the form of coke from which the by-products have been recovered) is sufficient to produce a ton of iron. This is the reason why aluminium reduction works are usually erected at or near hydro-electrical generating stations, and particularly in situations where there is little other demand for the power and it is correspondingly cheap. Four tons of bauxite are needed to make two tons of alumina, to yield in its turn one ton of the metal.

As long ago as 1883, F. R. Mallet of the Geological Survey of India found that a variety of laterite from Jabalpur district, in Madhya Pradesh, contained a large proportion of aluminium and, in 1903, H. and F. J. Warth proved that many Indian laterites from various parts of Bihar, Bombay, Madras, Vindhya Pradesh and Madhya Pradesh are, in reality, bauxites. Sir Cyril Fox's memoir on the bauxite and aluminous laterites of India appeared in 1923.

Bauxite is not a distinct mineral species but rather a generic term for a number of aluminium hydroxides often in a colloidal condition, including diaspore (common in the Kashmir occurrences), boehmite, and gibbsite (common in both pisolites and matrices of the Indian material generally). Indian geologists apply the term to those varieties of laterite sufficiently rich in aluminium oxide, and free enough from undesirable impurities, to be acceptable as an aluminium ore. Laterite is a residual product of rock decay in tropical climates subjected to alternating wet and dry seasons, during which silica, lime, magnesia and alkalis are removed in solution and the iron, aluminium, manganese and titanium are left behind and rearranged, usually as hydrated oxides. The greater proportion of the larger spreads of laterite are far too ferruginous to be of any value as aluminium ore, though exceptionally they have been utilized both as ores of iron and of manganese. Between laterite and bauxite there is no sharp dividing line and one may gradually pass into the other. Almost all the bauxites (aluminous laterites) are of primary origin and were formed in the situations that they now occupy; moreover, most of the better-known occurrences are connected with the decomposition of the basaltic flows of the Deccan Trap.

It is customary to regard members of the group as ferruginous laterites when the percentage of iron is greater than 40 per cent, and as aluminous laterites (or bauxites) when the percentage of aluminium passes the same figure. The flat-topped hills so characteristic of regions occupied by Deccan Trap, and particularly the uppermost 10 feet or so of them, are favourable locations for bauxite occurrences. It is common to find that the very top of a scarp is made of the iron-bearing variety of latcrite, but just under this ferruginous mantle, the best grey bauxite occurs at depths of from 1 to 5 feet. If an extensive plateau exists, good bauxite is frequently found at the commencement of the stream courses which drain it, either in the bed itself, or close to its margins, taking the form of a rough pavement. In such instances there may be a slight development of the red ferruginous covering as well.

Recent investigations have resulted in the following estimates of the reserves of titaniferous bauxite, containing over 50 per cent of alumina, on such flat-topped, laterite-capped plateaus or similar situations. (See table on p. 260.)

It is to be noted that India's reserves of bauxite containing less than 50 per cent of alumina are several times this total of $25\frac{3}{4}$ tons. High-grade ore is also known to occur in Rewa, Vindhya Pradesh, and further deposits, usually of lower grade, are to be found in Ratnagiri and Gujerat, Bombay; Bastar, Madhya Pradesh; Bhopal;

RESERVES OF BAUXITE IN INDIA
(with 50% or more Al$_2$O$_3$)

STATE	DISTRICTS	RESERVES (Tons)
BIHAR	Ranchi and Palamau	9,000,000 (approx.)
MADHYA PRADESH	Surguja-Jashpur-Bilaspur ..	6,374,000
	Balaghat-Mandla-Kawardha ..	2,135,000
	Bilaspur-Shahdol (Amarkantak area)	620,000
	Jabalpur	525,000
BOMBAY	Belgaum	670,000
	Kolhapur	2,142,000
MADRAS	Salem (Shevaroy Hills)	2,000,000
MYSORE	Bababudan Hills	100,000
ORISSA	Sambalpur-Kalahandi	200,000
KASHMIR	Jammu and Poonch	2,000,000 (approx.)
	TOTAL ..	25,766,000 tons

Note :—The Shahdol district into which the Amarkantak plateau stretches from Bilaspur lies in Vindhya Pradesh.

Bikaner, Kotah and Tonk, Rajasthan. Quite recently bauxite enrichments have been discovered on Tungar Hill, near Bassein, Bombay, where there are about 100,000 tons of all grades with 30 to 50 per cent Al$_2$O$_3$; and near Mewasa in Nawanagar, Saurashtra, where samples analysed 42 to 64 per cent Al$_2$O$_3$, though the extent of the deposit has not yet been proved. According to the *United States Bureau of Mines Mineral Trade Notes* Vol. 36 (1), 1953, the Geological Survey of Pakistan reported the discovery in 1951 of about 500,000 tons of bauxite along the North-West Frontier Province and Kashmir border.

Quarrying for bauxite started in the Katni district of Madhya Pradesh in 1908, and in the Khaira district of Gujerat in 1920, in other districts of Bombay such as Thana and Belgaum considerably later and on a large and continuous scale in Bihar in 1946. Other areas contributing to the total include Nagod in Vindhya Pradesh and various districts of Mysore and Madras. The total recorded output between 1909 and 1950, inclusive, was 415,260 tons, most of which was drawn from the Katni district, until the manufacture of aluminium was successfully inaugurated, since when greater attention has been directed to the Lohardaga deposits of Bihar. Up to that time the bauxite had been used for refining kerosene, manufacturing alum and making refractory products. Of the 113,547 tons won during the decade 1934 to 1943, Madhya Pradesh contributed 94·3 per cent and Bombay 5·5 per cent, but in the next quinquennium, 1944 to 1948, with its total of 83,127 tons, the percentage from Madhya Pradesh had dropped to 65·5, Bihar had entered the list of producers with 21 per cent, while Vindhya

Brown & Dey, *India's Mineral Wealth, facing p.* 260

BAUXITE QUARRY ON THE SCARP OF A PLATEAU, CAPPED BY LATERITE, NEAR LOHARGADA, BIHAR

Pradesh and Mysore added the remainder. In 1949 and 1950 of 106,940 tons returned, Bihar gave 51·6 per cent, Madhya Pradesh 43 per cent while Bombay and Madras followed with 3·1 and 2·3 per cent respectively. Of the 64,400 tons raised in 1950, 23,000 tons went to the aluminium reduction works and the remainder was mainly consumed in the manufacture of alum and related chemicals, high alumina cement, refractories, and in kerosene refining. For some years the average declared ' pit's mouth ' value was about Rs 3-5-0 per ton, though this was little guide to the real worth of any particular variety and probably merely represented the approximate cost of extraction; by 1950 the average declared value had risen to Rs 12-10-0 per ton.

The first ingot of aluminium made in India from Indian bauxite was cast on 10 July 1944 at the works of the Aluminium Corporation of India Ltd, a company registered in 1937 which has its works at Jaykaynagar, near Asansol, West Bengal. These have a capacity of 3,000 tons of sheets and circles per annum and rely on steam power. The associated alumina plant commenced operations in October, 1942. Another concern, The Indian Aluminium Company, has its bauxite quarries at Lohardaga, its alumina works at Muri, in the Ranchi district of Bihar, its hydro-electric reduction works at Alwaye, near Alupuram in Travancore and its rolling mills at Belur, near Calcutta. It has been producing the metal since 1943, but as the last war interfered with the erection of its plant at Muri, imported alumina was used for the purpose. The projected capacity in this case is 5,000 tons per annum, but is unlikely to exceed 2,700 tons per annum until more power is made available from the Pallivassal hydro-electric undertaking. The combined production of the two companies has grown from 1,272 tons in 1943 to 3,594 tons in 1950, with a total production of 22,170 tons of aluminium over that period. In 1951, the Planning Commission considered it necessary that the output of aluminium should be increased within the next five years to 25,000 tons per annum. The two producing companies are therefore required to increase their capacity to 5,000 tons per annum each, and another reduction works is to be installed in the Hirakud area with a yearly output of 15,000 tons. Plant for the manufacture of aluminium wires and cables has been erected at Kundara, Travancore, while a factory to produce aluminium paste for paints has been constructed near Bombay. Aluminium hollow-ware has been made in India from imported metal and scrap since 1912, when a small plant was erected in Madras.

For the decade ending 1938, India's imports of aluminium in the form of unwrought ingots, circles, sheets and other manufactures, averaged 3,636 tons yearly, but during the three years ending 1946, they reached 5,423 tons per annum, valued at Rs 87,62,392. In 1950, 7,052 tons of wrought and unwrought aluminium, valued at over Rs 2 crores, were imported. This gives some idea of the scope

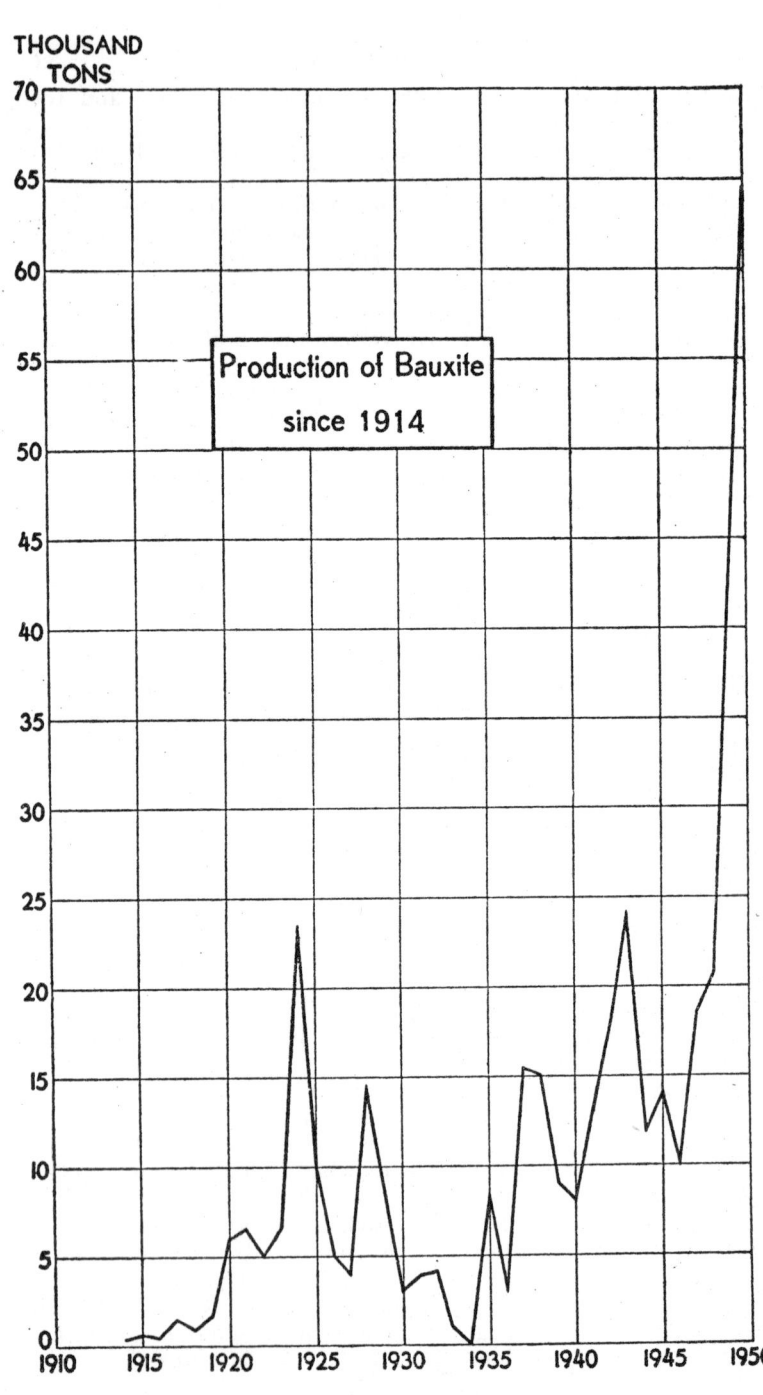

for the development of the indigenous aluminium industry, without considering the substantial increase to a consumption of 30,000 to 50,000 tons per annum within the next ten or fifteen years which is anticipated. The economics of aluminium manufacture in India have been discussed by Dara P. Antia, of the Directorate of Industry and Supply, who has concluded that unless the industry is backed by concerns already engaged in it elsewhere its rapid growth in this country is doubtful.

The world's annual production of bauxite in the period 1934-8, before the last war, was in the neighbourhood of 2¾ million tons, supplied by France, Hungary, the United States of America, British Guiana, Yugoslavia, Italy, Dutch Guiana, the Soviet Union, the Netherlands East Indies and Greece in order of magnitude of output, and two-thirds of this total is believed to have been turned into metallic aluminium. The war stimulated production enormously; by 1941 it had reached over 6¼ million tons, the average for the five years ending 1943 being 7,017,000 tons approximately, according to statistics issued by the United States Bureau of Mines, which do not include countries with an annual output of less than 100,000 tons. Production during that period was shared as follows: United States 29 per cent of the total, France 10 per cent, British Guiana 15 per cent, Surinam 14·7 per cent, Hungary 12·7 per cent, Italy 6·5 per cent, U.S.S.R. 4 per cent, Yugoslavia 3·7 per cent, Netherlands Indies 3 per cent and the remainder divided about equally between the Gold Coast and Ireland. The world's production in 1948 was considerably over 8 million tons, about half of which came from the Guianas and under one quarter from the United States of America. The U.S.A. is the largest aluminium producer in the world and is followed by Canada, which relies mainly on ore from British Guiana.

The use of bauxite in the manufacture of chemicals is described under ALUM, but it remains to add that the varieties most suitable for this purpose should contain less than 3 per cent of ferric oxide. Chemical grades of bauxite with 55 to 58 per cent of alumina and 1·5 to 2·5 per cent of ferric oxide command prices at least half as high again as the cruder kinds.

The crystalline variety of alumina, corundum, is a natural abrasive second only to the diamond in hardness, and its distribution in India is described under ABRASIVES. Artificial corundum is made by fusing bauxite in the electric furnace and for this particular purpose some of the lower grades of the mineral are acceptable, the finished product being marketed as powder, grains and special shapes under a great variety of trade names.

The use of bauxite in the manufacture of refractory bricks and other articles is described under REFRACTORIES. The aluminous cements, made by grinding fused mixtures of bauxite and chalk, possess very high early strength and are immune from many forms of chemical action which attack Portland cement and concrete made from it. The rapid-hardening properties, the resistance to sea-water, and to ground-water containing sulphates in solution, together with the general impermeability of aluminous cement and concrete made from it, have led to their extended use in the construction of reservoirs and foundations in marshy conditions, of piers and harbour works, of pipes and sewers for large drainage schemes, of internal linings for water tunnels, of power-station flues and of situations in general where strength is desirable in the shortest possible time. We are indebted to the Lafarge Aluminous Cement Co. Ltd, the makers of ' Ciment Fondu ', for this information.

Bauxite filters are installed in oil refineries for the purification and decolorization of kerosene, and the mineral from the Khaira district of Bombay has been largely used for this purpose.

Bauxite production in India will expand with the growth of the aluminium industry, especially as the imports of foreign alumina ceased in 1950, and with the further utilization of the mineral for the various purposes described.

MAGNESIUM

Magnesium is a silvery white, ductile metal which, with a density of 1·74, compared with that of 2·7 for aluminium, is also an uncommonly light one, but, although its compounds abound both in the crust of the earth and in the waters of the sea, it is not easy to extract from them. Its strong affinity for oxygen causes it to burn fiercely with an intense white light and accounts not only for its uses in photographic flashlight powders and as a deoxidizing agent in the refining of other metals and alloys, but also for its presence in the incendiary bombs of warfare. Incendiary bomb casings are alloys of magnesium with 5 to 7 per cent of aluminium, and the powdered metal is also a constituent of the filling of some types. The same affinity for oxygen leads to the employment of the metal in the form of ribbon or wire to remove the last traces of gases from radio valves.

It is made on a commercial scale by the electrolytic reduction of fused magnesium chloride, obtained from sea-water, natural brines or bitterns, and also by the thermal reduction of its oxide, magnesia, by means of ferro-silicon, coke or calcium carbide. The minerals used as a starting-point include magnesite, the carbonate, $MgCO_3$, with 28·9 per cent magnesium; dolomite, magnesium-calcium carbonate, $MgCO_3.CaCO_3$, with 13 per cent of magnesium, and brucite, magnesium hydrate, $Mg(OH)_2$, with 41·6 per cent of the metal. The carbonates magnesite and dolomite are sources of basic refractory materials and are further described under RE-FRACTORIES. The silicate olivine $2(MgFe)O.SiO_2$, its decomposition product serpentine, and the hydrated silicate talc, also have refractory and other industrial applications and are considered separately.

The pure metal is of little use in engineering, but its commercial alloys, with a general specific gravity of 1·84, are the lightest structural materials available, being about one quarter the weight of iron and two-thirds that of aluminium alloys. They are indispensable for aircraft frames, landing wheels, propellor blades, and aero-engine castings. They are also employed in gear-box castings as well as for tractor wheels, bodywork and other parts of motor vehicles of all descriptions. Their light weight, strength and excellent machining properties are noteworthy, whilst the strength-to-weight ratio of their castings is the highest for all cast materials, making them of great present and potential importance in many branches of engineering. For the construction of portable tools, machine parts and textile machinery and for all kinds of appliances that have to be moved, either manually or mechanically, they possess definite advantages. The high electro-chemical equivalent of magnesium has led to its growing use in the anodic protection of underground oil pipelines, and the buried foundations of cast iron and steel structures, for by this means corrosion which cannot be prevented is largely brought under control. Considerable quantities of pure magnesium are consumed in alloys of aluminium, for from 2 per cent to 10 per cent of the metal in their composition renders them completely resistant to corrosion by sea-water.

Aluminium, zinc and manganese are the metals most widely used in the past for alloying with magnesium itself, the two former for imparting hardness and other improved physical properties, and the latter as a corrosion-resisting agent. The chief alloys are of the quaternary type and contain 3 per cent to 10 per cent of aluminium besides zinc and manganese, but many different varieties are made, each designed for its own special purpose. The wrought forms are available as rolled sheets, plates and strips; extruded bars, sections and tubes, pressed or impacted forgings; rolled bars and sections: other types are made for use in sand, gravity-die and pressure-die castings. Only one of many examples can be quoted here, the alloy known as ' Elektron A8 ' which contains about 8 per cent of aluminium, 0·5 per cent of zinc and 0·2 per cent of manganese, and which, after solution heat-treatment, develops remarkable resilience and high shock-resistance, so that it is almost exclusively used in the construction of the landing wheels of aircraft.

More recently zirconium and the rare earth metals have been developed as magnesium alloying agents by Magnesium Elektron Ltd, to whom we are indebted for particulars. These new alloys are remarkable for their extremely fine grain and improved properties; the ternary casting alloys with about 0·7 per cent zirconium and 2·5 to 6·5 per cent zinc, possessing proof stresses nearly double those of the magnesium-aluminium-zinc series, while the related wrought types, with zirconium, exhibit substantial improvements over those of the older group. These alloys have actually been cast into ingots in normal steel ingot moulds and rolled down into bars in rolling mills in exactly the same way and at the same speeds as the steel ingots replaced. The quaternary alloys contain magnesium, zinc, zirconium and 2·5 per cent to 4 per cent of the rare earth metals ('cerium'), the introduction of the latter having been found to confer a remarkable resistance to creep at elevated temperatures. They can also be cast pressure-tight, in most complicated shapes to withstand high pressures, and have proved capable of heavy duty on full loads at elevated temperatures. Magnesium is so reactive chemically that it combines easily not only with the oxygen of the air to form its oxide, but also with the nitrogen to form its nitride; in melting it or its alloys it is essential to protect them completely to prevent combustion. This is done by means of special fluxes, mainly mixtures of the chlorides of magnesium, calcium, sodium and potassium, yielding fluxes of fluid types, or these chlorides to which magnesia and calcium fluoride are added to give viscous and thicker mixtures. Care is also needed in the preparation of the moulding sands for the casting processes, but treated correctly the metal and its alloys can be handled safely without any undue risk of fire. Unprotected magnesium-base alloys are very resistant to atmospheric attack except in salt-laden atmospheres, but like other erosive metals, such as iron and steel, they must be protected by suitable paints if the maximum immunity is to be achieved.

The second world war created an unprecedented demand for magnesium and it was met by a phenomenal increase in production, which increased from about 32,000 tons in 1939 to 265,000 tons in 1943, when in the United States of America alone 63 plants were either making, or preparing to make, the metal and over 183,000 tons were produced. Mounting stocks and decreasing requirements for war materials soon made their effects apparent, a number of reduction works were closed, and by 1945, as far as the States were concerned, magnesium was plentiful for all war requirements with only 50,000 tons of the total 300,000 tons capacity in use. The end of the war found the world supplied with a production capacity far beyond its existing peace-time needs, together with a legacy of stocks and secondary metal which had not been entirely absorbed by 1950. In that year it was reported that only one primary producer was in part-time operation in North America, with an output of some 10,000 tons per annum. The world's production for 1950 has been provisionally estimated at about 20,000 tons, excluding the Soviet Union, and even this figure represents an increase of nearly 40 per cent on the output for 1949. To what extent the growing rearmament programmes of the nations will affect the situation is not yet clear.

It is for these reasons that the question of magnesium production in India, despite her abundant supplies of high-grade raw materials, should be approached with caution, and the wise recommendation of the Non-Ferrous Metal Industries Panel in 1947, to defer the matter for the time being, upheld.

Besides its uses as a refractory material, dolomite serves many other purposes; some varieties are used in iron smelting as fluxes, others as building stones, statuary marbles and lithographic stones. The mineral is suitable as a source of carbon dioxide and of basic magnesium carbonate, which blended with asbestos is employed as a heat-insulating covering for boilers and hot-pipe laggings.

Magnesite and dolomite are the starting materials for the preparation of many magnesium salts, which are essential chemicals in many industries including ceramics, glass manufacture, paper making, sugar refining, as well as in fire-resisting paints, water treatment agents, the glue and rubber trades and pharmacy. The chloride of magnesium is of special importance in India, where it is widely employed in the sizing of cotton yarns before they are woven into cloth, particularly in the hot and dry textile centres where its hygroscopic character promotes softness and pliability in the mill yarns. This country has for many years produced its own supplies of this compound and its manufacture is described separately in Chapter XIV. The application of the chloride in the preparation of oxychloride cements is also described elsewhere, but it may be added here that jointless composition floorings of these materials are extensively employed in India for railway carriages and vans. Magnesium chloride has other uses, including the part it plays in refrigerating media, wood treatment compounds, fire extinguishers and dust-laying preparations.

Epsom Salt, the sulphate of magnesium, is also of some importance in India, in the finishing of cotton fabrics, the dyeing of textiles and in the paper and leather trades, as well as in medicine. At one time upwards of 600 tons per annum were regularly imported, mainly from Germany, but it is now recovered from bitterns and made from magnesite. The present production is about 3,500 to 4,000 tons per annum.

Dr M. S. Krishnan, in a recent paper, has summarized the magnesium resources of the State of Madras in which the largest deposits of the carbonate, magnesite, occur.

BERYLLIUM

Beryl, a silicate of beryllium and aluminium, $3BeO.Al_2O_3.6SiO_2$, is the only commercial source of the metal beryllium known today. Its precious varieties, the emerald and the aquamarine, are described under GEMS. Theoretically the mineral contains 14 per cent of beryllium oxide, or beryllia, and only 5 per cent of the metal, while in actual practice the amount extracted is considerably less than this. With a specific gravity of 1·84 the metal is but slightly heavier than magnesium (1·74) and considerably lighter than aluminium (2·7), but it possesses a much higher melting point than either of these metals—1280° C., compared with 651° and 660° C.; moreover, it is harder and has a higher corrosion-resistance than either of them.

Beryllium is described as a brittle, steel-grey metal and hitherto its chief use has been in alloys with copper to which it imparts great strength after suitable heat-treatment. A copper alloy with 2·25 per cent of beryllium possesses six times the tensile strength of copper alone and has in addition a high fatigue-resistance. Such alloys are marketed as wires, rods and strips and are fabricated into springs of many kinds, gears, cams and bearing bushes, membrane discs of delicate instruments, watch and camera parts, valve guides, vibrating mechanisms and all manner of mechanical devices in which resilience, coupled with resistance to hard wear and fatigue, are essential. These alloys are also non-sparking and are used for tools, switch gear and other purposes in situations where fire hazards exist. Beryllium in small amounts greatly increases the tensile strength of nickel and it can also be alloyed with other metals, including aluminium, magnesium, iron, silver and platinum.

It is also employed in windows of X-ray tubes, and in conjunction with a compound of radium is a convenient source of neutrons for experimental work in nuclear physics. The development of atomic energy programmes in various countries has greatly increased the demand for beryllium, and it is of considerable potential importance as a moderator and sheathing metal for the uranium rods in slow neutron reactors. The metal is made on a commercial scale either by the electrolysis of chloride melts, or by the reduction of the fluoride with magnesium.

Some of the salts of beryllium such as the oxide, and the compound, zinc beryllium silicate, are used as coatings of the tubes used in fluorescent lamps, screens and electric signs. About 0·5 per cent of beryllium, added in the form of a soluble salt to the thorium-cerium solutions used for the impregnation of gas mantles, is said to strengthen the resulting body. Beryllium compounds are toxic and workers with them are liable to suffer from acute respiratory disorders unless suitable industrial health precautions are observed.

Ground beryl has been employed in the United States of America as a partial batch substitute for feldspar in the manufacture of electrical ceramic specialities, particularly of sparking-plug insulators. Beryllia itself is an excellent refractory, superior not only in this quality, but also in thermal conductivity and dielectric properties to alumina, especially at temperatures above 1900° C. when alumina softens, but its cost restricts its development and use.

The productive beryl deposits of India are found in the pegmatites associated with the granites of Rajasthan, but the mineral also occurs in the mica-bearing pegmatites of Bihar and Andhra, and is recoverable in small amounts as a by-product of mica mining, particularly from the Koderma Forest area of Hazaribagh and the mica mines around Gudur in Nellore.   Other localities are known, both in India and in Pakistan, and more will be found as the granitic tracts of the Peninsula and the Himalayas come to be mapped in detail.

K. L. Bhola described the Ajmer-Merwara occurrences in 1934; A. M. Heron contributed the Rajasthan deposits in 1938; H. Crookshank added his observations in 1948, while Dr M. S. Krishnan, the present Director of the Geological Survey of India, had reviewed the whole position in a special bulletin published in 1942 and reprinted in 1946.   Although these Rajasthan pegmatites had provided material for generations of Jaipur lapidaries, their commercial exploitation did not really commence until 1930, and by 1932, 281 tons of beryl, valued at Rs 5,281, had been collected through the pioneer enterprise of Nusserwanji Contractor.   This increased to 324 tons and Rs 7,261, in 1933, and then decreased again, so that the average annual production for the five years 1934-8 was but 67 tons, valued at Rs 3,984.   The industry, by that time in a moribund condition, raised only 9 tons (Rs 900) in 1939, but war demands and better prices soon caused a revival—during 1940-2, a total of 171 tons was produced—and by 1943 output was 1,463 tons, valued at Rs 45,565.   In 1944 and 1945 a total of 606 tons was won, and in 1946 exports were banned, all stocks of beryl in India were acquired by the Atomic Energy Commission, and the publication of statistics relating to the mineral ceased.

Beryl occurs sporadically as hexagonal or rounded crystals from half an inch to many feet in length, in wide pegmatite veins, generally where zoning is prominently developed and large quartz cores exist.   Although most prevalent at the edges of these cores and in the feldspathic zones adjoining them, the mineral is also found in unzoned pegmatites of the coarse, granitic type.   Shades of blue and green are its commonest colours, but it is a very deceptive mineral liable to assume other tints and is frequently mistaken for quartz, while a milky white variety is easily confused with feldspar and a black one with tourmaline.   Most of the crystals are cloudy, but clear patches can sometimes be found suitable for the lapidary, though they are not in much demand.   Giant crystals up to 20 feet in length and 4 feet in width, weighing upwards of 20 tons, have been seen and even larger ones reported to exist. Medium-sized crystals have been made use of locally as readymade gate-posts and built into the walls of castles, shrines and wells. Clean Rajasthan beryl generally contains over 12 per cent beryllia (BeO).

The mineral is won from eluvial deposits on the outcrops of the pegmatites, as well as from large quarries within them, which have been responsible for about half the output in the past, and as a by-product of mica mining to the extent of about 10 per cent.   H. Crookshank believed that considerable quantities could be obtained from this source if the terms of the mining leases concerned were made more encouraging.

Owing to the capricious distribution of the mineral, mining had nowhere been continued deeper than the bases of exposed pockets; methods of working are primitive in the extreme and quarries were not opened unless many crystals each weighing 100 lb. or so could be seen. Small crystals, even if numerous, were considered worthless unless of gem quality. Considerable quantities of eluvial ore are still recoverable from ground already picked over, while large areas of Mewar, in Bhowat, are virgin ground as far as quarrying is concerned.

If beryl mining is to be firmly established in India not only will proper mining methods have to be adopted, but some system of concentration will have to be evolved, by which low-grade ores can be successfully treated and the valuable mineral separated from its gangue. It may then well be found that those pegmatites in which the mineral is ' well though thinly distributed ' are more profitable sources of supply than the erratic, though rich, ore shoots roughly excavated in the past.

As the demand for beryllium in connexion with work on atomic energy projects has grown, so it has become increasingly difficult to obtain statistical information regarding beryl mining, as most countries now exercise strict control over exports and no longer publish figures of production. Some authorities give the world's output in 1940 as about 5,000 tons of beryl, but by 1944 it appears to have been nearer 3,000 tons, of which Brazil was responsible for some 40 per cent, and India for about 17 per cent; Australia was third on the list with 14 per cent, followed by Argentina with 11 per cent, the remainder coming from various parts of Africa. In later years supplies from South America are known to have declined while those from South Rhodesia and other States in South Africa have increased. There was an output of 490 tons in the United States of America in 1952 in an estimated world production of 6,500 tons. The Atomic Energy Commission for India offers rewards for new discoveries of beryllium ores.

LITHIUM

Lepidolite, or lithia mica, a hydrated fluo-silicate of aluminium, potassium and lithium, with a lithia (Li_2O) content ranging from 2 to 6 per cent, has long been known as a constituent of certain Indian mica-bearing pegmatites and vein granites. F. R. Mallet, in 1874, though not finding it widely distributed in such rocks in northern Hazaribagh, proved its existence in considerable quantities in some places, as, for example, in a dyke passing into a greisen near Pihra, where it occurs with cassiterite in irregular, scaly masses of violet-red to greyish violet and lead-grey tints. The former variety contained 3·71 per cent of lithia and 5 per cent of fluorine, the latter 1·75 per cent of lithia, 8·59 per cent of potash, 0·7 per cent of rubidium oxide and doubtful traces of caesium. About a mile south of Manimundar in the same neighbourhood, the sides of a hillock are strewn with blocks of the mineral, one of which was estimated to weigh about 8 cwt.

In 1934, H. Crookshank found boulders of lepidolite near Mundaval, in Bastar, Madhya Pradesh, derived from a pegmatite some 30 feet in width, in which the mineral is confined to a zone of 15 feet in the centre. He estimated that this particular vein is capable of yielding several hundreds of tons of lepidolite containing 3·3 per cent of lithia and 4·8 per cent of fluorine.

Very large, deep lilac-coloured plates of lepidolite, up to six inches across, occur in a pegmatite vein at Sakangyi, Katha district, Burma, and it is probably to be found in some of the cassiterite-bearing greisens of Tenasserim in the same country.

Other important minerals containing lithium are spodumene, a silicate of lithium and aluminium, $LiO_2.Al_2O_3.4SiO_2$, with 8·4 per cent of lithia and amblygonite, a fluo-phosphate of aluminium and lithium, $AlPO_4.LiF$, with 10·1 per cent of lithia. La Touche found a few lilac-coloured blocks of ' spodumene ' in a valley close to the sapphire mines in Kashmir, but F. R. Mallet proved that some at least of the mineral was amblygonite. A green lithia-tourmaline and cookeite, a rare variety of lepidolite, also occur there, but the isolation of the locality would probably prevent the commercial extraction of the minerals, even if systematic prospecting proved their presence in large quantities. Spodumene analysing 5·8 per cent LiO_2, and associated with some lithium-mica, has been recorded in the pegmatites of the Ooregum mine in Mysore. All the minerals named are used as sources of lithium and its compounds, and it is also recovered in the form of lithium sodium phosphate from the brines of Searles Lake in California.

Lithium, with a specific gravity of 0·543, is the lightest of all the metals, weighing only 37 lb. per cubic foot, as against 109 lb. for magnesium, 167 lb. for aluminium and 450 lb. for cast iron, but it is soft enough to be cut with a knife and rapidly deteriorates through oxidation on exposure to the air. It is produced commercially by the electrolysis of its chloride, in the presence of potassium chloride, and is preserved in airtight containers after being coated with a light hydrocarbon oil.

It is an important degassing, deoxidizing and general purifying agent in metal refining, especially of copper and the bronzes. Very small quantities of lithium impart hardness, toughness and tensile strength to other metals and alloys and it is employed for this reason in extruded lead products, lead cable sheaths, copper electrodes and bearing metals. The *Bahnmetall* of the German metallurgists is a lead base alloy with only 0·04 per cent of lithium. Lepidolite is useful to the glass-maker for its fluxing, toughening and strengthening properties; in larger quantities it is an opacifier for both opal and white glasses. It is also employed in the manufacture of special porcelains and in glazes and enamels. Lithium chloride is a very hygroscopic substance which finds application in air-drying plants; the chloride and the fluoride in fluxes for the electrical welding of the light metals; the hydroxide in alkaline accumulators; the hydride in the preparation of hydrogen; while other compounds have minor uses in pyrotechny, photography, mineral waters and pharmacy. The hydride has recently been suggested as a component of the hydrogen bomb.

Most of the lithium minerals are produced and consumed in the United States of America, the domestic production there rising from 113 tons in 1940 to 848 tons in 1944, expressed in terms of lithia content. Other producing countries include South-West Africa, Brazil, Argentina, Australia, Sweden and Germany. In 1948, exports of lepidolite from South-West Africa reached 2,266 tons compared with 2,535 tons in 1947.

CHAPTER VII

THE ATOMIC METALS AND THEIR ASSOCIATES

URANIUM

THE observations on uranium ores given below are based on information published officially before the second world war, in the course of which the development of atomic power from them was inaugurated. It is not permissible to discuss later developments but attention can be directed to the statement in Parliament, by the Minister for Natural Resources and Scientific Research, on 24 March 1951, that 'two uranium-bearing belts have recently been discovered in Eastern and Central India' and that a detailed examination of these areas was then in progress.

The earliest reference to a uranium mineral in India appeared in a German publication in 1860, in which Emil Stoehr recorded the occurrence of copper uranite ($Cu(UO_2)_2. (PO_4)_2. 8H_2O$), an old name for torbernite, a hydrated phosphate of uranium and copper, also known in Indian literature as 'uranium mica', at Lopso Hill in Singhbhum. Many years later it was found again with uranium ochres as encrustations on magnetite-apatite rocks at Sungri, in Dhalbhum, associated with libethenite, a hydrated phosphate of copper.

Pitchblende or uraninite, the substance which started the development of atomic energy, a complex mineral with 69 to 91 per cent of uranium oxide, U_3O_8, and the chief source of the metal, was first recognized in India by Sir Thomas Holland in 1901. It came from a mica mine, two miles south-east of Singar, in the Gaya district of Bihar, a locality examined by R. C. Burton in 1912. He found pitchblende in a wide pegmatite vein, mined for many years for mica, intrusive in mica schists, at Abraki Pahar. The mineral occurs as rounded nodules of all sizes up to a maximum of 36 lb. in weight, distributed in basic segregations in the pegmatite. Triplite, a phosphate and fluoride of iron and manganese, generally associated with large masses of ilmenite, usually forms the outer ring of these basic patches, though occasionally the pitchblende lies in the centre of feldspathic masses. White and yellow micas, tourmaline, zircon and torbernite also occur. The pitchblende is normally surrounded by a rim of uranium ochre. About 6 cwt of the mineral were recovered from this place during prospecting operations between 1913 and 1915.

Another locality lies five miles to the north-north-west, near Pichhli. Here, according to G. H. Tipper, the mode of occurrence is much the same and small nodules of pitchblende, two inches or so in diameter, deeply altered into uranium ochres, are found, while bright green torbernite and lemon-yellow autunite also occur. The latter mineral has a similar chemical constitution to torbernite but with its copper replaced by calcium. Other accessory minerals include columbite, monazite, black tourmaline and pink garnet.

Pitchblende was found again about 1935 in a pegmatite quarried for beryl at Bisundi, Ajmer-Merwara. Nodules of the massive black mineral, with its typical pitch-like lustre, occur there in a kaolinized, laminated variety of albite feldspar known as cleve-landite. They are invariably surrounded by brightly coloured alteration products, the black or brownish kernel being followed by layers of scarlet or bright orange-red colours, passing outwards into gamboge and presumably composed of gummite, hydrated oxides of uranium and other bases of uncertain composition. The outermost crusts are formed of lemon-yellow, crystalline autunite.

A number of other minerals, niobates, tantalates and titanates of the rare earth elements frequently contain uranium and are sometimes referred to as its refractory ores. Indian examples include samarskite, fergusonite, euxenite and others, more fully described under TANTALUM and NIOBIUM.

According to Dr C. F. Davidson, Chief Geologist of the Atomic Energy Division, Geological Survey of Great Britain, well over a thousand localities are on record at which uranium-bearing pegmatites have been discovered, but not one has yet been found capable of yielding a significant tonnage of uranium minerals at an economic price, although many attempts have been made to work them in Tanganyika, Madagascar, Norway, the United States of America, Manchuria and elsewhere. Only where economics do not matter, or where production is possible as a by-product, is a small output of uranium ore likely to be practicable from such a source.

India's occurrences of pitchblende and other uranium-bearing minerals are of pegmatitic origin and unless mining costs are shared by some other product, such as mica or beryl, from the same vein, output from the pegmatites can only be small and fortuitous.

There is, however, another potential source of uranium in India, for commercial monazite concentrates commonly contain $0 \cdot 3$ to $0 \cdot 4$ per cent of U_3O_8. Dr D. N. Wadia, Geological Adviser to the Government of India, in a publication dated 1949, mentions a content of about $0 \cdot 3$ per cent U_3O_8 adding, ' since considerable reserves of monazite sands exist (in association with the ilmenite sands of the west and east coasts), extraction of a notable quantity of uranium will be possible when the monazite sands are utilized for the manufacture of thorium metal '.

Uranium, the heaviest element occurring naturally, is described as a silvery white, malleable metal which burns easily in the air and is made by the reduction of its tetrafluoride with calcium in an inert atmosphere. It is said to have four different atomic weights, namely 233, 234, 235 and 238, of which the last is by far the most abundant variety; uranium 235 which occurs with it being present in the ratio of only one part in one hundred and forty. These two varieties are isotopes and cannot be separated by chemical means; they can, however, be divided by physical processes.

Uranium is radioactive; its atomic nuclei undergo spontaneous and ceaseless disruption, emitting alpha, beta and gamma rays in the process, and giving birth by transmutation to a whole series of other elements including helium, radium, actinium and lead. The alpha rays are charged helium particles; beta rays consist of electrons, while gamma rays are described as very short electromagnetic rays of the same nature as X-rays but of more penetrating effect.

Until the discovery, in 1898, that pitchblende contained radium there was little demand for the uranium ores, a state of affairs that continued for some years afterwards, but as the demand increased, and in spite of the fact that there is only about one part of radium present in these ores for every three million parts of uranium, its unique properties made its extraction profitable and led to the exploitation of ore deposits in Colorado and Utah, United States of America, in the Belgian Congo and in Arctic Canada. Professor W. R. Jones has estimated that about 1932 the total weight of radium that had been extracted from uranium ores was less than one pound in weight, and that even by the end of 1942 all the world's supply would weigh little more than about 1,000 grams (2·2 lb.). He adds that about 85 per cent of this was employed for medicinal purposes, especially in the treatment of malignant diseases, and about 10 per cent in the preparation of luminous paints, generally consisting of zinc sulphide with minute amounts of radium, used for gun sights, aircraft instruments and so forth. Uranium and its salts in those days were by-products of the radium refineries and were not always saleable. The compounds found outlets to some extent in the manufacture of fluorescent glass, of an opalescent, yellow transparency but turning green by reflected light, in ceramic glazes, in photographic and analytical chemicals and as mordants in calico printing and dyeing. The metal had been tried in various alloys, as a deoxidizer of steel and as a catalyst in the fixation of nitrogen, but apparently without much success.

It was not until 1939, when the nucleus of the uranium atom was first split by bombardment with neutrons, with the freeing of more neutrons capable of developing further fissions, that the possibility of the chain reaction, ' the key to the release of atomic power on a large scale ', was realized. ' The energy released from the fission of a pound of fissionable material is about that resulting from the explosion of eight thousand tons of T.N.T.', writes Professor Morrison, 'and it momentarily creates enormous pressures and temperatures of millions of degrees Centigrade.' (T.N.T., or trinitrotoluene, is a high explosive adopted extensively for military purposes, particularly as a bursting charge in shells, bombs and mines.) Sir John Cockcroft, Director of the Atomic Energy Research Establishment in Great Britain, has stated that ' the complete destruction [by fission] of one ton of uranium releases as much energy as the burning of three million tons of coal '.

Thus uranium from being little more than a chemical curiosity has become the most eventful metal in the world and statistics of the production of its ores are now jealously guarded secrets in the countries concerned. It is required for the separation of its isotope, uranium 235, and for the preparation of plutonium, another powerful atomic fuel, and used, like uranium 235, in atom bombs.

Atomic energy is liberated under controlled conditions in nuclear reactors, or piles, in which chain reactions are allowed to develop in natural uranium, embedded in moderators such as graphite which have the power of slowing down neutrons. These piles are used for research purposes and to investigate the effects of intense radiation on the properties of materials. In less than a decade uranium has been responsible for the creation of vast new industries involving enormous expenditure and employing many thousands of workers. For accounts of the processes employed the reader is referred to the official account in *Britain's Atomic Factories*, published in 1954 and dealing with the design, construction and organization of the headquarters at Risley in Lancashire, and the three large operating units which produce uranium from its ores at Springfields in Lancashire, plutonium at Windscale in Cumberland and uranium 235 at Capenhurst in Cheshire. A companion publication is entitled *Harwell: the British Atomic Energy Research Establishment* (1952).

Though most of the work done in the atomic factories of the world to date has been to direct this new source of power into weapons of destruction, to quote the words of the British Minister of Supply in December, 1953: ' At the same time impressive progress has been made in applying the forces of nuclear fission to peaceful and constructive uses, thus opening up to this and future generations an ever-expanding prospect of material betterment.'

The most striking development in this direction is the proposed construction of large ' fast reactors ', which use no moderators, can be used as sources of power and in which at the same time, there are prospects that more secondary fuel in the form of plutonium can be bred than the amount of primary fuel, uranium 235, consumed in the process. The first experimental, power-producing, fast-breeder reactor of this type has been operating in the United States of America since early 1953. In the same country a large submarine to be driven by atomic power has already been launched. In January 1953, an extensive programme was adopted in England to include the immediate building of a reactor to produce power and of a full-scale breeder reactor, the combined objective being set at 50,000 kilowatts. In June 1954, the British Electricity Authority announced its belief that a significant contribution will become available to the nation's power supplies from nuclear energy stations within the next 20 years, and its hope soon to begin the construction of such stations as part of its normal activities.

Though the primary object of large nuclear reactors so far operating in the world has been the transmutation of uranium into plutonium, radioactive isotopes of many elements are also being made on a large scale and there is now an extensive chemical industry engaged in the transmutation of one element into another. Mention must also be made of the new synthetic transuranic elements such as neptunium, americum and others formed by secondary reactions in atomic piles. Radioactive isotopes are increasingly used in industry, biochemistry and medicine. Among many other applications they can be used as ' tracers ' in animals and plants, for the detection of air and gas leaks, to measure the wear of bearings, for the examination of metal castings and for the dispersal of static electrical charges in textile mills and other manufacturing processes. Cobalt 60, made in the atomic pile, is an efficient substitute for radium in conventional therapy, but while radium still costs the equivalent of over Rs 66,000 per gram, cobalt 60 of equivalent activity costs about Rs 260 for the same quantity.

At the official opening of the monazite processing factory of the Rare Earths Ltd, near Alwaye, in Travancore-Cochin, on 24 December 1952, by Pandit Jawaharlal Nehru, the Prime Minister stated that the plan drawn up by the Atomic Energy Commission for the development of atomic energy in India had been approved by the Government of India. This plan provides for the construction of a medium-sized reactor in India within the next three years.

Ores of uranium and other radioactive minerals in India are under the control of the Atomic Energy Commission and rewards are offered for the discovery of new deposits, with grants-in-aid for mining developments.

THORIUM

Monazite, the principal ore of thorium, is a monoclinic phosphate of cerium and other rare earth metals, including lanthanum, praseodymium, neodymium and samarium, $Ce(La, Pr, Nd, Sm)PO_4$, with small amounts of the rare earth elements of the terbium and yttrium groups, in addition to thorium and, occasionally, uranium. It also contains minute quantities of radium and mesothorium. The thoria content may vary from nothing to as high as 33 per cent, and that of urania from nil to 4·5 per cent. Travancore monazite varies in thoria content from about 8 to 10·5 per cent: Ceylon material averages about 10 per cent.

In its original situations monazite is found in pegmatites, as in the prismatic crystals, associated with pitchblende and columbite, near Pichhli, Gaya district, Bihar; in similar rocks in the vicinity of Bangalore, Mysore; or, again, in small grains in pegmatites traversing the gneisses of south Travancore, and in parts of Ceylon, where it is also a constituent of biotite and hornblende granites and of gneisses. A new member of the monazite group was described in 1953 as ' cheralite ' (from *Chera* the ancient name of Travancore). It is a dark green mineral found sparingly in brittle masses with black tourmaline, small greenish yellow chrysoberyls, partly meta-mict dark zircon and much smoky quartz, in a kaolinized pegmatite at Kuttakushi, Kalkulam taluk, about 25 miles east-south-east of Trivandrum. Similar material was collected from Cootykad Pothay in the adjoining Vilavancod taluk by E. Masillamani about 1914. Almost all monazite contains some thorium and a little uranium replacing the cerium-lanthanum earths in the crystal lattice of the mineral, but in cheralite, with 29·45 per cent of thoria and 6·56 of urania, this substitution has been carried far beyond normal quantities. We wish to thank Messrs Bowie and Horne of the Geological Survey of Great Britain for giving us this informa-tion preparatory to its publication. Cheralite does not occur in sufficient quantities to be of any economic importance. Dr D. N. Wadia, in 1952, gave the provisional name ' travancorite ' to a mineral rich in thorium and uranium called green monazite from Travancore.

Monazite deposits of commercial importance are generally confined to the sands of sea beaches; the mineral has a high enough specific gravity, sufficient hardness and chemical stability, to permit of its transport there after its liberation from its parent rocks by weathering agencies, accompanied by its constant associates ilme-nite, arizonite and magnetite, garnet, zircon and rutile. Its com-bination of suitable properties is also responsible for its concentra-tion, with its companion minerals, in favourable locations on the beaches where wave action can bring its sluicing effects into play, and the bulk of the lighter minerals is removed by tidal currents.

In such natural, coastal concentrates the monazite exists as small, rounded, translucent grains of an amber-yellow colour, averaging 0·1 to 0·2mm. in diameter. Twenty-five years ago, Sir Edwin Pascoe gave the average percentage of monazite in the Travancore beach sands as about 10 per cent, yet today, it is stated by Dr C. F. Davidson, Chief Geologist to the Atomic Energy Divi-sion, Geological Survey of Great Britain, that ' probably no beach deposit workable on a large scale, can yield ore with more than about three per cent '. Old sand dunes near the coast sometimes carry monazite and such wind-borne deposits are occasionally cemented into compact masses by infiltrated carbonate of lime. In older strata still, such as the Warkalli Beds, there are, according to G. H. Tipper, dark brown, ferruginous grits composed of the same minerals as those of the existing beaches with monazite in some quantity.

The monazite sands lying between Cape Comorin and Quilon were discovered in 1909 by C. W. Schomberg, and eventually five major deposits were located at Liparam, Pudur, Kovilam, Varkala (Warkalli) and Nindikari, respectively. Fuller descriptions of them will be found under TITANIUM. Their exploitation commenced in 1911 and from that date until the end of 1944, 51,211 tons had been produced. Their site values are not given, owing to their great variations, which in any case probably bore little relation to the value of the mineral in the world's markets at the time. The record year was in 1938 with its output of 5,221 tons, valued at Rs 2,33,700, and after 1944, ordinary trade exports and the publication of statistics relating to them have ceased for strategic reasons. Dr D. N. Wadia stated, however, in 1949 that output had risen progressively to 5,000 tons per annum, while Dr W. D. West, Director of the Geological Survey of India at that time, had, in 1945, given the reserves of the Travancore beaches alone at over two million tons. The firms engaged in monazite winning are Travancore Minerals Ltd, Hopkins and Williams (Travancore) Ltd, F. X. Pereira & Sons Ltd, and The Associated Minerals Co. Ltd, acting as agents of the State which took over the control of the deposits in 1946. A factory capable of processing 1,500 tons of monazite per annum has been built at a cost of about Rs 80 lakhs at Alwaye, by Indian Rare Earths Ltd, a company financed jointly by the Government of India and the Government of Travancore-Cochin.

Before 1911, the world's supplies of monazite were almost entirely derived from Brazil, but India obtained the lead in 1914 and probably kept it until the decline in the demand supervened as a result of the spread of electricity for lighting purposes, and reduced output to a fraction of its former figures. For the years 1911 to 1915 inclusive, Indian production was fairly steady at about 1,000 tons per annum. It then rose rapidly and passed a peak of 2,118 tons, valued at Rs 8,82,285, in 1918. A severe fall took place in 1922, and the average annual production over the decade ending 1931 only amounted to 172·5 tons. The export of the sand was suspended in 1929 and 1930, but in 1932 production had increased to 654·3 tons and to 1,009 tons in 1934. The decade from 1934 to 1943 witnessed the greatest activity in the monazite industry, the average annual production over the ten years concerned being 3,090 tons. In 1938, the world's production of monazite was 5,926 tons, of which India supplied 88 per cent, the Netherlands East Indies 6·5 per cent and Brazil 5·5 per cent. Of 19,204 tons of monazite imported into the United States of America, over the 4 years 1939 to 1943, three-quarters came from India and one quarter from Brazil.

With the growth of electric lighting thorium lost much of its earlier industrial importance, for its nitrate, made from monazite, was used in the manufacture of incandescent gas mantles as it

yields the oxide, thoria, on heating. At the same time this outlet
has not entirely ceased for such mantles are still utilized on a large
scale in petrol and paraffin-burning lamps, particularly in India
and China. Thoria, a heavy white powder, is one of the most
refractory substances known, with its melting point of 3050°C., and
is employed in the manufacture of special refractories, such as
crucibles for the laboratory melting of vanadium and titanium.
It is also added to tungsten, intended for use in lamp filaments, as
it inhibits excessive crystal growth and so improves the mechanical
properties of the wire at the incandescent temperatures to which
it is subjected.   Thoria, in the proportion of five parts per hundred
parts of cobalt, is used as an activator in the mixed catalysts for the
Fischer-Tropsch synthesis of hydrocarbons.   It is also an important
constituent of optical glasses for special photographic lenses, as
described under Cerium. Another application of thorium is in
electron-emissive elements and it is used too as an anode coating
in special types of radio bulbs.

In recent years the metal has assumed a new role for it is a
radioactive element and a potential source of atomic energy. Just
as uranium in the course of its atomic disintegration produces a
new series of daughter elements, so thorium gives rise to a closely
parallel one: in the same way as natural uranium (U 238) can by
capture of a neutron be changed into plutonium, so thorium with
its atomic weight 232 can be transmuted in a nuclear reactor into
uranium 233, an isotope which is said to possess properties similar
to those of uranium 235 and plutonium.   It has been described by
Sir John Cockcroft as an alternative secondary nuclear fuel, and
one of the problems facing the metallurgist today is the preparation
of thorium metal in a form suitable for use in reactors.

Thorium, described as a very ductile, soft, lead-like metal, can
be obtained by the reduction of its oxide with calcium and calcium
chloride in an inert atmosphere. The powder so obtained is com-
pacted, sintered and processed generally in a similar manner to
that adopted in the case of tungsten.   It is available on the market
in ingot and sheet form containing about 98 per cent thorium. The
commercial salts of thorium include the oxide, ThO_2, in which the
rare earth metals and iron are absent; the hydoxide $Th(OH)_4$,
about 99 per cent pure; the sulphate, $Th(SO_4)_2.9H_2O$ and two
forms of the nitrate, $Th(NO_3)_4.12 H_2O$ and $Th(NO_3)_4.4H_2O$. The
latter grade contains about 6 per cent of the sulphate and is the
variety used in the manufacture of gas mantles.

The radioactive substance mesothorium is a natural disintegration product of thorium and is recovered as a by-product in the
course of thorium nitrate manufacture. One ton of monazite
containing 5 per cent of thoria is said to yield about 3 milligrams
of mesothorium.   It has a half-life of but $5\frac{1}{2}$ years and was used as
a substitute for radium in the treatment of malignant diseases and
in the preparation of luminous materials.

Other thorium-bearing minerals include the oxide thorianite, ThO_2, and the silicate, thorite $(ThO_2.SiO_2)$. Thorianite is an end member of an isomorphous series of mixed cubic minerals, the other end member of which is an oxide of uranium. A black cubic mineral from Thadagay Hill, Travancore, with the high specific gravity of 10·3, which contains 32·3 per cent thoria and 39·6 per cent uranium oxide, may be uranothorite, a member of this series. Both thorianite and thorite are known from Ceylon and there can be little doubt that sooner or later they will also be found in southern India.

In prospecting for radioactive minerals with the Geiger counter, it should be remembered that the instrument does not distinguish between radiation due to uranium and that due to thorium minerals, though the gamma emission of the thorium series is less intense than that due to the uranium series.

Inquiries from Dr Davidson of the Atomic Energy Division, Geological Survey of Great Britain, in February 1951, to whom we wish to express our indebtedness, confirmed the fact that the demand for thorium in British atomic energy developments is still limited to experimental quantities. The United States Atomic Energy Commission is interested almost wholly in uranium. It is a reasonable assumption that the capital invested in uranium plant is now so enormous that a change-over to thorium is highly unlikely, so long as adequate supplies of uranium are available, and there is no foreseeable prospect of a shortage of this element as new sources of supply are continually being developed. In this connexion it is as well to remember that uranium is not a particularly uncommon constituent of the earth's crust, being about one-twelfth as abundant as lead and twenty times as abundant as silver. Many problems remain, however, connected with its concentration and profitable recovery from very low-grade ores.

Since 1951, however, more attention has probably been directed to thorium as knowledge of fast reactors (see URANIUM) has grown and their construction been undertaken. This depends on the proposals made by some authorities to use thorium as a blanket around the cores of such reactors and its own transmutation into uranium 233 in the process. The latter is described as an alpha-active, fissile isotope and as good a nuclear fuel as uranium 235 or plutonium 239. It may well be, therefore, that as more breeder and power reactors come to be built that the demand for thorium (and for monazite its parent mineral) will increase. It should be added that natural uranium can also be used as a blanket around the cores of plutonium or of uranium 235 mixed with uranium 238. Looking farther ahead, we have to thank Dr R. Spence, Director of the Chemical Laboratories of the British Atomic Energy Research Establishment at Harwell, for permission to quote his view that ' the long-term future of atomic energy as at present conceived depends on the successful transmutation on an industrial scale of natural thorium into the fissionable uranium 233 and of natural uranium into plutonium '.

CERIUM AND THE RARE EARTH METALS

There are some 17 elements grouped under the term ' rare earths ', so called in the past on account of the scarcity of their natural compounds at that time and the general resemblance of their oxides to lime and magnesia.   The rare earths are similar to one another in many respects, are always found together, are often associated with uranium and thorium and are only separately isolated with extreme difficulty, so much so that practically not one of them has yet been prepared in a state of high purity.   It should be stated that in the latest classifications the three elements scandium (originally found in the mineral euxenite), yttrium and lanthanum, are no longer definitely grouped with the rare earth elements, though their properties are very closely related and they occur in nature together.   In this note the older system is followed.   Though found sparingly in many mineral species, monazite, the orthophosphate of the cerium elements with thorium, is their only important ore.   Its distribution and economics are considered under TITANIUM and THORIUM, and it remains to describe briefly the applications of such members of the earths as find places in industry today.

They are divided arbitrarily into the three groups of the cerium, terbium and yttrium earths between each of which there are no sharp distinctions.   Ceylon monazite averages about 27 per cent of ceria, 30 per cent of lanthana and the allied oxides, and 2·5 per cent of the yttria and terbia earths: there is no reason to suppose that the Travancore mineral differs greatly from this composition.

The cerium group, the only one of practical importance at present, includes, besides cerium itself, lanthanum, praseodymium, neodymium, and samarium.   An analysis of a typical monazite sand, quoted by H. E. Kremers, shows thoria 6·5 per cent, ceria 28·8, lanthana etc. 31·8, yttria etc. 0·32, terbia etc. 0·8 and urania 0·2 per cent.   The 31·8 per cent of the lanthana earths are distributed in the following proportions: lanthanum oxide (La_2O_3) 15·6 per cent, neodymium oxide (Nd_2O_3) 11·4 per cent, praseodymium oxide (Pr_6O_{11}) 3·6 per cent and samarium oxide (Sm_2O_3) 1·2 per cent.   Commercial metallic cerium may contain the metals in the following proportions: cerium 45 to 50, lanthanum 20 to 25, neodymium and praseodymium 15 to 20, and samarium 5 to 10 per cent, with small amounts of iron.   They are so closely related and the separation of their salts by repeated fractional crystallizations is so tedious a process that for most industrial uses a mixture of them all is considered suitable.

This alloy, often referred to by its German name of *Mischmetall*, is prepared by the electrolysis of the rare earth chlorides with the chlorides of calcium, magnesium and sodium as fluxes.   The crude product is remelted under molten fluxes, with alloying additions, and then cast into grooved steel moulds to form the rods which, cut into suitable lengths, form the familiar but misnamed ' flints ' of mechanical lighters, the pyrophoric alloys that emit sparks when struck with an abrasive substance. Most of them are alloys of the rare earth metals with iron contents varying from 15 to 25 per cent, with small quantities of zinc, magnesium, copper or aluminium. Cerium itself is a soft and ductile metal and the addition of iron is necessary to increase both hardness and brittleness in the finished product. Alloys of these types have been employed as tips to tracer shells and bullets which, igniting as the projectile is fired, enable its path through the air to be traced. Ferro-cerium has been tried as a scavenging agent for the removal of oxygen and other unwanted impurities from cast iron. Small amounts of cerium are constituents of certain aluminium and magnesium alloys, and the metal is also used in the evacuation of radio bulbs. The applications mentioned are said to account for about one quarter of the monazite derivatives.

About half the total production of cerium salts, however, is said to be consumed in the cores of arc carbons, as they increase the luminosity of searchlights, cinema projectors, therapeutic lamps, etc., and at the same time act as stabilizers and smooth out fluctuations in lighting intensity.

We have to thank Messrs Thorium Ltd for much of the following information on the chemical compounds manufactured from monazite. They are marketed either as ' pure ' salts of cerium, lanthanum, samarium and thorium, in which contamination by the other elements is kept below certain definite limits, in the case of cerium itself not more than 0·1 per cent of the other earths of the group, and in some cases not more than 0·05; or as ' technical ' rare earth compounds which contain varying proportions of the other elements as well as cerium, ' didymium ', neodymium and yttrium, as the case may be. The applications of cerium salts include their uses in volumetric chemical analysis as oxidizing agents; in the preparation of organic compounds such as aldehydes and quinones; as waterproofing and fungicidal agents for textiles and leather; as catalysts, for example in the manufacture of acetone from acetylene; as commencing materials in the manufacture of resinates, naphthenates, etc., for paint driers; as constituents of magnesium flashlight powders, and in medicine for the prevention of sickness. The glass-maker uses cerium salts both as decolorizing agents and in the production of yellow glasses, as well as opacifiers for vitreous enamels. Finally, apart from their use in arc-lamp carbons already referred to, the average gas mantle contains about 1 per cent of ceric oxide.

· A number of pure lanthanum salts made from monazite are marketed, including the acetate; the double lanthanum ammonium nitrate, with not more than 0·02 per cent of cerium, and in which neodymium and praseodymium are practically absent; the chloride, suitable for the electrolytic preparation of the pure metal, and the oxide, a constituent of special optical glasses. Samarium oxide, containing about 99·0 per cent of Sm_2O_3, is yet another derivative of monazite which finds its uses in fluorescent tube lighting.

Commercial didymium compounds include the carbonate with 0·6 per cent ceria, as well as the chloride, a suitable material for the preparation of resinates for paint driers, the nitrate and the oxide, from which special coloured glasses both for decoration and for the use of welders as spectacle lenses are made. The pink neodymium oxide is also available and is 87 per cent pure. It is an excellent glass decolorizer and a source of other neodymium salts. Another ceria-enriched, rare earth oxide mixture is prepared with special attention to its physical properties for polishing high-grade optical glass. It is faster in effect and cleaner in handling than rouge.

Many of the rare earth elements yield sharp and narrow absorption bands in the visible and ultra-violet parts of the spectrum, a characteristic property taken advantage of by prospectors in the field, as a confirmatory test for monazite which displays well-marked didymium bands in the yellow, green and blue sections.

The following account of the uses of certain rare earths in the glass industry is based on information kindly supplied by Messrs Chance Brothers Ltd. Both lanthanum and thorium oxides are used in optical glasses which have been developed in recent years, their effect being to produce a glass with a high refractive index coupled with a low dispersion. These properties are desirable from the point of view of correcting photographic lenses, and are normally obtained by the use of barium which gives a series of glasses known as the dense barium crowns. Lanthanum and thorium oxides, however, have the advantage that the refractive index is increased relative to that of the barium glasses. Typical compositions of these new glasses are as follows:

			per cent	per cent	per cent	per cent
SiO_2	..	..	21·5	10·3	15·0	11·3
BaO	..	..	45·0	26·9	31·3	14·7
PbO	..	..	..	..	9·0	12·7
B_2O_3	..	..	19·0	24·8	15·4	19·5
La_2O_3	..	..	..	18·4	13·0	18·0
ThO_2	..	..	14·5	13·5	11·3	13·3
ZnO	..	..	..	4·0	2·5	3·1
ZrO_2	..	..	..	2·1	2·5	7·5
Nd	..	..	1·650	1·691	1·717	1·744
V	..	..	58·5	54·8	47·7	44·7

Nd is the refractive index for the helium D line.
V is the reciprocal dispersive power.

Cerium oxide in glass has the property of absorbing ultra-violet light and use is made of it in the so-called Haze Filter, employed

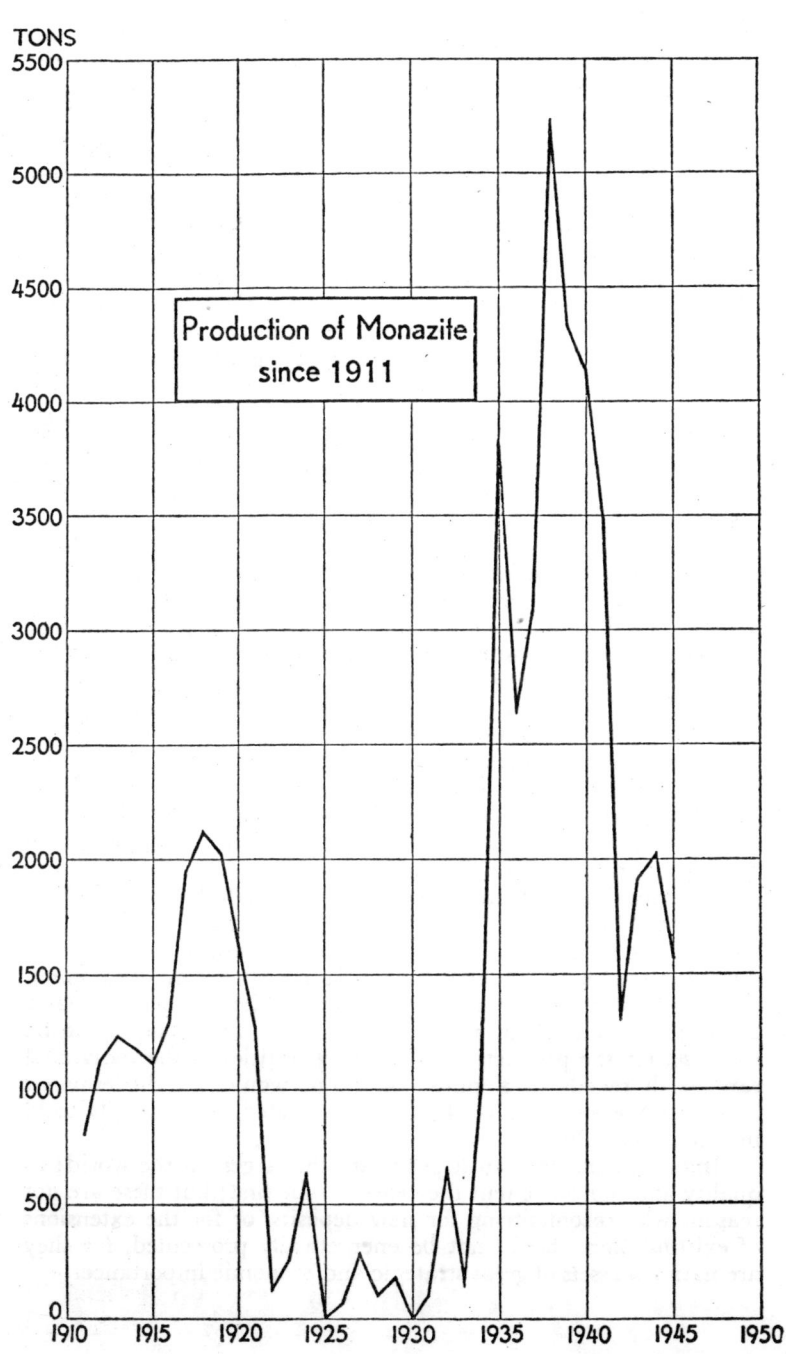

TONS

Production of Monazite
since 1911

in photography for absorbing the ultra-violet light which is scattered by atmospheric haze.   Both didymium and cerium oxides are constituents of didymium filter glass, which not only absorbs ultra-violet light, but also possesses an absorption band corresponding to. the sodium D band, and is for this reason used in the manufacture of spectacle lenses for glass-blowers and others exposed to the glare of sodium excitation.   The well-known Crookes' lenses also contain both these oxides.

The other groups of the rare earths are not yet utilized industrially; that trifling amounts of yttria and erbia were at one time employed among other rare earths in the glowers of Nernst lamps, before the introduction of the tungsten filament lamp, is merely a matter of historical interest.   Inquiries in London in 1951 elicited the information that only a few pounds of the yttria earths are sold annually, mainly to scientific institutions for research purposes. Commercial yttrium oxide is a light fawn-coloured powder containing 80 per cent of yttria and 15 per cent of other rare earth oxides.   The remaining 5 per cent is represented by loss on ignition.

Besides occurring in monazite, yttrium and its associates, lucetium, ytterbium, thulium, erbium and holmium are found in a number of other minerals, including samarskite and fergusonite, niobates and tantalates of yttrium, cerium and uranium, already mentioned under NIOBIUM and TANTALUM.   More important from the yttrium point of view, however, are xenotime, its natural phosphate, $Y_2O_3.P_2O_5$, and gadolinite, a silicate of yttrium, beryllium and iron $FeO.2BeO.Y_2O_3.2SiO_2$.   A mineral related to xenotime has been found in the apatite deposits of Kanyaluka, in Singbhum, and it contains yttria and the related earths $47 \cdot 6$ per cent, ceria earths $5 \cdot 8$ per cent and thoria $6 \cdot 92$ per cent.   Gadolinite was discovered in 1903, by Baidyanath Saha, in a tourmaline pegmatite at Hosainpura, Palanpur, Bombay.

The vicissitudes of the Indian monazite trade furnish excellent examples of how mineral products which, having become of little consequence for their primary purposes, are needed once more as fresh uses are found for them; and, again, of the manner in which apparently worthless by-products of an earlier period may later become the mainstay of a mineral industry.   Such may again be the case, for the production of larger quantities of the individual rare earth metals in a pure condition, would, as the eminent American metallurgist, W. J. Kroll, has stated, undoubtedly yield unexpected results.

India's monazite sand deposits are the largest in the world; in quality and thoria content they easily come first; but these are not reasons why reconnoitring for new deposits, or for the extensions of existing ones, should not be energetically prosecuted, for they are national assets of great strategic and economic importance.

CHAPTER VIII

THE RARER ELEMENTS OF INDUSTRIAL IMPORTANCE

ANTIMONY

STIBNITE, or antimonite, the natural trisulphide of antimony, Sb_2S_3, with 71·8 per cent of the metal, occurs in quartz veins traversing slates of Palaeozoic age, near Krinj and Partson, about 13 miles from Chitral, in Pakistan, in a mineralized zone which, according to V. P. Sondhi, extends for several miles. S. Tayyab Ali, of the Geological Survey of Pakistan, later reported deposits $3\frac{1}{2}$ miles south-west and 5 miles west of Krinj, in the Owiret and Monia areas. Mining was started in 1939, at first in haphazard fashion, but regular exploitation commenced in 1942, by the Parekh Varani Syndicate and later by the Chitral Mining Corporation of Bombay, only to cease after partition in 1947. Before dispatch to the Star Metal Refinery at Vikhroli, near Bombay, high- and low-grade ores were blended at the mines so as to give an average of 35 to 40, per cent of antimony in each batch. Experiments by the Utilization Branch of the Geological Survey of India have proved that the run-of-mine ores, containing some 16 per cent of antimony, are readily amenable to beneficiation by tabling and froth flotation, yielding a concentrate containing over 93 per cent of stibnite. Zinckenite, the double sulphide of lead and antimony, $PbS.Sb_2S_3$, is reported to occur, while jamesonite, a related mineral, $2PbS.$ Sb_2S_3, was identified by G. H. Tipper, from Awi, near Shogar, a few miles from Krinj. The development of these deposits is handicapped by their location at an elevation of about 8,000 feet in an inaccessible region, and by the long lead to Dargai, the nearest rail-head. From other parts of Pakistan old antimony mines are reported to exist in the Zaimukht Hills, north of Thal, in the Kurram valley, and, with lead ores, at Sekran, near Khuzdar in Kalat.

The existence of antimony ores near the Shigri glacier in Lahul, East Punjab, has been known for upwards of a century, and a consignment of 15 tons of stibnite from this locality reached England in 1905. The lodes are thick, contain stibnite with its decomposition products, cervantite, $Sb_2O_3.Sb_2O_5$, and kermesite, $2Sb_2S_3.$ Sb_2O_3, occur in gneissose granite and are associated with argentiferous galena, zinc blende, pyrite and manganiferous siderite. It is reported that some of the stibnite contains small amounts of gold. The inaccessibility of the neighbourhood, its elevation of 13,500 feet beyond the Hamta pass (14,500 feet), and its climate, which is rigorous enough to limit work to two or three months in the year, have hindered any active exploitation up to the present time.

The stibnite deposits of Thabyu, in the extreme south-east of the Amherst district of Lower Burma, are close to the Thailand frontier. A. M. Heron states that the veins are very large, the biggest measured being at least 20 feet thick and traceable for 600 feet. The ore consists of radiating or parallel crystals, or massive aggregates of stibnite, superficially oxidized to cervantite and stibiconite, $H_2Sb_2O_5$. The vein stuff is a calcareous chert showing distinct brecciation and often a cellular structure. The country rocks are black, fissile slates of unknown age. Small angular fragments of slate occur in the veins, which are believed to fill tension cracks, and to have been deposited during periods of upheaval, at moderate depths, from solutions at comparatively low temperatures. During times when high prices have ruled in the markets for metallic antimony, large quantities of ore have been obtained from Thabyu and other places in the Amherst district. Thus, in 1916, they supplied upwards of 1,000 tons, but in more normal years the distance of the deposits from any modern ways of transportation renders their working unprofitable. According to the Mining and Mineral Production Reports of the Government of Burma, 101 tons of antimony ore were produced in 1949, falling to 54 tons in 1950, and rising again to 286 tons in 1951.

A narrow quartz vein containing stibnite has been traced for 600 or 700 feet, in the slates forming the crest of a low ridge, on the western slopes of the eastern of the two parallel ranges of the Thaton-Martaban hills, seven miles to the east of Katun railway station, in the Thaton district of Lower Burma, which adjoins the Amherst district on the north.

The stibnite deposits of the Southern Shan States were examined by H. C. Jones, who concluded that none of them appear to be large or of much economic importance. They occur at the following localities: Naking and Loi Hke in Mong Hsu, Mong Ing in Kengtung, Hkomhpok and Loi Hsang in Mong Kung. The stibnite usually exists in a bladed, striated variety and more rarely in drusy and massive forms. The oxidized ores cervantite and valentinite, Sb_2O_3, are common. The Naking deposit, from which about 1,000 tons of ore were taken in 1908, consists of stibnite irregularly deposited through a vein in sandstone, perhaps of Jurassic age. Some of the others appear to be quartz-stibnite veins in Plateau Limestone.

Small quantities of stibnite and antimony ochre have been won from veins and patches in the quartzose rock of a schist series at Chikkannanahalli, in the Chitaldrug district of Mysore. The veins are about two inches in thickness, swelling in places to wider lenses up to a foot or so in width. Prospecting operations have shown that the grade of the orebody would have to improve considerably before mining under normal conditions could be entertained.

Antimonial lead was produced as a by-product at the Nam Tu smelters of the Burma Corporation until the Japanese invasion of the country stopped their operations. During the first world war the requirements of the Indian Ordnance Department were met from this source, and large quantities were exported to the United States of America after that time. Official statistics only commenced in 1924, and from that year until the end of 1941, 21,617 tons had been made. Up to about 1933 the composition of the product used to vary between the following limits: lead 72 to 77 per cent, antimony 21 to 24 per cent and 6 to 8 oz. of silver to the ton. From 1934 onwards it was more consistent, with lead about 81·75 per cent, antimony 17·75, copper 0·22 and 3 to 4 oz. of silver per ton. It is estimated that over 4,000 tons of metallic antimony were contained in the total product. The run-of-mill ore at Nam Tu sometimes averaged over 1 per cent of antimony and it was doubtless derived from the presence of one or more of the following minerals, all of which have been identified in the lead-copper-silver-zinc ores of Bawdwin: boulangerite, a sulphantimonite of lead, $5PbS.2Sb_2S_3$; bournonite, a sulphantimonite of lead and copper, $3(Pb,Cu_2)S.Sb_2S_3$; pyrargyrite, a sulphantimonite of silver $3Ag_2S.Sb_2S_3$, and tetrahedrite, a sulphantimonite of copper $4Cu_2S.Sb_2S_3$.

Antimony is too brittle a metal to be used alone, but it has many important alloys, particularly with lead and tin. To the former it imparts hardness and tenacity, and such 'hard lead', with from 5 to 12 per cent of antimony, is used in the grids of storage batteries. Other alloys of the same type find applications in the chemical industry in acid storage tanks, pumps and valves; in shrapnel bullets and the fillings of small-arms ammunition; in the sheathings of telegraph and telephone cables; in certain alloys used for collapsible tubes and foils, as well as for many architectural and ornamental purposes for which lead alone is too soft.

Metallic antimony is an essential component of most of the 'anti-friction', 'white' or 'bearing-metals', which also contain tin or lead. 'Babbitt metal', for instance, contains 83 to 89 per cent tin, 7 to 11 per cent antimony and 4 to 6 per cent copper. The lead base alloys may contain up to 15 per cent antimony. The type metals of the printer are essentially alloys of lead (50 to 80 per cent), with varying amounts of antimony (up to 30 per cent), in which small percentages of tin, bismuth and copper may also be incorporated. They are characterized by their fusibility and power of slight expansion on solidification. The Britannia metals, which by reason of their silvery appearance are employed in the manufacture of table-ware, are alloys of tin or lead and antimony in varying amounts, with smaller quantities of copper and zinc. Pewter is a related alloy of tin, lead and antimony.

Compounds of the metal have widely spread applications. Surma is the vernacular name for the powdered natural sulphide, sold in the bazaars of northern India and Pakistan as a cosmetic for the beautifying of the eyes and eyelashes. The more prosaic services of the sulphide include its use as a dark pigment in camouflage paints; it is said to possess the same infra-red reflecting power as green foliage. Incorporated in the charges of shells it produces a dense white smoke when they explode, a property which it shares with the oxide. The red trisulphide, or Antimony Red, is a useful pigment, and both it and the pentasulphide are employed in the vulcanization of rubber. Many of the compositions of the heads of safety matches contain about 3 per cent of antimony trisulphide, while the striking surfaces of the box itself contain about 8 per cent of the same substance, which is also employed in pyrotechny and as an ingredient of percussion-cap mixtures. The oxides of antimony have many uses, not only as white pigments and opacifiers for the vitreous enamels of iron and steel articles and in the glass and ceramic industries, but also in the composition of special flame-retarding paints and of sprays for the fire- and mildew-proofing of various textiles. Other compounds form the basis for a number of yellow pigments. The trichloride is used for the ' browning ' and ' bronzing ' of gun barrels. Tartar emetic, potassium antimony tartrate, and other salts are employed as mordants in dyeing. Finally, the medicinal preparations of antimony should be mentioned, especially those used in the fight against *kala azar* and bilharziosis.

The Star Metal Refinery at Vikhroli, Bombay, completed during the second world war, is the only antimony-producing concern in India, deriving its ores from Chitral until the mines passed to Pakistan on the partition of the country in 1947. In that year 238 tons of the metal were made, rising to 330 tons in 1948 and falling to 100 tons in 1949. Indian imports of antimony ore totalled 571 tons in 1948 and 250 tons in 1949, derived from Burma, Siam, the United States of America and China (in 1948). For the six months ending June 1950, India imported 417 tons of antimony ore. The consumption of metallic antimony before partition is estimated to have been approximately 300 tons per annum, and it is expected to be doubled in the near future. During the five years 1939-43, inclusive, the average annual production of antimony ore from the Chitral mines was 442 tons; for the four years ending 1947 it was 1,167 tons, of a spot value of Rs 1,81,045, and since that time no further output has been reported.

The average annual world production of antimony ore, in terms of metal, for the five years ending 1938, was approximately 34,000 tons, about three-quarters of which came from China, Bolivia and Mexico. Until the invasion by the Japanese in 1942, China was the leading antimony-producing country, responsible for about 70 per cent of the world's supply, and in earlier years still for a good deal more than this. The chief ore deposits are in the provinces of Hunan, Kwangtung and Kwangsi. In the former a series of sediments, ranging from Silurian to Carboniferous in age, have been strongly folded and fractured, resulting in the shattering of certain quartzite bands, the joints and cracks of which have been recemented by antimonite, which also replaces the rock to some extent. In other localities the stibnite is found in quartz veins of a more normal type. The decrease in Chinese production has led to the large-scale development of antimony ore deposits elsewhere, particularly in South America, so that of the world's production of 37,327 tons of antimony ore, representing say 26,000 tons of the metal, approximately 32 per cent came from Bolivia, 20 per cent from Mexico, 15 per cent from the United States and over 4 per cent from Peru; outside the Americas, South Africa is the largest producer with 11 per cent of the total in 1947, the stibnite here occurring in the auriferous reefs of the Murchison Range in the Transvaal. Antimony ores are widely distributed and eighteen other countries appear in the list of producers for 1948.

Stibnite is one of the most fusible of minerals and can be melted very easily, a property taken advantage of in the preliminary treatment of this ore, in which heat is applied and the molten sulphide run off into receivers as it drains away from the gangue and waste rock. It contains about 70 per cent of the metal and is referred to in the trade as Crude Antimony. The unrefined metal is termed Regulus, while Star Antimony is the name applied to the comparatively pure refined metal, doubtless from the characteristic markings on the surface of the ingots. It generally contains over 99 per cent of the metal, often, in the case of special brands, rising to 99·6-99·8 per cent antimony.

ARSENIC

Arsenic is a steely-grey, brittle metal with a bright lustre and scaly structure, a very widely distributed element and a constituent of a great number of mineral species, such as the sulpharsenides of copper, lead and silver and the various arsenates. Its chief primary mineral is arsenopyrite or mispickel, the sulpharsenide of iron, $FeS_2.FeAs_2$, which contains 46 per cent of arsenic; closely related to it are the arsenides of iron, löllingite, $FeAs_2$, and leucopyrite Fe_3As_4. They are all members of the marcasite group of minerals, marcasite being the orthorhombic form of iron pyrites, FeS_2, and it is likely that mixed crystals exist which may contain any of them. The simple sulphides, realgar, AsS, with 70 per cent of arsenic and orpiment, As_2S_3, with 61 per cent of arsenic, occur in Chitral and elsewhere. Practically all the arsenical compounds of commerce, with the exception of these natural coloured sulphides, are recovered as by-products in the roasting of the arsenical ores of other metals, such as copper, silver, gold and tin. Soots and flue dusts from such operations contain the crude oxide, which after purification is marketed as White Arsenic, arsenious oxide, As_2O_3.

The orpiment mines of Chitral are of great age, and small quantities of the mineral are still obtained from them from time to time, though for a great many years no returns of production were available, until 1945 and 1946, when a total of 11 tons was returned. According to G. H. Tipper, there are six principal areas in which they are situated—Mirgasht Gol, Aligot, Londku, Wizmich, Mogomo Zom and Stach and all lie between 10,000 and 16,000 feet above sea level. The bright yellow trisulphide, orpiment, is usually associated with the brilliant aurora-red monosulphide, realgar, and with fluorspar, the minerals occurring close to a band of basic rock, intrusive into calcareous shale accompanied by marble. V. P. Sondhi visited the region in 1943 and found the occurrences extremely variable, ranging from mere stringers to local expansions up to 10 feet across. Small quantities of the sulphides were then being won at Aligot. For nine months of the year the workings are buried under deep snow, so that any large-scale developments in the foreseeable future are unlikely. Arsenical pyrites is also well known in Chitral, but as a source of arsenic or its oxide it could not compete with cheap imported products.

Both orpiment and realgar occur in scattered fragments on the moraines of the Shankalpa glacier in the Kumaun Himalayas, where they are collected and sold locally, doubtless furnishing part of the supplies of the cities in northern India, for the minerals can be purchased in specimen quantities in almost any bazaar.

Orpiment has been imported into Burma from the Chinese province of Yunnan for a great many years. Coggin Brown was the first foreigner to locate, visit and describe the mines, which lie at an elevation of 8,000 feet, in mountainous country, two days' journey to the south-west of Tali. The deposit is confined to a band of quartzite about four feet thick, of Permo-Triassic age, which has been thoroughly shattered in all directions. Orpiment and realgar have been deposited in the bedding, joint and fracture planes, and to some extent have replaced the minerals of the rock itself, forming irregular strings which swell into lumps and bands of solid sulphides. The quantity of orpiment coming into Burma from Yunnan used to fluctuate between 200 and 500 tons per annum, but the discontinuation of the compilation of the trans-frontier trade returns in 1924 makes it impossible to comment on what may have happened since that time.

The occurrence of arsenical pyrites on Sampthar Hill, in the Kalimpong subdivision, Darjeeling district, West Bengal, originally described by F. R. Mallet in 1882, was re-examined during the second world war and found to consist of two seams, seven and six inches thick respectively, separated by a band of quartz schists, but their lenticular character did not favour further exploration. Samples of the seams contained from 9·7 to 27·17 per cent of arsenic. The occurrences of the iron arsenides, löllingite and leucopyrite, in the mica-bearing pegmatites of the Hazaribagh district, Bihar, possess no economic importance.

The most important metallurgical use of arsenic is in the preparation of arsenical copper, for with 0·1 to 0·5 per cent of arsenic the metal becomes harder and stronger and has better heat- and corrosion-resistance than the purer form. Arsenical copper is accordingly used for locomotive firebox plates and stays, for calico-printing rollers, for motor-car radiators and other articles that are assembled by soldering. Deoxidized arsenical copper is mainly used for welded vessels. The usual method of making arsenical copper is by the addition of arsenious oxide to the molten metal, followed by poling. Amounts up to 1 per cent of arsenic are added to lead which is to be used in the manufacture of shot. Arsenious oxide, or white arsenic, is an extremely poisonous compound and upwards of 70 per cent of the total world production is said to be used in the preparation of insecticides, such as the lead and calcium arsenates, for the protection of crops of various kinds from the attacks of injurious pests, while a further 20 per cent enters into the composition of weed killers. Fungicides, bactericides, sheep and cattle dips, preservatives for timber, skins, hides and leather, as well as arsenical soaps, are other outlets. White arsenic also has its uses in opalescent glass-making, in calico printing, in the fixation of aniline dyes and in many drugs for veterinary and general medical practice. Some of the lethal substances proposed for chemical warfare, such as lewisite (chlorovinyl dichlorarsine), owe their destructive power to the presence of arsenic. As its name indicates, orpiment (a corruption of the Latin *auri pigmentum* or 'golden paint') finds a direct use in the manufacture of Indian ornamental lac wares and of Burmese lacquer work. Powdered and mixed with gum it produces a so-called 'gold lacquer', while with indigo it forms green tints. In the designs of Afridi wax cloths advantage is taken of the colour of orpiment. The mineral is also widely used in the East as a depilatory.

There is a small but steady demand in India for arsenical compounds. Thus during the five years 1913-14 to 1917-18, approximately 100 tons of arsenic and its oxide were imported annually, while over the decade ending 1943, this had risen to 185 tons, valued at Rs 4,31,043 per annum. The world's production of white arsenic in 1948 was 41,880 tons, out of which the United States were alone responsible for 17,290 tons. The severe competition from countries where white arsenic is produced as a cheap by-product would have to be met if it became possible to manufacture the oxide in India, in connexion with some future development of her base metal industry.

BISMUTH

Bismuth is closely related to arsenic and antimony and like these elements is found in the native state and in a number of similar natural compounds. Native bismuth is a very brittle, lustrous, silvery-white metal with a pinkish tinge, a well-developed, straight, brilliant cleavage and a platey structure. On exposure its fresh surfaces tarnish rapidly. It can be cut with a knife and melts easily below a red heat, possessing the power of expansion on solidification. The ores which have been identified in India, or Burma, include the native metal itself, Bi; bismuthinite, bismuth sulphide, Bi_2S_3, with 81·2 per cent of the metal; bismite or bismuth ochre, bismuth trioxide, Bi_2O_3, with 89 per cent of the metal; bismutite, a basic carbonate of uncertain composition, but probably $Bi_2O_3.CO_2.H_2O$, and bismutosphärite, another basic carbonate with the formula $Bi_2(CO_3)_2.2Bi_2O_3$.

Small quantities of bismuth have been reported from some of the copper ores of Singhbhum, with the nickel-cobalt ores of Bhorle in Nepal and with manganese ore at Siri on the borders of Kulu, E. Punjab. Bismuthinite and bismutosphärite have been found associated with galena, cerussite (the carbonate of lead) and barytes at Malthol, near Purulia, Manbhum.

A few hundredweights of bismuth ores have been exported from the Tavoy district of Burma from time to time: here both native bismuth and its sulphide occur in small amounts in some of the wolfram and cassiterite veins, as, for example, in those of Kanbauk, Kalonta, Zimba and Putletto. They have also been found in the adjoining districts of Mergui and Amherst. The bismuth minerals originated from the granites of Tenasserim, as those of tin and tungsten have also done, but they belong to a later phase of the ore-forming processes, as the metal is often found in thin filaments deposited on, or cutting through, the wolfram. The quantity of the bismuth minerals found in the veins is far too insignificant to permit of their profitable extraction on this account alone, and the small parcels of ore which have left Burma have been recovered as by-products in the sluicing of eluvial deposits for wolfram and tinstone, the heavy bismuth compounds accumulating in the sluice boxes with these concentrates. Under these conditions the native metal is always very oxidized and its coatings of bismuth ochres cause it to resemble small rounded pieces of dirty, yellowish-grey stone, which are often carefully picked out by tributors ignorant of their value and thrown away, although on breaking the larger pieces there is often a bright, metallic kernel within. It is well known that some of the tin-tungsten ores, not only of Burma, but also of Thailand and China, contain appreciable amounts of oxidized bismuth compounds, mainly in the form of the carbonates, and that they remain with the cassiterite when the wolfram is removed from the mixed concentrates by magnetic separation. From such tin ores the bismuth is recoverable by suitable chemical means, but no information is obtainable as to the quantities of Burmese ores so treated or of the amounts of bismuth so obtained. As far as existing methods on the mining fields themselves are concerned, the output from known sources is likely to remain extremely small. It remains to add that large nodules of native bismuth are occasionally found in the gem-bearing detritus of the Ruby Mines region in Upper Burma, and that their source is completely unknown.

In normal times it is said that upwards of three-quarters of the world's production of bismuth is employed in the manufacture of medicinal and cosmetic preparations, but the metal is also used on a large scale for alloying with lead, tin, cadmium and other metals such as antimony. Such alloys are characterized by their low melting points and non-shrinking properties; for example the familiar Wood's metal with bismuth 50 per cent, lead 25 per cent, tin 12·5 per cent and cadmium 12·5 per cent, melts at about 70° C.; another, known as Rose's metal, with bismuth 50 per cent, lead 25 per cent and tin 25 per cent, melts at 94° C. Their industrial applications include fuses for automatic water-sprinklers which operate in the case of accidental fires, safety plugs for boilers, safety fuses for electrical apparatus, moulding and pattern metals, mountings for dies, punches and so forth, special solders, and fillers for bending thin-walled tubing of other metals from which they can afterwards be steamed out. Large quantities of bismuth and its alloys are said to be used in the production of atomic bombs and radar equipment. Bismuth amalgams are used in dentistry; the carbonate and nitrate are the chief pharmaceutical compounds.

It is estimated that before the second world war the total consumption of bismuth was in the neighbourhood of 1,300 or 1,400 tons annually and it has probably increased greatly since then, but complete and accurate data are not available. Twenty years ago Bolivia was the main source of supply, the bismuth ores forming part of a tin-tungsten-base metal sulphide assemblage recalling that of Lower Burma. Peru is now the leading producer, the bismuth being obtained as a by-product in the smelting and refining of lead and lead-silver ores. The Mexican output comes largely from the flue dusts of smelters treating copper and copper-silver ores. The Canadian production too is a by-product recovery from lead and copper ores. Bismuth ores seem to have been reported from most of the important mining fields of the world, though rarely in substantial quantities; at the same time the list of producing countries is a long one including as it does Spain, Yugoslavia, Sweden, Germany, France, the Soviet Union, China, Australia, the Belgian Congo and South Africa.

The price of metallic bismuth, which had fallen from 12s. 6d. in 1920 to 3s. 6d. per lb. in September 1935, had risen again to 17s. per lb. in December 1950.

CADMIUM

Cadmium has been described as ' the rarest of the common metals '. It is soft and silvery-white in appearance, malleable, ductile and easily fusible. A close relative of zinc, it normally occurs in zinc ores to the extent of from 0·1 to 0·4 per cent, probably in the form of the sulphide, greenockite, CdS. It is also found in very small amounts in other metallic ores, and is recovered on a commercial scale not only from the products volatilized during the roasting of zinc ores and from the leach liquors of the electrolytic process of zinc manufacture, but also from the dust- and fume-collecting equipments of copper and lead smelters.

The zinc blende of the Bawdwin orebody in Burma is known to contain small quantities of cadmium. Zinc concentrates from the Zawar mines of Rajasthan average 0·2 per cent of the metal. A specimen of zinc blende from the Great Limestone, near Darabi, Riasi *tahsil*, Kashmir, contained 0·17 per cent cadmium.

Just as the major use of zinc in normal times is in thin coatings to protect iron and steel sheets from atmospheric corrosion and to be seen all over the world in the form of 'galvanized' corrugated sheets, wire netting and fencing, pipes, tubes, bolts, nuts, screws and so on, so the major use of the rarer and much more expensive sister metal cadmium in the past has been to electro-plate more important iron and steel articles with a resistant, rust-proof coating, to be found for example in aircraft parts and the fittings of motor cars. Cadmium is also an essential component of the high duty alloys used for the bearings of internal combustion engines, lowering the coefficient of friction, adding strength and increasing fatigue-resistance, particularly when coated with small amounts of indium, another rare metal not as yet identified in India. Such alloys may contain from 95 to 98 per cent of cadmium with small additions of nickel, or of silver and copper. Cadmium lowers the melting point of solders, and with bismuth, lead and tin is a component of the fusible alloys more fully described under BISMUTH. Small amounts of cadmium are added to pure copper to be used in the form of wires for long-span overhead cables, for by this means the strength of the metal is greatly increased with a minimum sacrifice of electrical conductivity. Similar cold-worked copper with about 0·9 per cent of cadmium is extensively employed for trolley wires and other purposes. As cadmium has a high absorption capacity for neutrons it has been made into rods for the control of some types of atomic piles, the reactions within which can be decreased or intensified by winding the rods in or out as required, but it is not the only element adopted for this purpose.

Salts of cadmium, apart from those used in electro-plating, have a number of industrial uses; the sulphide forms the brilliant pigment known as Cadmium Yellow, the sulphoselenide is Cadmium Red. These, and a whole range of related colours, are used in paint-making as well as for ceramics and inks and the processing of rubber and leather goods. Other compounds are used in luminescent pigments and in photography. The colouring agents most frequently used by Indian bangle-makers are cadmium sulphide and selenium, besides the oxides of cobalt and copper. Cadmium sulphate is employed in standard electric cells for the accurate determination of electric pressures.

The average world production of cadmium for the five years ending 1938 was a little more than 4,000 tons, which came, of course, from the countries mining and smelting zinc ores or from others which make zinc from imported ores. Thus about half of the 4,000 tons came from the United States of America and the remainder from Mexico, Canada, Germany, Australia, Poland and Belgium. In 1947 the United States alone produced over 3,600 tons, Mexico over 760 tons and Canada about 330 tons. For a number of years the Australian production has averaged about 230 tons per annum.

Cadmium is a costly metal; its production figures are usually stated in pounds avoirdupois or kilograms and in the American and British markets it is sold by the pound. The London price of 5s. 4d. per pound in 1945 had risen to 17s. 3d. per pound by the end of 1950, the equivalent of £1,932 per ton.

GALLIUM

Gallium, a member of the family of elements which also includes aluminium, indium and thallium, is one of the scarcest metals although traces of it are to be found in many common ores. Its existence was predicted by the Russian chemist Mendeléeff in 1871, under the name eka-aluminium, and it was discovered by the French chemist L. de Boisbaudran in 1875, in a zinc blende from the Pyrenees. Today, it is recovered from the flue dusts of zinc smelters, from the residues of zinc refineries, and, like germanium, from the flue dusts of gases from producers burning certain types of coal. It occurs in some bauxites, the ores of aluminium, and has, indeed, been identified in specimens from Salgipat north of Lohardaga, Bihar, by B. Mukherjee and R. Dutta. Residues from the various industrial processes using bauxite in India, including those of the aluminium works, merit examination as possible sources of supply. Gallium has also been found in quartz from the Kangundi gold mine in Chittoor, Andhra, and in both manganese ore and mica from Nagpur, Madhya Pradesh. The metal itself, which is most conveniently obtained by the electrolysis of aqueous solutions of sodium gallate, has some unusual properties, for it is a silvery-white crystalline solid which melts at 30° C., so that it liquifies when held in the hand. It behaves rather like mercury in forming amalgams, and it alloys easily with other metals, but it does not boil below 1200° C., compared with 357° C. for mercury. Apart from its use in the construction of high-temperature thermometers it has no outstanding industrial applications at present, but its unique properties will no doubt be turned to commercial account when larger supplies become available.

GERMANIUM

Germanium is a greyish-white crystalline and brittle metal allied to tin, and originally isolated by the German chemist Winkler from the sulphogermanate of silver, argyrodite, thirteen years after Mendeléeff had predicted its properties with remarkable accuracy. It also occurs in a few other rare natural compounds of similar character, but on a commercial scale is obtained mainly from the residues of zinc refining works in America and from the flue dusts of coal in Britain. Many English coals are reported to contain germanium to the extent of 10 to 20 parts per million, which becomes concentrated chiefly in the dusts of flues of installations burning producer gas made from them. Such dusts, according to A. R. Powell of Johnson Matthey & Co., may contain up to 1 per cent of germanium and of gallium, though their general content is from 0·25 to 0·75 per cent of each of the two elements. The germanium is separated from them as its tetrachloride, a liquid which boils at 85° C., which is then hydrolized to obtain the dioxide. This, on reduction by hydrogen, yields the metal. According to B. Mukherjee and R. Dutta, ashes from coals of the Garo Hills of Assam contain from 0·095 to 0·122 per cent of germanium, while those from coals of the Singareni and Tandur fields of Hyderabad contain from 0·055 to 0·065 per cent and 0·017 per cent respectively of the same element. The whole question of the occurrence of germanium in Indian coals needs fuller investigation.[1]

Germanium is a semi-conductor and its resistance to the passage of an electric current decreases with a rise in its temperature, a reversal of the behaviour of a normal metallic conductor, and a property which can be utilized in the construction of thermistors. These are small and extremely sensitive devices for measuring temperatures. The metal is also used in instruments for the determination of the strength of magnetic fields, but it is in the field of electronic developments that it is becoming of increasing importance. Herein, it is used as a crystal rectifier in the detection of very high-frequency electric waves, such as those used in radar, and in various types of transitors which amplify currents and perform other functions usually done by thermionic valves. Radio broadcasting receivers have been demonstrated which employ a germanium crystal rectifier, as well as germanium crystal triode valves as amplifiers, in both radio-frequency and audio-frequency stages. Germanium diode and triode assemblies have advantages over the thermionic valve in that they require no heating, are of small size, rugged construction and operate instantly when switched on. They are of great service in many types of electronic circuits including computing machines, small radio receivers, deaf-aid amplifiers and in general industrial work of this kind. In August

---

[1] Prof. S. N. Bose and R. K. Datta have recently recorded 0·24 per cent germanium in magnetite associated with sphalerite from Nepal.

1953 germanium metal was quoted on the United States market at 65 cents per gram or $295 per pound and germanium dioxide at $142 per pound; the approximate sterling equivalents of these three dollar prices at prevailing rates of exchange being £0-4-8, £105-7-0 and £50-14-0 respectively.

MERCURY

Mercury, or quicksilver, one of the heaviest of the elements and the only pure metal that is liquid at ordinary climatic temperatures, occurs naturally in small quantities, but is for the most part obtained from its sulphide, cinnabar, HgS, a mineral which is mined chiefly in Italy, Spain and the Americas. Various occurrences, both of mercury and of cinnabar, have been reported from India and Burma, but the evidence for their existence is not trustworthy and those that have been examined have proved spurious. P. Viswanathan has recorded ' crimson grains of cinnabar ' in the black beach sand concentrates from Needakara near Quilon, Travancore-Cochin state. Recently, a reported occurrence of mercury near Sakoli in the Bhandara district of Madhya Pradesh has been found on investigation to be a case of salting. In Pakistan, however, cinnabar has been definitely identified in the concentrates of the gold washings from the Chitral river, ' pointing ', to use the words of Sir Lewis Fermor, ' to the existence of a deposit of this mineral somewhere in the State '. In most parts of the world, the ores of mercury are geologically young and their distribution is related to the folding and fracturing associated with the Alpine-Himalayan mountain systems. It is, therefore, not beyond the bounds of probability that they may occur in the as yet vast unprospected region which stretches from Assam to Kashmir and beyond, especially as they are known to exist in north-west Yunnan to the east and in Afghanistan to the west.

Mercury has manifold uses ranging from scientific instruments such as thermometers and barometers, electrical contacts, arc rectifiers, automatic switches and control devices to mercury-vapour lamps and the mercury-vapour boilers of large power installations. It is employed in the electrolytic preparation of chlorine, caustic soda, acetic acid and acetone. Many metals, including gold, silver and tin, dissolve in mercury to form alloys known as amalgams, and advantage is taken of this in the recovery of gold from its ores and in the preparations used in dentistry. Many salts of mercury are of great utility: the red mercuric oxide in dry battery cells, and in anti-fouling paints for ships; the fulminate as a powerful detonating explosive; the bright scarlet sulphide as a pigment in paints and printing inks; both mercurous and mercuric chloride play an important part in medicine, the former being the well-known drug, calomel, and the latter corrosive sublimate, an antiseptic, fungicide and insecticide of note. Other compounds of mercury are employed in the manufacture of plastics, dyestuffs and other chemicals.

The average annual world production of mercury during the period 1934-8 was 3,950 tons, upwards of 70 per cent of which was represented by the combined output of Spain and Italy, with smaller amounts from the United States of America, the Soviet Union, Mexico, China and other countries. The 1947 production was estimated at about 5,300 tons, to which Spain and Italy contributed approximately 60 per cent. In 1950, the output from the Almaden deposits of Spain rose to between 118,000 and 120,000 flasks, the wrought iron receptacles in which the metal is stored and transported. The standard flask contains about 76 lb. of mercury and forms the market unit of quantity. In December 1950 the London price was a nominal one of £37-10-0 per flask.

RUBIDIUM AND CAESIUM

The elements lithium, sodium, potassium, rubidium and caesium together constitute the alkali group of metals. They are all silvery-white in colour, exceptionally light in weight (lithium being only about half the weight of water), soft enough to be cut with a knife, tarnish rapidly in air and decompose in water at ordinary temperatures. Lithium, rubidium and caesium are the rarer members of the group, in the order named, and they are generally found together in their natural compounds, though lithium is far more abundant than either of the other two. The lithium-bearing minerals so far identified in India, lepidolite, spodumene and amblygonite, have been described under LITHIUM, but in only one of the occurrences, that of the lepidolite, or lithium mica, from Pipra in Bihar, has the presence of rubidium, to the extent of 0·07 per cent of its oxide, Rb_2O, and of traces of caesium, been confirmed. In the lepidolite from Mundaval in Bastar only rubidium has been detected spectrographically. This is probably because the others have not been fully investigated chemically. Traces of caesium are also suspected in the composition of the green, roscoelitic micas, described by S. K. Chatterjee, from Mahalgaon, Bhandara district, Madhya Pradesh. When investigations into the prevalence of these rare alkali metals in India are undertaken, the microcline feldspars from the mica-bearing pegmatites of Bihar, Andhra and Rajasthan should be particularly examined, as well as the beryls from the last named State. Such feldspars from pegmatites in south-west Maine, U.S.A., have been found to carry up to 3 per cent of rubidium oxide and over 0·5 per cent of caesia. A publication by the Principal Mineralogist of the United States Bureau of Mines and others, gives the information that rubidium occurred in at least fractional percentages in every specimen of forty-four microclines tested from the pegmatites of Maine, Massachusetts, Connecticut and New Hampshire, and that in twenty-two of the forty-four, a content of 1 to 3 per cent of rubidia was indicated. Lepidolite from the same States nearly always contains some caesium and rubidium. An amazonite (green microcline) from the Ilmen Mountains of the Soviet Union contains over 3 per cent of rubidia, while a microcline from Varutrask, Sweden, is reported to carry 3·3 per cent rubidia, 0·6 per cent caesia and 0·34 per cent lithia. In such feldspars the rarer alkali metals replace part of the normal potassium in the formula $K_2O.Al_2O_3.6SiO_2$. Although rubidium is more plentiful than caesium it is not known to form any definite mineral species of its own. Caesium has only one natural compound, its hydrated silicate with aluminium, pollucite, an exceedingly rare mineral which has been found in a pegmatite on the Isle of Elba, in another in Sweden and in a few in Maine and Dakota, U.S.A., as well as at Karibib in South-West Africa.

The metals themselves can be prepared by the electrolysis of fused chloride melts, or by the vacuum distillation of their oxides with aluminium, but they are usually marketed as chlorides or nitrates. Rubidium compounds are stated to have importance as microchemical reagents. Caesium salts are chiefly employed in the manufacture of photo-electric cells, electron multipliers, the screens of television cameras and in the so-called 'black light' and other signalling devices.

SELENIUM

Selenium is a non-metallic element, closely allied to sulphur, which forms the natural selenides such as clausthalite, the selenide of lead, PbSe, and berzelianite, the selenide of copper, Cu_2Se, the analogues of the sulphides, galena, the sulphide of lead, PbS and chalcocite, Cu_2S, a sulphide of copper, respectively. Selenium occurs in native sulphur and in most ores of a pyritic character, though often in very small quantities. There is reason to suspect its presence in the copper ores of Singhbhum and in the lead-zinc-copper ores of Bawdwin, in the Shan States, but in neither case are analyses of the waste products forthcoming, in which it may have accumulated during their treatment. The element is never abundant enough to be mined alone for its own sake and commercial supplies are obtained as by-products during the electrolytic refining of blister copper, as both selenium and tellurium remain in the sludges from which they are recovered. Smaller quantities are also obtained from deposits which accumulate in the lead chambers during the manufacture of sulphuric acid.

The principal application of selenium is in the glass industry, as a neutralizing agent of the greenish colour imparted to glass by small amounts of iron, and for this purpose it is said to be displacing manganese dioxide. Larger percentages give pink, red and ruby tints to glasses which are manufactured for such purposes as railway signal lights, the rear lights of motor vehicles and the like. Mixtures of selenium and varying amounts of cadmium sulphide afford a whole series of glass and ceramic pigments, ranging from yellow to red, and are, in fact, the colouring agents most frequently used by Indian bangle-makers.

Selenium, like sulphur, exists in several allotropic forms, and one of them, a silvery-grey crystalline solid, the so-called ' metallic selenium ', varies in electrical resistance with the intensity of the light to which it happens to be exposed, and for this reason is used in the construction of photo-electric cells. These play an essential part in the ' talking pictures ' of the cinema, in the transmission of photographs and sketches by ' wire ', as well as in photographic exposure meters, scanners, counters, remote control apparatus, optophones, smoke and turbidity measuring instruments, automatic devices for lighting street lamps and buoys at sea, electric signs, as well as those for the opening and closing of doors, for burglar alarms and mechanical safety devices. Selenium is also employed in recti-fiers for the conversion of alternating into direct electric currents. It is added to some forms of stainless steel and to certain copper alloys to improve their machining properties. The rubber industry uses it as a toughening agent for such products as cable coverings for mines and ships, for machine beltings and shock-resisting blocks and pads. In such examples it is said to confer on rubber a number of desirable attributes unobtainable by the use of sulphur alone.

The world's annual production of selenium is probably in the neighbourhood of 550 tons, and it is derived almost entirely from the major copper refining countries whose output is usually ex-pressed in pounds avoirdupois. Thus in 1947, the United States produced 612,600 lb., and Canada 501,090 lb., falling to 327,500 lb. in 1948, while the slimes of the Northern Rhodesian copper re-fineries yielded 27,056 lb. in 1950. About the middle of 1950, selenium was obtainable at a cost of 14s. per lb., but by the end of the same year this had risen to £1-5-0 per pound.

TELLURIUM

Tellurium is a brittle silvery-white element, resembling antimony in outward appearance, which lies on the borderline between the metals and non-metals: closely related to selenium and sulphur in many of its chemical properties, it does, at times, act like a true metal. It occurs in the native state and is widely distributed in small amounts, often in association with the ores of gold, silver, lead and copper. Altaite, the telluride of lead, $PbTe$, the analogue of the selenide clausthalite, $PbSe$, and of the sulphide, galena, PbS, occurs with gold at Kyaukpazat, Katha district, Upper Burma. Tellurides are also known to occur with the gold of the Oriental Lode of the Kolar goldfield; with copper sulphides in the gold-bearing quartz veins of Lawa, Manbhum, Bihar, and with the copper ores of Sikkim, but to which particular mineral species these Indian tellurides belong still awaits determination, except in the case of Sikkim, where tetradymite, the telluride of bismuth, Bi_2Te_3, has been identified.

At the present time copper ores are the chief source of tellurium, and it is recovered as an oxide from the slimes of the electrolytic copper refineries, after their selenium contents have been removed. The oxide is reduced in crucible furnaces by means of flour and borax and the dark grey tellurium cast into 80-lb. bars.

Tellurium, like selenium, is used in the vulcanizing of rubber, to increase its toughness and abrasive resistance, as well as to improve the quality of certain ferrous and non-ferrous alloys. Minute quantities added to cast iron are said to increase its resistance to abrasion and to make it more suitable for such purposes as car and gear wheels. Small percentages of tellurium added to lead augment its strength and toughness, as well as its resistance to heat, vibration and corrosion. Pipes made of such alloys can, after suitable treatment, be made one third thinner then ordinary lead piping and yet possess greater strength. Tellurium-lead, however, finds its chief outlets in chemical engineering, as, for example, in pickling-tanks to contain hot sulphuric acid. One half of one per cent tellurium is reported to double the life of lead apparatus in sulphuric acid plants.

Fifteen years ago the total annual world production of tellurium is reported to have been less than one ton, but by the 1936-9 period this had risen to about 33 tons annually. The United States and Canada are the chief producers, the former giving 52,290 lb. in 1947 and the latter 32,100 lb. in 1948. At the end of 1950 the London price of tellurium was 14s. 4d. per pound.